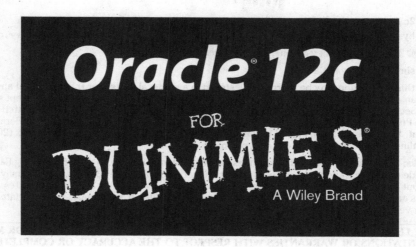

Oracle® 12c

FOR DUMMIES®

A Wiley Brand

by Chris Ruel and Michael Wessler

FOR DUMMIES®
A Wiley Brand

Oracle® 12c For Dummies®

Published by: **John Wiley & Sons, Inc.,** 111 River Street, Hoboken, NJ 07030-5774, www.wiley.com

Copyright © 2014 by John Wiley & Sons, Inc., Hoboken, New Jersey

Published simultaneously in Canada

Library of Congress Control Number: 2013949553

ISBN 978-1-118-74531-1 (pbk); ISBN 978-1-118-74527-4 (ebk); ISBN 978-1-118-74530-4 (ebk); ISBN 978-1-118-74543-4 (ebk)

Manufactured in the United States of America

V10009195_040319

Contents at a Glance

Table of Contents

Part III: Caring for and Feeding an Oracle Database ... 153

Introduction

Welcome to the exciting world of Oracle 12c database administration! Few things are as exciting as starting a new journey, and you certainly have a thrilling ride ahead of you. Luckily, the authors of this book, your guides in this adventure, can help smooth out any bumps in the road and point out the things you want to see. With decades of combined Oracle experience managing hundreds of databases for many clients, we hope to make understanding the Oracle database a fun, enlightening experience.

Oracle is a large company with a diverse portfolio of software and hardware. It seems like every other week Oracle releases some new product or acquires another company. Don't let the overwhelming nature of the big picture discourage you. This book imparts the fundamental knowledge of database administration. An Oracle career is a constant learning process. Establishing a solid understanding of the building blocks behind the database engine will vault you into a successful Oracle career.

The foundation of almost all of Oracle's products is the database, and Oracle databases are the best in the world. Understanding how Oracle databases work and how to manage them successfully is the first step to opening an awful lot of doors. Starting at this level is key. After reading this book, you will be well on your way to an interesting career filled with challenges and plenty of opportunity.

Every year we see companies grow and accumulate data at a staggering rate, and that rate is accelerating. Relational database theory first came out in the early 1970s, and database design and technology continue to evolve and become more powerful every year. Oracle is at the forefront of this evolution, and the knowledge of Oracle 12c that you gain from this book puts you in the driver's seat for your database career. Hop into your high-performance Oracle ride for an exciting journey!

About This Book

Oracle 12c For Dummies focuses on the tenets of Oracle database administration in the Oracle 12c environment. Not only do we cover many of the features released with the 12c version of the database, but we also explain the fundamental building blocks database administration. Many of these concepts and techniques apply to past versions of Oracle and almost certainly to future releases. Our goal is to make you a *smarter* and more *functional* DBA by explaining Oracle technology from the perspective of folks who manage Oracle software for a living.

 Sometimes we refer to directories and file locations on both Linux/UNIX and Windows. Essentially the two can be interchanged with a couple of things in mind. For example, here is an ORACLE_BASE value that you might come across on Linux/UNIX:

```
$ORACLE_BASE: /u01/app/oracle
```

In Windows, /u01 is much like a drive letter. They call it a *mount point* in Linux/UNIX.

Also, variables in Linux/UNIX are frequently prefixed with a dollar sign. Furthermore, the slashes are in opposite directions for each operating system. On Linux/UNIX, you use a *forward slash*, /. In Windows, you use a *back slash*, \. Lastly, Windows encapsulates the variable in percent signs. The same previous setting might look like this in Windows:

```
%ORACLE_BASE%: C:\app\oracle
```

We give examples of both environments throughout this book.

Who Are You?

People who find themselves needing or wanting a skill set for Oracle databases come from all backgrounds. You might be an application developer, a system administrator, or even a complete newbie. Many of the folks that we come across in this industry became a *database administrator* (DBA) by accident. One day, your company finds itself without a DBA, and the next thing you know, that's you! One trick is to be ready. Above all else, learn on your own and *think* rather than just react.

Icons in This Book

You see these icons throughout this book. They're a heads-up for different situations. These are items we wished someone told us when we were learning Oracle.

Warnings, if not heeded, will cause you to lose data or maybe even your job.

Remembering these bits of information can help you in the long run. And even the short run. Even on a brief walk.

Tips can save you time, energy, resources, or your weekend. We realize all these items are in short supply.

Technical Stuff icons indicate things we think are interesting and want to share with you, but you can skip them if you'd rather get straight to the nitty-gritty.

Beyond the Book

We've provided additional information about Oracle online to help you on your way:

- ✔ **Cheat Sheet:** Check out www.dummies.com/cheatsheet/oracle12c to grab some handy reminders for syntax and commands you'll use on a regular basis. We also include some tips for items to monitor to ensure you don't get caught by surprise.

- ✔ **Online articles:** On several of the pages that open each of this book's parts, you'll find links to what the folks at *For Dummies* call Web Extras, which expand on some concept we've discussed in that particular section. You'll find them at www.dummies.com/extras/oracle12c. There we've provided information to help you upgrade databases with the Database Upgrade Assistant (DBUA), gather database statistics to improve performance, and use Automatic Storage Management (ASM).

Where to Go from Here

Dive in and get started! Keep an open mind and try not to get overwhelmed. Like any skilled profession, it isn't always easy, but you can do it. We think you'll find it rewarding. This book is written so you can avoid the "too-much-information" reaction. Look at each section as a piece of a big puzzle, and you will soon see how everything starts to take shape. And remember to have fun!

Part I
Getting Started with Oracle 12c

getting started
with
Oracle
12c

For Dummies can help you get started with lots of subjects. Visit www.dummies.com for more great content online.

In this part . . .

✔ New to databases? New to Oracle? Find out how databases and Oracle fit into the modern IT infrastructure in Chapter 1.

✔ A solid foundation is the best way to start any project. Chapter 2 helps you understand the architecture behind the Oracle software, which goes a long way toward helping you be a successful database administrator.

✔ Chapter 3 shows you how an Oracle database fits in a typical IT application environment. You also find out about the requirements you need to meet before installing Oracle database.

Chapter 1

Discovering Databases and Oracle 12c

Welcome to the exciting world of databases, specifically Oracle 12c. Oracle is a recognized hardware and software giant on par with Microsoft in terms of size and influence. Oracle Corporation made its reputation and initial wealth with database technology and is still a recognized leader in databases. Many information technology (IT) professionals would agree Oracle databases provide the most advanced and capable means of storing, accessing, and managing data in the world today. As you read this book, you find out why many professionals hold that belief.

In this chapter, we explain what databases are, how they work, and why they're a core component of any computer system. Next, we introduce Oracle databases and guide you on when to use Oracle 12c. Finally, we examine database administration and what a database administrator's (DBA) role entails.

Discovering Databases

Since the earliest days of *information technology* (that's data processing for you old-timers), data has been at the heart of everything computers do. Users input data; and programs process, analyze, and perform calculations on the data. Then data output occurs. Notice a common theme? Everything relates to data! As technology increasingly becomes a part of daily life, you can expect almost every aspect of your life to have a data element associated with it.

Data comes from different sources in various formats. Every year, new types of data are created as technology evolves. Consider this partial list of data sources:

- ✔ Order information from your favorite online shopping application
- ✔ Trouble ticket information entered into a computer by a person in a call center
- ✔ Financial data including calculations for interest, taxes, and investments generated by banks and investment companies
- ✔ Multidimensional scans captured by complex medical imaging equipment
- ✔ Inventory data captured by tracking products by their RFID tags and point of sale information
- ✔ Images, videos, and audio files uploaded to social media and video sharing websites

The amount of data in the world is growing at an explosive rate. Consider the number of online sales transactions every day in addition to the Twitter tweets and Facebook posts from smartphones. Additionally, almost every retail sale is tied to an automated sales tracking and inventory control system. Almost anything you do that involves interaction, communication, or commerce generates data.

The size and number of data elements created are also increasing as technology evolves. Pictures, sound files, and videos take far more space on computer disk storage than simple text data (letters and numbers). Scientific and medical devices, such as satellite images and MRI scans, are common examples of how large data is generated rapidly and are part of peoples' lives.

Defining a database

All this data needs to reside somewhere; specifically, within a *database*. Databases are complex software programs that catalog and provide access to data. Although the data is usually stored on a disk storage system, the database software manages how that data is stored and managed.

Businesses use databases to store their data because the size and complexity of their data often exceed what can be stored on a spreadsheet. Most business and scientific activities, and many social activities involving technology will require the creation, access, updating, or deleting of data at some level. It is database software that allows these activities occur in a fast, efficient manner.

Databases provide these primary functions:

- **Storage:** Data must be kept within a computer system, usually disk storage, so that the data is available when needed. Disk storage technologies can vary, but they must be fast and large and are often expensive and complex.

- **Organization:** Data must be stored in a logical manner on disk so it can be found quickly and efficiently. Compare an organized desk and file cabinet with a child's messy bedroom; where would you prefer to work?

- **Access:** Finding the requested data in a fast and efficient manner and returning that data to the requestor is a key function of databases.

- **Security:** A database determines who can access the data and what they can do with that data. Security must be established and enforced.

- **Adding, updating, and deleting:** After data is added to the database, it can be modified and deleted. The database software manages the complex rules for how data is manipulated.

- **Safekeeping:** Databases keep data safe and available when failures occur such as a disk drive crashing. Backup and recovery are the processes used by databases to ensure data is not permanently lost if there is a failure.

Here's the general process:

1. You open the database and enter your data.

2. The database determines how best to store and catalog that data in a secure manner on the computer system's disk storage.

3. When you (or a computer application) want to access, update, or delete that data, the database checks your security permissions and then implements your request in the fastest manner based on the rules that have been defined.

Databases can look more like full operating systems (OSs) than simple applications you start and stop. Advanced databases (such as Oracle) have users, detailed security privileges, network configuration settings, performance tuning for memory, CPU, and disk options, and robust backup and disaster recovery (DR) options.

Examining how databases work

Databases have evolved over the years but have stabilized into the *relational model*. A relational database management system (RDBMS) stores data in logical structures called *tables*. A table is a logical container of similar data. A *table definition* is the set of rules or characteristics for each row of data stored in table. When data is loaded into a database, it is loaded as rows within one or more tables based on the characteristics of the data.

Each row of unique data exists only once in a table. For example, there will only be one row of data for each individual customer in a table. Each row is identified by its *primary key,* which is a unique identifier for that specific row. This uniqueness is a fundamental component of the relational aspect of databases. In Figure 1-1, each customer exists as a single row in the CUSTOMER table as identified by its unique primary key (CUST_ID) and is defined by *columns* specific to that table.

Tables are joined together by connecting the primary key of one table to a related table where it is defined as a *foreign key.* You implement relationships between tables by joining a row of one table to one or more rows in another table. (Remember: This is a relational database).

Figure 1-2 shows how a customer stored in a CUSTOMER table is joined to an ORDER table via the foreign key relationship.

CUSTOMER	
CUST_ID (Primary Key)	Number
LAST_NAME	Text
FIRST_NAME	Text
PHONE_NUMBER	Number
EMAIL_ADDR	Text
ADDRESS	Text
CITY	Text
STATE	Text
ZIP	Number
ORDER_ID (Foreign Key)	Number

Figure 1-1: Defining rows in the CUSTOMER table.

CUSTOMER			ORDER	
CUST_ID (Primary Key)	Number		CUST_ID (Primary Key)	Number
LAST_NAME	Text		PRODUCT	Text
FIRST_NAME	Text		QUANTITY	Text
PHONE_NUMBER	Number		PRICE	Number
EMAIL_ADDR	Text		TAX	Number
ADDRESS	Text		DATE_ORDERED	Date
CITY	Text		DATE_SHIPPED	Date
STATE	Text		IN_STOCK	Boolean
ZIP	Number		PAYMENT_RCVD	Boolean
ORDER_ID (Foreign Key)	Number		PAYMENT_DATE	Data

Figure 1-2:
Establishing relationships between CUSTOMER and ORDER tables.

The CUSTOMER table contains a single row for each customer, and each customer has a unique primary key identifier. The ORDER table stores all the orders for the company and each order is identified by its primary key ORDER_ID. A customer may have zero (new customer), one, or many (repeat customer) orders, and each order must have a customer. (You can't have an order without a customer.) Each row in the ORDER table is tied to the CUSTOMER table by the CUST_ID column which acts as the foreign key joining the ORDER and CUSTOMER table.

Databases have hundreds or even thousands of tables, keys, and relationships, and tables can have millions of rows of data consuming gigabytes or even terabytes of disk storage. To speed access when searching for a specific row of data, an *index* is created on one or more columns in a table. Indexes work similarly to the indexes in a book. On a daily basis, it is common for thousands of rows of data to be inserted, updated, or deleted within the database. The RDBMS software, managed by the database administrator (DBA), supports the overall management, functioning, and performance of the database. We talk about DBAs in the upcoming "Keeping a Database Safe and Sound" section.

Structured Query Language (SQL) is the language used to query (SELECT), create (INSERT), modify (UPDATE), and remove (DELETE) data in a database. SQL is the core language that DBAs and database application developers work in; you need a working knowledge of SQL to effectively manage a database. SQL is further defined as data manipulation language (DML) for querying, creating, modifying, and removing data and data definition language (DDL) for changing database and table structure. Oracle offers a programming extension of SQL called PL/SQL used to implement application logic within an Oracle database.

Oracle gained a big advantage early in the database market by successfully implementing *row locking* inside tables. That is, when one or more people update the same row in a database at the same time, the RDBMS software ensures that everyone's changes are made without conflicts and the data is visible with read consistency throughout the life of the transaction. Not all database vendors handled this issue cleanly.

Finding the right database for the job

The traditional saying, "If all you have is a hammer, everything looks like a nail," is appropriate to the selection of IT toolsets. Whether people are storing the addresses, phone numbers, and e-mails for a family reunion or they're maintaining an online shopping application, they need a data store. The size, complexity, and scope of that data store determines whether a database is even necessary and, if so, what characteristics (and vendor) of the database are appropriate.

The data requirements for people and businesses vary greatly in size, complexity, and importance. Different technologies exist based on these factors to meet users' data needs.

- ✔ Small, individual, or limited-use data stores, such as address information, are best served by a Microsoft Excel spreadsheet or a Microsoft Access database because both are inexpensive and easy to use.

- ✔ Small or medium size data stores, such as those found at small or medium sized businesses, could make good use of Microsoft SQL Server, Oracle MySQL, or Oracle Enterprise or Standard Edition. These implementations are commonly small, less complex databases where keeping costs low is an important factor.

- ✔ Medium to large data stores, such as those found at medium and large businesses, are commonly the realm of Microsoft SQL Server, IBM DB2, and Oracle Enterprise Edition. This medium to large database market is what many people think of as a typical database environment.

- ✔ Large and extremely large data stores, such as those found at large and multinational businesses, are commonly served by Oracle Enterprise Edition and IBM DB2. The large and complex database environments are special creatures and require very specialized software and hardware.

Review your current computer system environment and projected future needs to make the best decision for your mission. Vendors might try to upsell you on their product, so do your homework before making a decision. However, understand that as your data requirements change, your database environment might require change. We often see systems that started as small, departmental desktop applications grow until the old software is no longer functional. The result is an upgrade to a larger-scaled database system, and that system is often Oracle.

Choosing Oracle

Many seasoned IT people agree that Oracle makes the most advanced and reliable databases in the world. Your authors happen to agree with that opinion, too. Oracle offers several databases targeted for different uses and audiences at varying price points, including Oracle Enterprise Edition, Oracle Standard Edition, Oracle Berkley DB, Oracle NoSQL, and MySQL. (This book focuses on Oracle Enterprise Edition, Release 12c, although what you learn will be relevant to previous versions of Oracle.) Additionally, Oracle offers a programming extension of SQL called PL/SQL, which is used to implement application logic within an Oracle database.

Oracle as a database

Oracle databases are extremely advanced and sophisticated software components that are state of the art for RDBMS. Many features and options are available, and we guide you through the features you need for most implementations. The highly advanced features, such as Real Application Clusters (RAC), remote data replication, and engineered solutions such as Exadata, are for customers who require the cutting edge of technology for specialized implementations. Visit www.oracle.com for more details on these advanced technologies.

The sophistication and technological advancement that make Oracle databases so great can also make them very complex. Skilled DBAs devote their entire careers to learning the finer points of Oracle databases — it's a never-ending (but often rewarding) process.

Fortunately, Oracle understands that not everyone wants to commit themselves to learning the complexities of Oracle databases. Therefore, Oracle provides a robust, web-based administration tool, Enterprise Manager, where you manage and monitor your databases and the environment supporting them. Leveraging Enterprise Manager to make your job easier is a theme you can find throughout this book.

What is the "c" in Oracle 12c?

Following on the success of the previous Oracle database, release 11g (*g* is for *grid*), the most recent Oracle database release is 12c; the *c* stands for *cloud computing*, but what is that?

Oracle just does databases, right?

Wrong! At one point in time, if any Oracle product came into an IT shop, it got passed straight to the DBAs for implementation because it had to be database related. Those times are long gone, and understanding the history of Oracle is important so you're not confused by the myriad of Oracle products.

Oracle Corporation started as a database software company but, through remarkable success and a series of acquisitions of other companies, now has a bunch of products. The acquisition of Sun Microsystems yielded SPARC UNIX server hardware, the Solaris operating system, storage systems, and the Java programming language. The purchase of BEA Systems provided the well-respected WebLogic Java application server. Other purchases, such as PeopleSoft and Siebel, provided Oracle with new applications software.

Today, Oracle products include (but are not limited to) databases, operating systems (Linux and Solaris), database and web application server hardware, disk and tape storage devices, web and application server software, Business Intelligence (BI) software, Java programming language and supporting software, and multiple business applications. As you design your next computer system, you likely will have the option to have most, if not all, the components supplied by Oracle. You can consider the pros and cons of that (end-to-end support versus vendor commitment, for example), based on your mission requirements.

Cloud computing is an architecture where services (such as databases, applications, development environments, or even server infrastructure) are available over the network to the consumer (user). The cloud service provider supplies the product and bills the consumer based on usage. For example, say you wanted to use a type of computer server but you didn't want the overhead of buying and maintaining physical computer hardware and software. A cloud provider could sell you access to that computer server hosted in their cloud. You would pay the cloud service provider a fee based on your usage and the provider would give you access to the servers in their cloud. You get the benefits of having access to the cloud based server without the hassle and costs of buying and maintaining your own servers.

Cloud architecture allows consumers to choose only the services they need and pay for only what they use. Benefits to the consumer include lower cost, not having to provide their own IT service, and generally faster delivery of services than if they built the computing environment themselves.

Oracle 12c is engineered to run on the cloud and be accessible as a service. Through virtualization and multi-tenant architecture, each database application can appear to have its own private database but, in reality, the system is a shared database environment. The use of shared resources and virtualization is a method used by companies and database providers to reduce costs. However, there is no requirement that Oracle 12c must run in the cloud; you may run Oracle 12c just like you run other versions of Oracle without the cloud.

Keeping a Database Safe and Sound

The person who installs and configures a database, manages user access and accounts, ensures space for database objects, and (we hope) makes backups, among many other responsibilities, is the *database administrator,* or DBA.

Medium to large IT shops have one or more DBAs, sometimes even a large team of DBAs. Smaller IT shops may have a person working as a DBA part-time but doing system administration or application development as well. Regardless of whether you're a full-time or part-time DBA, you need to understand the responsibilities and common tasks involved with the care and feeding of a database.

Try not to confuse the DBA with the *application developer.* The process of defining tables, columns, relationships, and rules is application design, data modeling, and ultimately application development. The DBA is peripherally involved with these tasks, but they're typically the application developers' responsibilities.

DBA responsibilities

A DBA has multiple responsibilities around which individual tasks are created to support. Work comes in the form of technical, non-technical, database-centric, and business-centric tasks, but they generally relate to a set of core areas. As a DBA, you have to

- **Protect the data.** You are the gatekeeper and protector of the data you are entrusted to defend. Data must be protected from theft, damage, and destruction. Protecting the data encompasses both security and backup and recovery. This responsibility commonly comes in the form of establishing, testing, and monitoring backups and implementing security policies and technologies.

- **Provide access to the data.** You must ensure that the data is available to those users and programs which are authorized to access it. Speedy, quick access is necessary because if a query takes too long to execute and the user gives up, it might as well never finish. Data must be accessible as well; if the database is shutdown or otherwise unavailable, it does the users no good. Providing access to the data involves performance tuning and High Availability (HA).

- **Maintain the software.** You are responsible for ensuring the general maintenance and housekeeping of the database is kept up to date. Databases must be monitored for errors, ensuring there is enough space to grow as new data is loaded, and monitor processing jobs for success. Furthermore, there is always a new version of software to upgrade to or apply a patch (often after hours). These are generally mundane items and much of it can be automated via scripts or Enterprise Manager, but they still are your responsibility.

✔ **Support the business.** Databases do not exist in isolation. They are part of an overall business objective, and that business objective is usually evolving. New application code is being generated requiring developer assistance, audits of your processes are being conducted, and users always have miscellaneous issues. The most common example is applying a new application release to the database or implementing new technology to enable a new business capability. These efforts periodically correspond to database maintenance, but they are in support of moving the business objectives forward, and the wise DBA supports these efforts.

Common tasks

Life as a DBA varies based on the nature of the business and the IT environment. Here's how the core responsibilities can manifest themselves within a common task:

✔ **Protect the data by**

  • Reviewing output logs and messages to ensure the previous night's backups ran successfully.

  • Responding to questions about user access and database auditing procedures. (This task also falls under *support the business.*)

  • Researching and applying Critical Patch Update (CPU) patches to ensure security and vulnerability fixes are made. (This task also falls under *maintain the software.*)

✔ **Provide access to the data by** checking Enterprise Manager and your cell phone texts for alerts showing down databases or listeners, which would impact user access to the databases.

✔ **Maintain the software by** using Enterprise Manager and log files to search for database alerts, errors, and space usage threshold concerns.

✔ **Support the business by**

  • Reviewing output logs and messages to ensure the previous night's application batch jobs and processes completed.

  • Checking e-mail and responding to any application or user issues.

  • Applying application updates to development, test, and production databases to provide additional functionality and bug fixes for users.

Database administration is a respected profession in the IT field. Many people make a comfortable living as an Oracle DBA. Some would say Oracle wouldn't be where it is today if not for the legions of dedicated Oracle professionals worldwide.

Chapter 2

Understanding Oracle Database Architecture

. . . .

In This Chapter

▶ Structuring memory

▶ Checking the physical structures

▶ Applying the irreducible logic of the logical structures

. . . .

*U*nderstanding the Oracle architecture is paramount to managing a database. If you have a sound knowledge of the way Oracle works, it can help all sorts of things:

✔ Troubleshooting

✔ Recovery

✔ Tuning

✔ Sizing

✔ Scaling

As they say, that list can go on and on. That's why a solid knowledge of the inner workings of Oracle is so important.

In this chapter, we break down each process, file, and logical structure. Despite the dozens of different modules in the database, you should come away with a good understanding of what they are, why they're there, and how they work together. This chapter is more conceptual than it is hands-on, but it gives you a solid base for moving forward as you begin working with Oracle.

Defining Databases and Instances

In Oracle speak, an *instance* is the combination of memory and processes that are part of a running installation. The *database* is the physical component or the files. You might hear people use the term *database instance* to refer to the entire running database. However, it's important to understand the distinction between the two.

Here are some rules to consider:

- **An instance can exist without a database.** Yes, it's true. You can start an Oracle instance and not have it access any database files. Why would you do this?

  - This is how you create a database. There's no chicken-or-egg debate here. You first must start an Oracle instance; you create the database from within the instance.

  - An Oracle feature called Automatic Storage Management uses an instance but isn't associated with a database.

- **A database can exist without an instance but would be useless.** It's just a bunch of magnetic blips on the hard drive.

- **An instance can access only one database.** When you start your instance, the next step is to mount that instance to a database. An instance can mount only one database at a time.

- **You can set up multiple instances to access the same set of files or one database.** *Clustering* is the basis for the Oracle Real Application Clusters feature. Many instances on several servers accessing one central database allows for scalability and high availability.

Deconstructing the Oracle Architecture

You can break down the Oracle architecture into the following three main parts:

- **Memory:** The memory components of Oracle (or any software, for that matter) are what inhabit the RAM on the computer. These structures exist only when the software is running. For example, they instantiate when you start an instance. Some of the structures are required for a running database; others are optional. You can also modify some to change the behavior of the database, whereas others are static.

✔ **Processes:** Again, Oracle processes exist only when the instance is running. The running instance has some core mandatory processes, whereas others are optional, depending on what features are enabled. These processes typically show up on the OS process listing.

✔ **Files and structures:** Files associated with the database exist all the time as long as a database is created. If you install only the Oracle software, no database files exist. The files show up as soon as you create a database. As with memory and process, some files are required, whereas others are optional. Files contain your actual database objects: the things you create as well as the objects required to run the database. The logical structures are such things as tables, indexes, and programs.

Maybe you could say that the Oracle architecture has two-and-a-half parts. Because files contain the structures, we lump those two together.

The following sections get into more detail about each of these main components.

Walking Down Oracle Memory Structures

Oracle has many different memory structures for the various parts of the software's operation.

Knowing these things can greatly improve how well your database runs:

✔ What each structure does

✔ How to manage it

In most cases, more memory can improve your database's performance. However, sometimes it's best to use the memory you have to maximize performance.

For example, are you one of those power users who likes to have ten programs open at once, constantly switching between applications on your desktop? You probably know what we're talking about. The more programs you run, the more memory your computer requires. In fact, you may have found that upgrading your machine to more memory seems to make everything run better. On the other hand, if you are really a computer nerd, you might go into the OS and stop processes that you aren't using to make better use of the memory you have. Oracle works in much the same way.

Trotting around the System Global Area

The *System Global Area* (SGA) is a group of shared memory structures. It contains things like data and SQL. It is shared between Oracle background processes and server processes.

The SGA is made up of several parts called the *SGA components:*

- ✔ Shared pool
- ✔ Database buffer cache
- ✔ Redo log buffer
- ✔ Large pool
- ✔ Java pool
- ✔ Streams pool

The memory areas are changed with initialization parameters.

- ✔ You can modify each parameter individually for optimum tuning (only for the experts).
- ✔ You can tell Oracle how much memory you want the SGA to use (for everyone else).

Say you want Oracle to use 1GB of memory. The database actually takes that 1GB, analyzes how everything is running, and tunes each component for optimal sizing. It even tells you when it craves more.

Shared pool

Certain objects and devices in the database are used frequently. Therefore, it makes sense to have them ready each time you want to do an operation. Furthermore, data in the shared pool is never written to disk.

The shared pool itself is made up of four main areas:

- ✔ Library cache
- ✔ Dictionary cache
- ✔ Server Result cache
- ✔ Reserved Pool

A *cache* is a temporary area in memory created for a quick fetch of information that might otherwise take longer to retrieve. For example, the caches mentioned in the preceding list contain precomputed information. Instead of a user having to compute values every time, the user can access the information in a cache.

The library cache

The library cache is just like what it's called: a library. More specifically, it is a library of ready-to-go SQL statements.

Each time you execute a SQL statement, a lot happens in the background. This background activity is called *parsing*. Parsing can be quite expensive in terms of processing power.

During parsing, some of these things happen:

- ✔ **The statement syntax is checked to make sure you typed everything correctly.**
- ✔ **The objects you're referring to are checked.** For example, if you're trying to access a table called EMPLOYEE, Oracle makes sure it exists in the database.
- ✔ **Oracle makes sure that you have permission to do what you're trying to do.**
- ✔ **The code is converted into a database-ready format.** The format is called *byte-code* or *p-code*.
- ✔ **Oracle determines the optimum path or plan.** This is by far the most expensive part.

Every time you execute a statement, the information is stored in the library cache. That way, the next time you execute the statement not much has to occur (such as checking permissions).

The dictionary cache

The dictionary cache is also frequently used for parsing when you execute SQL. You can think of it as a collection of information about you and the database's objects. It can check background-type information.

The dictionary cache is also governed by the rules of the *Least Recently Used* (LRU) algorithm: If it's not the right size, information can be evicted. Not having enough room for the dictionary cache can impact disk usage. Because the definitions of objects and permission-based information are stored in database files, Oracle has to read disks to reload that information into the dictionary cache. This is more time-consuming than getting it from the memory cache. Imagine a system with thousands of users constantly executing SQL . . . an improperly sized dictionary cache can really hamper performance.

Like the library cache, you can't control the size of the dictionary cache directly. As the overall shared pool changes in size, so does the dictionary cache.

The server result cache

The server result cache has two parts:

- ✔ **SQL result cache:** This cache lets Oracle see that the requested data — requested by a recently executed SQL statement — might be stored in memory. This situation lets Oracle skip the execution part of the, er, execution, for lack of a better term, and go directly to the result set if it exists.

  What if your data changes? Well, we didn't say this is the end-all-per-formance-woes feature. The SQL result cache works best on relatively static data (like the description of an item on an e-commerce site).

  Should you worry about the result cache returning incorrect data? Not at all. Oracle automatically invalidates data stored in the result cache if any of the underlying components are modified.

- ✔ **PL/SQL function result cache:** The PL/SQL function result cache stores the results of a computation. For example, say you have a function that calculates the value of the dollar based on the exchange rate of the Euro. You might not want to store that actual value since it changes constantly. Instead, you have a function that calls on a daily or hourly rate to determine the value of the dollar. In a financial application, this call could happen thousands of times an hour. Therefore, instead of the function executing, it goes directly to the PL/SQL result cache to get the data between the rate updates. If the rate does change, Oracle re-executes the function and updates the result cache.

The reserved pool

When Oracle needs to allocate a large chunk (over 5 KB) of contiguous memory in the shared pool, it allocates the memory in the reserved pool. Dedicating the reserved pool to handle large memory allocations improves performance and reduces memory fragementation.

Least Recently Used algorithm

If the library cache is short on space, objects are thrown out. Statements that are used the most stay in the library cache the longest. The more often they're used, the less chance they have of being evicted if the library cache is short on space.

The library cache eviction process is based on what is called the _Least Recently Used_ (LRU) algorithm. If your desk is cluttered, what do you put away first? The stuff you use the least.

Heap area

There aren't a lot of interesting things to say about the heap area within the context of this book. Basically, the *heap area* is a bunch of smaller memory components in the shared pool. Oracle determines their sizes and tunes them accordingly.

Only the nerdiest of Oracle DBAs search the dark nether-regions of the Internet for heap area information. It's not readily available from Oracle in the documentation, and the information you do find may or may not be accurate. If all I have done was make you more curious, look at the dynamic performance view in the database called V$SGASTAT to get a list of all the other heap area memory component names.

You can't change the size of the library cache yourself. The shared pool's overall size determines that. If you think too many statements are being evicted, you can boost the overall shared pool size if you're tuning it yourself. If you're letting Oracle do the tuning, it grabs free memory from elsewhere.

Database buffer cache

The *database buffer cache* is typically the largest portion of the SGA. It has data that comes from the files on disk. Because accessing data from disk is slower than from memory, the database buffer cache's sole purpose is to cache the data in memory for quicker access.

The database buffer cache can contain data from all types of objects:

✔ Tables

✔ Indexes

✔ Materialized views

✔ System data

In the phrase *database buffer cache,* the term *buffer* refers to database blocks. A *database block* is the minimum amount of storage that Oracle reads or writes. All storage segments that contain data are made up of blocks. When you request data from disk, at minimum Oracle reads one block. Even if you request only one row, many rows in the same table are likely to be retrieved. The same goes if you request one column in one row. Oracle reads the entire block, which most likely has many rows, and all columns for that row.

It's feasible to think that if your departments table has only ten rows, the entire thing can be read into memory even if you're requesting the name of only one department.

Buffer cache state

The *buffer cache* controls what blocks get to stay depending on available space and the block state (similar to how the shared pool decides what SQL gets to stay). The buffer cache uses its own version of the LRU algorithm.

A block in the buffer cache can be in one of three states:

- ✔ **Free:** Not currently being used for anything
- ✔ **Pinned:** Currently being accessed
- ✔ **Dirty:** Block has been modified but not yet written to disk

Free blocks

Ideally, free blocks are available whenever you need them. However, that probably isn't the case unless your database is so small that the whole thing can fit in memory.

The LRU algorithm works a little differently in the buffer cache than it does in the shared pool. It scores each block and then times how long it has been since it was accessed. For example, a block gets a point each time it's touched. The higher the points, the less likely the block will be flushed from memory. However, it must be accessed frequently or the score decreases. A block has to work hard to stay in memory if the competition for memory resources is high.

Giving each block a score and time prevents this type of situation from arising: A block is accessed heavily at the end of the month for reports. Its score is higher than any other block in the system. That block is never accessed again. It sits there wasting memory until the database is restarted or another block finally scores enough points to beat it out. The time component ages it out very quickly after you no longer access it.

Pinned blocks

A block currently being accessed is a *pinned block*. The block is locked (or pinned) into the buffer cache so it cannot be aged out of the buffer cache while the Oracle process (often representing a user) is accessing it.

Dirty blocks

A modified block is a *dirty block*. To make sure your changes are kept across database shutdowns, these dirty blocks must be written from the buffer cache to disk. The database names dirty blocks in a dirty list or write queue.

You might think that every time a block is modified, it should be written to disk to minimize lost data. This isn't the case — not even when there's a *commit* (when you save your changes permanently)! Several structures help prevent lost data.

Furthermore, Oracle has a gambling problem. System performance would crawl if you wrote blocks to disk for every modification. To combat this, Oracle plays the odds that the database is unlikely to fail and writes blocks to disk only in larger groups. Don't worry; it's not even a risk against lost data. Oracle is getting performance out of the database *right now* at the possible expense of a recovery taking longer *later*. Because failures on properly managed systems rarely occur, it's a cheap way to gain some performance. However, it's not as if Oracle leaves dirty blocks all over without cleaning up after itself.

Block write triggers

What triggers a block write and therefore a dirty block?

- The database is issued a shutdown command.
- A full or partial *checkpoint* occurs — that's when the system periodically dumps all the dirty buffers to disk.
- A recovery time threshold, set by you, is met; the total number of dirty blocks causes an unacceptable recovery time.
- A free block is needed and none are found after a given amount of searching.
- Certain *data definition language* (DDL) commands. (DDL commands are SQL statements that define objects in a database. You find out more about DDL in Chapter 6.)
- Every three seconds.
- Other reasons. The algorithm is complex, and we can't be certain with all the changes that occur with each software release.

The fact is the database stays pretty busy writing blocks in an environment where there are a lot changes.

Redo log buffer

The *redo log buffer* is another memory component that protects you from yourself, bad luck, and Mother Nature. This buffer records every SQL statement that changes data. The statement itself and any information required to reconstruct it is called a *redo entry*. Redo entries hang out here temporarily before being recorded on disk. This buffer protects against the loss of dirty blocks.

Dirty blocks aren't written to disk constantly.

Imagine that you have a buffer cache of 1,000 blocks, and 100 of them are dirty. Then imagine a power supply goes belly up in your server, and the whole system comes crashing down without any dirty buffers being written. That data is all lost, right? Not so fast. . . .

The redo log buffer is flushed when these things occur:

- ✔ Every time there's a commit to data in the database
- ✔ Every three seconds
- ✔ When the redo buffer is 1/3 full
- ✔ Just before each dirty block is written to disk

Why does Oracle bother maintaining this whole redo buffer thingy when instead, it could just write the dirty buffers to disk for every commit? It seems redundant.

- ✔ **The file that records this information is sequential.** Oracle always writes to the end of the file. It doesn't have to look up where to put the data. It just records the redo entry. A block exists somewhere in a file. Oracle has to find out where, go to that spot, and record it. Redo buffer writes are very quick in terms of I/O.
- ✔ **One small SQL statement could modify thousands or more database blocks.** It's much quicker to record that statement than wait for the I/O of thousands of blocks. The redo entry takes a split second to write, which reduces the window of opportunity for failure. It also returns your commit only if the write is successful. You know right away that your changes are safe. In the event of failure, the redo entry might have to be re-executed during recovery, but at least it isn't lost.

Large pool

We're not referring to the size of your neighbor's swimming pool. Not everyone uses the optional *large pool* component. The large pool relieves the shared pool of sometimes-transient memory requirements.

These features use the large pool:

- ✔ Oracle Recovery Manager
- ✔ Oracle Shared Server
- ✔ Parallel processing
- ✔ I/O-related server processes

Because many of these activities aren't constant and allocate memory only when they're running, it's more efficient to let them execute in their own space.

Without a large pool configured, these processes steal memory from the shared pool's SQL area. That can result in poor SQL processing and constant resizing of the SQL area of the shared pool. Note: The large pool has no LRU. Once it fills up (if you size it too small) the processes revert to their old behavior of stealing memory from the shared pool.

Java pool

The Java pool isn't a swimming pool filled with coffee (Okay, we're cutting off the pool references.) The *Java pool* is an optional memory component.

Starting in Oracle 8i, the database ships with its own *Java Virtual Machine* (JVM), which can execute Java code out of the SGA. In our experience, this configuration is relatively rare. In fact, we see this where Oracle-specific tools are installed.

However, don't let that discourage you from developing your own Java-based Oracle applications. The fact is, even though Oracle has its own Java container, many other worthwhile competing alternatives are out there.

Streams pool

The streams pool is used only if you're using Oracle Streams functionality. Oracle Streams is an optional data replication technology where you replicate (reproduce) the same transactions, data changes, or events from one database to another (sometimes remote) database. You would do this if you wanted the same data to exist in two different databases. The streams pool stores buffered queue messages and provides the memory used to capture and apply processes. By default, the value of this pool is zero and increases dynamically if Oracle Streams is in use.

Program Global Area

The *Program Global Area* (PGA) contains information used for private or session-related information that individual users need.

Again, PGA used to be allocated out of the shared pool. In Oracle 9i, a memory structure called the *instance PGA* held all private information as needed. This alleviated the need for the shared pool to constantly resize its SQL area to meet the needs of individual sessions. Because the amount of users constantly varies, as do their private memory needs, the instance PGA was designed for this type of memory usage.

The PGA contains the following:

- ✔ **Session memory**
  - Login information
  - Information such as settings specific to a session (for example, what format to use when dates are displayed)
- ✔ **Private SQL area**
  - Variables that might be assigned values during SQL execution
  - Work areas for processing specific internal SQL actions: sorting, hash-joins, bitmap operations
  - Cursors

Managing Memory

You have basically three ways to manage the memory in your instance:

- ✔ **Automatically** by letting Oracle do all the work
- ✔ **Manually** by tuning individual parameters for the different memory areas
- ✔ **Combination of automatic and manual** by using your knowledge of how things operate, employing Oracle's advice infrastructure, and letting Oracle take over some areas

First, a quick note on Oracle automation. Through the last several releases of Oracle, the database has become more automated in areas that were previously manual and even tedious at times. This isn't to say that soon it will take no special skill to manage an Oracle database. Exactly the opposite: When more mundane operations are automated, it frees you up as the DBA to focus on the more advanced features.

We've had great success implementing automated features for clients. It frees up our resources to focus on things such as high availability and security, areas that require near full-time attention. Thank goodness we don't have to spend hours watching what SQL statements are aging out of the shared pool prematurely, resulting in performance problems.

We recommend that you manage memory automatically in Oracle 12c. For that reason, we cover only automatic management in this chapter.

Managing memory automatically

When you create your database, you can set one new parameter that takes nearly all memory tuning out of your hands: MEMORY_TARGET. By setting this parameter, all the memory areas discussed earlier in this chapter are automatically sized and managed. After you type **show parameter memory_ target** in SQL*Plus (the SQL command-line interface available in Oracle), you see this output on the screen:

```
NAME TYPE VALUE
------------------------------------- ----------- -------------------------------
memory_target big integer 756M
```

Automatic memory management lets you take hold of the amount of memory on the system and then decide how much you want to use for the database.

It's never obvious what value you should choose as a starting point. Answer these questions to help set the value:

✔ How much memory is available?

✔ How many databases will ultimately be on the machine?

✔ How many users will be on the machine? (If many, we allocate 4MB per user for process overhead.)

✔ What other applications are running on the machine?

Before the users get on the machine, consider taking no more than 40 percent of the memory for Oracle databases. Use this formula:

(GB of memory × .40) / Number of Eventual Databases = GB for MEMORY_ TARGET per database

For example, if your machine had 8GB of memory and will ultimately house two databases similar in nature and only 100 users each, we would have this equation: (8 × .40) / 2 = 1.6GB for MEMORY_TARGET per database.

To help determine whether you have enough memory, Oracle gives you some pointers if you know where to look. It's called the Memory Target Advisor. Find it from the command line in the form of the view V$MEMORY_TARGET_ ADVICE. As seen in Figure 2-1, find it in the Database Control home page by clicking Advisor Central➪Memory Advisors➪Advice.

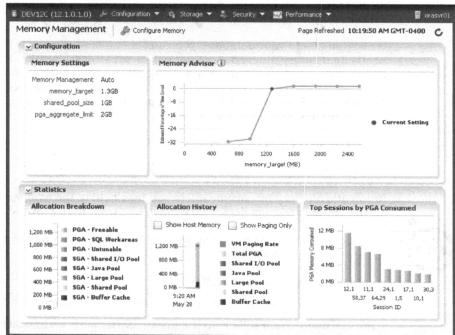

Figure 2-1:
MEMORY_
TARGET
offers
advice.

Whatever you choose for the MEMORY_TARGET setting isn't all the memory Oracle uses. That's why you should have an idea of how many sessions there will be *before* you make the final determination.

For instance, this parameter covers only memory used by the SGA and PGA. Every single session that connects to the database requires memory associated with its OS or server process. This memory requirement adds up. One of our clients has nearly 3,000 simultaneous connections eating up about 16GB of memory outside the SGA and PGA. The client's machine has 64GB of memory, and the MEMORY_TARGET is set at 16GB.

Following the Oracle Processes

When you start and initiate connections to the Oracle instance, many processes are involved, including

- ✔ The component of the Oracle instance that uses the Oracle programs
- ✔ Code to gain access to your data

There are no processes when the Oracle instance is shut down. Some of the processes are mandatory, and others are optional depending on the features you've enabled. It can also depend on your OS.

Three types of processes are part of the instance:

- **Background processes** are involved in running the Oracle software itself.
- **Server processes** negotiate the actions of the users.
- **User processes** commonly work outside the database server itself to run the application that accesses the database.

Background processes

In Oracle 12c, you can have over 200 background processes. We say "over 200" because it varies by operating system. If this sounds like a lot, don't be scared. Many are multiples of the same process (for parallelism and taking advantage of systems with multiple CPUs). Table 2-1 shows the most common background processes.

TIP

By default, no processes have more than one instance of their type started. More advanced tuning features involve parallelism. To see a complete list of all the background processes on your OS, query V$BGPROCESS.

Table 2-1	Common Background Processes
Background Process Name	**Description**
PMON	The *process monitor* manages the system's server processes. It cleans up failed processes by releasing resources and rolling back uncommitted data.
SMON	The *system monitor* is primarily responsible for instance recovery. If the database crashes and redo information must be read and applied, the SMON takes care of it. It also cleans and releases temporary space.
DBW*n*	The *database writer's* sole job is taking dirty blocks from the dirty list and writing them to disk. There can be up to 20 of them, hence the *n*. It starts as DBW0 and continues with DBW1, DBW2, and so on. After DBW9, it continues with DBWa through DBWj. An average system won't see more than a few of these.

(continued)

Table 2-1 *(continued)*

Background Process Name	Description
LGWR	The *log writer* process flushes the redo log buffer. It writes the redo entries to disk and signals a completion.
CKPT	The *checkpoint process* is responsible for initiating check points. A check point is when the system periodically dumps all the dirty buffers to disk. Most commonly, this occurs when the database receives a shutdown command. It also updates the data file headers and the control files with the check point information so the SMON know where to start recovery in the event of a system crash.
ARC*n*	Up to 30 *archiver* processes (0–9, a–t) are responsible for copying filled redo logs to the archived redo storage area. If your database isn't running in archive mode, this process shuts down.
CJQ0	The *job queue* coordinator checks for scheduled tasks within the database. These jobs can be set up by the user or can be internal jobs for maintenance. When it finds a job that must be run it spawns the following goodie.
J000	A *job queue process slave* actually runs the job. There can be up to 1,000 of them (000–999).
DIA0	The *diagnosability* process resolves deadlock situations and investigates hanging issues.
VKTM	The *virtual keeper of time* sounds like a fantasy game character but simply provides a time reference within the database.
LREG	The *listener registration* process, which registers database instance and dispatcher information with the Oracle listener process. This allows incoming user connections to get from the listener to the database.
MMON	The *manageablity monitor process* supports the Automatic Workload Repository (AWR) by capturing statistics, monitoring threasholds, and taking snapshots. This is related to performance tuning and troubleshooting.
MMNL	The *manageability monitor lite*'s job is to write Active Session History (ASH) statistics from ASH buffer in the SGA to disk. This is related to performance tuning and troubleshooting.

Other background processes exist, as you can tell by the "over 200" number we stated at the beginning of this section. However, those described in Table 2-1 are the most common, and you will find them on almost all Oracle installations. When you engage some of Oracle's more advanced functionality, you'll see other processes.

It's very easy to see these background processes if you have an Oracle installation available on Linux or UNIX. In Figure 2-2, the ps –ef | grep ora_ portion lists the background processes. This situation works very well because all background processes begin with ora_.

User and server processes

Because user and server processes are intertwined, we discuss the two together. However, they are distinct and separate processes. As a matter of fact, they typically run on separate machines. A very simple example: When you start SQL*Plus on a Windows client, you get a *user process* called sqlplus.exe. The user process represents a user's session in the database. When a connection is made to the database on a Linux machine, you get a connection to a process named something like oracle<*database_name*> or ora_S000_<*database_name*>.

Figure 2-2: The Oracle background process list.

```
oracle@orasvr01:~

[oracle@orasvr01 ~]$ ps -ef|grep ora_
oracle    2161    1   0 10:06 ?        00:00:00 ora_pmon_dev12c
oracle    2163    1   0 10:06 ?        00:00:00 ora_psp0_dev12c
oracle    2165    1   8 10:06 ?        00:02:11 ora_vktm_dev12c
oracle    2169    1   0 10:06 ?        00:00:00 ora_gen0_dev12c
oracle    2171    1   0 10:06 ?        00:00:00 ora_mman_dev12c
oracle    2175    1   0 10:06 ?        00:00:00 ora_diag_dev12c
oracle    2177    1   0 10:06 ?        00:00:00 ora_dbrm_dev12c
oracle    2179    1   0 10:06 ?        00:00:02 ora_dia0_dev12c
oracle    2181    1   0 10:06 ?        00:00:00 ora_dbw0_dev12c
oracle    2183    1   0 10:06 ?        00:00:00 ora_lgwr_dev12c
oracle    2185    1   0 10:06 ?        00:00:00 ora_ckpt_dev12c
oracle    2187    1   0 10:06 ?        00:00:00 ora_smon_dev12c
oracle    2189    1   0 10:06 ?        00:00:00 ora_reco_dev12c
oracle    2191    1   0 10:06 ?        00:00:00 ora_lreg_dev12c
oracle    2193    1   0 10:06 ?        00:00:03 ora_mmon_dev12c
oracle    2195    1   0 10:06 ?        00:00:01 ora_mmnl_dev12c
oracle    2197    1   0 10:06 ?        00:00:00 ora_d000_dev12c
oracle    2199    1   0 10:06 ?        00:00:04 ora_s000_dev12c
oracle    2211    1   0 10:06 ?        00:00:00 ora_tmon_dev12c
oracle    2213    1   0 10:06 ?        00:00:00 ora_tt00_dev12c
oracle    2215    1   0 10:06 ?        00:00:00 ora_smco_dev12c
oracle    2217    1   0 10:06 ?        00:00:00 ora_fbda_dev12c
oracle    2219    1   0 10:06 ?        00:00:00 ora_aqpc_dev12c
oracle    2221    1   0 10:06 ?        00:00:00 ora_w000_dev12c
oracle    2225    1   0 10:06 ?        00:00:00 ora_p000_dev12c
oracle    2227    1   0 10:06 ?        00:00:00 ora_p001_dev12c
oracle    2229    1   0 10:06 ?        00:00:00 ora_p002_dev12c
oracle    2231    1   0 10:06 ?        00:00:00 ora_p003_dev12c
oracle    2233    1   0 10:06 ?        00:00:00 ora_cjq0_dev12c
oracle    2263    1   0 10:07 ?        00:00:00 ora_qm02_dev12c
oracle    2267    1   0 10:07 ?        00:00:00 ora_q002_dev12c
oracle    2269    1   0 10:07 ?        00:00:00 ora_q003_dev12c
oracle    2339    1   0 10:12 ?        00:00:00 ora_w002_dev12c
oracle    2442    1   0 10:24 ?        00:00:00 ora_w001_dev12c
oracle    2527 2501   0 10:31 pts/1    00:00:00 grep ora_
[oracle@orasvr01 ~]$
```

The *server process* serves and exists on the database server. It does anything the user requests of it. It is responsible for reading blocks into the buffer cache. It changes the blocks if requested. It can create objects.

Server processes can be one of two types:

- ✔ Dedicated
- ✔ Shared

The type depends on how your application operates and how much memory you have. You're first presented with the choice of dedicated or shared when you create your database with Oracle's *Database Configuration Assistant* (DBCA). However, you can change it one way or the other later on.

Dedicated server architecture

Each user process gets its own server process. This is the most common Oracle configuration. It allows a server process to wait on you. If the resources can support dedicated connections, this method also is the most responsive. However, it can also use the most memory. Even if you're not doing anything, that server process is waiting for you.

Not that it's a bad thing. Imagine, though, 5,000 users on the system sitting idle most of the time. If your applications can't use connection pools (similar to shared server processes), your database probably won't survive and perform adequately for more than a day.

Shared server architecture

Just as the name implies, the *server processes* are shared. Now, instead of a server process waiting on you hand and foot, you have only one when you need it.

Think of a server process as a timeshare for Oracle. It's more cost-effective (in terms of memory), and you almost always have one available when you need it (provided the infrastructure is properly configured).

On a system with 5,000 mostly idle users, you might be able to support them with only 50 server processes. You must do these things for this to work properly:

- ✔ Make sure the number of concurrent database requests never exceeds the number of shared servers configured.

- ✔ Make sure users don't hold on to the processes for long periods. This works best in a fast transaction-based environment like an e-commerce site.

✔ Have a few extra CPU cycles available. All the interprocess communication seems to have small CPU cost associated with it over dedicated server processes.

The fact is shared server configurations are less common in today's environment where memory is cheap. Most applications these days get around the problems associated with too many dedicated servers by using advanced connection pooling on the application server level.

You should know about some other limitations: DBA connections must have a dedicated server. Therefore, a shared server environment is actually a hybrid. Shared servers can coexist with a dedicated server.

Many different types of files are required (and optional) to run an Oracle database:

✔ Data files

✔ Control files

✔ Redo log files

✔ Archive log files

✔ Server and initialization parameter files

Knowing what each of these files does greatly increases your database management success.

Getting Physical with Files

Many types of files are created with your database. Some of these files are for storing raw data. Some are used for recovery. Some are used for housekeeping or maintenance of the database itself. In the next few sections, we take a look at the various file types and what they're responsible for storing.

Data files: Where the data meets the disk

Data files are the largest file types in an Oracle database. They store all the actual data you put into your database as well as the data Oracle requires to manage the database. Data files are a physical structure: They exist whether the database is open or closed.

Data files are also binary in nature. You can't read them yourself without starting an instance and executing queries. The data is stored in an organized format broken up into Oracle blocks.

Whenever a server process reads from a data file, it does so by reading at the very least one complete block. It puts that block into the buffer cache so that data can be accessed, modified, and so on.

It's also worth noting that the data file is physically created using OS blocks. OS blocks are different from Oracle blocks. *OS blocks* are physical, and their size is determined when you initially format the hard drive.

You should know the size of your OS block. Make sure that it's equal to, or evenly divisible into, your Oracle block.

Most of the time Oracle data files have an extension of .DBF (short for database file). But the fact of the matter is that file extensions in Oracle don't matter. You could name it .XYZ, and it would function just fine.

We feel it is best practice to stick with .DBF because that extension is used in 95 percent of databases.

In every data file, the very first block stores the block header. To be specific, depending on your Oracle block size, the data file header block may be several blocks. By default, the header block is 64k. Therefore, if your Oracle block size is 4k, then 16 header blocks are at the beginning of the file. These header blocks are for managing the data file's internal workings. They contain

✔ Backup and recovery information

✔ Free space information

✔ File status details

Lastly, a *tempfile* is a special type of database file. Physically, it's just like a regular data file, but it holds only temporary information. For example, a tempfile is used if you perform sorts on disk or if you're using temporary tables. The space is then freed to the file either immediately after your operation is done or as soon as you log out of the system.

Figure 2-3 shows that by executing a simple query against V$TEMPFILE and V$DATAFILE you can see a listing of the data files in your database.

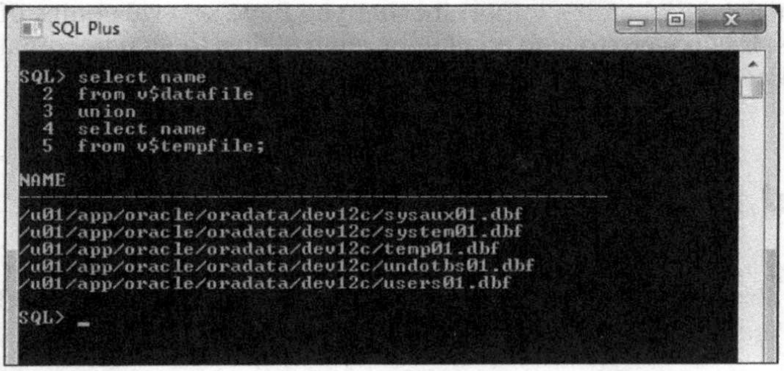

Figure 2-3:
Data files
listed.

```
SQL Plus                                        — □ X
SQL> select name
  2   from v$datafile
  3   union
  4   select name
  5   from v$tempfile;

NAME
_____
/u01/app/oracle/oradata/dev12c/sysaux01.dbf
/u01/app/oracle/oradata/dev12c/system01.dbf
/u01/app/oracle/oradata/dev12c/temp01.dbf
/u01/app/oracle/oradata/dev12c/undotbs01.dbf
/u01/app/oracle/oradata/dev12c/users01.dbf
SQL>
```

Control files

The control file is a very important file in the database — so important that
you have several copies of it. These copies are placed so that losing a disk on
your system doesn't result in losing *all* of your control files.

Typically, *control files* are named with the extension .CTL or .CON. Any extension will work, but if you want to follow best practice, those two are the most
popular.

Control files contain the following information:

- ✔ Names and locations of your data files and redo log files
- ✔ Recovery information
- ✔ Backup information
- ✔ Checkpoint information
- ✔ Archiving information
- ✔ Database name
- ✔ Log history
- ✔ Current logging information

Control files contain a host of other internal information as well. Typically,
control files are some of the smaller files in the database. It's difficult to tell
you how big they are because it varies depending on the following:

- ✔ How many files your database has
- ✔ How much backup information you're storing in them
- ✔ What OS you're using

As mentioned earlier, it's important that you have several copies of your control files. If you were to lose all of your control files in an unfortunate failure, it is a real pain to fix.

Redo log files

Redo log files store the information from the log buffer. They're written to by the *Log Writer* (LGWR). Again, you can't read these binary files without the help of the database software.

Typically, redo log files are named with the extension .LOG or .RDO. It can be anything you want, but best practice indicates one of those two extensions. Also, redo log files are organized into groups and members. Every database must have at least two redo log groups.

Redo log files contain all the information necessary to recover lost data in your database. Every SQL statement that you issue changing data can be reconstructed by the information saved in these files.

Redo log files don't record select statements. If you forget what you selected, you're just going to have to remember that on your own!

The optimal size for your redo log files depends on how many changes you make to your database. The size is chosen by you when you set up the database and can be adjusted later. When the LGWR is writing to a redo log file, it does so sequentially. It starts at the beginning of the file and once it is filled up, it moves on to the next one. This is where the concept of *groups* comes in. Oracle fills each group and moves to the next. Once it has filled all the groups, it goes back to the first. You could say they are written to in a circular fashion. If you have three groups, it would go something like 1,2,3,1,2,3, . . . and so on.

Each time a group fills and the writing switches, it's called a *log switch operation*. These things happen during a log switch operation:

  ✔ The LGWR finishes writing to the current group.

  ✔ The LGWR starts writing to the next group.

  ✔ A database check point occurs.

  ✔ The DBWR writes dirty blocks out of the buffer cascade.

How fast each group fills up is how you determine its size. By looking at all the things that occur when a log switch happens, you might agree that it is a fairly involved operation. For this reason, you don't want frequent log switches.

The general rule is that you don't want to switch log files more often than every 15–30 minutes. If you find that happening, consider increasing the size of each group.

Because these redo log files may be involved in recovery operations, don't lose them. Similar to control files, redo log files should be configured with mirrored copies of one another. And, as with control files, each member should be on a separate disk device. That way, if a disk fails and the database goes down, you still have recovery information available. You should not lose any data.

Each copy within a group is called a *member*. A common configuration might be three groups with two members apiece, for a total of six redo log files. The group members are written to simultaneously by the log writer.

✔ **How many groups are appropriate?** The most common configuration we come across is three. You want enough that the first group in the list can be copied off and saved before the LGWR comes back around to use it. If it hasn't been copied off, the LGWR has to wait until that operation is complete. This can severely impact your system. Thankfully, we rarely see this happen.

✔ **How many members are appropriate?** It depends on how paranoid you are. Two members on two disks seems to be pretty common. However, it isn't uncommon to see three members on three disks. More than that and you're just plain crazy. Well, not really. It's just that the more members you have, the more work the LGWR has to do. It can impact system performance while at the same time offering very little return.

We commonly get this question: "If my disks are mirrored at the hardware level, do I need more than one member on each group? After all, if a disk fails, I have another one right there to pick up the slack."

Unfortunately, you get different answers depending on who you ask. Ask us, and we'll recommend at least two members for each group:

✔ Oracle still recommends two members for each group as a best practice.

✔ Depending on how your hardware is set up, you may have the same disk controller writing to your disk mirrors. What if that controller writes corrupt gibberish? Now both your copies are corrupted. Separating your members across two different disks with different controllers is the safest bet.

Moving to the archives

Archive log files are simply copies of redo log files. They're no different from redo log files except that they get a new name when they're created.

Most archive log files have the extension .ARC, .ARCH, or .LOG. We try to use .ARC as that seems most common.

Not all databases have archive log files. It depends on whether you turn on archiving. By turning on archiving, you can recover from nearly any type of failure providing two things:

- ✔ You have a full backup.
- ✔ You haven't lost all copies of the redo or archive logs.

There is a small amount of overhead with database archiving:

- ✔ **I/O cost:** The ARCn process has to copy each redo log group as it fills up.
- ✔ **CPU cost:** It takes extra processing to copy the redo logs via the ARCn process.
- ✔ **Storage cost:** You have to keep all the archive logs created between each backup.

Relatively speaking, each of these costs is small in terms of the return you get: recovering your database without so much as losing the dot over an *i*. We typically recommend that, across the board, all production databases archive their redo logs.

Sometimes, archiving isn't needed, such as in a test database used for testing code. You can easily just copy your production database to revive a broken test. We're not recommending *not* archiving on test databases. Sometimes the test database is important enough to archive. We're just saying that sometimes you can get by without incurring the extra overhead.

You should keep archive log files for recovery between each backup. Say you're doing a backup every Sunday. Now say that your database loses files due to a disk failure on Wednesday. The recovery process would be restoring the lost files from the last backup and then telling Oracle to apply the archive log files from Sunday all the way up to the failure on Wednesday. It's called *rolling forward,* and we talk about it in Chapter 8.

Like control files and redo log files, it's best practice to have more than one copy of each of your archive log files. They should go to two different destinations on different devices, just like the others. You can't skip over a lost archive log.

Server and initialization parameter files

Server and initialization parameter files are the smallest files on your system:

- ✔ **PFILE,** or *parameter file,* is a text version that you can read and edit with a normal text editor.
- ✔ **SPFILE,** or *server parameter file,* is a binary copy that you create for the database to use after you make changes.

Typically, these files end with an .ORA extension. Personally, we have never seen anything but that. It's best practice for you to continue the tradition.

PFILEs and SPFILEs have information about how your running database is configured. This is where you configure the following settings:

- ✔ Memory size
- ✔ Database and instance name
- ✔ Archiving parameters
- ✔ Processes
- ✔ Over 1,900 other parameters

Wait, what was that? Over 1900 parameters to configure and tweak? Don't be frightened. The fact is 99 percent of your database configuration is done with about 30 of the main parameters. The rest of the parameters are for uncommon configurations that require more expert adjustment. As a matter of fact, of those 1,900, over 1,600 are hidden. Sorry if we scared you a little there. We just want you to have the whole picture.

Whenever you start your database, the very first file read is the parameter file. It sets up all your memory and process settings and tells the instance where the control files are located. It also has information about your archiving status.

In Chapter 4, we cover how the PFILEs and SPFILEs are located under the directory where you installed the database software. This directory is called the ORACLE_HOME:

- ✔ **Linux/UNIX:** $ORACLE_HOME/dbs
- ✔ **Windows:** %ORACLE_HOME%\database

It should have a specific naming structure. For example, if your database name is dev12c, the files would be named as follows:

- ✔ The PFILE would be called initdev12c.ora.
- ✔ The SPFILE would be called spfiledev12c.ora.

By naming them this way and putting them in the appropriate directory, Oracle automatically finds them when you start the database. Else, you have to tell Oracle where they are every time you start the database; that just isn't convenient.

We recommend you keep the PFILE and SPFILE in the default locations with the default naming convention for ease of administration.

Applying Some Logical Structures

After you know the physical structures, you can break them into more logical structures. All the logical structures that we talk about are in the data files. Logical structures allow you to organize your data into manageable and, well, logical, pieces.

Without logical breakdown of the raw, physical storage, your database would

- ✔ Be difficult to manage
- ✔ Be poorly tuned
- ✔ Make it hard to find data
- ✔ Require the highly trained and special skill set of a madman

Figure 2-4 shows the relationship of logical to physical objects. The arrow points in the direction of a one-to-many relationship.

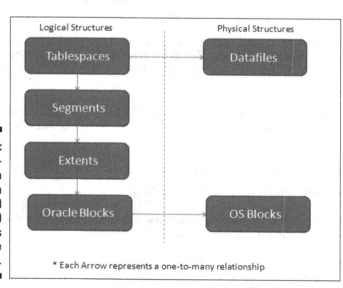

Figure 2-4:
The relationship between logical and physical structures in the database.

Tablespaces

Tablespaces are the first level of logical organization of your physical storage.

Every 12c database should have the following tablespaces:

- ✔ **SYSTEM:** Stores the core database objects that are used for running the database itself.
- ✔ **SYSAUX:** For objects that are auxiliary and not specifically tied to the core features of the database.
- ✔ **UNDO:** Stores the rollback or undo segments used for transaction recovery.
- ✔ **TEMP:** For temporary storage.

Each tablespace is responsible for organizing one or more data files. Typically, each tablespace might start attached to one data file, but as the database grows and your files become large, you may decide to add storage in the form of multiple data files.

So what's the next step to getting your database up and running? You create some areas to store your data. Say your database is going to have sales, human resources, accounting data, and historical data. You might have the following tablespaces:

- ✔ SALES_DATA
- ✔ SALES_INDEX
- ✔ HR_DATA
- ✔ HR_INDEX
- ✔ ACCOUNTING_DATA
- ✔ ACCOUNTING_INDEX
- ✔ HISTORY_DATA
- ✔ HISTORY_INDEX

Separating tables and indexes both logically and physically is common in a database.

- ✔ Because tablespaces must have at least one data file associated with them, you can create them so data files are physically on separate devices and therefore improve performance.

✔ You can harden our databases against complete failure. Tablespaces can be backed up and recovered from one another independently. Say you lose a data file in the SALES index tablespace. You can take only the SALES_INDEX tablespace offline to recover it while human resources, accounting, and anyone accessing historical data is none the wiser.

We discuss actual tablespace creation in Chapter 7.

Keep in mind that when deciding on the logical organization, it pays to sit down and map out all the different activities your database will support. If possible, create tablespaces for every major application and its associated indexes.

If your database has especially large subsets of data, sometimes it pays to separate that data from your regular data as well. For example, say you're storing lots of still pictures. Those pictures probably never change. If you have a tablespace dedicated to them, you can make it read only. The tablespace is taken out of the checkpointing process. You can also back it up once, and then do it again only after it changes. That reduces the storage required for backups, plus it speeds up your backup process.

Segments

Segments are the next logical storage structure after tablespaces. *Segments* are objects in the database that require physical storage and include the following:

✔ Tables

✔ Indexes

✔ Materialized views

✔ Partitions

These object examples are *not* segments and don't store actual data:

✔ Views

✔ Procedures

✔ Synonyms

✔ Sequences

The latter list of objects don't live in a tablespace with segments. They're pieces of code that live in the SYSTEM tablespace.

Whenever you create a segment, specify what tablespace you want it to be part of. This helps with performance.

For example, you probably want the table EMPLOYEES stored in the HR_DATA tablespace. In addition, if you have an index on the LAST_NAME column of the EMPLOYEES table, you want to make sure it is created in the HR_INDEXES tablespace. That way, when people are searching for and retrieving employee information, they're not trying to read the index off the same data file that the table data is stored in.

Extents

Extents are like the growth rings of a tree. Whenever a segment grows, it gains a new extent. When you first create a table to store items, it gets its first extent. As you insert data into that table, that extent fills up. When the extent fills up, it grabs another extent from the tablespace.

When you first create a tablespace, it's all free space. When you start creating objects, that free space gets assigned to segments in the form of extents. Your average tablespace is made up of used extents and free space.

When all the free space is filled, that data file is out of space. That's when your DBA skills come in and you decide how to make more free space available for the segments to continue extending.

Extents aren't necessarily contiguous. For example, when you create an items table and insert the first 1,000 items, it may grow and extend several times. Now your segment might be made up of five extents. However, you also create a new table. As each table is created in a new tablespace, it starts at the beginning of the data file. After you create your second table, your first table may need to extend again. Its next extent comes after the second extent. In the end, all objects that share a tablespace will have their extents intermingled.

This isn't a bad thing. In years past, before Oracle had better algorithms for storage, DBAs spent a lot of their time and efforts trying to coalesce these extents. It was called *fragmentation*. It's a thing of the past but we still see people getting all up in arms about it. Don't get sucked in! Just let it be. Oracle 12c is fully capable of managing such situations.

I also want to mention situations where you have multiple data files in a tablespace. If a tablespace has more than one data file, the tablespace automatically creates extents in a round-robin fashion across all the data files. This is another Oracle performance feature.

Say you have one large table that supports most of your application. It lives in a tablespace made of four data files. As the table extends, Oracle allocates the extents across each data file like this:

1,2,3,4,1,2,3,4,1,2,3,4 . . . and so on

This way, Oracle can take advantage of the data spread across many physical devices when users access data. It reduces contention on segments that have a lot of activity.

Oracle blocks

We've mentioned Oracle blocks at least twice before. We had to mention them when talking about the buffer cache and data files. Here in this section we can fill in a little more information.

An *Oracle block* is the minimum unit that Oracle will read or write at any given time.

Oracle usually reads and writes more than one block at once, but that's up to Oracle these days. You used to have more direct control of how Oracle managed its reads and writes of blocks, but now functionality is automatically tuned. You can tune it manually to a certain extent, but most installations are best left to Oracle.

Regardless, blocks are the final logical unit of storage. Data from your tables and indexes are stored in blocks. The following things happen when you insert a new row into a table:

✔ Oracle finds the segment.

✔ Oracle asks that segment if there's any room.

✔ The segment returns a block that's not full.

✔ The row or index entry is added to that block.

If no blocks are free for inserts, the segment grabs another free extent from the tablespace. By the way, all this is done by the server process to which you're attached.

Oracle blocks also have a physical counterpart just like the data files do. Oracle blocks are made up of OS blocks. It is the formatted size of the minimum unit of storage on the device.

Oracle blocks should be evenly divisible by your OS block size. Oracle blocks should never be smaller than your OS block size. We discuss Oracle block sizing more in Chapter 4.

Pluggable Databases

Now that you have a good understanding of the pieces and parts of databases and instances, we've saved the best for last as we throw a new concept at you in an attempt to muddy the waters. Welcome to *pluggable databases*. New in Oracle 12c is an optional architecture where you have one or more smaller subsets of schemas, data tables, indexes, and data dictionaries running as Pluggable Databases (PDB) inside a larger, superset Container Database (CDB).

The Container Database acts as a root database instance and each of the Pluggable Databases run within that single Container Database as *tenants*. We call this a multi-tenancy architecture where one CDB contains multiple tenant PDBs. Each PDB contains only the schemas, database, indexes, and mini split data dictionary to remain self-contained within the larger supporting CDB. For example, we could have separate PDBs for our sales, Human Resources, and new products departments withing our larger CDB. This breaks a previous database "rule" where now we have multiple databases (the PDBs) inside a single database instance (the CDB).

Why in the world would you want to do this? Well, the first reason is to be cool kid within your group of Oracle friends. The reason you tell your boss is you are supporting the cloud in 12c via multi-tenancy; he may not know what that means but he'll put it in his report to his boss. Seriously, think about the benefits of off-loading rudunant physical structures and overhead memory and background processes to a larger CDB rather supporting multiple copies for each PDB. This allows you to consolidate more databases as PDB tenants into a CDB while consuming few resources. In very larger environments such as data center consolidation or where server resources are constrained, these saves are very useful.

Also consider the *pluggable* part of PDBs; you can create them easily by cloning exiting PDB copies and you can move them between CDBs (unplug and plug) as needed to support migrations, upgrades, and testing. The pluggable architecture gives you a high degree of granular control of your PDBs. The self-contained architecture of the PDBs make this pluggable flexibility possible and is a great potential benefit as you manage multiple databases.

Chapter 3

Preparing to Implement Oracle

· ·

In This Chapter

▶ Implementing Oracle

▶ Verifying system requirements

▶ Planning server and disk configuration

▶ Taking care of post-software-installation setup

· ·

*B*efore you create databases and store your data, you need to plan your steps, which will make your implementation much easier. First and foremost, you need to determine your overall database architecture. Databases don't exist as standalone entities; they're part of an *information system,* and you need to understand how that system is laid out. This chapter looks at two of the most common implementation methods and helps you determine which method is right for you.

After you determine the right overall implementation plan, you need to make sure that your target environment meets the necessary requirements to host Oracle. This chapter not only looks at obvious requirements, such as server hardware and software, but it also looks at less reviewed (yet critical) requirements, such as user, configuration, and storage considerations. This chapter gives you the knowledge to make good judgments of where and how you implement your Oracle database.

Understanding How an Oracle Database Fits into a System's Architecture

Oracle databases don't simply exist in isolation; they act as part of a computer system. Before installing the Oracle software and configuring your database, you need to know how your database fits into the overall system architecture. Some systems are more complex than others, but most fall into the following basic categories:

   ✔ Client-server

   ✔ Multi-tier

   ✔ Component configurations

Knowing which category your database fits into will make a big difference during your system setup because you'll know the specific needs of your database.

Client-server applications

Client-server applications (sometimes called *two-tier applications*) are those in which the user's workstation has the application program installed and, during execution, the program accesses data stored on a remote database server. Although you have some wiggle room here, the workstation handles the presentation and application logic, and the database server acts as a data store. Figure 3-1 shows how a client-server configuration works.

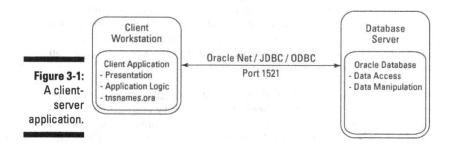

Figure 3-1:
A client-server application.

In Figure 3-1, the workstation (client-tier) handles the application logic and presentation to the user. Application logic may be implanted via many different languages, but common examples include PowerBuilder, MS Visual Basic, Java applications, and even some versions of Oracle Forms and Reports. When these client-side applications need data, they access the database via ODBC (Open Database Connectivity), JDBC (Java Database Connectivity), or Oracle Net by using client-side tnsnames.ora files. These database communication protocols allow connectivity from any client to any database, including Oracle.

On the database tier, the database stores the data and, via users, roles, and permissions, it provides that data to the application in response to SQL queries and data manipulation language (DML) statements (which are simply

SQL statements that manipulate, or change, the data). Depending on whether you're using a fat or thin client, some of the application logic and processing may be off-loaded to the database tier. Processing on the database server often makes sense because a database server can do much more intensive processing and number-crunching than even the largest workstation. Data processing is commonly executed via database procedures, functions, and packages, which process the data into a smaller result set to be returned to the client for presentation to the user.

Many people have claimed that client-server is dead. If it is, why are so many client-server applications still out there? Sure, the client-server architecture is older, and many newer applications exist in the multi-tier world. However, a simple client-server application still meets the immediate needs of a business in many situations. Also, the client-server application may be an existing legacy application that does its job — so, the business has no need to upgrade. Regardless, although we don't recommend developing new, large-scale systems on this model, we can't deny that client-server applications still exist in many organizations. Lastly, as a reader of this book, you may not be here to implement a new system. You may be here because you have to understand Oracle and how it works in an existing client-server application environment.

Multi-tier applications

Multi-tier applications are the current industry standard and compose multiple web, application, and database servers providing content to thin clients with presentation via a web browser. Ever wonder what's behind the scenes when you log in to a web application for online purchases or banking? Well, it looks something like Figure 3-2.

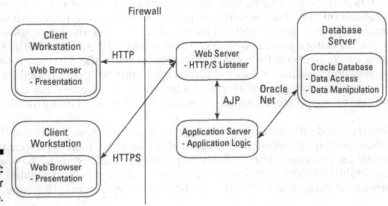

Figure 3-2:
Multi-tier
architecture.

In Figure 3-2, the client-tier is merely a web browser accessing a web server. Displaying content to the user is the primary purpose of the client in this architecture; no actual processing occurs at this layer within the browser. Presentation occurs most commonly via HTML (HyperText Markup Language), but it can also be within a Java applet or an ActiveX component and use JavaScript for more dynamic formatting and content.

Communication from the browser to the web server occurs via HTTP (HyperText Transfer Protocol) or HTTPS for secure (encrypted) data. Web servers conceptually act as web listeners; they receive requests from browsers and return formatted result sets with little processing on their own. Once on the web server, the browser request is parsed and sent to the appropriate application server for processing. The application server component may be on the same physical server as the web server, or it may be on another physical server. By far, the most common web server is Apache, or one of its commercial derivatives, with over 50 percent of the market share according to http://news.netcraft.com/archives/web_server_survey.html.

At the application server level, the user request is processed using the relevant application logic. One very common method is to use a Java application server, such as Tomcat, Orion, or Glassfish. In this case, the program logic is executed inside a Java Virtual Machine (JVM), which acts as the runtime environment for the program code.

Another popular tool is Oracle Fusion Middleware (OFM). Within OFM, the program may run as Oracle Forms, Reports, Discoverer, or even Java via Oracle Containers for J2EE (OC4J). Regardless of the product, it's within the application server component that the application logic is executed.

During processing on the application server, it's common to need database access to query, create, update, or delete data. The application server communicates with the database server via protocols, such as JDBC or Oracle Net, to access the data. During this time, the application server is accessing the database on behalf of the user making the application request. Rather than connecting as a named, distinct user such as JSMITH, the application server connects using a generic web account (such as WEB_USER). Multiple simultaneous connections from the application server to the database form a *connection pool* that allows any database connection to access data for a request. Connection pooling is a performance benefit because only a few database connections can service thousands of requests on behalf of many users.

When logged into the database instance, the generic web user queries or executes DML on behalf of the application server, which is processing an actual user request. The connection pooled web user doesn't have schema ownership into the database; it has only those permissions needed to access or update data on behalf of the application server. During this time, normal database roles, permissions, and grants are used. Additionally, database program logic implemented in PL/SQL via procedures, functions, and packages is often executed.

After the data result set is generated on the database-tier, it's passed back to the application server for more processing. Next, the results are relayed back through the web server and across the network for presentation to the user via their web browser.

Sounds complicated with all the various components? You may think so at first, but good reasons exist for breaking the system into web, application, and database components:

✔ You can use components from different vendors in a "best of breed" configuration. For example, you can use a free Apache web server instance coupled with Tomcat or Glassfish for a cheap application server component. Then tie that to the power of the Oracle database, and you have a solid system at lower costs!

✔ As more users come online, you can add more web, application, or database server instances to boost your processing power. Rather than buying bigger servers, just buy smaller servers.

✔ After you have a series of multiple servers, you gain fault tolerance. This is called clustering. If a web server crashes or the application server needs maintenance, no problem — the redundant servers will pick up the workload.

Hopefully, these benefits show why multi-tier system architectures are the industry standard and have surpassed client-server systems.

Component configurations

In client-server and multi-tier systems, the Oracle database was the core of the system because it holds the data. Existing as the primary data store for the entire system is the most common use of an Oracle database, but it's not the only time you'll have to install Oracle. For example, often, these databases are in a supporting role, acting as secondary data stores for larger Commercial Off-The-Shelf (COTS) applications. In these cases, Oracle databases act as repositories storing specialized data for use within a larger system. During installation of the larger system, the Oracle database is installed as a supporting component.

One common example of an Oracle repository you may be familiar with is Oracle Designer. You can use this Oracle developer tool to design, create, and store application code (among other things), and it resides on the user's desktop. When the user starts Oracle Designer, it prompts for an Oracle repository to connect to, and the user specifies that information. It is within that repository that all the objects to be used by the Designer desktop are stored. In this case, Designer is following the client-server model described in the section "Client-server applications," earlier in this chapter.

Oracle Internet Directory (OID) is a more current example of Oracle acting as a subcomponent within a multi-tiered environment. OID is the Oracle implementation of an LDAP (Lightweight Directory Access Protocol). LDAPs are hierarchically defined (not relational) data-stores (not databases) that allow systems quick lookup access of data. A common example is an e-mail address book, which doesn't contain a lot of updates or deeply layered data — it's just a need for quick lookups of a piece of data, which is the core use of an LDAP.

Another common LDAP use is to store users and their credentials so that web application servers can simply look up a person to see whether she is authorized to access a system. After all, you don't want to allow just anyone into your system! This credential verification creates a need for the Oracle Fusion Middleware products (OFM), and an LDAP is the solution. And, of course, with Oracle being a database company first and foremost, it opted to put its LDAP implementation inside an Oracle database, which is OID. (See Figure 3-3.)

Figure 3-3 shows how a specialized Oracle database can provide authentication via OID/LDAP for a larger system that also happens to use Oracle for the backend database where traditional customer data is stored. The OID is just a necessary component in a larger system.

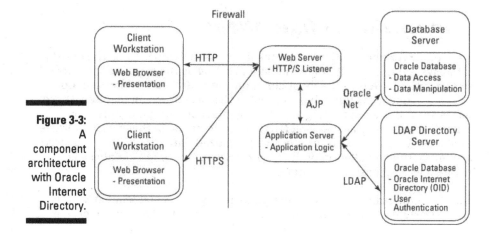

Figure 3-3:
A component architecture with Oracle Internet Directory.

The idea of this section isn't to make you an authority on Oracle Designer or OID. Rather, it's to show you that Oracle is more than just "the database" for large applications; Oracle also appears in critical support roles. Your Oracle installation may be for one of these support components, but don't discount the importance of such a database. Without the supporting Oracle component database, the overall system would not be functional.

Verifying System Requirements

Oracle databases are very good at storing and accessing data, but a little prep work helps them to run even better. Before installing the Oracle software, you need to do some homework to ensure that your server can support the software. We cover a basic Linux installation in Appendix A, but read and understand this chapter before jumping to the software installation.

Each release of Oracle databases is better than the previous one, but each version also has minor updates to the installation requirements. Oracle does a good job of documenting these updates for the myriad versions it supports. This information can be found on the documentation website at

www.oracle.com/technology/documentation/database.html

Pay particular interest to the Installation Guide and Quick Installation Guide for your operating system (OS).

You can avoid many of the installation problems people experience by just spending a few minutes reviewing the Oracle Installation Guide for your specific OS and meeting those requirements. A quick review of this guide before installing a new version can save you hours troubleshooting issues because you're not making mistakes that Oracle has already documented.

User and directory requirements

On UNIX- and Linux-based systems, the software is installed and configured as a specific user and group. In most cases, the user is called *oracle,* the primary group *oinstall,* and the secondary group *dba.* Here's a sample of how this user is defined:

```
$ id
uid=501(oracle) gid=501(oinstall) groups=501(oinstall),502(dba))
```

On Windows systems, the software should be installed as a member of the Local Administrators group for the machine.

It's common to have multiple versions of Oracle running on the same machine simultaneously. To avoid chaos, you need to organize how and where each version is installed. The framework commonly used to organize and install Oracle software is called Optimal Flexible Architecture (OFA). As the DBA, you can use this organizational hierarchy to install the Oracle software based on software versions and common directories used by all versions.

Key to the OFA is the directory environment variables ORACLE_BASE and ORACLE_HOME:

- ORACLE_BASE is where you can find common software used by all Oracle software versions; it's the base of underlying Oracle code trees.

- ORACLE_HOME is a subdirectory and denotes the location where a specific version of Oracle database software is installed, often associated with one or more database instances.

Here's the hierarchy:

```
/directory name/app/oracle/product/version number/actual software_version_number
```

Table 3-1 describes each level of the hierarchy.

Table 3-1	OFA Hierarchy
Level	*Description*
directory name	Base directory, file system, or drive name.
app	Directory name denoting application software will be located in this tree.
oracle	Owner of the software and is defined as ORACLE_BASE.
product	Holding directory for software trees.
version number	Directory with unique version number containing the actual software installation. Defined as ORACLE_HOME.

Here's an example of how this hierarchy may exist on UNIX or Linux:

```
/u01/app/oracle/product/12.1.0
```

And on Windows:

```
d:\app\oracle\product\12.1.0
```

When you install the database software with the Oracle installation tool (Oracle Universal Installer), it guides you through identifying these locations, but, you need to understand why each location is defined so you can better organize your software installations. We introduce the Oracle Universal Installer in Appendix A.

In the ORACLE_BASE directory, an Oracle Inventory directory is created as *oraInventory*. Within this directory, Oracle logs a record of all Oracle software that has been installed, patched, and removed from the server. This information is used so that the *Oracle Universal Installer* (OUI) and the OPatch utility can track software dependencies during installation and patching operations. The Oracle Inventory is managed automatically by the OUI and OPatch utilities.

Underneath ORACLE_BASE is an admin directory with named subdirectories for each Oracle database, as well as backup, config tool logs, the Fast Recovery Area, and product directories:

```
$ ls $ORACLE_BASE
admin  backup  cfgtoollogs  diag  fast_recovery_area  product
```

Of particular importance, under each ORACLE_BASE/admin/*database name* subdirectory is directories for auditing, Data Pump configuration files, configuration, and Oracle Security Wallet files:

```
$ ls $ORACLE_BASE/admin/*
/u01/app/oracle/admin/db01:
adump  dpdump  pfile  xdb_wallet

/u01/app/oracle/admin/dev12c:
adump  dpdump  pfile  xbd_wallet
```

Table 3-2 shows you directories for auditing, Data Pump, configuration, and Oracle wallets.

Table 3-2	Database admin Directories
Directory	*Purpose*
adump	Audit file location. Can generate many files, but are generally not very large.
dpdump	Location for Data Pump utility.
pfile	Location for database startup configuration files.
xdb_wallet	Oracle wallets storage area. These are security devices.

In previous versions of Oracle, bdump, cdump, and udump directories appeared underneath each database admin directory storing alert, trace, and core dump files. However, starting in Oracle 11g and continuing so in 12c, these directories appear in trace, alert, and incident subdirectories under the $ORACLE_BASE/diag/rdbms/*database name* directory. In Figure 3-3, you see the location of key trace and alert files.

Table 3-3	Trace and Alert File Locations
Directory	*Purpose*
alert	Location of the ever-important activity log file for your database (XML Format).
cdump	Location of core dump files.
trace	Location of database or user-generated trace files reflecting an error event. Replaces bdump and udump directories.
incident	Location of additional trace files (Plain Text Format).

Oracle manages software installations based on their ORACLE_HOME directories. Multiple ORACLE_HOME directories can exist on a server, each corresponding to a different version of the database. Different versions can generally coexist without conflict as they only share the Oracle Inventory, oratab file, and database listener process. This separation of the software into different directories allows this separation and management to occur. Here's an example of multiple ORACLE HOME directories:

```
$ ls -1 $ORACLE_BASE/product
12.1.0
11.1.0
10.2.0
```

In the preceding example, you see multiple ORACLE_HOME directories installed into different directories. Defining your environment variable settings to point to a specific ORACLE_HOME determines which one you're using.

Database files (data, index, control, redo) are preferably stored in separate file systems allocated specifically for this purpose and separated by database names:

```
/u02/oradata/dev12c
/u03/oradata/dev12c
/u04/oradata/dev12c
```

The oracle user in group dba needs to be able to read, write, and execute to the ORACLE_BASE and ORACLE_HOME directories, subdirectories, and files, as well as the database files themselves. If other users on this server need to execute programs on the server side, such as SQL*Plus or export/import or SQL*Loader, they need execute permissions on corresponding executables and, in some cases, libraries.

Hardware requirements

Oracle software requires a minimum amount of memory, virtual memory, CPU speed, and disk space to install successfully. If you lack these requirements, at best, the software will run slowly; at worst, it may not even install at all.

Don't forget to consider what other software is executing on the machine, too, both now and in the foreseeable future. It does little good to meet the database requirements and then add more software that will consume hardware resources beyond what the server can support.

Several vital server requirements to check include the following:

- ✔ **Memory:** The working area for programs as they execute, memory is key to fast performance. The kind you care about here is Random Access Memory (RAM), and it's measured in megabytes (MB) or, more commonly, gigabytes (GB). Oracle database SGAs are memory pools. Having large amounts of memory available allows you to have larger SGAs. The more memory you have available, the more options you have when managing the ever important SGA.

- ✔ **Virtual memory:** When a program or data is being executed, it's stored in memory. When that same program isn't actively being executed but will be momentarily, it's stored in virtual memory (for MS Windows) or swap (for UNIX/Linux operating systems). This system administrator-defined disk area operates as a slower extension of memory. Generally, virtual memory is sized to between ¾ to twice the size of installed memory.

✔ **CPU speed:** The clock speed of your *CPU* (central processing unit) is important. If the CPU is old (and slow) and is laboring just to keep the OS running, then adding an Oracle database isn't a good idea. Additionally, if so many other programs are running and consuming the CPU, you can have problems trying to run Oracle. For as much hype as you hear about CPU speeds, a better solution than having one fast CPU is having multiple CPUs; even if they are a little slower, more CPUs are better than fewer.

✔ **Disk:** The disk is where the Oracle database software is stored — essentially on your hard drive. The disk is only where your Oracle software itself is installed; it's not where your actual database files will exist with all your data. Oracle software installations take only a few gigabytes, but actual databases can take terabytes.

Like most software, a minimum value is listed by the vendor but more is generally better. Table 3-4 lists the *minimum* hardware requirements for 12c databases.

Table 3-4		Minimum Hardware Requirements		
Operating System	*RAM*	*Virtual Memory/Swap*	*CPU*	*Disk*
Windows	2GB	2 times RAM	550 MHz	6GB
Linux	2GB	1 to 2 times RAM	550 MHz	6GB

When identifying where you're going to install the software, make sure that you allow space for growth — don't just go with the minimum hardware requirements. After you install the software, you may have patches to apply (which take space), and log files will grow as the software runs; you don't want to run out of space!

Software requirements

Your OS version must meet the Oracle requirements. Being close isn't good enough. Oracle 12c is currently supported to operate on the following requirements in these specific Windows and Linux operating environments:

- Windows Server 2008 x64 — Standard, Enterprise, Datacenter, Web, and Foundation editions

- Windows Server 2008 R2 x64 — Standard, Enterprise, Datacenter, Web, and Foundation editions

- Windows 7 x64 — Professional, Enterprise, and Ultimate editions

- Oracle Enterprise LINUX 5.0 and 6.0

- Red Hat Enterprise LINUX 5.0 and 6.0

- SUSE LINUX Enterprise Server 11.0 SP2

Oracle is also supported on multiple UNIX operating environments, such as Sun Solaris, HP HP-UX, and IBM AIX. Obtain the most current information about kernel requirements on the Oracle Technology Network at the following URL:

`www.oracle.com/technetwork/indexes/documentation/index.html`

Also consider that an OS has software bug fixes applied to it in the form of patches, which create a patch level. Patches aren't a negative reflection of any particular operating system; they're simply part of the software development lifecycle. Oracle requires a specific minimum patch level per OS for the database software to even install.

It's common to have the system administrator apply software patches before the Oracle installer will execute. Hopefully, your system administrator routinely applies patches as they become available so that your OS is relatively current. Keep in mind that often a server needs to be restarted for the OS patches to take effect. The ramification is that if you need a patch applied, you may have to schedule time for a server to be restarted, which, depending on your organization's policies, may take several days or weeks.

How do you know what patches need to be applied? One way is to check the Oracle Documentation Installation and Configuration Guide as it lists the minimum requirements. Sometimes, though, the requirements change faster than the documentation, and you need to check the Release Notes for detailed updates. These notes appear on the Oracle website under Installing and Upgrading for your specific OS version (`www.oracle.com/pls/db121/homepage`) or on the software installation media.

An easier method is to let the Oracle Universal Installer (executed via the run-Installer program) check for you. With the `-executeSysPrereqs` option flag, the OUI program runs checks on the OS for version, patching, and hardware requirements prior to installing any software. It makes sure that at least the minimum requirements are met before software is installed, thus reducing problems during installation. The OUI is also a great way to generate a list of necessary patches so that you can have your system administrator install them. To run the OUI, execute it like so:

```
$ runInstaller -executeSysPrereqs
Starting Oracle Universal Installer...

Checking Temp space: must be greater than 500 MB.    Actual 27861 MB    Passed
Checking swap space: must be greater than 150 MB.    Actual 3924 MB     Passed
Checking monitor: must be configured to display at least 256 colors
```

Storage requirements

Your ORACLE_HOME directory hosts your software files and binaries. When installed, the ORACLE_HOME doesn't grow excessively except for when patches are applied. The ORACLE_BASE grows some during logging operations and even more if trace and core dump files are generated. However, it's the actual database files that can take lots of space and grow rapidly.

Database files (data, index, redo, and temp) should be stored separately from the installation files and binaries for management, growth, and performance reasons.

Many smaller databases are installed on whatever disk space is available on the server (called *internal drives*). Cramming multiple, smaller databases onto internal drives is often not optimal for several reasons:

- ✔ You have negative performance impacts when database files are on non-dedicated disks.
- ✔ Internal disks are often not as fast or flexible as external disk solutions.
- ✔ You need to consider special backup and recovery issues because these files have different backup requirements than other files. (See Chapter 8.)

Despite these issues, many people still cram their databases onto internal disks until their databases grow too large.

One downside of having a large or medium-sized database is that it takes a lot of disk space. Often the database will be larger than the internal disk that comes with your server, so you need another option, such as storing your database on a large disk farm or disk storage array attached to your database server.

Storage arrays can be complex devices, but they offer many benefits. Using attached storage allows your database to grow because the storage administrator can allocate more space as needed. The reading and writing of data is often buffered in memory on the array to increase performance. Advanced configurations of disk mirroring and stripping are also available.

Disk optimization basics

Planning and configuring storage for a large database is an art and science, but everyone should understand a few basic concepts. First, not all data files are accessed equally. Some types of files are read/written to far more often than others. Classify your files into either high- or low-utilization categories and then isolate the high-utilization files onto separate disks. The idea is not to have all your high-utilization files on the same physical disk; spreading them out over multiple disks balances the read/write operations to reduce contention and improve performance. Not all disks are the same speed, so make sure that your high-utilization files are on the fastest disks you have.

A second key item deals with disk redundancy and RAID levels. Redundancy Array of Inexpensive/ Independent Disks is a categorization of how your data is spread across multiple disks. *Striping* is data written across multiple disks to speed up read/write access because there is less contention on an individual disk. *Mirroring* is maintaining multiple redundant copies of data on multiple disks so that if one disk fails, the data is still available (providing *fault tolerance*). *Parity* is a mathematical technique of maintaining special bits of data to re-create data if a disk is lost. The following table shows the most common RAID levels in use today.

RAID Level	Description	Benefit
0	Striping with no mirroring or parity	Performance benefit only
1	Mirroring with no striping	Improved fault tolerance
0+1	Striping and mirroring	Improved fault tolerance and performance
5	Striping with parity over multiple disks	Performance and fault tolerance without doubling needed disk space

Other RAID levels exist, but most times people use RAID 0+1 or RAID 5. You can achieve the best performance and fault tolerance with RAID 0+1, but it comes at the price of doubling your storage requirements because you're writing your data twice (mirroring). RAID 5 provides improved performance and fault tolerance while using less disk space, but the benefits aren't as pronounced due to the overhead of maintaining parity bits.

In addition to internal drives or attached storage, Oracle provides you three choices when determining what kind of disk to store your Oracle database files on:

✔ **Raw devices:** These unformatted *(uncooked)* disk partitions don't have an existing file system structure. While they're necessary for some advanced Oracle configurations and offer a performance improvement, they're difficult to manage and administer. Many people feel those negatives outweigh the benefits.

✔ **Automatic Storage Management (ASM):** A step up from raw devices, with ASM, Oracle manages the disk for you. It uses partitioned disks, but Oracle sets up the disk groups and spreads the data across them to improve performance by balancing disk Input/Output (I/O) operations. The idea is to offload the work of managing the disks from the system administrator and place it in control of Oracle.

✔ **File system:** The opposite of raw devices, these formatted _(cooked)_ disk partitions have traditional mount points and directories like most people would expect. This disk is by far the most common type of disk configuration because it's easy to use, intuitive, and standard for most servers. Although raw and ASM-based systems offer benefits, traditional file systems are still the de facto standard.

Planning the storage for your database is one of the most critical factors for your database. If you get it right, performance will be fast, and management of the database growth will be simple. Mess it up or don't pay attention to it, and you'll have slow performance, and management will be difficult. You can almost always add more memory or CPUs if you need them, but if a large database is stored incorrectly, fixing it can be a large undertaking.

Other requirements

Oracle databases don't operate in isolation merely for the edification on the DBA; they operate to support a computer system, which in turn meets a business need. Identifying the details of the computer system the database must support will likely identify some unique requirements.

The following sections describe common examples of additional requirements and questions to ask yourself, the application team, or other infrastructure personnel before installation.

Oracle version

What version of Oracle is needed for this system? It's common to use the newest version of the database available, but is the application software certified for that version? Often times, a Commercial Off-The-Shelf (COTS) software package may not be tested and certified by the vendor to run with the latest version of a database. Although it may work fine, you don't know until it's tested. Plus, many organizations are mandated to operate only in _vendor-supported configurations_. Running a vendor supported configuration means you use a certain version of Oracle database to support the application software, even if it's not the most recent release.

Oracle patches

Oracle software comes as a base release, such as 12.1.0.1.1, but then you're expected to apply patches to get a more stable and secure version, such as 12.1.0.1.2. These patches typically come in the form of Oracle Security Patch

Updates (SPUs) or Patch Set Updates (PSUs), which are released quarterly (January, April, July, and October).

These patches may fix both software bugs and security vulnerabilities. Oracle expects you to install the base version of the software first, and then apply whatever is the most recent SPU patch (such as July SPU 2013). You don't have to apply previous SPU patches; the fixes are cumulative, so the most recent SPU will do.

Although SPUs are the most common patch, sometimes Oracle provides what are commonly referred to as *one-off patches*. These patches fix only a specific bug and are included in future Oracle versions or non-security related patches.

SPU in this book refers to what was formally called a CPU (Critical Patch Update). Consider the terms interchangeable.

Oracle patches are commonly applied using the OPatch (opatch) utility. This is an Oracle-provided, Perl-based program that applies patches but also runs dependency and conflict checks between your patches and can undo (roll-back) patches. This utility stores a log of all patches applied in the oraInventory directory located in ORACLE_BASE. The opatch utility is a critical part of databases, and the rollback feature is great, but the wise DBA will still run a good backup of the software and databases before running any patch!

Network connectivity

Who is connecting to the database and how? Connecting to the database has more to it than just updating the local tnsnames.ora files with the connection information.

If you're operating in the two-tier client/server model, people will be connecting to the database directly by using OracleNet protocol (sometimes still called SQL*Net) and connecting on port 1521 or 1526. If you're operating in a multi-tiered web architecture, the application server is connecting to the database on behalf of the users, probably via JDBC.

While the default port for Oracle to listen on is 1521 (formerly 1526 in older versions), it is best to change this to a non-default port for security reasons. After all, anyone with the Oracle documentation will know what port to flood if they want to cause trouble for you. Choosing a non-default port is one more thing a hacker has to figure out. In essence, don't make it easy for them. See Chapter 5 for more on changing ports.

The question is, are these communication ports open on the firewalls for the users or application servers to access the database? Getting firewall ports open for users requires coordination with the network staff and security, which can sometimes be an issue.

Security

You need to follow any company wide security procedures for before, during, and after installation, and verify these procedures have been followed. Know whether an audit trail is required and, if so, completed. For example, is your company bound by any regulatory compliance such as Sarbanes-Oxley or HIPPA?

Many organizations have additional security procedures that need to be applied. You should consider these procedures before installation, as well as any impact they may have on the end product. It's not uncommon to have to uninstall some components, lock accounts, or change file and directory permissions after the installation.

Application

The database holds data, but it also contains PL/SQL packages, procedures, users, and grants/privileges to control access and processing of that data. Via SQL scripts and data loads, the DBA will load these objects and data into the finished database itself. You generally have either a client-based application or a web application server that accesses the database. The DBA and other application administrators will compile, install, and configure these components to access the database.

Automated batch jobs or programs may also be part of the build process. If the application is part of a commercial package, these steps are likely well documented along with any special requirements that need to be met. In cases of a home-grown application, the application developers and architects will develop the documentation and then provide the DBA with the proper steps to execute the application configuration. When you're done, don't forget to test and validate that the system works properly before turning it over to the users.

Backups

No planning session would be complete without consideration for database backups. The size and activity level of the database, sensitivity of the data, and availability and recovery requirements all drive the type and frequency of backups. In some cases, these backups take the form of traditional cold and hot backup scripts written in-house or downloaded off the web. In many other cases, you're using Oracle's preferred backup utility, Recovery Manager, to schedule and run various backups. And, of course, you need to store these backups somewhere or write them to tape or other media. (For more on backup methodology, see Chapter 8.)

One final note on backups: Planning and executing backups isn't enough; you need to actually test them to ensure that they work as planned before relying on them!

Part II
Implementing an Oracle Database

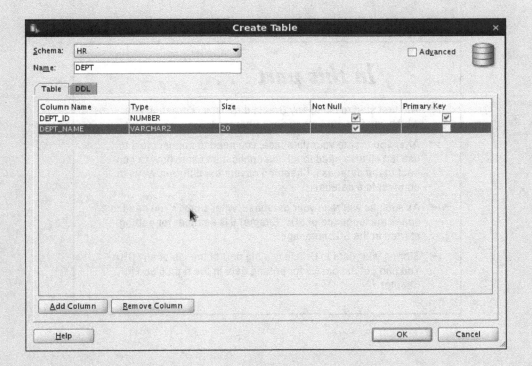

Visit www.dummies.com/extras/oracle12c to see how to upgrade an existing database with the Database Upgrade Assistant.

In this part . . .

✔ The first step to using any Oracle database is creating one, which you find out how to do in Chapter 4.

✔ After you create your database, you need to connect to it to use it. You also need to tell the application users how to connect to the database. Chapter 5 covers the different ways to connect to a database.

✔ As soon as you're in your database, what's next? You need to speak the language of SQL. Chapter 6 is a primer for getting started in the SQL language.

✔ Storing your data in Oracle is a big part of the job of any DBA. You find out the basics for putting data in the right place in Chapter 7.

Chapter 4

Creating Your Database

● ●

In This Chapter

▶ Familiarizing yourself with the Oracle environment

▶ Configuring an Instance

▶ Using the Database Configuration Assistant to create databases

▶ Post database creation checkup

● ●

Creating a database takes a lot of work. Thankfully, a graphical tool called the *Database Configuration Assistant* (DBCA) helps you point and click your way to victory. However, as its name implies, it only assists. Just like any software wizard-type tool, it can't cover every option; it can't explain everything. It *does* cover up some of the ugly syntax and other required activities (like creating directories and setting permissions) commonly forgotten by someone new to Oracle. It truly is a wonderful tool . . . as long as you know what options to use and what values are appropriate for the questions that it asks you.

With that said, this chapter goes over some of the details necessary to make the right decisions up front when creating a database. Doing so saves you from having to go back and do things twice . . . or even three times. In addition, when you understand why you make certain choices, it helps you create a robust and scalable database that serves you for a long time to come.

Feeling at Home in Your Environment

You should get familiar with a few things before working in your Oracle environment:

▮ ✔ Oracle software owner

▮ ✔ Oracle version

▮ ✔ Oracle base

✔ Oracle home

✔ Oracle SID (instance/database name)

✔ Path

Knowing how to find and work with these, you will better be able to manage not only your database but also databases and Oracle installations on other machines.

If Oracle was properly installed, these items should be relatively similar across most installations. Furthermore, if they're not similar, understanding what they are and how to find their values makes it easier for you to adapt.

Some slight differences exist between Oracle installations on Windows versus a Linux/UNIX environment. We point out some of those differences as well.

Finding the Oracle software owner

The Oracle software owner is a user on the operating system.

Linux/UNIX

On Linux/UNIX, you typically create a new user to own the installation files. Most commonly, this user is called oracle.

In addition, you create two OS groups:

✔ **oinstall** should be the user's primary group. This group will contain any users whom you would like to allow the ability to install and patch the Oracle software.

✔ **dba** contains any users whom you would like to have the power to manage the database in its entirety. Be very careful who you put into these groups — they could wreak havoc on your system and/or have access to all your data.

Windows

Windows has gone a long way to simplify running complex software on their system, and Oracle developed its software to play along. Installing Oracle on Windows only requires that the user be a member of the Local Administrators group on the machine where Oracle is installed.

Consider these tips, however, which include more creation:

✔ You don't have to create a user specifically to own the software in Windows, but we do it anyway because Oracle runs on Windows through a series of services. This way you can start those services as a specific owner.

✔ If you use the Windows task scheduler, consider using the Oracle software account to run the jobs. Jobs are easier for people to identify when they're owned by a named account.

✔ In Windows, you may sometimes want to map a drive for Oracle to use. It's easier if you assign it to a central Oracle management account so it isn't removed by someone else or forgotten about if passwords change.

You don't have to create any groups on Windows, but during the installation it creates a group on its own called ORA_DBA. This group behaves much the same way as the dba group on Linux/UNIX, so be careful who you add to it.

Oracle versions

This book is about Oracle 12c, but you may have to deal with environments that have multiple versions of Oracle installed. This issue with multiple versions is especially evident when you're upgrading your database from one release to the next. You may also encounter it when you're testing new releases against existing applications.

When you upgrade a database to the same machine, you install the new version of Oracle in parallel with the existing one. It's important to know how to change the environments around and tell which one is active. You find out how to do so on both Windows and Linux/UNIX in the later section "Setting your environment with oraenv."

Getting to home base

On systems where Oracle is installed, an important part of managing the Oracle installation is understanding environment variables. *Environment variables* tell

✔ The OS what software to run

✔ Oracle where to store certain files

✔ Oracle what database you want to connect to

The four most important variables are

- ORACLE_BASE
- ORACLE_HOME
- ORACLE_SID
- PATH

ORACLE_BASE

ORACLE_BASE is the top directory where all Oracle files on the machine are going to exist. If you have multiple versions of Oracle on the same machine, the ORACLE_BASE is likely the same.

Unless you have extraordinary circumstances and want everything to stay separate, we recommend having your ORACLE_BASE be the same for all installations.

Here are a few common ORACLE_BASE settings:

/opt/oracle

/u01/app/oracle

/app/oracle

Oracle documentation uses /u01/app/oracle in most examples, so we stick with that here.

Keep the following advice in mind when setting ORACLE_BASE:

- Don't install anything else under ORACLE_BASE.
- Choose a mount point that's not used for any other major OS or other third-party software.
- The final directory in the ORACLE_BASE should be oracle.

When you create your database, Oracle creates a series of directories underneath the ORACLE_BASE and uses them for management, logging, and troubleshooting.

ORACLE_HOME

ORACLE_HOME is where you have Oracle installed. Not only that, but it tells your session which Oracle installation you want to use.

If you have multiple Oracle installations on the same machine, set this variable to the location of the one that you want to work with.

Typically, ORACLE_HOME values contain the major release number of the Oracle version installed in the directory. It's created as a subdirectory off ORACLE_BASE. For example:

/u01/app/oracle/product/12.1.0

/u01/app/oracle/product/11.2.0

/opt/oracle/product/9.2.0

$ORACLE_BASE/product/12.1.0

The last example shows how you should use your ORACLE_BASE to define your ORACLE_HOME.

ORACLE_SID

ORACLE_SID is simply set to the name of the database that you want to connect to. If the database doesn't exist, set it to the name of the database you're about to create.

Limit your ORACLE_SID to 8 characters beginning with a letter. Also, on some operating systems, ORACLE_SID is case sensitive. We recommend sticking with lowercase.

You can change the ORACLE_SID within your session if you're moving around to different databases. Just be very careful and note which database you're connecting to. I'd be lying if I said the authors of this book have never made that mistake.

PATH

The PATH variable is typically already set for all sessions on the system. However, when you're using Oracle, you have to add to the path. You simply have to remember to put ORACLE_HOME/bin in front of your path.

ORACLE_HOME/bin is where the Oracle binaries are located. It contains tools such as the DBCA, SQL*Plus, and Data Pump.

By putting ORACLE_HOME/bin in front of your path, you can execute these tools without always having to

✔ Be in the ORACLE_HOME/bin directory.

✔ Type the full path every time to want to launch a tool.

The OS checks your PATH locations sequentially to find the tool you're trying to launch. By putting your ORACLE_HOME/bin first, you guarantee not launching some other software package that has a tool with the same name as one of your Oracle tools.

Setting your environment with oraenv

All the environment settings are stored in your OS user profile on Linux/ UNIX. That way, the appropriate parameters are configured every time you log in to the system to use the database.

If you're constantly switching your environment to connect to different databases and different Oracle versions, it might suit you to create a script where you name your various environments and then run the script and input your choice.

Oracle provides a script to change the environment on Linux/UNIX installations: oraenv. (Windows has no such handy little script.) You simply run the script, and it asks what database you want to connect to. Then it sets the rest of your environment accordingly.

This output asks whether you want to set the environment for the dev12c database. That happens to be the first database created on the machine by default. We override the default by choosing prod12c and it set the environment accordingly.

```
[oracle@classroom ~]$ oraenv
ORACLE_SID = [dev12c] ? prod12c
The Oracle base for ORACLE_HOME=
/u01/app/oracle/product/12.1.0/db_1 is /u01/app/oracle
```

In Windows, all the environment settings are also set in the registry. You can override them by setting variables from the DOS command line or by setting system-level environment variables. Of course, if you're lucky enough to have only one environment and one database on your machine, you only have to mess with this once, when setting Oracle up. For most people, that doesn't seem to be the case.

Configuring an Instance

Certain files in the database can completely change the way your database behaves. They can influence everything from performance and tuning as well as troubleshooting. Maintaining and configuring these files are a major component of database administration.

Using PFILE and SPFILES

These are the files that set up your database operating environment:

✔ PFILE

✔ SPFILES

In Chapter 2, we talk a bit about PFILE and SPFILES. In this section, we go through many of the common parameters you find in these files. The *parameter file* is the first file read when you start your database; the parameters within it configure how your database operates.

First, take a look at an example of a PFILE and some of the commonly set parameters:

```
*.audit_file_dest='/u01/app/oracle/admin/dev12c/adump'
*.audit_trail='db'
*.compatible='12.0.0.0.0'
*.control_files='/u01/app/oracle/oradata/dev12c/control01.ctl',
                '/u02/app/oracle/oradata/dev12c/control102.ctl',
                '/u03/app/oracle/oradata/dev12c/control103.ctl'
*.db_block_size=8192
*.db_domain='lfg.com'
*.db_name='dev12c'
*.db_recovery_file_dest='/u01/app/oracle/fast_recovery_area'
*.db_recovery_file_dest_size=4815m
*.diagnostic_dest='/u01/app/oracle'
*.memory_target=1280m
*.open_cursors=300
*.processes=300
*.undo_tablespace='UNDOTBS1'
```

The parameters have a * in front of them because you can use the parameter file to set parameters in more than one Oracle instance. In a file that serves multiple Oracle instances, you may see the instance name in front of some of the parameters, denoting that particular parameter only applies to one instance.

Follow these steps to see the parameters that are modified in an existing Oracle database:

1. **Log in to SQL*Plus as a SYSDBA.**

2. **Type** create pfile from spfile; **(including the semicolon).**

   The command dumps a text version of your SPFILE.

After you create your PFILE, you want to turn it into an SPFILE. Essentially, you do the reverse of what you did before:

1. **Log in to SQL*Plus as a SYSDBA.**

2. **Type** create spfile from pfile; **(including the semicolon).**

   You get a file called spfileORACLE_SID.ora in the same directory as your PFILE, where ORACLE_SID is your instance_name.

Setting parameters in the pfile and spfile

Whether you use PFILES or SPFILES determines how you set your parameters. This next section explains the common parameters in Oracle 12c and how they're configured in the files themselves.

With a new database, you always start with a PFILE. If you end up wanting to use an SPFILE, you create it from the PFILE (shown at the end of the chapter).

The first thing you need to do is find your PFILE. For whatever reason, despite all the other similarities, Linux/UNIX and Windows store it in different locations.

Find your PFILE on Windows, where ORACLE_SID is your instance name:

```
ORACLE_HOME\database\initORACLE_SID.ora
```

Find your PFILE on Linux/UNIX, where ORACLE_SID is your instance name:

```
ORACLE_HOME/dbs/initORACLE_SID.ora
```

These parameters are some of the most commonly customized. Most parameters suit most databases at their default value.

The * means to apply the parameter to all instances that read this file.

- ✔ **audit_file_dest:** This parameter tells Oracle where to put auditing information on the file system. All connections to the database as SYSDBA are audited and put into this directory. Furthermore, if you're auditing other operations in the database, those audit records may be dumped here as well.

- ✔ **audit_trail:** This tells Oracle where you want audit records written. Audit records are written to the database or the file system. They can be in text format or XML. Records written to the database are stored in the AUD$ system table. The valid values for this parameter follow:

  - *db:* Normal audit records written to the AUD$ table

  - *os:* Normal audit records written to the audit_file_dest directory

- *db_extended:* Audit records written to the AUD$ table in extended format, including SQLTEXT and bind variable values

- *xml:* XML-formatted normal audit records written to the database

- *xml, extended:* Normal auditing and includes all columns of the audit trail, including SqlText and SqlBind values in XML format to the database

✔ **compatible:** Set it to force the database to behave like a version earlier than Oracle 12c. In Oracle 12c, you can set it back as far as 10.0.0. However, it can be set back only before the database is created or before upgrading from an earlier version. After you migrate this parameter to 12.1.0 and open the database, you can no longer go back. The parameter is useful for testing before an upgrade is complete. Most of the time you find it set on the latest version for your software. If you try using a feature from a database version later than what you've configured, it results in an Oracle error.

✔ **control_files:** Just what is says. It tells the instance where to look for the control files during the startup phase. If the instance doesn't find even one of them, you can't mount your database. Notice in the parameters listing that the control files are spread across three different mount points.

✔ **db_block_size:** This parameter is really the only one you can't easily change without recreating the database, so choose it carefully. It tells the database what block size you want your Oracle blocks to be formatted on disk. We discuss block size in the upcoming "Taking the DBCA steps" section.

✔ **db_domain:** If you want your network domain to be part of your database name for identification purposes, fill in the domain name here. This won't be your actual database name, but an alias to identify it from other databases with the same name that might exist in another domain.

✔ **db_name:** The database name. Choose this name carefully. Although you can change it, doing so is a pain. The name can be up to eight alphanumeric characters. Avoid the urge to use special characters other than #, $, and _.

✔ **db_recovery_file_dest:** This sets what's known as the *Fast Recovery Area.* The area can hold files such as

- Backups

- Archive log files

- Control files

- Redo log files

✔ **db_recovery_file_dest_size:** This determines how much space is dedicated to your Flash Recovery Area. If it fills up, you get an error message and the database could come to a halt — especially if you're storing archive log files here. If archive log files can't be written, redo log files can't be overwritten. User sessions hang until the situation is resolved.

✔ **diagnostic_dest:** This location is known as the *Automatic Diagnostic Repository* (ADR) home. It contains files that Oracle support may use to resolve issues with your database. This parameter was new in 11g. You can use a new tool called ADRCI to access the files in this directory. It contains

- • Trace files
- • Core files
- • Alert logs
- • Incident files

✔ **memory_target:** This parameter sets the memory that the Oracle instance is allowed to use for all *System Global Area* (SGA) and program global area activities described in Chapter 2. It doesn't include memory consumed by server and user processes.

✔ **open_cursors:** Limits the number of open SQL cursors a session can have.

✔ **processes:** Limits the number of OS users' processes that can connect to the instance.

✔ **undo_tablespace:** This parameter tells the instance to which tables it will write its transaction undo. It must be an undo type tablespace.

Creating Your Oracle Database

You can create a database one of four ways:

✔ **Manually with SQL commands:** If you're on an ancient release like Oracle 8i, we recommend manual SQL commands; the DBCA wasn't as good back then. However, with Oracle 9i and up, it has really become a robust and useful tool. Furthermore, with more features being added to the database, the manual method isn't a laundry list of scripts. Back in the day, you had to run only an SQL command and two scripts. Not anymore. There are upwards of a dozen creation scripts depending on what features you want to install.

✔ **With the graphical tool called Database Configuration Assistant (DBCA):** We recommend Database Configuration Assistant (DBCA) to make your Oracle database. This recommendation is especially important for beginners. If you use DBCA to create the database, you don't have to make the PFILE; the DBCA creates it for you. You may want to alter your setting later, however.

✔ **A combination of SQL commands and DBCA:** Even old-timers like us prefer DBCA or SQL and DBCA. Using SQL to create the database gives you control over every aspect of the creation, but it also leaves open a lot of areas for mistakes and accidental omissions.

✔ **Cloning an existing database:** This book doesn't cover the topic because it's a more advanced topic for, uh, smarties?

Using the Database Configuration Assistant (DBCA) to Create Databases

Launch the Database Configuration Assistant (that's right; you're in charge) from the command line of the operating system where the database resides.

The DBCA walkthrough in this chapter chooses the Advanced and Custom Database option (versus General Purpose or Data Warehouse options). This option is for when you really want to get your hands dirty and have complete control. We like this option for a few reasons:

✔ You don't have to install the features that you aren't going to use. They just take up more space and give you more things to manage.

✔ You can specify a lot more options that the other templates don't allow.

✔ Customizing isn't that hard. You're reading the book, right? It'll be easy.

The only drawback to the Custom Database method is the time it takes while creating the data files. How much time? We've seen it take anywhere from 2 to 30 minutes. It depends on

✔ The number of CPUs your system has

✔ What features you select

Taking database control

Oracle Enterprise Manager is an option you can choose during database creation. Don't get too attached to this invaluable resource. Take some time to get to know the basic SQL commands for managing your database. I've seen Enterprise Manager crash where the only thing left was a blinking SQL prompt. A well-rounded DBA knows how to manage her database both ways.

> ## Database Configuration Assistant
>
> Not only does this tool create databases, but it also lets you delete and modify them and create database templates. The top in the title bar reads 1 of 13 steps. We kid you not that in Oracle 9i it was 1 of 8 steps, and in 10g it was 1 of 12 steps. This is what we mean: Creating the database with the DBCA is the way to go as Oracle gets heavier with features.

Taking the DBCA steps

If you're ever unsure about an option on the DBCA screen, click the Help button. It does a good job of explaining what each item does.

One of the things we have noticed in Oracle 12c is that Oracle has done a good job of speeding up the Help function. In past versions, it took forever to load. Also, in 12c, the look and feel has changed a lot to be more consistent with the Oracle Universal Installer.

The DBCA has a lot of screens with all kinds of information. The following steps take you through creating a database with the Database Configuration Assistant:

1. **Log in as the Oracle software owner.**

2. **Go to a command prompt.**

3. **Type** dbca.

   You see a splash screen, as shown in Figure 4-1, and another screen with options.

4. **Select the Create a Database option.**

   You are presented with the option of using a default configuration or an advanced one.

5. **Select the Advanced option.**

6. **Click Next.**

   You see the output shown in Figure 4-2. Optional database templates are shown:

   - General Purpose
   - Data Warehouse
   - Custom Database

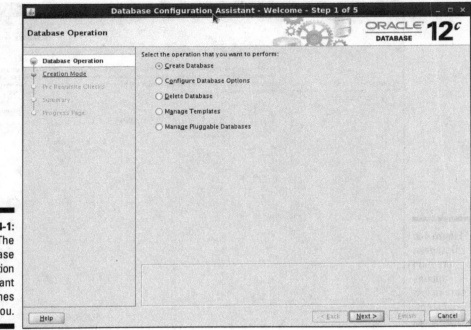

Figure 4-1:
The
Database
Configuration
Assistant
welcomes
you.

The first two include the data files. You supply a few custom settings, and it unzips the database from the Oracle installation directory. Use these options only when you're new to Oracle and aren't sure what to do with some of the more advanced parameters. You should select Custom here; we go over all the options in the rest of the steps.

7. Select the Custom Database option.

Click Show Details if you want to see the features, parameters, and files chosen by default for each type of database.

8. Click Next.

A screen asks you to choose the database name.

9. Fill in these fields:

- *Global Database Name:* Your database name with your network domain attached. If you don't want to attach your network domain, leave this field blank. Doing so just sets the initialization parameter db_domain. It helps uniquely identify your database on the network. For example, you might have a database named prod in two different domains. A global database name allows that without confusing some of the Oracle networking features.

- *SID:* This is the short name for your database. It equates to your environment variable ORACLE_SID.

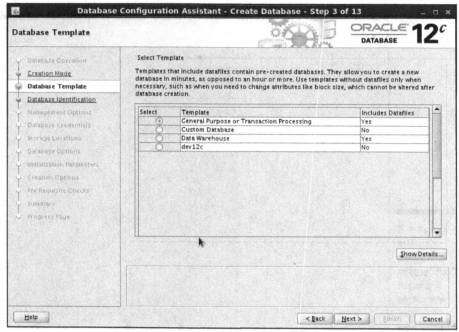

Figure 4-2:
Database
creation
options
require lots
of steps.

10. **Click Next.**

You're asked whether you want to manage your database with Oracle Enterprise Manager, as shown in Figure 4-3. (You can read more about Oracle Enterprise Manager in Chapter 13.)

You can configure this two ways:

- *Configure Enterprise Manager (EM) Database Express:* Database Express is a management package that runs locally on the database machine and has many of the features of Cloud Control. However, it controls only one database. We caution you only when configuring Database Express. If you're setting up Oracle on a machine with limited resources, you're going to feel Database Express, if you know what we mean. The good news is, in 12c, Database Express is much better in resources usage than prior versions (known then as Database Console).

- *Register with Enterprise Manager (EM) Cloud Control:* An Oracle software package that typically runs on its own server elsewhere on your network. It can manage many databases, many versions of Oracle, servers, application servers, and even other non-Oracle software, such as Microsoft SQL server, and firewalls. You must have the Grid Control Management Agent installed to get this option.

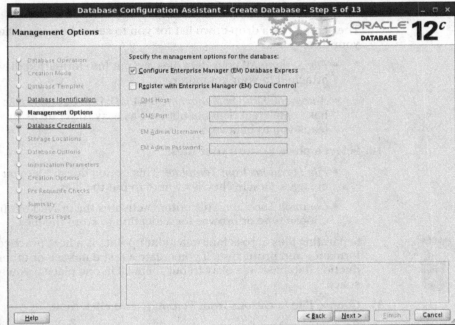

11. **Select the Configure Enterprise Manager (EM) Database Express option.**

12. **Click Next to continue.**

13. **Set the database credentials (passwords).**

    You have two choices here. You can set the passwords individually for the users that are created with the database or set the same password for all users. We ask that you select *Use the same administrative password for all accounts* to keep things simple for now. Fill in the Password and Confirm Password text boxes.

    Here are some good password practices:

    - Use different password for each user. If this is a test database, it may not matter that much. Even if you want to keep it simple now and make all the passwords the same, you can easily go back change them later.

    - Set the same password for everyone. If this is production, it's in your best interest to have separate passwords for all the users.

14. **Click Next.**

    You're asked whether you want to register your database with a listener. If you do, choose the correct listener and click Next.

15. Select an option for how you want to store your files.

The screen has a drop-down list for you to select how you want to store your files:

- *File System:* All your data files are put into formatted drives attached to your computer.

- *Automatic Storage Management (ASM):* Don't choose this now. ASM has some great benefits but isn't as easy to set up as the DBCA leads you to believe.

16. Select a place to store your files:

- *File Locations from Template:* This option doesn't let you make any changes. Oracle chooses where to put the files.

- *Common Location:* This option activates the grayed-out field. You choose type or browse for a location to store the files.

Separating files across multiple mount points is a best practice for performance and protection. If you create a test database or other nonproduction database, it's okay to put them all in one place if you have the space.

17. Choose File Locations from Template and click Next.

You're in the Fast Recovery Area (FRA) configuration. The FRA is a storage area that resides on disk which can house backups, archive logs files, control files, and redo log files.

18. Choose to configure the FRA.

Doing so simplifies the storage of backups and archive log files. We don't typically use it for the control or redo files; we manually separate those files ourselves.

19. Determine what FRA space you have available and increase it accordingly.

The default value is about 5GB. This might be okay for the archive log files of small databases. However, an FRA of this size fills up very quickly. You can resize the FRA anytime without taking down the database.

20. Choose to archive later and click Next.

Archiving adds drain on the system while creating the database. It's easy enough to enable later on.

TIP

Filing that away

We could buy the argument that it's okay to put files in the same location if later on you were going to separate your application data files accordingly. Also, it's relatively easy to move them. The other possibility is that you're going to use a large chunk of storage on a SAN (a high-speed *storage area network*) that presents its storage to you as one location, and then you'll manage the performance in the background by spreading the files across many disks.

You're asked what features you want to install on the screen. Depending on what software you installed, not all are available. Luckily, you can add later. Click the Help button if you want a more detailed description:

- *Oracle Text:* This indexing feature allows custom indexing of large text-type documents. It can index pages of data. It also allows advanced searching against rich media objects.

- *Oracle OLAP:* This is Oracle's business intelligence tool.

- *Oracle Spatial:* This mapping tool is for geospatial mapping.

- *Oracle Label Security:* Label security is for securing data in a way that gives users levels of access to restricted data.

- *Sample Schemas Tab:* This is a bunch of test data that you can use for training or trying new features. We usually install this on test and training databases. It includes several schemas with varying degree of complexity.

- *Oracle Database Vault:* Basically, this option locks down the database to extreme measure, disallowing activities we take for granted in a normal system. It protects your database against your own people, in essence. It significantly creates more management overhead. However, in a system that must remain ultra-secure, it's the price you pay.

- *Oracle JVM:* This is the Oracle Java Container for running Java out of the database.

- *Oracle Multimedia:* This feature extends Oracle's capabilities to offer better support for multimedia data.

- *Oracle Application Express:* This is the kind of a development environment that allows you to develop applications in a web-based framework. It runs on top of the database and allows creating hosted applications that can be quite robust.

If you're testing to get a basic environment up and running, deselect everything. However, if you're going to work with one or more of these options, install them. Remember that they take space and time during the database creation process — some more so than others.

21. **Click Next.**

    Figure 4-4 shows the screen where you begin choosing the initialization parameters discussed earlier in the chapter. The Memory tab has two options: Typical Settings and Custom Settings.

22. **Select the Typical Settings option.**

    Because we're talking Oracle 12c, selecting Typical Settings sets the memory target as one large chunk and lets Oracle figure out where everything goes.

23. **Click the Sizing tab.**

24. **Select the block size.**

    If you get this wrong, your only option is to re-create your database (if the performance problems haven't gotten you fired).

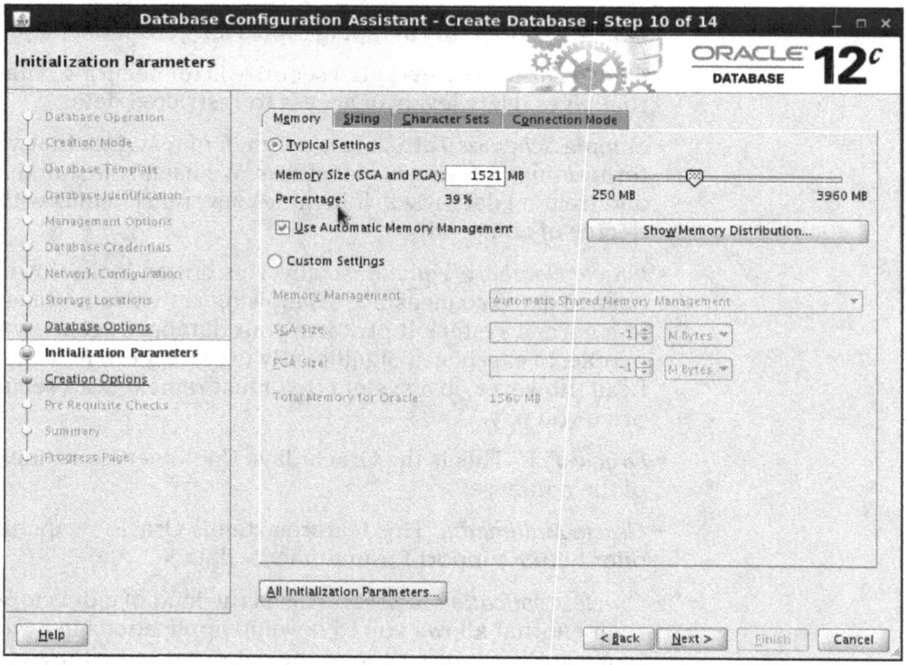

Database Configuration Assistant - Create Database - Step 10 of 14

Initialization Parameters

ORACLE **12**^{c}
DATABASE

- Database Operation
- Creation Mode
- Database Template
- Database Identification
- Management Options
- Database Credentials
- Network Configuration
- Storage Locations
- Database Options
- **Initialization Parameters**
- Creation Options
- Pre Requisite Checks
- Summary
- Progress Page

Memory | Sizing | Character Sets | Connection Mode

⦿ Typical Settings

Memory Size (SGA and PGA): [1521] MB

Percentage: 39 %

☑ Use Automatic Memory Management

250 MB   3960 MB

[Show Memory Distribution...]

○ Custom Settings

Memory Management   Automatic Shared Memory Management

SGA Size   -1   M Bytes

PGA Size   -1   M Bytes

Total Memory for Oracle   1560 MB

[All Initialization Parameters...]

[Help]   [< Back] [Next >] [Finish] [Cancel]

Figure 4-4:
Choosing database initialization parameters.

Keep the following details in mind as you decide on your block size:

- If you're creating a database that will have many users with smaller quick transactions, go with a block size of 4k.

- If you're creating a data warehouse-type database with large SQL queries that retrieve heaps of data at once for analysis, choose the largest block size you can. The largest block size you can choose is OS dependent.

- If you're somewhere in the middle of the first two, go with 8k.

- Make sure the block size is divisible evenly by the OS block size or OS I/O size. You don't want your OS to read a minimum of 8k but choose a 4k block size. That would waste 4k for every read.

25. Click the Character Set tab.

You can change the character set after creating the database, but it's time consuming and tedious. Select a character set that will house all the characters that your application may use.

- *Database Character Set:* For all the standard-language columns in your database. Also encompasses the character set that Oracle messages will display in, and the characters you may use in program code.

- *National Character Set:* For special datatypes that may house data only used in your applications. For example, what if you work at a primarily English-speaking university and the Greek department wants to create an application to storage indexable, searchable Greek manuscripts? No programming or database message will be displayed in Greek.

- *Unicode Character Sets:* Select this option if you're going to support multiple languages.

26. Click the Connection Mode tab.

You have two options:

- Dedicated Server Mode
- Shared Server Mode

We discuss this in Chapter 2. Most current systems use dedicated server connections. In most cases, we recommend starting that way. If memory is constantly running short (while at the same time supporting thousands of users), investigate shared server configuration.

The All Initialization Parameters button lets you adjust all parameters discussed earlier in the chapter (as well as others we didn't); see Figure 4-5 for the All Initialization Parameters screen. By default, the screen shows only what Oracle considers basic parameters. Oracle considers some parameters advanced. You don't need them, but if you're curious, click the Show Advanced Parameters button.

	All Initialization Parameters			✕
Name ▲	Value	Override Default	Category	
cluster_database	FALSE		Cluster Database	▲
compatible	12.0.0.0.0	✔	Miscellaneous	
control_files	("/u01/app/oracle/oradata/{DB_UN...	✔	File Configuration	
db_block_size	8	✔	Cache and I/O	
db_create_file_dest			File Configuration	
db_create_online_log_dest_1			File Configuration	
db_create_online_log_dest_2			File Configuration	
db_domain		✔	Database Identification	
db_name	dev12d	✔	Database Identification	
db_recovery_file_dest	{ORACLE_BASE}/fast_recovery_area	✔	File Configuration	
db_recovery_file_dest_size	4800	✔	File Configuration	
db_unique_name			Miscellaneous	
instance_number	0		Cluster Database	
log_archive_dest_1			Archive	
log_archive_dest_2			Archive	
log_archive_dest_state_1	enable		Archive	
log_archive_dest_state_2	enable		Archive	
nls_language	AMERICAN		NLS	
nls_territory	AMERICA		NLS	
open_cursors	300	✔	Cursors and Library ...	
pga_aggregate_target	390		Sort, Hash Joins, Bitm...	
processes	300	✔	Processes and Sessions	
remote_listener			Network Registration	
remote_login_passwordfile	EXCLUSIVE	✔	Security and Auditing	
sessions	172		Processes and Sessions	▼

Help   Close   Show Advanced Parameters   Show Description

Figure 4-5:
The All
Initialization
Parameters
page lets
you make
adjustments.

27. **Breathe.**

    You're almost done.

28. **Click the Customize Storage Button to make storage adjustments.**

    Now is a good time to make sure the files spread across multiple mount points. Click each menu: Controlfile, Tablespaces, Datafiles, and Redo Log Groups. Change the directories (on the right) so they're not all in the same place.

    As you can see in Figure 4-6, the screen lists the file and storage objects. The screen currently shows the Controlfile choices.

    About file locations: In the past, we've encountered problems with some directories not being there when you change where the files are created. Sometimes Oracle complains about permissions.

    Make sure the permissions on the directories where you store your files are set for the Oracle user to read and write. For example, if you move a control file to /u01/oradata/dev12c and that directory isn't there, some systems give an error and the database creation stops.

    We create all the directories where files are going to go ahead of time. This might resolve some headaches when you launch the actual database creation.

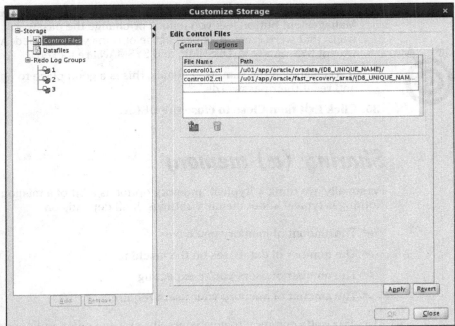

Figure 4-6:
The storage
configura-
tion page
lists file and
storage
objects.

29. **Click the Close button when you are finished adjusting any files.**

30. **Decide if you want to save your decisions as a template for future use.**

    If you think you may create a similar database again, this step is a good idea. You can give it a name and a description.

31. **Save everything you did in a set of scripts and decide where you want them.**

    It's a good idea to keep these around just in case. Also, if you're curious about all the scripting work you just avoided by using the DBCA, have a look.

32. **Decide whether you want to create the database now.**

33. **Click Next to go to the summary screen.**

34. **Click Finish.**

    A screen shows all the options you just chose and the parameters you set.

    The creation status screen appears. A status bar and options also appear. You can watch it go through everything until it's done.

When the database is complete, a screen shows the details. A Password Management button lets you unlock or change the passwords of the users that were created as part of the options you installed. All users except SYS, SYSTEM, DBSNMP, and SYSMAN are locked.

If you installed the sample schemas, this is a good place to unlock them and reset their passwords.

35. Click Exit then Close to close the DBCA.

Sharing (a) memory

Personally, we think a "typical" memory option is a bit of a misnomer. Nothing is typical about memory settings. It all depends on

- The amount of memory you have
- The number of databases on the machine
- The number of users you're expecting
- The amount of memory your users require

Also, it is quite common to give yourself a starting point and then go from there. Oracle suggests using 40 percent of your memory for the shared and private areas of your database. This is an interesting choice. What if this machine were destined to house ten databases? Hmmm. . . .

Think about how the memory on this machine is going to be shared. These points might help you decide:

- Never start with the combination of shared and private memory areas of all your databases on the machine consuming more than half the memory. Therefore, if you have 8GB of memory and will have two databases, both memory_target parameters combined *shouldn't exceed* 4GB. This setup gives plenty of room for error.

  The reason for this is to make sure you have plenty of room for other processes on the system to run. For each database you add, you may need to go back and resize your memory components to make sure they all fit and there's enough left-over memory for the day to day operations of the system. This is not a hard and fast rule; we are giving you an example of leaving half the memory available because it is a relatively safe approach. If you know your system and its memory better, you can be more liberal with your memory usage.

- If your database is going to be extremely large, figure out how many users will have server sessions at once. Take that number and multiply it by 8MB. Add 2GB for your OS and then add 20 percent more of the available memory. Split what is left over amongst the rest of the databases.

10g memories

If you were on Oracle 10g, the Custom option on the Memory tab gives you a choice. You can set separate shared and private areas. It still gives you the typical 40 percent option, but it then sets the two in the background. If you were back in Oracle 9i, you'd have to set all the memory areas yourself. Man, how did we get by back in 2001? If you want to set everything yourself, or you want to see what it looked like in 9i just for the fun of it, select Custom and change the drop-down list to Manual Shared Memory Management. Ah, the memories. . . .

This still might not be right for you, so Chapter 11 discusses tuning and performance management. Ultimately, the memory you need boils down to monitoring and adjusting. We wanted to give you a starting point. It is one of the most common user questions yet is difficult to quantify without real application environment data.

Doing a Post-Creation Check-Up

When everything is complete, we recommend that you log in to your database for the first time and check everything out.

- ✔ Look in the directories where the files were supposed to go.

- ✔ Check your initialization parameters.

- ✔ Perform a backup if this is a soon-to-be production database. That way you don't have to create the entire database again if something goes wrong.

Chapter 5

Connecting to the Database

In This Chapter

▶ Starting and stopping the database

▶ Connecting to the database instance

▶ Avoiding pitfalls

*Y*ou can't use a database until it's running and you connect to it. In this chapter, we cover how to make that happen. First, we cover the setup of your DBA environment so you can log in to the database and begin your startup work. Next, we cover the various startup modes and states that a database can be in depending on your type of work. Furthermore, shutting down a database can happen in several ways. We cover all the options so that you can start up and shut down with the proper parameters.

You can connect locally or remotely to a database with Oracle Net. We examine the role of the database listener process and how to configure, start, and stop it. Next, we show how to set up client-side connections to the database. Finally, we cover a few common problems you might encounter when setting up Oracle Net.

Starting and Stopping the Database

Before users connect to a database instance to do work, it obviously must be running. Starting up entails allocating the database instance memory, starting the database processes, and opening the control and database files in a mode accessible and appropriate for the users. Depending on the type of work being done, there are several states a database can be in for the users or DBA to access. Alternatively, sometimes you need to shut down a database instance for a multitude of reasons. When you have to do a shutdown, though, what happens to users logged in and doing work? When performing a shutdown, you can handle existing users and the state of their work in several ways.

Environmental requirements

Before starting or stopping an Oracle database instance, a few environmental requirements must be met. These environment requirements get you logged in to the server as the correct user with the right environment variables so that you can do your DBA work.

Log in to the database server

Log in to the server where the database resides to do your key *database administrator* (DBA) work. Yes, you can do some of this via Enterprise Manager but only after you've set up your environment and created your database in the first place.

Most critical DBA work occurs on the database server itself because it provides the most flexibility and is the simplest for starting DBAs.

Log in as the Oracle DBA account

You should be in the operating system DBA account that owns the Oracle software to start and stop the database. Commonly this is the oracle user account and is in the DBA group:

```
$ id
uid=501(oracle) gid=501(oinstall) groups=501(oinstall),502(dba))
```

The oracle user is in groups oinstall and dba.

Set up your environment variables

Many environment variables exist for your oracle user, and we cover them in detail in Chapter 4. However, at a minimum you want to have these variables set:

- ORACLE_BASE
- ORACLE_HOME
- ORACLE_SID

```
$ echo $ORACLE_BASE
/u01/app/oracle
$ echo $ORACLE_HOME
/u01/app/oracle/product/12.1.0/dbhome_1
$ echo $ORACLE_SID
dev12c
```

Be sure to verify the ORACLE_BASE, ORACLE_HOME, and ORACLE_SID variables before you do any type of DBA work. It is very easy to define the wrong ORACLE_HOME, in which case you work with the wrong database software. Worse yet, it's even easier to incorrectly define ORACLE_SID and stop the wrong database! If it occurs frequently, you're making what we refer to as a "career-limiting move."

Start SQL*Plus as a DBA

The command-line interface into Oracle databases is SQL*Plus. To do serious DBA work such as startup or shutdown, you need to be logged in as SYSDBA.

To log in this way, you must be the oracle operating system user as described earlier in this chapter. Then start SQL*Plus with the "/ as sysdba" option:

```
$ sqlplus "/ as sysdba"

SQL*Plus: Release 12.1.0.1.0 - Production on Sun May 19 07:46:53 2013

Copyright (c) 1982, 2013, Oracle.  All rights reserved.


Connected to:
Oracle Database 12c Enterprise Edition Release 12.1.0.1.0 - 64bit Production
With the Partitioning, OLAP, Advanced Analytics and Real Application Testing
options

SQL>
```

An alternative: When you're in SQL*Plus, issue connect as sysdba to log in as SYSDBA, provided you're on the database server as the oracle operating system user.

```
SQL> connect / as sysdba
Connected.
SQL>
```

When you're connected as SYSDBA, you can begin your DBA work.

Database parameter file

Before starting the database, you must have a parameter file listing all the different runtime parameters, such as SGA configuration. This is covered in detail in Chapter 4, so we don't rehash the details here. However, we assume you have your SPFILE created and in a default location so that Oracle can find it. If it isn't in a default location, or you want to use a different parameter file, you may use the pfile=`'PATH TO SPFILE/FILENAME'` syntax with your startup commands.

Improper environment setup is a common error and is something you should correct before beginning your database work. Doing so will save you time and frustration troubleshooting unnecessary errors.

Starting the database

You don't actually *start* a database per se; you start the instance.

A *database* is defined as the actual data, index, redo, temp, and control files that exist on the files system. The *instance* consists of the processes (PMON, SMON, DBWR, LGWR, and others) and the SGA (memory pool) that access and process data from the database files. The instance is what accesses the database, and it is the instance that users connect to. Thus, it is the instance (not the database) that you actually start.

Are we splitting hairs here? Not in this case; you need to understand the relationship between the instance and the database to understand startup and shutdown.

As an Oracle instance starts, it proceeds through various states until it and the database are fully open and accessible to users. At each state, different components are started and opened. Furthermore, at each state you may perform different types of DBA or user work. You may specify your startup command to take the database instance into a specific state depending on what you need to do.

In ascending order, during startup the database instance goes through these states:

NOMOUNT

- ✔ Read Parameter File
- ✔ Allocate SGA
- ✔ Start Background Processes
- ✔ Only SGA and Background Processes Running
- ✔ Used for CREATE DATABASE (only SYS can access)
- ✔ Specified by STARTUP NOMOUNT

MOUNT

- ✔ Read Parameter File
- ✔ Allocate SGA
- ✔ Start Background Processes
- ✔ Open and Read Control File

- ✔ SGA and Background Processes Running and Control Files Open
- ✔ Used for database maintenance and recovery operations (only SYS can access)
- ✔ Specified by STARTUP MOUNT

OPEN

- ✔ Read Parameter File
- ✔ Allocate SGA
- ✔ Start Background Processes
- ✔ Open and Read Control File
- ✔ Open All Database Files
- ✔ SGA and Background Processes Running, Control Files Open, All Database Files Open
- ✔ Default OPEN state for database and is accessible by users and applications
- ✔ Specified by STARTUP or STARTUP OPEN

Unless you're performing specialized maintenance, the default is as follows:

- ✔ STARTUP with the parameter file read
- ✔ Background processes and SGA started
- ✔ Control files open and read
- ✔ All database files open

In this open state, users access the database normally.

Here's what it looks like when starting the database into the default OPEN mode. Because we're using the default parameter file, we don't need to specify one.

```
$ sqlplus "/ as sysdba"

SQL*Plus: Release 12.1.0.1.0 - Production on Sun May 19 09:59:12 2013

Copyright (c) 1982, 2013, Oracle.  All rights reserved.

Connected to an idle instance.
SQL> startup
ORACLE instance started.

Total System Global Area  789172224 bytes
Fixed Size                  2148552 bytes
Variable Size             557844280 bytes
Database Buffers          218103808 bytes
Redo Buffers               11075584 bytes
Database opened.
SQL>
```

Although we normally go straight to the fully open mode, you can increment the modes. For example, you could do database maintenance with the database in MOUNT mode and, once done, issue ALTER DATABASE OPEN to take the database to open mode so users can start work.

That's what's done here:

```
SQL> startup mount
ORACLE instance started.

Total System Global Area   789172224 bytes
Fixed Size                   2148552 bytes
Variable Size              570427192 bytes
Database Buffers           205520896 bytes
Redo Buffers                11075584 bytes
Database mounted.
SQL> alter database open;

Database altered.

SQL>
```

Note that you can only go forward to a more open state; you can't move to a more restrictive state without issuing a shutdown.

In most cases, when you open a database you want it open for every user. Sometimes, however, you want to block all or some users even though the database is in the OPEN state.

To do this, put the database in RESTRICTED SESSION mode via one of these ways:

✔ STARTUP RESTRICT

✔ ALTER SYSTEM ENABLE RESTRICTED SESSION

```
SQL> startup restrict;
ORACLE instance started.

Total System Global Area   789172224 bytes
Fixed Size                   2148552 bytes
Variable Size              570427192 bytes
Database Buffers           205520896 bytes
Redo Buffers                11075584 bytes
Database mounted.
Database opened.
SQL>
SQL> alter system enable restricted session;

System altered.
```

✔ When the database is OPEN, you must grant users CREATE SESSION to connect.

✔ When the database is RESTRICTED, users must have CREATE SESSION *and* they also must have RESTRICTED SESSION to connect.

The only backdoor is if the user was already logged in when an ALTER SYSTEM ENABLE RESTRICTED SESSION was issued; then the user can remain logged in. Therefore, you should kill all user sessions after putting the database in RESTRICTED mode to kick them out. If they don't have RESTRICTED SESSION, they get this Oracle error when they try to log in:

```
$ sqlplus barb/test123

SQL*Plus: Release 12.1.0.1.0 - Production on Sun May 19 11:26:41 2013

Copyright (c) 1982, 2013, Oracle.  All rights reserved.

ERROR:
ORA-01035: ORACLE only available to users with RESTRICTED SESSION privilege
```

Why would you want to do this (other than just to frustrate your users)? Although frustrating users is the secret pleasure of every administrator (especially security administrators), some valid technical reasons exist. Major data, table, or application updates often need a stable system with no updates or locks to contend with so they can process successfully. Some database maintenance operations also require a restricted session.

If you need to allow in a subset of users or perhaps the application user processing a database job, you may grant them RESTRICTED SESSION:

```
SQL> grant restricted session to barb;

Grant succeeded.

SQL> connect sdeas/test123
Connected.
```

Revoke the RESTRICTED SESSION from any non-DBA user once the user's work is done. Also, don't forget to take the instance out of restricted session.

```
SQL> alter system disable restricted session;

System altered.
```

Starting up database instances isn't terribly difficult, and most times you use the default STARTUP command to take the database instance to the OPEN state. Only occasionally does the situation require a RESTRICTED SESSION.

If the database startup seems to take a few minutes, it may be because of a large SGA during which time memory is being allocated. Or there may be many database files to open.

If the database crashed or a SHUTDOWN ABORT occurred prior to the startup, database instance recovery is occurring, which can take time. If this occurs, leave your screen with the STARTUP command open; let it run. View the alert log with another window. We cover the alert log in Chapter 12. If more severe errors occur (such as media recovery), they appear both on the startup screen and in the alert log file. Of course, you can prevent many of these issues if you stop the database in a clean manner. Carry on to the next topic.

Stopping the database

Just as there is an order of events to starting a database instance, there is also an order for how a database instance is stopped. Ideally, this is what happens during a database shutdown:

- ✔ New connections to the database are denied.
- ✔ Existing transactions are either committed or rolled back with proper updates to online redo log files.
- ✔ User sessions are terminated.
- ✔ Database file headers are updated and files are closed.
- ✔ SGA is shut down.
- ✔ Background processes are terminated.

It is preferable for all the steps to occur naturally during shutdown, which ensures that

- ✔ All transactions are neatly committed or rolled back.
- ✔ Online redo log files are properly updated.
- ✔ All files are closed properly without corruption.

If the preceding steps *don't* occur during shutdown because of a server or database instance crash or SHUTDOWN ABORT, the cleanup operations must occur during startup in a phase called *instance recovery.*

During instance recovery, Oracle won't open a database instance until it's satisfied that all transactions are accounted for and all data files are opened. If it can't complete these tasks, error messages appear and the DBA must address them. Instance recovery is successful most of the time, but it may take several minutes to process the cleanup.

Shutdown types

When a database needs to be shut down, several methods exist to do so with varying effects on current users and their transactions.

SHUTDOWN [NORMAL]

- New connections to the database are denied.
- Existing transactions continue normally until either they roll back or commit.
- Users log out normally on their own.
- After the last user logs out, database file headers are updated and files are closed.
- SGA is shut down.
- Background processes are terminated.
- Specified by the SHUTDOWN or SHUTDOWN NORMAL command.

SHUTDOWN TRANSACTIONAL

- New connections to the database are denied.
- Existing transactions continue normally until they either roll back or commit.
- After an existing transaction is completed, user sessions are terminated.
- Database file headers are updated and files are closed.
- SGA is shut down.
- Background processes are terminated.
- Specified by the SHUTDOWN TRANSACTIONAL command.

SHUTDOWN IMMEDIATE

- New connections to the database are denied.
- Existing transactions are rolled back.
- User sessions are terminated.
- Database file headers are updated, and files are closed.
- SGA is shut down.
- Background processes are terminated.
- Specified by the SHUTDOWN IMMEDIATE command.

SHUTDOWN ABORT

- ✔ New connections to the database are denied.
- ✔ Existing transactions are not rolled back.
- ✔ User sessions are terminated.
- ✔ SGA is shut down.
- ✔ Background processes are terminated.
- ✔ Specified by the SHUTDOWN ABORT command.
- ✔ Instance recovery is required on startup.

Shutdown decisions

When do you use each shutdown type?

- ✔ Generally, SHUTDOWN IMMEDIATE is what you want because it cleanly commits or rolls back existing transactions, terminates user sessions when they are complete, and then closes the database in a clean manner.
- ✔ Don't use SHUTDOWN NORMAL very often because even one user still logged in (after he's left for the day) can hang the shutdown.
- ✔ SHUTDOWN TRANSACTIONAL doesn't buy you much because it forces you to wait on users to finish their transactions. If you want to wait, you can just enter SHUTDOWN NORMAL. However, if you want to force them off the database instance, you use SHUTDOWN IMMEDIATE. There are times SHUTDOWN TRANSACTIONAL is useful, but it's not as common as you might think. This method is most commonly used in clustered environments.

  Here's how a typical SHUTDOWN IMMEDIATE executes. Keep in mind that you must be logged in as SYSDBA to run the shutdown command.

  ```
  SQL> shutdown immediate;
  Database closed.
  Database dismounted.
  ORACLE instance shut down.
  SQL> exit
  ```

- ✔ Use SHUTDOWN ABORT only when you have to. It essentially crashes the database and expects instance recovery to pick up the pieces. You may have to do that if the system is hung, but it shouldn't be your first choice (unless you want to do real database recovery sometime). If you can issue commands on the database instance, issue an ALTER SYSTEM SWITCH LOGFILE to force a checkpoint to close file headers and flush the online redo logs before issuing the SHUTDOWN ABORT. Forcing a check point allows for an easier instance recovery during the next startup.

Before you issue any commands changing the running state of the instance, make sure you're connecting to the correct instance. On Linux, if the instance is not started yet, type the following at the command line:

```
$ echo $ORACLE_SID
```

If the instance is already running and you want to shut it down or restrict it, type this:

```
$ sqlplus / as sysdba

SQL> select instance_name from v$instance;
INSTANCE_NAME
----------------
dev12c
```

Connecting to the Database Instance

A database instance isn't much good if you can't connect to it. Establishing a reliable, persistent, and secure connection to the database from the client is essential.

Oracle has established a network architecture of protocols, processes, utilities, and configuration files to support communication into the database. Oracle Net (formally called SQL*Net or Net8) is the Oracle networking protocol.

Oracle Net is supported by

✔ DBA-managed listener processes

✔ Client- and server-side configuration files

✔ Command-line utilities

✔ Optional GUI administration tools

Additionally, connections can come into the database via several lighter-weight non-Oracle protocols such as ODBC or JDBC. However, even these non-Oracle protocols use the same underlying server-side Oracle components as Oracle Net connections. For these reasons, we focus on the Oracle specific components.

Local versus remote connections

Connections into the database can be one of two kinds:

- ✔ **Local (bequeath):** A local connection originates from the same server the database is on and doesn't use the database listener process. When you connect to SQL*Plus as "/ as sysdba", you're connecting locally.

- ✔ **Remote:** All other connections from outside the database server or those from the server using the listener are remote connections. The easy way to determine whether a user is connecting remotely is if you have @TNS_ALIAS in the connect screen. For example, sqlplus scott@ dev12c indicates a remote connection to the dev12c database.

Communication flow

Connections to an Oracle database typically come across from a client located away from the database; over a network infrastructure; to the database server; through a database listener process; and, finally, into the database itself.

On the client side, the program calling the database references tnsnames. ora to find the database server host and protocol to send the request to. The request then leaves the client and goes onto the network utilization OracleNet. The default port for Oracle Net communications is 1521, although that's configurable. Over this Oracle Net protocol is where database communications traffic flows between the client and database server.

After a client's communication request reaches the database server host, it's handed off to the listener. The database listener is a separate Oracle software process on the database server that listens for incoming requests on the defined OracleNet port (1521). When it gets a request, the listener identifies which database instance is targeted for that request and establishes a connection to that database instance. On the server side, the listener uses the listener. ora file to make this determination. When the connection is established and the session begins, the listener steps out of the picture and allows communication between the database and client. Each client session has a dedicated server process on the server side. Within this dedicated server process, the user's session code is executed. Figure 5-1 represents the communication flow.

The client contains the client application and tnsnames.ora file. It communicates to the database server over Oracle Net on port 1521. On the database server, a listener process is configured by way of the listener.ora file. The listener routes the incoming request to the target database instance (either dev11g or db01) and establishes the initial connection handshake between the database instance and client.

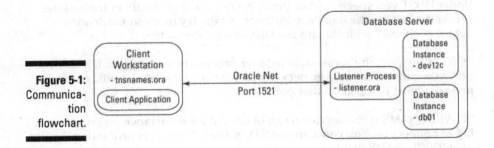

Figure 5-1: Communication flowchart.

Setting up tnsnames.ora

You must provide the address or location of the database you're trying to connect to. This information is often stored in the tnsnames.ora text file, which exists on the client you're connecting from. Other methods of locating your database exist such as referencing an Oracle Internet Directory (OID), but tnsnames.ora is the most common method for clients.

Note this "client" can be a user's workstation, a web application server, or even another database server.

Here is a sample tnsnames.ora file that can be found in ORACLE_HOME_DIRECTORY/network/admin:

```
dev12c =
  (DESCRIPTION =
    (ADDRESS_LIST =
      (ADDRESS = (PROTOCOL = TCP)(HOST = orasvr01)(PORT = 1521))
    )
    (CONNECT_DATA =
      (SERVICE_NAME = dev12c)
    )
db01 =
  (DESCRIPTION =
    (ADDRESS_LIST =
      (ADDRESS = (PROTOCOL = TCP)(HOST = orasvr02)(PORT = 1521))
    )
    (CONNECT_DATA =
      (SERVICE_NAME = db01)
    )
```

This particular tnsnames.ora contains 2 TNS (Transport Network Substrate) aliases, one for dev12c and one for db01. When connecting to a database instance, you actually specify the TNS alias (not database name). For example, sqlplus barb@dev12c uses dev12c as the alias. The TNS alias can be any name (such as dev12c or something more generic like dev or trainingdb); it doesn't have to be the actual database name. That flexibility means you can have a generic alias and not hardcode the database name.

Under HOST you specify either the DNS host name or the IP address of the server containing the database instance. Again, try to avoid hardcoded values such as IP address and use DNS names if possible.

PORT is the port the server-side listener process is listening on. It's also the port you connect across the network on for your OracleNet traffic (thus the firewalls must be open on that port).

SERVICE_NAME is the service name of the database instance you're attempting to connect to. You can also use SID, although Oracle is promoting the use of SERVICE_NAME instead.

The tnsnames.ora file is text based, and you can edit it by hand. After making changes, it's not necessary to restart the database or listener process.

Configuring the database listener with listener.ora

The key file to the listener process is the listener.ora configuration file. This file identifies two things:

- Each database it will listen for
- On what ports (default 1521)

The file is located in ORACLE_HOME/network/admin.

Here's a sample listener.ora file:

```
# listener.ora Network Configuration File: /u01/app/oracle/product/12.1.0/
               dbhome_1/network/admin/lis
tener.ora
# Generated by Oracle configuration tools.

SID_LIST_LISTENER =
  (SID_LIST =
    (SID_DESC =
      (GLOBAL_DBNAME = db01)
      (ORACLE_HOME = /u01/app/oracle/product/11.1.0/db_1)
      (SID_NAME = db01)
    )
    (SID_DESC =
      (GLOBAL_DBNAME = dev12c)
      (ORACLE_HOME = /u01/app/oracle/product/12.1.0/dbhome_1)
      (SID_NAME = dev12c)
    )
  )
```

```
LISTENER =
  (DESCRIPTION_LIST =
    (DESCRIPTION =
      (ADDRESS = (PROTOCOL = TCP)(HOST = orasvr01)(PORT = 1521))
    )
    (DESCRIPTION =
      (ADDRESS = (PROTOCOL = IPC)(KEY = EXTPROC1521))
    )
  )
```

In the preceding code, you see two main sections: SID_LIST_LISTENER and
LISTENER. The SID_LIST_LISTENER section identifies each database instance
that the listener will service connections for. It lists the global database
name, ORACLE_HOME, and SID.

As you need more databases, simply add the following section and then customize the relevant information:

```
(SID_DESC =
  (GLOBAL_DBNAME = dev12c)
  (ORACLE_HOME = /u01/app/oracle/product/12.1.0/dbhome_1)
  (SID_NAME = dev12c)
)
```

The LISTENER section identifies what host the database exists on and what
port it accepts connections on:

```
(DESCRIPTION =
  (ADDRESS = (PROTOCOL = TCP)(HOST = orasvr01)(PORT = 1521))
)
```

Here you see the listener will listen on the HOST (server) orasvr01, and the
port is 1521. Requests on other ports will not be acknowledged.

You can add more databases, even if they're different database versions to
the listener.ora. If you have multiple database versions, run your listener
with the highest version of the database software you have. You can also add
additional LISTENER processes (if you want to listen on multiple ports, for
example).

You should be aware of one configuration option we don't necessarily recommend: *Shared Servers* (also known as *Multi-Threaded Servers,* or MTS). With
this method, each user connection uses a shared process rather than a dedicated server process on the database server. In theory, having connections
share a server-side process reduces memory use and is good for systems with
lots of concurrent users. However, we've never seen it provide a noticeable
benefit, and we wouldn't consider it a common configuration.

Note that this is different from connection pooling with application servers, which we *do* recommend. What we outline in the earlier "Communication flow" section is the *dedicated server* mode, which is more common, provides better performance, and is required for DBA connections.

The sqlnet.ora file is one additional configuration file. It can be client or server side, usually located with the listener.ora or tnsnames.ora file. The sqlnet.ora file is a *special options* file where you can add parameters to the Oracle Net architecture. This file can exist both on servers to impact the listener process and on clients to influence TNS settings. For example, you can

- ✔ Add commands to force increased tracing, logging options, or encryption.
- ✔ Tell the listener to add a domain name to each database.
- ✔ Direct the listener to look up connection information in an LDAP instead of a tnsnames.ora file.

Here is a simple sqlnet.ora file:

```
$ more sqlnet.ora
NAMES.DIRECTORY_PATH=TNSNAMES
```

The setting simply tells the client to use the tnsnames.ora file instead of any other resource (such as an LDAP).

If you're experiencing connection issues and your tnsnames.ora and listener.ora files look fine, don't forget the sqlnet.ora. There may be a forgotten setting there causing issues.

Starting and stopping the database listener

The database listener process reads the listener.ora and sqlnet.ora files for its configuration; the DBA manages it by using the lsnrctl command-line utility. You can use the utility to do these things to the listener:

- ✔ Start
- ✔ Stop
- ✔ Check status

There is no direct relationship between the listener process and the database itself; the processes operate independently. That means you can start the listener before or after the database.

However, remember that the listener must be started before the database can service remote connections.

To start the listener, issue the lsnrctl start command:

```
[oracle@orasvr01 dbs]$ lsnrctl start

LSNRCTL for Linux: Version 12.1.0.1.0 - Production on 19-MAY-2013 12:10:44
Copyright (c) 1991, 2013, Oracle.  All rights reserved.
Starting /u01/app/oracle/product/12.1.0/dbhome_1/bin/tnslsnr: please wait...

TNSLSNR for Linux: Version 12.1.0.1.0 - Production
System parameter file is
/u01/app/oracle/product/12.1.0/dbhome_1/network/admin/listener.ora
Log messages written to
/u01/app/oracle/diag/tnslsnr/orasvr01/listener/alert/log.xml
Listening on: (DESCRIPTION=(ADDRESS=(PROTOCOL=tcp)(HOST=192.168.1.66)
            (PORT=1521)))
Listening on: (DESCRIPTION=(ADDRESS=(PROTOCOL=ipc)(KEY=EXTPROC1521)))

Connecting to (DESCRIPTION=(ADDRESS=(PROTOCOL=TCP)(HOST=192.168.1.66)
            (PORT=1521)))
STATUS of the LISTENER
------------------------
Alias                     LISTENER
Version                   TNSLSNR for Linux: Version 12.1.0.1.0 - Production
Start Date                19-MAY-2013 12:10:44
Uptime                    0 days 0 hr. 0 min. 0 sec
Trace Level               off
Security                  ON: Local OS Authentication
SNMP                      OFF
Listener Parameter File
/u01/app/oracle/product/12.1.0/dbhome_1/network/admin/listener.ora
Listener Log File
/u01/app/oracle/diag/tnslsnr/orasvr01/listener/alert/log.xml
Listening Endpoints Summary...
  (DESCRIPTION=(ADDRESS=(PROTOCOL=tcp)(HOST=192.168.1.66)(PORT=1521)))
  (DESCRIPTION=(ADDRESS=(PROTOCOL=ipc)(KEY=EXTPROC1521)))
(DESCRIPTION=(ADDRESS=(PROTOCOL=tcps)(HOST=orasvr01)(PORT=5500))(Security=(my_
            wallet_directory=/u01/app/oracle/admin/dev12c/xdb_wallet))
            (Presentation=HTTP)(Session=RAW))
Services Summary...
Service "dev12c" has 1 instance(s).
  Instance "dev12c", status READY, has 1 handler(s) for this service...
Service "dev12cXDB" has 1 instance(s).
  Instance "dev12c", status READY, has 1 handler(s) for this service...
Service "prod12c" has 1 instance(s).
  Instance "prod12c", status READY, has 1 handler(s) for this service...
```

```
Service "prod12cXDB" has 1 instance(s).
  Instance "prod12c", status READY, has 1 handler(s) for this service...
The command completed successfully
```

If you need to stop the listener, you can issue the lsnrctl stop command:

```
$ lsnrctl stop

LSNRCTL for Linux: Version 12.1.0.1.0 - Production on 19-MAY-2013 12:10:40
Copyright (c) 1991, 2013, Oracle.  All rights reserved.
Connecting to (DESCRIPTION=(ADDRESS=(PROTOCOL=TCP)(HOST=192.168.1.66)
          (PORT=1521)))
The command completed successfully
$
```

After changing the listener.ora file, you must restart the listener process. You can do this via the stop and start commands. An easier method is the lsn-rctl reload command. It effectively restarts the listener process without the explicit stop and start.

To determine what databases the listener is configured to service requests, you can read the listener.ora configuration file. Or, more easily, you can issue the lsrnctl status command:

```
$ lsnrctl status
LSNRCTL for Linux: Version 12.1.0.1.0 - Production on 19-MAY-2013 12:13:09
Copyright (c) 1991, 2013, Oracle.  All rights reserved.
Connecting to (DESCRIPTION=(ADDRESS=(PROTOCOL=TCP)(HOST=192.168.1.66)
          (PORT=1521)))
STATUS of the LISTENER
------------------------
Alias                     LISTENER
Version                   TNSLSNR for Linux: Version 12.1.0.1.0 - Production
Start Date                19-MAY-2013 12:10:44
Uptime                    0 days 0 hr. 2 min. 25 sec
Trace Level               off
Security                  ON: Local OS Authentication
SNMP                      OFF
Listener Parameter File   /u01/app/oracle/product/12.1.0/dbhome_1/network/admin/
          listener.ora
Listener Log File         /u01/app/oracle/diag/tnslsnr/orasvr01/listener/alert/
          log.xml
Listening Endpoints Summary...
  (DESCRIPTION=(ADDRESS=(PROTOCOL=tcp)(HOST=192.168.1.66)(PORT=1521)))
  (DESCRIPTION=(ADDRESS=(PROTOCOL=ipc)(KEY=EXTPROC1521)))
  (DESCRIPTION=(ADDRESS=(PROTOCOL=tcps)(HOST=orasvr01)(PORT=5500))(Security=(my_
          wallet_directory=/u01/app/oracle/admin/dev12c/xdb_wallet))
          (Presentation=HTTP)(Session=RAW))
Services Summary...
```

```
Service "dev12c" has 1 instance(s).
  Instance "dev12c", status READY, has 1 handler(s) for this service...
Service "dev12cXDB" has 1 instance(s).
  Instance "dev12c", status READY, has 1 handler(s) for this service...
Service "prod12c" has 1 instance(s).
  Instance "prod12c", status READY, has 1 handler(s) for this service...
Service "prod12cXDB" has 1 instance(s).
  Instance "prod12c", status READY, has 1 handler(s) for this service...
The command completed successfully
$
```

This code shows listening for connections for the dev12c and prod12c databases.

Logs for the listener process are stored in the listener.log file. Depending on database setup, the listener.log may be in one of these two spots:

✔ In ORACLE_HOME/network/admin

✔ Under the ADR infrastructure in ADR_BASE/diag/tnslsnr tree

For more information on this file, see Chapter 12.

Testing the connection

The best way to test a connection is via the application, but that isn't always possible. Preferably, you're on the client tier and actually go through the same network path as the client applications. If you don't do that, you may not be executing a valid test.

To execute a connectivity test, follow these steps to determine whether you can connect to the database instance:

1. **Go to the client tier.**

2. **See whether Oracle client software such as SQL*Plus and tnsnames. ora is installed.**

3. **Execute a sqlplus** *username@tns_alias*, **such as sqlplus mwhalen@ dev12c.**

4. **Enter the password to connect to the database.**

Using the tnsping utility is an even faster method that doesn't require a password. This utility connects over the network via the listener and establishes a handshake. It then terminates the connection and reports the results, which you see here:

```
$ tnsping dev12c

TNS Ping Utility for Linux: Version 12.1.0.1.0 - Production on 19-MAY-2013
            12:20:07
Copyright (c) 1997, 2013, Oracle.  All rights reserved.
Used parameter files:
/u01/app/oracle/product/12.1.0/dbhome_1/network/admin/sqlnet.ora

Used TNSNAMES adapter to resolve the alias
Attempting to contact (DESCRIPTION = (ADDRESS = (PROTOCOL = TCP)(HOST =
            localhost)(PORT = 1521)) (CONNECT_DATA = (SERVER = DEDICATED)
            (SERVICE_NAME = dev12c)))
OK (20 msec)
```

Testing connections is a good verification step for the DBA. If problems occur, it lets you catch them first instead of relying on users to report them later.

Oracle Net Configuration Assistant

It's important to understand how the listener works and what different files control the communication process; that's why we explain those parts first in this chapter.

Many DBAs simply copy the same template files from one server to the next, making only minor changes. However, Oracle does provide a GUI database assistant tool called Oracle Net Configuration Assistant to preconfigure tnsnames.ora and listener.ora for you on the server side. It can also be executed on the client side. It walks you through generating your configuration files and even tests the connection for you.

We encourage you to test the Oracle Net Configuration Assistant and see whether it's easy for you, but we caution you to understand the files themselves. Through that understanding, you can better fix problems and gotchas.

Sidestepping Connection Gotchas

Setting up connections to an Oracle database doesn't have to be difficult, but sometimes initial setup can be tough. Most of the time, you, as the DBA, review the configuration and figure out the issue. In other cases, you need to work with the network people to trace connections or open firewalls. In still other cases, you work with the application experts and determine who the client application is attempting to connect to the database.

Many people fall into several gotchas:

- ✔ **Remember to start the listener.** This sounds obvious, but it's not uncommon to start the database and forget to start the listener process. Scripting these steps helps eliminate these errors.

- ✔ **Keep open the firewall on the listener port.** It is common to have a firewall separating the database server from the users or web application servers. That means Oracle Net traffic may be blocked; in fact, you should assume that you need to have the firewall opened until proven otherwise. Using the tnsping utility can help you test these connections.

- ✔ **Watch out for multiple tnsnames.ora files.** On users' workstations, multiple installations of Oracle client software are likely to have multiple tnsnames.ora files. That becomes a problem when an update to tnsnames.ora is necessary, but not all the tnsnames.ora files are updated. This issue manifests itself in some applications working and others that don't. Either have one common file or a script to update all the files.

- ✔ **Copy and paste existing entries and change only the key parameters.** Because tnsnames.ora is a text file, it invites people to edit it by hand. That's fine, but it's easy to transpose a number (1512, for instance), misspell a server name, or insert an extra parenthesis somewhere. Also, avoid using IP addresses for host information unless you really need to. Use the DNS server name instead and you won't have to worry about the IP address changing without warning.

None of these errors is insurmountable, but checking these items may save you some time.

Although we use the default port of 1521 in many of our examples, best practice says to modify this port. If you listen with your database on the default port, you make your system more vulnerable to hackers. Choose an unused port that no one has common knowledge of.

Chapter 6

Understanding the Language of Databases: SQL

▶ Learning the basics of SQL
▶ Using the data dictionary
▶ Programming with PL/SQL

C ommunicating with most relational databases is done with Structured Query Language, or just SQL for short. SQL can be used against many types of relational databases, not just Oracle. However, most databases have their own little differences with SQL. As a budding Oracle database administrator (DBA), you should have a good grasp on the SQL language.

SQL can be very simple to learn. In fact, some people say that it's one of the easiest programming languages. You will see in this chapter that to begin functioning as an Oracle DBA, the basic commands aren't difficult. With that said, keep in mind that this chapter is meant only as a high-level introduction to the fundamentals of SQL. The SQL language is very large and powerful. And although most of your DBA tasks won't require you to know the more advanced SQL features, you should continue your learning beyond what this chapter offers.

The second part of this chapter focuses on the *data dictionary,* which is the key component to understanding how your database is organized and how it runs. All good DBAs have a strong understanding of the data dictionary. Understanding the data dictionary will keep you secure, tune, troubleshoot, and configure your database.

Last, we take a look at the PL/SQL programming language. PL/SQL is SQL with more traditional programming constructs. Some say the PL stands for Procedural Language, and others might say Programming Language. Either way, PL/SQL extends the SQL language to be more powerful. It's not always a focus of DBAs, but often more a focus for developers. However, as a DBA, understanding at least some PL/SQL will go a long way to making you a successful DBA.

Learning the Basics of SQL

The first step to learning SQL is to understand the different types of commands.

- ✔ **Data Manipulation Language (DML)** statements manage data within schema objects.
- ✔ **Data Definition Language (DDL)** statements create or alter structures (not data) in the database.
- ✔ **Data Control Language (DCL)** statements manage security in the database.
- ✔ **Transaction Control Language (TCL)** statements manage transactions in the database.

You can see that SQL can be broken down into different areas. This chapter focuses mostly on DML and TCL within the context of SQL. In Chapter 7, we touch on DDL and DCL.

SQL calling environments

There are many environments in which you can use to execute your SQL statements. The Oracle database is typically delivered with two:

- ✔ **SQL*Plus:** Command line
- ✔ **SQL*Developer:** A more graphically enhanced environment

So as to not confuse matters any more than we have to, we focus on the SQL*Plus environment. That way, we can direct our attention toward the commands themselves and not the other fancy features that SQL*Developer offers, which can be distracting. After you become familiar with the SQL language, you may decide that exploring a more powerful environment can lead to better productivity.

SQL*Plus comes installed on the database server itself or as part of the Oracle client installation. Again, to keep things simple, we show using the SQL*Plus environment directly on the server. As a DBA, you may find that this is also where a lot of your work will be done.

Follow these steps to connect to your database with SQL*Plus in a UNIX/ Linux environment:

1. **Open a terminal to your OS as the Oracle software owner.**

2. **Set your environment with oraenv, as shown in Chapter 4.**

3. **Type \<sqlplus\> and press Enter.**

4. Type your username and press Enter.

5. Type your password and press Enter.

For the examples in this chapter, we use the provided demo schema, HR. This schema should be installed if you selected it as part of the database creation. Here is an example of what you see as a result of following the above login procedure:

```
[oracle@orasvr01 admin]$ . oraenv
ORACLE_SID = [dev] ? dev12c
The Oracle base remains unchanged with value /u01/app/oracle
[oracle@orasvr01 admin]$ sqlplus

SQL*Plus: Release 12.1.0.1.0 Production on Fri Jun 28 19:23:27 2013

Copyright (c) 1982, 2013, Oracle.  All rights reserved.

Enter user-name: hr
Enter password:
Last Successful login time: Fri Jun 28 2013 18:32:41 -04:00

Connected to:
Oracle Database 12c Enterprise Edition Release 12.1.0.1.0 - 64bit Production
With the Partitioning, OLAP, Advanced Analytics and Real Application Testing
            options

SQL>
```

SQL statement clauses

Your SQL statements can be broken into sections called clauses. Not all statements contain all the clauses. It depends on what you're trying to do. See Table 6-1 for the basic architecture of the SQL SELECT clauses.

Table 6-1	SELECT Statement Clauses
Clause	*Description*
SELECT	Contains the columns and operators to display the data
FROM	Contains one or more tables from which the data originates
WHERE	Determines what data will be returned or restricted
GROUP BY	Groups the data according to certain values
ORDER BY	Orders the output of the data based on specified columns

The only mandatory clauses in a statement are SELECT and FROM. The rest are optional, as you will see throughout the chapter as we discuss the other clauses.

Case sensitivity in the database

SQL commands themselves are called *key words*. For example, some key words are

- ✔ SELECT
- ✔ FROM
- ✔ TABLE
- ✔ WHERE
- ✔ CREATE
- ✔ DELETE

You may notice that we frequently use uppercase when writing key words. You don't have to, though. As a matter of fact, all SQL commands are case-insensitive. The reason we use uppercase is because typing key words in uppercase is common in the SQL language and makes them a little easier to read.

Additionally, object names aren't case-sensitive. However, we often use lowercase when typing object names in statements. Again, this is only to help make things easier to read. The fact is all object names and attributes are converted to uppercase when they're stored in the database.

The only thing that is truly case-sensitive in your database is the data. Whatever you store in the database goes in and comes out with the specified case during the operations themselves. Of course, you can influence this one way or the other, which we will show later when we talk about functions.

Even though object names are case-insensitive, you can technically force them to be case-sensitive by putting the names in double quotes (" "). However, that practice is highly discouraged because you could end up with three different objects in the database with essentially the same name: for example, EMP, emp, Emp. That is confusion that no one needs.

Viewing your objects and data with the DESCRIBE and SELECT statements

Perhaps the most common statements you will run as a DBA are the DESCRIBE and SELECT commands. After all, a big part of your job will be researching what is in the database and analyzing the current conditions.

For the examples in this chapter, we start out using objects in the HR (demo) schema. In the next section, we start using the data dictionary.

Say you want to get some information about the jobs in your company.

1. **Open a terminal to your OS as the Oracle software owner.**
2. **Set your environment with oraenv, as shown in Chapter 4.**
3. **Type <sqlplus> and press Enter.**
4. **Type <hr> and press Enter.**
5. **Type <your password> and press Enter.**
6. **Type <DESCRIBE jobs> and press Enter.**

   The following output appears:

   ```
   SQL> DESCRIBE jobs
    Name                             Null?     Type
    ------------------------------   --------  ---------------------
    JOB_ID                           NOT NULL  VARCHAR2(10)
    JOB_TITLE                        NOT NULL  VARCHAR2(35)
    MIN_SALARY                                 NUMBER(6)
    MAX_SALARY                                 NUMBER(6)
   ```

7. **To see the job_id and job_title, type**

   ```
   <SELECT job_id, job_title FROM jobs;>
   ```

   and press Enter.

   You should see the following output:

   ```
   SQL> select job_id, job_title from jobs;

   JOB_ID      JOB_TITLE
   ----------  ----------------------------------
   AD_PRES     President
   AD_VP       Administration Vice President
   AD_ASST     Administration Assistant
   FI_MGR      Finance Manager
   FI_ACCOUNT  Accountant
   AC_MGR      Accounting Manager
   AC_ACCOUNT  Public Accountant
   SA_MAN      Sales Manager
   ```

```
SA_REP     Sales Representative
PU_MAN     Purchasing Manager
PU_CLERK   Purchasing Clerk
ST_MAN     Stock Manager
ST_CLERK   Stock Clerk
SH_CLERK   Shipping Clerk
IT_PROG    Programmer
MK_MAN     Marketing Manager
MK_REP     Marketing Representative
HR_REP     Human Resources Representative
PR_REP     Public Relations Representative

19 rows selected.
```

The DESCRIBE command allows you to see the table structure. This includes the column names, the data types, and whether the columns are allowed to be empty (null). This information can be very important when constructing various SQL statements. For example, if you were inserting a row, you would need to supply values for job_id and job_title because they are NOT NULL.

The SELECT statement is very simple. Notice that it was typed all on one line. SQL doesn't really care how you break up statements line by line, as long as you don't break words in half.

Break up SQL statements by clause. For longer, more complex statements, you may use many line breaks. These breaks can help make statements easier to read.

Here are two SELECT statements and their output:

```
SQL> select *
  2  from jobs
  3  where job_title = 'President';

JOB_ID     JOB_TITLE                           MIN_SALARY MAX_SALARY
---------- ----------------------------------- ---------- ----------
AD_PRES    President                                20080      40000

SQL> select *
  2  from jobs
  3  where job_title like 'P%';

JOB_ID     JOB_TITLE                           MIN_SALARY MAX_SALARY
---------- ----------------------------------- ---------- ----------
AD_PRES    President                                20080      40000
AC_ACCOUNT Public Accountant                         4200       9000
PU_MAN     Purchasing Manager                        8000      15000
PU_CLERK   Purchasing Clerk                          2500       5500
IT_PROG    Programmer                                4000      10000
PR_REP     Public Relations Representative           4500      10500

6 rows selected.
```

Note that instead of using a list of columns, we use an asterisk (*). That tells the SELECT clause is to return all the columns, as opposed to what we show earlier where we select just two columns.

Notice the use of the WHERE clause. The WHERE clause restricts what data is returned. In this example, we use the WHERE clause in two ways:

✔ As an equality (=): You search for exactly what you want to find.

✔ As a fuzzy search (LIKE): You can use wild cards to complete search terms. Oracle uses the percent sign as a wild card symbol.

The use of the % symbol specifies that we want to select all rows that begin with capital P and then have anything after them. Often, on operating systems, you see an asterisk used as a wild card. That's not the case inside an SQL statement, though; instead, use a percent sign (%).

Adding to our SELECT statement, you see

```
SQL> select lower(job_id), upper(job_title) title, max_salary
  2  from jobs
  3  where job_title like 'P%'
  4  and max_salary < 14000
  5  order by max_salary ASC;


LOWER(JOB_ TITLE                                    MAX_SALARY
---------- ------------------------------------     ----------
pu_clerk   PURCHASING CLERK                               5500
ac_account PUBLIC ACCOUNTANT                              9000
it_prog    PROGRAMMER                                    10000
pr_rep     PUBLIC RELATIONS REPRESENTATIVE               10500
```

We added some functions to our columns in the SELECT clause. Functions take and input to produce an output: in this case, job_id and the job_title. We used the character functions UPPER and LOWER. Can you guess what they do? In this case, it's pretty obvious. Oracle has dozens of functions for you to use to act on your data in all kinds of ways. In this case, we demonstrate how it is not necessarily important how your data is stored; you can display it however you want.

Notice the names of the columns for job_id and job_title in the output. job_id seems to be a mix of our function and the column_name. That's because Oracle automatically uses whatever you type in the SELECT clause for your column heading. On the second column, job_title, we use an "alias" to make the output is a little prettier. An alias comes after the column construct but before the comma. In this example, *title* is the alias. The alias will always default to uppercase unless you put double quotes (" ") around it. You also need to use double quotes if your alias is more than one word. For example

```
SQL> select upper(job_title) "Job Title"
  2   from jobs
  3   where job_title like 'P%';

Job Title
-----------------------------------
PRESIDENT
PUBLIC ACCOUNTANT
PURCHASING MANAGER
PURCHASING CLERK
PROGRAMMER
PUBLIC RELATIONS REPRESENTATIVE
```

The use of the AND statement is a construct of the WHERE clause. The AND statement allows us to use multiple conditions to restrict our data.

Last, the ORDER BY clause sorts the output on the column specified, either numerically or alphabetically, depending on the data type. By default, it sorts in ascending order. We added the ASC (ascending) key word for clarification. We could have used DESC instead to order the results in descending numeric order of max_salary.

Add to your data with the INSERT statement

To add rows to your database, you use the INSERT statement. An INSERT statement acts on one table at a time. The INSERT statement has three clauses, of which one is optional:

✔ INSERT clause

✔ Column clause (optional)

✔ VALUES clause

Here's how you would insert a new row into the jobs table:

1. **For the INSERT clause, type**

   ```
   <INSERT INTO jobs>
   ```

   and press Enter.

2. **For the columns clause, type**

   ```
   <(job_id, job_title)>
   ```

   and press Enter.

3. **For the VALUES clause, type**

```
<VALUES ('TRN_MGR','TRAINING MANAGER');>
```

and press Enter.

You see

```
SQL> INSERT INTO jobs
  2  (job_id, job_title)
  3  VALUES ('TRN_MGR','TRAINING MANAGER');

1 row created.
```

After you add one row to your table, the results appear as follows:

```
SQL> SELECT *
  2  FROM jobs
  3  WHERE job_id = 'TRN_MGR';

JOB_ID     JOB_TITLE                            MIN_SALARY MAX_SALARY
---------- ------------------------------------ ---------- ----------
TRN_MGR    TRAINING MANAGER
```

The salary columns are empty. Remember when we describe the table earlier? Those columns didn't have a constraint on them specifying that they cannot be null. Therefore, we left them out as an example. In the next exercise, we show you how to fix that.

Single quotes (' ') must be used around character fields. Anything that contains characters (such as a, b, or c) needs to have single quotes around it if you're talking about data. Numeric fields can be left without quotes.

Changing data with the UPDATE statement

If you have data which you want to modify, use the UPDATE statement. The UPDATE statement acts on columns. Here are the clauses of the UDPATE statement:

- ✔ UPDATE clause
- ✔ SET clause
- ✔ WHERE clause

The first two clauses are required. Technically, the last clause is optional albeit highly recommended.

Because we "forgot" the salary information in our INSERT statement, here's how to fix it with an UPDATE statement:

1. **Type**

   ```
   <UPDATE jobs>
   ```

   and press Enter.

2. **Type**

   ```
   <SET min_salary = 10000, max_salary = 20000>
   ```

   and press Enter.

3. **Type**

   ```
   <WHERE job_id = 'TRN_MGR';>
   ```

   and press Enter.

   You see

   ```
   SQL> UPDATE jobs
     2   SET min_salary = 10000, max_salary = 20000
     3   WHERE job_id = 'TRN_MGR';

   1 row updated.
   ```

And the results are

```
SQL> SELECT *
  2  FROM jobs
  3  WHERE job_id = 'TRN_MGR';

JOB_ID     JOB_TITLE                               MIN_SALARY MAX_SALARY
---------- --------------------------------------- ---------- ----------
TRN_MGR    TRAINING MANAGER                             10000      20000
```

Always consider using a WHERE clause with an UPDATE statement, or else you update all the rows.

Use your WHERE clause with your UDPATE statement to form a SELECT statement. That way, you can verify that your WHERE clause is acting on the correct data before you run your update. (This would also apply to a DELETE statement.)

If you like what you see, you have to make your changes permanent. Type **<COMMIT;>** and then press Enter.

You see:

```
SQL> commit;

Commit complete.
```

And, your changes cannot be easily undone.

Removing data with the DELETE statement

The last DML-type statement to talk about is the DELETE statement. The DELETE statement allows you to remove rows from tables. DELETE acts on one table at a time. You should also carefully consider using a WHERE clause with your DELETE statement, or else all your rows will be removed.

The DELETE statement has two clauses:

- ✔ DELETE clause
- ✔ WHERE clause

Here's how to remove the last rows we just added to the database for the TRN_MGR job_id:

1. **Type**

   ```
   <DELETE FROM jobs>
   ```

   and press Enter.

2. **Type**

   ```
   <WHERE job_id = 'TRN_MGR';>
   ```

   and press Enter.

You see

```
SQL> DELETE FROM jobs
  2  WHERE job_id = 'TRN_MGR';

1 row deleted.
```

And the results appear as follows:

```
SQL> SELECT *
  2  FROM jobs
  3  WHERE job_id = 'TRN_MGR';

no rows selected
```

There are no longer any rows in the table for the job_id TRN_MGR. Additionally, all the columns were removed. To remove just one of the values, use an UPDATE statement and set the column to empty (null). DELETE always acts on all columns; it removes rows.

Oops! We did not mean to DELETE the TRN_MGR row! Luckily, we did not COMMIT our change yet. We can easily undo this change with a ROLLBACK statement:

```
SQL> ROLLBACK;

Rollback complete.

SQL> SELECT *
  2  FROM jobs
  3  WHERE job_id = 'TRN_MGR';

JOB_ID     JOB_TITLE                                     MIN_SALARY MAX_SALARY
---------- --------------------------------------------- ---------- ----------
TRN_MGR    TRAINING MANAGER                                   10000      20000
```

As long as you have not issued a COMMIT in your session, you can rollback any changes to the last COMMIT within your session. Also, until you commit your data, no one else in the database can see it.

Leaving data un-committed for long periods of time can cause *locking* problems in your database. Data that has been changed and not committed holds a lock on the row(s) in question. You should commit your changes as soon as possible.

The last section about DML was very brief; we encourage you to seek out further training on SQL. (Try *SQL For Dummies,* 8th Edition, by Allen G. Taylor.)

Using the Data Dictionary

Learning the in and out of the data dictionary is perhaps one of the most important things you can do to become a top-notch Oracle DBA. The *data dictionary* is a collection of tables and views inside the database that hold all the information about the current and past state of the database. Data in the data dictionary is modified only by Oracle itself through the running processes of the database. Oracle records millions of bits of information for which you can use to tune, secure, and troubleshoot the database. It may take years for you to master. Understanding the Oracle data dictionary is one of the measuring sticks between a junior or senior DBA.

The data dictionary can be broken into the categories noted in Table 6-2.

Table 6-2		Categories of Data Dictionary Objects
Prefix	**Type**	**Description**
USER_	View	Objects owned by current user
ALL_	View	All objects to which current user has access
DBA_	View	All objects in the database
V$	View	Dynamic performance view. Populated from memory and control files
GV$	View	Like V$, but, for multiple instances in a cluster environment
X$	Table	Internal tables containing cryptic but often useful data

Of the dictionary view types listed in Table 6-2, as a DBA, you will spend most of your time reading the DBA_ and V$ views. These views provide the most useful and most easily interpreted data. In fact, users who aren't DBAs often will not have access to the DBA_ and V$ views. On the other hand, all users have ACCESS to the USER_ and ALL_ views. Keeping the DBA_, V$, and X$ views hidden is an important part of database security. Some information in those views could be used by people to gain access to data in which they are not allowed.

Oracle 12c has thousands of data dictionary views in the database. We can't give you an exact number because it depends on what options you install and configure. In the database we're using for demonstration purposes, there are approximately three thousand.

Most, but not all, DBA_ and V$ views have names that are somewhat intuitive. For example, Table 6-3 has a sampling of useful views in the database.

Table 6-3	Useful Data Dictionary Views
Name	**Contents**
DBA_TABLES	Information about all tables
DBA_USERS	Information about all users
DBA_AUDIT_TRAIL	Information about captured audits
V$DATABASE	Information about the current database configuration
V$CONTROLFILE	Information about the current database control files

Despite the vast amount of data dictionary objects available to you, getting information about them is relatively easy with a little bit of practice. The Oracle documentation is going to be the definitive source of all information, listing the different views and describing the contents of the various columns. You can get the documentation for the view at

```
http://docs.oracle.com/cd/E16655_01/server.121/e17615/
          toc.htm
```

With a little bit of know-how and common sense, you can also get a lot of the information yourself. As we mention earlier, many of the views have names that are self-explanatory. With that information, you can look inside the database to see what views are available. There is actually a view of the views:

```
SQL> describe dictionary
 Name                            Null?    Type
 ------------------------------ -------- --------------------
 TABLE_NAME                               VARCHAR2(128)
 COMMENTS                                 VARCHAR2(4000)
```

You can sometimes find what you are looking for with a little bit of common sense and cleverness. Say you're looking for information about indexes:

```
SQL> SELECT table_name
  2  FROM dictionary
  3  WHERE table_name like 'DBA%INDEX%';

TABLE_NAME
-------------------------------------------------------------
DBA_INDEXES
DBA_INDEXTYPES
DBA_INDEXTYPE_ARRAYTYPES
DBA_INDEXTYPE_COMMENTS
DBA_INDEXTYPE_OPERATORS
DBA_PART_INDEXES
DBA_XML_INDEXES

7 rows selected.
```

As we mention earlier, getting familiar with the data dictionary is paramount. You might hear there's no need to worry about the data dictionary because all the GUI tools give you the information that you need. The fact is those GUI tools do read from the data dictionary views. However, don't let that give you a false sense of security. More than once, we've seen where the GUI tools have failed or gone offline. If you're not comfortable navigating the data dictionary by SQL, it could be the end of your DBA job in an emergency.

We would also advise you that despite the availability of the GUI tools, a DBA who is efficient at querying the data dictionary with SQL can often get accurate answers more quickly than someone using a tool like Database Express. As senior DBAs, we both agree that we actually prefer the data dictionary over Enterprise Manager for many of the day-to-day tasks.

Last, if you want very specific reports generated on a schedule, there is no better way than to write your own reports and schedule to run as a script through a scheduler, such as Windows Task Scheduler or UNIX/Linux crontab. Then, after generating the report, the script can send the results out via e-mail. You may like to have reports that are not canned in Enterprise Manager, such as Users with Failed Login's due to Wrong Password in the Last 24 Hours:

```
SQL> SELECT USERNAME, USERHOST, TIMESTAMP, ACTION_NAME, RETURNCODE
  2  FROM dba_audit_trail
  3  WHERE username = 'HR'
  4  ORDER BY timestamp;

USERNAME USERHOST         TIMESTAMP ACTION_NAME  RETURNCODE
-------- ---------------- --------- ------------ ----------
HR       orasvr01         06-JUN-13 LOGON                 0
HR       orasvr01         08-JUN-13 LOGON              1017
HR       orasvr01         09-JUN-13 LOGOFF                0
HR       orasvr01         16-JUN-13 LOGON                 0
HR       orasvr01         17-JUN-13 LOGON                 0
HR       orasvr01         17-JUN-13 LOGOFF                0
HR       orasvr01         18-JUN-13 LOGOFF                0
HR       orasvr01         28-JUN-13 LOGON                 0
HR       orasvr01         28-JUN-13 LOGON              1017
HR       orasvr01         28-JUN-13 LOGOFF                0

10 rows selected.
```

Or, Tables Created by User HR in the Last 100 Days:

```
SQL> SELECT object_name, created
  2  FROM dba_objects
  3  WHERE created > sysdate - 100
  4  AND object_type = 'TABLE'
  5  AND owner = 'HR';

OBJECT_NAME     CREATED
--------------- ---------
REGIONS         09-MAY-13
LOCATIONS       09-MAY-13
JOB_HISTORY     09-MAY-13
JOBS            09-MAY-13
EMPLOYEES       09-MAY-13
DEPARTMENTS     09-MAY-13
COUNTRIES       09-MAY-13

7 rows selected.
```

Programming with PL/SQL

PL/SQL is an SQL with more powerful programmatic contructs built around your code. For example, PL/SQL offers

- ✔ Looping control
- ✔ Variables
- ✔ If/then constructs
- ✔ Error handling

Normal SQL really doesn't have any of this. Normal SQL is good to use in code that acts on specific data in the "now." It can't make any data-driven decisions. You have to know what that data is — and how you want it to look.

PL/SQL is also more secure than regular SQL. As it stands, when users execute SQL, they have to have permissions on the underlying objects in which the data lives. However, with PL/SQL, named programs execute with the permissions of the owner. That way, the owner of the data could write a program to manage the data. The owner then gives access to the program to the user, not the underlying objects. For example, say you have a program that pulls a user's salary history for them to view. You don't want the user to be able to select on the employee salary table. And without a PL/SQL program, that's what you'd have to do. You can code it so that when the program runs, the program pulls in the connected user as a variable and collects the salary history for that user only.

PL/SQL is often the primary domain of application developers. As a DBA, however, you should also be familiar with the basic premises of the code and be able to read how the code functions. Even though DBAs may not be application developers, you will be called upon to help troubleshoot code or tune code that may be in the form of PL/SQL programs.

Furthermore, Oracle has provided the DBAs with hundreds of built-in programs written in PL/SQL to facilitate actions in the database. In some cases, these programs will be required for you to do your job. Understanding how PL/SQL functions will help you better understand how to use these built-in features.

Types of PL/SQL programs

PL/SQL programs come in many forms. PL/SQL programs are also sometimes referred to as "program units." See table 6-4 for a listing of the common types of PL/SQL constructs you'll come across.

Table 6-4	Type of PL/SQL Program Units
Name	**Description**
ANONYMOUS BLOCK	Un-named program that runs from the command line
PROCEDURE	Stored, named program that performs a tasks
FUNCTION	Program that takes input, acts upon it, and produces output
PACKAGE	Group of named procedures and/or functions which are related by task
TRIGGER	Program acts upon outcome of some other action; fires automatically

PL/SQL block structure

PL/SQL programs are built on the *block structure*. That is, they can be broken down into specific parts of the program based on function. The parts of the PL/SQL block differ slightly based on the type of program unit, but they all have similar characteristics. Here is a breakdown of the parts of a PL/SQL program unit:

✔ **Declarative:** This section contains the name of the unit (if it's named) and any variables. The variables are named, typed, and optionally initialized in the section. The program unit would not be named if it is coded as an *anonymous block*. An anonymous block is used when you are often writing a program for a one-time use.

✔ **Body:** This is the section that holds the meat of the program. It contains the functionality and the business logic needed to process the variables and data. You will see things like loops and if/then statements in this section.

✔ **Exception:** This section defines and handles any errors that come up during the processing of the body. If an error is properly handled, often the program can continue running. Or, at the very least, output a meaningful message to the end user. If an error is encountered and is not handled by the exception section, often the program aborts with a default error message.

✔ **End:** The end section doesn't contain anything. It just signifies that the program is at the end of its processing. And in a package of many procedures, the end section separates it from the next procedure in the list.

Calling PL/SQL programs

PL/SQL procedures, functions and packages are called in a couple of different ways. You can use the EXECUTE command, or you can call the program as part of another block. *Triggers,* as described in Table 6-4, on the other hand, are not called from the command line. They automatically execute only after some other process completes. For example, you might want a trigger to fire every time someone updates the salary column of the employees table. Then, perhaps that trigger shoots an e-mail to the HR manager to report the change.

The DESCRIBE command can also work against PL/SQL programs. This can prove helpful if you don't know the arguments or variables that the procedure may take for input. For example, say you have a procedure that gets the salary for an employee based on first and last name input. The procedure is called get_sal.

```
SQL> DESCRIBE get_sal
PROCEDURE get_sal
 Argument Name                   Type                   In/Out Default?
 ------------------------------  ---------------------  ------ --------
 P_LAST_NAME                     VARCHAR2               IN
 P_FIRST_NAME                    VARCHAR2               IN
```

The procedure takes to IN arguments of VARCHAR2 type.

Here's how you would execute the procedure with the EXECUTE command, using the employee Mike Whalen:

```
SQL> EXECUTE get_sal('Whalen','Mike')

Mike, Whalen - Makes:  $8300

PL/SQL procedure successfully completed.
```

As we mention earlier, Oracle has a plethora of pre-supplied packages, procedures, and functions for managing the database. To get a complete list, go to the following section of the documentation that outlines all the Oracle-supplied program units:

```
http://docs.oracle.com/cd/E16655_01/appdev.121/e17602/
           toc.htm
```

Table 6-5 offers some example Oracle-supplied programs.

Table 6-5	Example Oracle-Supplied Programs
Name	*Description*
DBMS_SCHEDULER	Manages the internal database scheduler
DBMS_STATS	Gathers statistics on users, objects, system, and whole database
SYSDATE	Outputs current time and date of system
UTL_MAIL	Utility for e-mail with features, such as attachments, Cc, and Bcc
DBMS_METADATA	Function for pulling object DDL out of database among other tasks
DBMS_DATAPUMP API	Manages Data Pump within a PL/SQL program

Chapter 7

Loading Data into Your Database

- -

In This Chapter

▶ Making tablespaces

▶ Understanding users and schemas

▶ Understanding database object types

- -

*I*t's no secret that databases hold data: typically, lots of it. However, data isn't just loose in the database; data lives in structures, which are owned by users. Furthermore, this isn't a random collection of data and objects; it supports a specific application.

In this chapter, we focus less on the actual data itself and more on the structures that hold the data and control access to that data. We explain tablespaces and their role in object storage. Objects must have an owner, and we explain how users have schemas that contain objects. Database objects that a user can own include — but are not limited to — tables, indexes, and views.

A database application includes the tables, indexes, PL/SQL code, and other objects executing the program logic inside the database. Depending on the application's size and nature, building an application structure within a database can be complex.

Here is the general order of operations for building an application environment:

1. Create the tablespaces that will contain the tables and indexes for the application.

2. Create the database account for who will own the database objects for the application.

3. Create the objects (tables, indexes, packages, and so on) in the application owner's schema.

4. Create any synonyms for object names to simplify access.

5. Create database roles to control access to the application schema owner's objects.

6. Load the data into the tables and generate indexes.

7. Create the application users and grant those users access roles so they can access the application objects.

The exact build instructions for an application environment should come from the vendor, or you should create them with the application developers. The requirements should be defined before the production environment is built — although in the "real world," the requirements are often subject to change.

In this chapter, we give you knowledge and tools to perform the steps for building an application environment.

Making Tablespaces

Database objects are logically contained within tablespaces. A *tablespace* is a logical storage container that houses physical data files in which database tables and indexes are stored.

In a database, tablespaces are created in two ways:

- By default for internal database structures
- By the database administrator (DBA) to store user objects

For example, a data tablespace has one or more database files on the OS's file system. Within that tablespace, one or more data table is created, and the data is stored in the tablespace's corresponding data files. In Figure 7-1, you can see a graphical example of a tablespace and its contents.

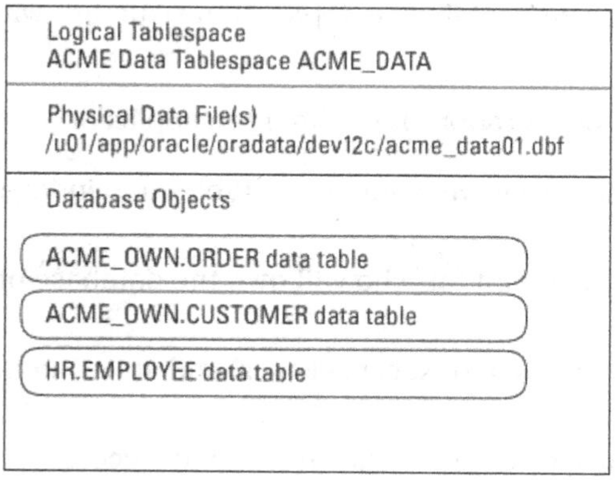

Figure 7-1:
The data
tablespace
hierarchy.

Logical Tablespace
ACME Data Tablespace ACME_DATA

Physical Data File(s)
/u01/app/oracle/oradata/dev12c/acme_data01.dbf

Database Objects

ACME_OWN.ORDER data table

ACME_OWN.CUSTOMER data table

HR.EMPLOYEE data table

Figure 7-1 includes the following:

- **Logical tablespace:** This stores data tables for the user.
- **Physical data file:** You can add data files as necessary.
- **Database objects:** Here you can see objects from different users.

Multiple users can store their objects in the same tablespace. Tablespaces are available to any user with objects in the database although organizing different users in different tablespaces is better for performance and manageability. Also, try to separate data and index objects into separate tablespaces (and thus database files) to reduce disk contention as index and table segments for the same object are accessed.

As you add objects and tables grow, Oracle manages the size of these things:

- **Segments** are any objects requiring storage.
- **Extents** are the unit of storage Oracle uses to allocate space for segments.

Oracle tracks the growth of segments and extents and knows where each object is stored. This segment management is covered in greater detail in Chapter 10.

These standard tablespaces are listed with their corresponding data files:

```
SYS@dev12c> SELECT TABLESPACE_NAME, FILE_NAME FROM DBA_DATA_FILES
  2  ORDER BY TABLESPACE_NAME;

TABLESPACE_NAME  FILE_NAME
---------------- -------------------------------------------------
EXAMPLE          /u01/app/oracle/oradata/dev12c/example01.dbf
MY_DATA          /u01/app/oracle/oradata/dev12c/my_data01.dbf
SYSAUX           /u01/app/oracle/oradata/dev12c/sysaux01.dbf
SYSTEM           /u01/app/oracle/oradata/dev12c/system01.dbf
UNDOTBS1         /u01/app/oracle/oradata/dev12c/undotbs01.dbf
USERS            /u01/app/oracle/oradata/dev12c/users01.dbf

6 rows selected.
```

The EXAMPLE tablespace is for Oracle demo objects, and MY_DATA contains a demo table. SYSAUX and SYSTEM are for internal database objects. UNDOTBS1 is for undo (rollback) objects. USERS is the default tablespace for objects created by users who didn't specify a tablespace when they created objects.

TIP

To see each tablespace, space available, type, and extent management, go to
Enterprise Manager Database Express and choose Storage⇨Tablespaces.
Figure 7-2 shows this data.

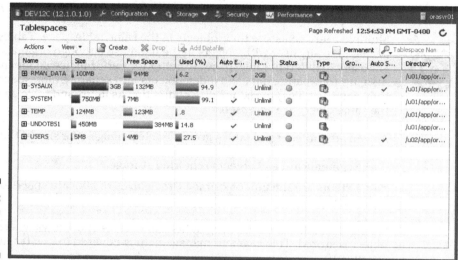

Figure 7-2:
Tablespace
manage-
ment.

From the Tablespaces management screen, you can choose Actions⇨Create to
create a tablespace for storing application data tables, as shown in Figure 7-3.

Figure 7-3:
The Create
Tablespace
General
options.

Then follow these steps:

1. **On the General options screen, type a tablespace name.**

   In this example, the tablespace name is MY_DATA.

2. **Select the tablespace type:**

   - *Permanent* for normal objects, such as tables and indexes.

   - *Temporary* for temp storage typically used for processing data. Data disappears from objects either after a commit or a session logs out.

   - *Undo* for storing undo segments.

   Do not select the Set as Default check box for this example unless you want this tablespace to be the default tablespace for all users.

3. **Select the Smallfile radio button (for data files less than 32GB).**

   These files are easier to manage than bigfiles.

4. **Select the Online radio button so the tablespace is available immediately.**

5. **Click the right arrow to go to the next screen.**

6. **On the Add Datafiles option screen, enter this name for your file:**

   `/u01/app/oracle/oradata/dev12c/my_data01.dbf`

   Set the remaining options as follows:

   - *File Size:* Leave File Size set at its default 100M.

   - *Reuse Existing File:* You should only check this box, for example, if you are re-creating the tablespace over an old one that was dropped.

   - *Auto Extend:* Allows the data file to grow if more space is needed. Leave this check box selected.

   - *Increment:* Tells Auto Extend how much to grow at a time. Leave this set at default 100M.

   - *Maximum File Size:* This allows the data file to grow to a specified size up to 32GB. Change that to 8G.

   Figure 7-4 shows an added data file and filename for my_data01.dbf.

7. **Click the right arrow to go to the next screen.**

8. **On the Space options screen (see Figure 7-5):**

   a. *Leave Block Size set as Database Default.*

   b. *For Extent Allocation, select the Automatic radio button.* This is best for databases that have normal, regular growth.

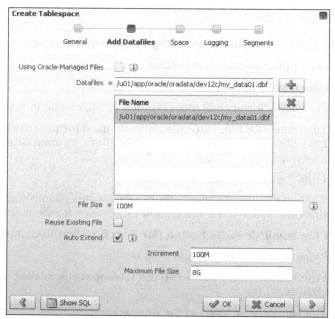

Figure 7-4:
Adding the
MY_DATA
data file.

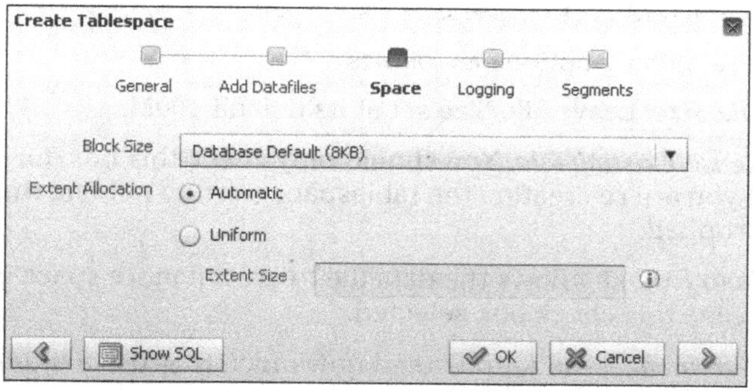

Figure 7-5:
MY_DATA
storage
options.

9. **Click the right arrow to go to the next screen.**

From the Logging options screen, you choose whether you want operations logged on the tablespace. You almost always want to choose
logging. The only time you may not want logging is if this tablespace is
going to store objects that are part of a load process, where every night
they are batch-loaded, and then the data is moved to other tablespaces
for long-term storage. Without logging, you compromise recoverability.
The Force Logging check box sets that even if someone tries to skip logging on an operation in this tablespace, Oracle will not allow the logging
to be skipped.

10. **Leave Logging selected and Force Logging unselected.**

11. **Click the right arrow to go to the next screen.**

12. **On the Segments option screen, choose a Segment Space Management and Compression option:**

    - *Automatic:* For ease of management, let Oracle manage the extent and segment growth.

    - *Manual:* Manually specify the size of each unit of allocation.

    - *Compression:* Choose from None (no compression), Basic (SELECT friendly compression, no so DML friendly), and OLTP (DML friendly, extra, licensed feature).

13. **Click the Show SQL button to see the actual SQL being executed:**

```
CREATE SMALLFILE TABLESPACE "MY_DATA" DATAFILE
'/u01/app/oracle/oradata/dev12c/my_data01.dbf'
SIZE 100M AUTOEXTEND ON NEXT 100M MAXSIZE 8G
LOGGING DEFAULT NOCOMPRESS ONLINE
EXTENT MANAGEMENT LOCAL AUTOALLOCATE
SEGMENT SPACE MANAGEMENT AUTO;
```

14. **When you're satisfied with your options, click OK.**

    The tablespace is created.

15. **Repeat Steps 1 through 14 to create the index tablespace.**

    If you name the second tablespace ACME_INDEX, you have these options when it's created:

```
TABLESPACE_NAME FILE_NAME
--------------- ------------------------------------------------
SYSTEM          /u01/app/oracle/oradata/dev12c/system01.dbf
SYSAUX          /u01/app/oracle/oradata/dev12c/sysaux01.dbf
UNDOTBS1        /u01/app/oracle/oradata/dev12c/undotbs01.dbf
USERS           /u02/app/oracle/oradata/dev12c/users01.dbf
MY_DATA         /u01/app/oracle/oradata/dev12c/my_data01.dbf
MY_INDEX        /u01/app/oracle/oradata/dev12c/my_index01.dbf
6 rows selected.
```

Now you have tablespaces and are ready to start creating users and objects.

Understanding Users and Schemas

Users not only access data in a database, but they own the objects that contain the data. The set of objects owned by a user is its *schema*. Not all users own objects, so schemas may be empty.

Other users can access or execute objects within a user's schema after the schema owner grants privileges. It's common practice to have one user own all of an application's objects (tables, indexes, views, and so on) and then provide access to those objects to all the application users within the database. This is done via database grants, roles, and synonyms.

For example, assume you have the ACME application. You'd create a user called ACME_OWN and create all objects as ACME_OWN. Then you'd create a database role called ACME_USER and grant SELECT, UPDATE, EXECUTE for the objects in ACME_OWN's schema to that role. Application users would be granted the ACME_USER role so they could access the ACME_OWN's objects. This way, one user owns the objects, but the actual database or application users access the data. This separation improves both security and manageability.

Users fall into one of two categories:

- ✔ Application owners whose schemas contain multiple objects
- ✔ Application users with few or no objects

The syntax for each user creation is the same, but grants and privileges for each are what separate the two categories.

Here's the simple syntax for creating a user:

```
CREATE USER <USERNAME>
IDENTIFIED BY "<PASSWORD>"
TEMPORARY TABLESPACE <TEMPORARY TABLESPACE>
DEFAULT TABLESPACE <DEFAULT TABLSPACE>;
```

For username, use something descriptive (such as *DATABASE TITLE*_OWN) for the owner of objects for the application. If a connection pooled web user (as explained in Chapter 3) is going to access the application, a name appended with _WEB is appropriate. Normal application users should be descriptive, such as first name, last initial; an example is VICKYB.

The password for the user should have the following characteristics:

- ✔ Be more than eight characters
- ✔ Include numbers and special characters
- ✔ Not be based on dictionary words
- ✔ Use uppercase and lowercase characters

Placing the password in double quotation marks (" ") allows special characters without disrupting the SQL syntax.

Two tablespaces need to be identified when creating a user: temporary and default:

- ✔ The TEMPORARY tablespace is where temporary segments are created. TEMP is the standard.

- ✔ The DEFAULT tablespace is where tablespace objects (such as tables or indexes) are created if you omit the TABLESPACE storage clause during the object create statement. Ideally, every table or index creation statement lists a tablespace. If a tablespace is missing, these objects go to the tablespace defined as DEFAULT. Generally, the USERS tablespace is defined as DEFAULT.

A user needs system privileges to be able to connect to the database and create objects. Granting the CREATE SESSION privilege or CONNECT role allows a user to log in to the database. Giving a user the RESOURCE role enables the user to create database objects. Roles and privileges are explained in greater detail in Chapter 9.

In the following steps, you create a user with SQL*Plus and grant the necessary roles and privileges to connect to the database:

1. **In SQL*Plus, type the following to create a user:**

   ```
   SYS@dev12c> create user acme_own
      2   identified by "acme_own2013!"
      3   temporary tablespace temp
      4   default tablespace users;

   User created.
   ```

   In this example, the user is schema owner ACME_OWN. The default tablespace is defined as USERS although the TABLESPACE storage clause is expected to specify ACME_DATA when objects are created. We also create a role to hold the necessary privileges that this user will need.

2. **Grant the user CONNECT and RESOURCE roles so that the user can log in to the database and create objects:**

   ```
   SYS@dev12c> grant connect to acme_own;

   Grant succeeded.

   SYS@dev12c> grant resource to acme_own;

   Grant succeeded.
   ```

3. **Create a new role:**

```
SYS@dev12c> create role acme_user;

Role created.

SYS@dev12c> grant create session to acme_user;

Grant succeeded.
```

In this example, ACME_USER is created. That user will receive object grants from the ACME_OWN account as objects are created.

4. **Grant the appropriate INSERT, UPDATE, DELETE, and EXECUTE privileges for each object to the second role.**

This lets you grant the role that has the grants to each application user. Each application user then has access to the ACME_OWN objects. This saves you from having to individually grant each user access to each object.

5. **Grant CREATE SESSION to the first role.**

When users receive the role, they can log in to the database.

You can create individual application users by using SQL*Plus. Use Enterprise Manager Database Express to create users:

1. **Choose Security⇨Users to get to the Create User screen shown in Figure 7-6.**

2. **Enter the username, profile, and password.**

VICKYB has DEFAULT profile and password authentication. The password you type appears as asterisks; you have to enter it twice to ensure you don't mistype it.

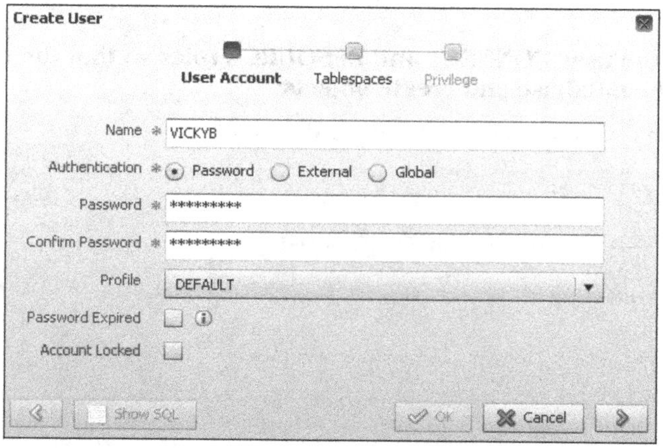

Figure 7-6:
The Create
User
screen.

3. Click the right arrow to go to the Tablespaces screen. (See Figure 7-7.)

Choose the new MY_DATA tablespace as VICKYB's default tablespace. Accept the Temporary Tablespace — TEMP tablespace default.

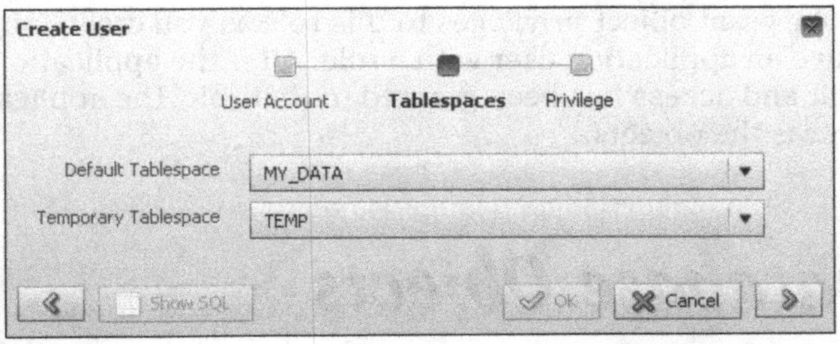

Figure 7-7:
The user creation tablespace selection.

4. Click the right arrow to go to the next screen.

The Privilege screen appears. On the left are system privileges or roles. Roles are denoted by a check mark. Figure 7-8 shows the new user with the CONNECT role.

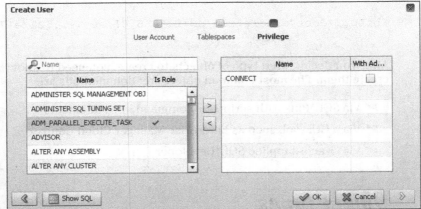

Figure 7-8:
The user creation privilege screen.

5. When you finish choosing roles and privileges, click OK.

The user is created.

If you need more application users, follow these steps:

1. From the main Security screen, select the user you want to use as a template.

2. Click the CREATE LIKE button.

This will take you back into the Create User wizard with the options already selected to reflect the user you are copying.

3. **Create a new user with the same roles and privileges but with a different username and password.**

   At this point, you have an application schema owner account and a database role; grant object privileges to this role as you create objects. You also have an application user with a role. After the application objects are built and access has been granted to that role, the application user can access the objects.

Creating Database Objects

Multiple object types exist in a database, and it's important to know what's available. Periodically, Oracle adds new object types to extend functionality. New options within each object type are regularly added as well.

The multitude of objects in Oracle grows with every release, and the options available for each object grow even faster. To get the most up-to-date listing of syntax and options, visit the Oracle Database SQL Language Reference 12c documentation at

```
http://docs.oracle.com/cd/E16655_01/server.121/e17209/
                        toc.htm
```

After you decide what type of objects to create, you need to know how to create them. The most common object creation methods are

- ✔ Via SQL*Plus with scripts or command line statements
- ✔ Via a GUI tool, such as Enterprise Manager Cloud Control
- ✔ Via Oracle-supplied SQL*Developer

Object types

The guts of a database are its objects; and tables are at the core because they contain the rows of data. However, other objects within the database are important. The following objects are common in an Oracle database.

Table

A *table* contains rows of data and is the core of the database. Tables are composed of column names, each with a defined data type. Data is loaded into the table as *rows*.

Create specific *constraints* on each column of data to restrict data. Create *primary keys* on one or more columns to enforce uniqueness for each row. *Foreign keys* generate relationships between rows in one table and rows in other tables.

Tables are contained within a tablespace and may be split between multiple tablespaces *(partitioning)* to improve performance and manageability.

View

A *view* is a SQL statement that joins one or more tables to form a logical representation of data. Rather than the user or program unit issuing a complex statement on multiple tables, the view allows that data to already be joined. That way, the user can select from the view to achieve the same result. Views provide the benefits of reduced complexity and improved performance when created as materialized views, in which data is already selected and stored.

Index

An *index* is an internal mechanism that allows fast access to selected rows within a table. Just as you look in a book's index to find a topic, a database index is a pointer to selected data within data tables.

You can use multiple types of indexes depending on the nature of the table and data:

- ✔ **B*Tree indexes** are the default and most common.

- ✔ **Bitmap indexes** are used for data with low cardinality or low levels of uniqueness, such as a YES/NO column.

- ✔ **Function-based indexes** exist on functions on SQL statements. For example, if you want to search for LAST_NAME in uppercase, you might create an uppercase function-based index.

Indexes are key to fast data access, but they come at a cost. The index must be updated every time data is inserted, updated, or deleted — and those are all performance hits. Indexes also consume disk space and are commonly stored in tablespaces separate from the corresponding data tablespaces. Bottom line: Index enough to speed up common searches, but, not so much as to slow down data modifications.

Like rows of data, you may partition indexes into multiple tablespaces to improve performance and manageability.

Procedure

A *procedure* is a PL/SQL program unit that executes program code to process rows of data. Application and business logic exist as procedures within a database.

A procedure can

- ✔ Stand alone within a schema
- ✔ Be part of a package
- ✔ Be an anonymous PL/SQL block

Function

A *function* is a PL/SQL program unit that executes and returns a value to the program unit that called it. Conceptually, an Oracle function isn't unlike functions in other programming languages. Functions typically accept input parameters from the calling program, perform some type of processing on that input, and return a value to the calling program unit.

Functions come in two ways:

- ✔ Oracle provides many useful built-in functions: for example, time, date, and mathematical functions.
- ✔ The user can write customized functions.

A function can exist in the following ways:

- ✔ Stand alone within a schema
- ✔ As part of a package
- ✔ As an anonymous PL/SQL block

Package

A *package* is a group of related PL/SQL procedures and functions that form a larger program unit. A package typically has procedures and functions related to a specific business purpose; that way, the functionality is contained to that package. A package contains two things:

- ✔ A package *spec,* or header, which lists the publicly exposed program units
- ✔ The package *body,* which holds the actual PL/SQL program code for each contained procedure or function

Trigger

A *trigger* is a PL/SQL program unit that is executed when a table is updated, inserted, or deleted, or when other database events occur. Here's a common trigger example:

Assume an insert on the sales table. Delete the appropriate amount on the inventory table; if it drops to a certain level, then order new inventory.

Database link

A connection from one database to another is a *database link*. It allows a user or program unit to select or modify data from another Oracle database. The link specifies a Transport Network Substrate (TNS; described in Chapter 5) alias to connect to a remote database. For example, if you execute

```
SELECT * FROM CUSTOMER@ROLLING_MEADOWS_DB;
```

You select all the data from the CUSTOMER table in the ROLLING_MEADOWS_DB database.

Synonym

A *synonym* in a database is just what it is in everyday life: a different name for the same thing. Synonyms can be

- ✔ **Private:** The name is available only to the owner of that synonym.
- ✔ **Public:** The name is more common and provides a short name for all users within a database so they don't have to list the schema owner for each object in their queries.

By default, objects are accessed by SCHEMA_OWNER.OBJECT_NAME. For example, ACME_OWN.CUSTOMER is the customer table for ACME_OWN and is how any other application user must access that table: for instance, SELECT * FROM ACME_OWN.CUSTOMER. A public synonym allows you to drop the ACME_OWN from the query.

Object creation methods

As a DBA, you're expected to create objects, but you seldom create them from scratch. Typically, the application developer or software vendor provides SQL scripts with the DDL and DML for the objects to be created. You simply log in via SQL*Plus and run the scripts provided.

SQL scripts are the recommended method for these reasons:

- ✔ A script isn't subject to typos.
- ✔ A script can be versioned, controlled, and re-executed as necessary.

We cover many of the fine points of SQL and SQL*Plus in Chapter 6.

Odds are that if you're creating multiple objects by hand, typing directly into SQL*Plus, something is wrong with your overall development process. Rarely is it okay to create ad hoc objects.

TIP

The easiest way to create objects is with a tool, such as SQL*Developer. SQL*Developer enables you to hand-code the SQL to create objects or use various wizards if you're not yet comfortable with the SQL language. The nice thing is that if you use a wizard, you can always see the SQL it created to help you learn.

The next section runs through some examples using SQL*Developer on Linux. First, launch SQL*Developer and get connected to your database with the HR demo schema. This example uses the Oracle software installed on our database server, and we are connecting to our local database, dev12c.

1. **Open a terminal window and navigate to sqldeveloper under your ORACLE_HOME directory.**

2. **Log in as your Oracle software owner, oracle.**

3. **From this point, type**

   ```
   cd $ORACLE_HOME/sqldeveloper
   ```

4. **Launch the SQL*Developer tool by typing the following.**

   ```
   ./sqldeveloper.sh
   ```

5. **Connect to your database by clicking the (+) sign under the Connections tab on the right side of the screen.**

6. **In the wizard that appears, give your connection a name and then fill in the username and password.**

7. **Select the Save Password check box.**

8. **Change the SID to dev12c, as shown in Figure 7-9.**

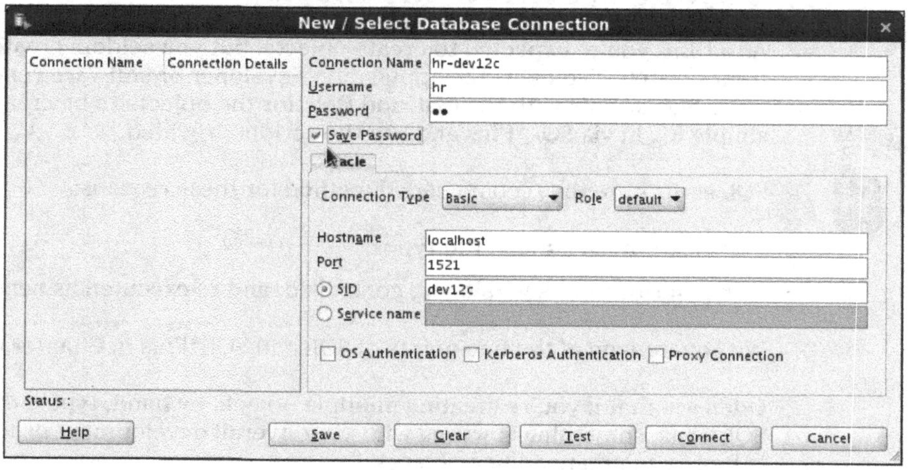

Figure 7-9:
Creating a
SQL*
Developer
Connection.

New / Select Database Connection		
Connection Name	Connection Details	

Connection Name: hr-dev12c
Username: hr
Password: ••
☑ Save Password

Oracle

Connection Type: Basic   Role: default

Hostname: localhost
Port: 1521
◉ SID: dev12c
○ Service name:

☐ OS Authentication ☐ Kerberos Authentication ☐ Proxy Connection

Status :

Help   Save   Clear   Test   Connect   Cancel

9. **Click the Test button. If everything works, click Save.**

10. **Click the Connect button to open a connection to the database.**

To create a database table in a schema, follow these steps:

1. **Open the drop-down menu from the plus sign (+) next to your connected username.**

2. **Right-click Tables and choose New Table from the context menu.**

   The Create Table screen appears.

3. **Fill in your column information.**

   Figure 7-10 shows a DEPT table with two columns.

4. **(Optional) Click the DDL tab to see the code generated in the background.**

5. **Click OK to create the table.**

6. **From the Connections panel, right-click Indexes and choose New Index from the context menu.**

   The Create Index screen appears, as shown in Figure 7-11.

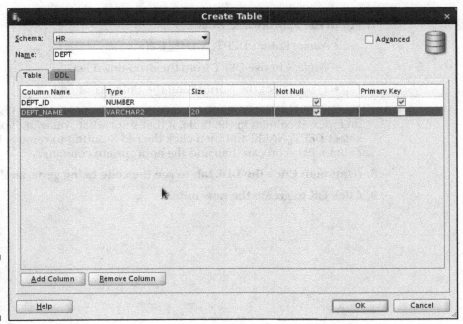

Figure 7-10:
Creating the
DEPT table.

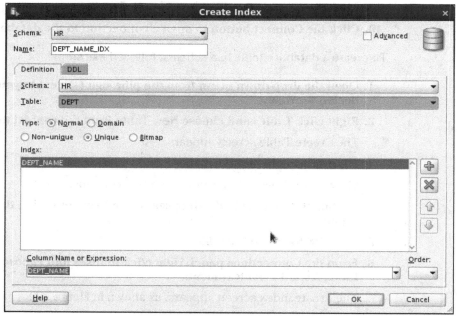

Figure 7-11:
Creating an
index on the
DEPT table.

7. **Fill in the appropriate values:**

   - *Name:* Enter **<DEPT_NAME_IDX>**.
   - *Table:* Choose DEPT from the drop-down list.
   - *Type:* Select the Normal and the Unique options.

   The DEPT_NAME column is automatically selected because it's the only un-indexed column in the table. If that's not what you want, you can select DEPT_NAME and then click the red X button to remove it from the column list. You can then add the appropriate columns.

8. **(Optional) Click the DDL tab to see the code being generated.**

9. **Click OK to create the new index.**

Part III

Caring for and Feeding an Oracle Database

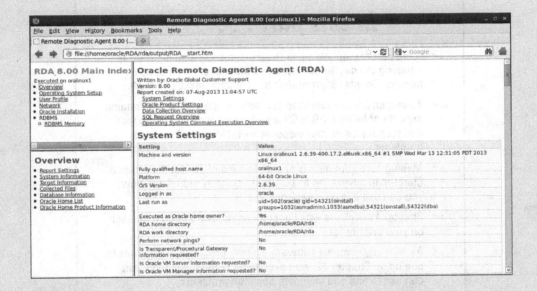

Visit www.dummies.com/extras/oracle12c to read about a focused approach to managing the statistics in a database.

In this part . . .

✔ A big part of your job as an Oracle database administrator is handling the day-to-day activities that keep the database healthy. Chapter 8 introduces the common tasks of a DBA.

✔ Tuning an Oracle database can be one of the most challenging aspects of being a DBA. Chapter 9 introduces you to the tools and techniques at your disposal for tackling performance problems.

✔ Making sure your data is secure is a job of utmost importance. Chapter 10 covers the basic Oracle security model and how you can use it in your environment.

✔ Chapter 11 explains why backup and recovery need to be high on your priority list.

✔ As with any complex software system, problems are bounds to pop up. In Chapter 12, we cover some of the basic tools you can use to find and eliminate common problems.

✔ One tool that may be of interest to you as a new DBA is Oracle Enterprise Manager. Chapter 13 overviews how to use and navigate this handy tool.

Chapter 8

Keeping the Database Running

In This Chapter

▶ Performing daily common tasks

▶ Automating jobs via the Oracle Scheduler

▶ Using Oracle Data Pump

*I*n most instances, managing an Oracle database is a full-time job. That's why some people have the job title Oracle *database administrator* (DBA). A DBA must keep on top of a plethora of activities to make sure the database runs smoothly and doesn't let people down when they most need it.

The 12c Oracle database needs less attention in areas that were traditionally very hands-on. However, each release has new features that require the coddling and care that more mature features do not require. Besides basic care and feeding, you might be asked to do some things on a regular basis: for example, loading data or scheduling jobs.

In this chapter, we investigate some of the daily maintenance tasks you will find yourself doing, how to use the Oracle Scheduler, and how to load and unload data by using Oracle Data Pump.

Doing Your Database Chores

The following sections identify some of the common activities you as DBA might perform. All databases are different. Each DBA has unique tasks and common management responsibilities. You might discover that not all the common tasks in these sections apply to you. However, we think most of them do.

On the other hand, you might do something every day that's unique to your environment (and maybe everyone else's too). We can't possibly cover such unique tasks. Still, this chapter's guidelines get you started on the road toward a well-maintained, reliable database.

Making way, checking space

A lot of areas in the database require you to check on space for growth and shrinkage. Most people need to watch out for growth. In our experience, most databases grow, not shrink, over time. With the business use of unstructured data (such as image, sound, and movie files) and more online activity than ever, you can expect storage requirements to increase.

Some environments are severely restricted regarding how much space is available. If that's the case for you, identify database resources that allow you to reclaim valuable space. Also, avoiding extraneous, empty blocks of storage in the database helps performance.

Chapter 7 explains that when you create a brand-new tablespace, you choose a file for that tablespace to store its data. A *tablespace* is just a logical pointer to a file or files on the operating system. The *file* is the physical component of storage in Oracle. Everything is ultimately stored in a file.

Say you create a tablespace called MY_DATA by typing

```
<create tablespace my_data
datafile '/u01/app/oracle/oradata/dev12c/my_data01.dbf'
size 10M;>
```

When this tablespace is created, Oracle allocates 10MB of space from the operating system. The OS sees this space as used. However, if you look in the database, this space is free. Essentially, the space disappears from the OS and appears in the database.

Again, when you create a tablespace, the system administrator sees that the space on the system has shrunk; to the DBA, the database has grown. (We're beating this to death because this distinction is important.)

Imagine that you have 100GB of space available on the OS, and you create a 99GB tablespace. Someone looking on the OS side would start sounding alarms: New space must be purchased! But the DBA can calm any fears by saying, "Don't worry. That 99GB is still free, but Oracle owns it now. The OS can't see it." DBAs do this because it is bad for tables and indexes to run out of space, so DBAs err on the side of having too much space.

Before you jump into adding space, how much space is actually unused in your database? Too often people add space to a system that has plenty of free space available.

You can monitor available real estate in a tablespace a couple of ways:

- ✔ Use the Enterprise Manager Database Express (EM Express) web-based management tool.

- ✔ Query the data dictionary.

Although we recommend the EM Express tool, we show you both ways so you have a better understanding of how this process works.

Enterprise Manager Database Express

The EM Express web-based management tool provides an easy way to check space.

1. **Log in to EM Express as a DBA user, such as SYSTEM.**

   The URL is typically https://*yourservername.com*:5500/em.

2. **Click the Storage tab.**

3. **Click the Tablespaces link in the Storage section.**

   A screen similar to Figure 8-1 appears.

A lot of information is available in this window:

- ✔ **Name:** By row, which tablespace contains information/data.

- ✔ **Size:** The amount of space that the tablespace has access to on the file system. It doesn't mean that much space is unused. It's the total amount of used *and* free space in megabytes (MB).

- ✔ **Free Space:** The amount of space, in megabytes, you've used creating objects and inserting/loading data.

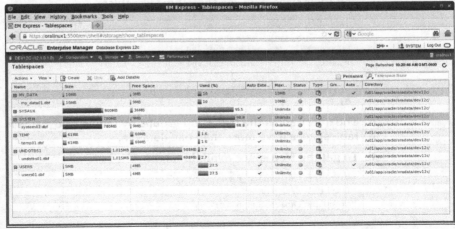

Figure 8-1:
Tablespace usage screen in EM Express looks like this.

✔ **Used (%):** A graphical representation of how much space is used. Nice for reports and showing to people who prefer pictures.

✔ **Auto Extend:** Setting to allow space to be added automatically as needed.

✔ **Maximum Size:** The maximum size the tablespace can grow.

✔ **Status:** A graphical representation of whether the tablespace is online or offline.

✔ **Type:** A graphical representation of the tablespace type; either permanent, undo, or temporary.

✔ **Group Name:** Storage group if assigned; often, this is null.

✔ **Auto Storage Management:** Indicator of whether automatic storage management is enabled for a tablespace.

✔ **Directory:** The directory where the data files for the corresponding tablespace are located.

To see the data file(s) and their size allocation, click the plus sign (+) under each tablespace name to expose this valuable information.

SQL

If EM Express isn't available in your environment, a couple of SQL queries can get you the same information.

1. **Log in to SQL*Plus.**

2. **Type the following code:**

```
< select tablespace_name, bytes
from dba_data_files;>
```

With this code you get the tablespace name, its associated data files, and their sizes. You see something like this:

```
TABLESPACE_NAME            BYTES
--------------- ---------------
UNDOTBS1           267,386,880
SYSAUX           1,200,553,984
USERS              101,777,408
SYSTEM             891,289,600
MY_DATA             10,485,760
```

The query sums the bytes and groups by tablespace_name in case the tablespaces have more than one data file.

3. **To get the free space available, type**

```
< select tablespace_name, sum(bytes) bytes
from dba_free_space
group by tablespace_name;>
```

You see something like this:

```
TABLESPACE_NAME           BYTES
---------------   ---------------
SYSAUX            264,503,296
UNDOTBS1          255,524,864
USERS              33,226,752
SYSTEM              6,422,528
MY_DATA            10,420,224
```

This information tells you how much available space remains in your tablespaces that you can use for creating objects and loading data.

4. Take those numbers and calculate your percentages.

If you're clever with SQL, you can do it all in one query. EM Express makes your work very easy here.

We'd love to say managing available space as simple as that. Alas, more goes into space management whether you use EM Express or SQL. You see, the preceding steps give you a rough estimate of the space you have available. It's a pretty good estimate, but it's not exact. Will it get you through the night knowing you have enough space for batch jobs to run? Yes, probably.

Beware the false numbers caused by the following situations:

✔ **When you create a tablespace, the OS considers the disk space allocated, even though within the database that space may not yet contain any objects.** (Similarly, misrepresentations can happen within the database, where you can allocate extents, but the space doesn't contain any objects.)

For example, when you create a table, by default it creates an extent that is 64k. That 64k is reserved for rows, so it no longer shows up in your free space allocation table. What if you took a 10MB tablespace and created 150 new tables with 64k initial extents? No data, just empty tables. Your free space view would tell you that only 0.1MB of that 10MB is left, yet you haven't put any data into the table

✔ **Autoextensible data files (described in Chapter 7).** A data file might say it's 10MB, but if it reaches that, it automatically grows up to the maximum size specified in the autoextend clause.

For a query that shows your tablespace sizes more accurately, type the following:

```
< select tablespace_name, file_name, bytes, autoextensible, maxbytes
from dba_data_files;>
```

You see something like this:

```
TABLESPACE_NAME           BYTES AUT       MAXBYTES
---------------  --------------- --- ---------------
USERS                101,777,408 YES     3.460E+10
UNDOTBS1             267,386,880 YES     3.460E+10
SYSAUX            1,200,553,984 YES     3.460E+10
SYSTEM              891,289,600 YES     3.460E+10
MY_DATA              10,485,760 NO              0
```

In this example, the AUT column stands for autoextensible. If the AUT column shows YES, the MAXBYTES column tells you how big the data file can automatically grow. This detail is important when you're deciding whether to add space.

Monitoring space in your segments

Segments are objects that take up space in the database. Segments are objects that, when created, allocated one or more extents from the free space in your tablespaces. The two most common database segments are

- ✔ Tables
- ✔ Indexes

Tables are what hold data, and indexes are access pointers to data elements within a table. Management of space for tables and indexes are very similar, so we focus on table management; however, the same concepts and techniques apply for index space management.

Before putting any data in a table, Oracle goes to the tablespace where it lives and allocates an extent. You can call this a *used extent* because it belongs to an object. The remaining space in the tablespace is free extents you can use when objects grow or new objects are created.

As you start putting data into that table, the extent that was allocated upon creation begins to fill up. When the extent reaches capacity, the table goes out to the tablespace and grabs another extent. This cycle continues until either you stop adding data or the tablespace runs out of free space. If the tablespace runs out of free space, the process requesting the space generates an error message and either fails or temporarily suspends until space is added.

To get a better idea of how objects grow, consider these guidelines:

- ✔ When you first create an object, the default extent size is 64k.
- ✔ The object continues to grow on 64k extents until it has 16 extents.
- ✔ The 17th extent is 1MB.

✔ The object continues to grow in 1MB extents for the next 63 extents (a total of 64, including the first 1MB extent).

✔ The 81st extent is 8MB.

✔ After 8MB extents, the last size Oracle uses is 64MB extents.

Knowing how your segments grow can help you predict space requirements. This skill is important to have when monitoring storage.

If you constantly insert data into your table, you've got it covered. However, that isn't always the case. Some tables grow and shrink. To be specific, they grow, but the shrinking, if necessary, is up to you.

Understanding how the objects in your application are used comes in handy. Consider these examples:

✔ What tables grow?

✔ What tables, if any, shrink over time?

✔ What tables receive inserts and are never added to again except for reads?

✔ What tables are under constant manipulation (INSERT, UPDATE, DELETE)?

Tables that stay the same are easy. You don't have to worry much about those tables unless you want to tune them for performance. We cover how to monitor a table's growth (in the earlier section "Making way, checking space"), so any tables that grow without getting any rows deleted are covered . . . unless, again, you want to tune them for performance (but that's another topic).

Growing and shrinking tables

A table that fits this category might be loaded every night and then deleted from throughout the day, like a batch processing table. For example, consider an ORDERS table that's batch loaded at night from all the orders that were taken from a website; as the orders are processed the next day, rows are deleted one by one. At the end of the day, all the rows are gone. What do you need to monitor for this table?

You should be most concerned with how big the table gets each day after the batch load. Businesses want orders to increase. What about the deletes? Should you shrink the table at the end of the day before the next batch load to free up space? Absolutely not. Although it's small, the growth of an object is overhead on the system processing. By leaving it the same size day to day, you know the space will be constantly reused. It's kind of like recycling. You mainly want to monitor this type of object for growth.

What about a table that you add to and delete from on a frequent basis? Say for every 1 million rows inserted in a week, 30 percent are deleted. This table can present an interesting challenge.

Take a quick look at how rows are inserted to better understand how objects grow and use space:

- You have a new table with one 64k extent.
- Your block size is 4k, so that extent is 16 blocks.
- You start inserting data; 100 rows fit in a block.
- By default, Oracle fills blocks to 90 percent full and then stops (so you can update the row later and have it grow). For example, some fields are left null until a later date, and then you fill them in. You don't want the block to get filled too easily by an update; otherwise Oracle has to move the row to a new block that fits it. This *rows migration* degrades performance.
- When all the blocks are filled in the free extents, the table allocates a new extent, and the process starts over.

What if you start deleting rows at the same time you're inserting? Will Oracle reuse the space where you deleted the row? It depends. Again, Oracle has a built-in feature that sacrifices space in favor of performance. Oracle inserts a row into a block that was once full, but only if the deletions bring the block to 40 percent full.

Oracle doesn't want to manage a block that teeters between full, not full, full, not full, and so on. Although Oracle has reduced the performance overhead that comes with managing blocks and which ones you can insert data into, managing block storage still has a cost associated with it. Imagine you have a table with 10,000 blocks and you're constantly inserting and deleting from that table. Oracle could spend all the CPU cycles managing what blocks can have inserts and which can't if there were only a one-row difference between full and not-full blocks.

That's why Oracle uses the 40-percent rule. A block takes all the inserts it can until it's 90 percent full, but the block can't get back in line until it's been reduced to 40 percent full.

Again, what if you insert 1 million rows a week and delete 30 percent of them? What if the 30 percent that you delete are randomly selected and spread evenly across the blocks? Over time, those blocks never get down to 40 percent full. After a year, you may have a table that is 10GB with 3GB of empty row space that won't be reused.

Shrinking tables

You must determine whether you can release an object's space after evaluating the object's usage pattern. Determining whether you can release an object's space requires a little arithmetic. Before you can decide whether to make room in a table, you need to analyze the table to gather statistics.

When we say analyze, we mean *analyze*. The ANALYZE command gets the necessary statistics to do this computation; DBMS_STATS doesn't get those stats.

This example uses the emp table. To analyze the table appropriately, take these steps:

1. **Log in to SQL*Plus and type**

   ```
   < analyze table emp compute statistics;>
   ```

   You see this:

   ```
   Table analyzed.
   ```

2. **Run a query against the USER_TABLES view by typing**

   ```
   <select table_name, avg_space, blocks
   from user_tables
   where table_name = 'EMP'>
   ```

   You see something like this:

   ```
   TABLE_NAME                                AVG_SPACE    BLOCKS
   ----------------------------------------- ---------- ----------
   EMP                                            3264       4528
   ```

   The AVG_SPACE column shows the average amount of free space per block.

3. **Use the following formula to calculate the amount of empty space in the emp table:**

   (AVG_SPACE – (DB_BLOCK_SIZE × FREE_SPACE)) × TAB_BLOCKS

   For this example, the formula looks like this:

   (3623 – (8192 × .10)) × 4528 = 11066432 (approximately 11MB)

4. **Decide whether there's enough space to make it worthwhile to shrink the object.**

5. **To enable Oracle to move rows around in the table type, issue this SQL command:**

   ```
   <alter table emp enable row movement;>
   ```

   You see this:

   ```
   Table altered.
   ```

6. **Issue this SQL command to do the shrink:**

```
<alter table emp shrink space;>
```

You see this:

```
Table altered.
```

7. **Re-analyze the table and re-execute the query to check the statistics.**

```
<select table_name, avg_space, blocks
from user_tables
where table_name = 'EMP'>
```

You should see something like this:

TABLE_NAME	AVG_SPACE	BLOCKS
EMP	933	2979

As you can see, the AVG_SPACE is about 10 percent of the block size. This is normal for default block space organization.

Check things like the Flash Recovery Area. Any day that produces a lot of archive logs or large backup files can quickly overcome the allocated space. If you don't have something like Enterprise Manager 12c watching this, you can encounter problems such as a hung database or failing backups. These situations can have dire consequences on your database system.

Checking users

Knowing what is going on within the database is part of your job as a DBA. You should regularly log in to your database to understand who is using it, what normal usage looks like, and whether anything unusual is occurring. Developing a baseline understanding of your database usage greatly helps you in your other DBA responsibilities.

If you check on your users on a regular basis, you'll be able to recognize the most active users. You can also find the following issues:

✔ Stale and abnormally long sessions

✔ Login abuse, such as people sharing accounts and unauthorized logins

Finding stale sessions

Stale sessions have been logged in to the system for a long time, and no one has done anything with them. Getting rid of stale sessions can help control resource usage.

Everyone's system is different, so you have to rely on some of your knowledge to decide whether the absence of activity is abnormal. To get a list of logged-in users and the last time they issued a command, connect to the database as a DBA user and type the following:

```
<select sid, serial#, username, last_call_et
from v$session
where username is not null;>
```

You might see something like this:

```
SID SERIAL# USERNAME          LAST_CALL_ET
--- ------- ----------------- ------------
 12    9853 SYSMAN                       3
 14    6552 HR                           0
 56      42 DBSNMP                       6
112   59271 SYSTEM                     160
 65   23451 MPYLE                   743160
 98    8752 CRM                          1
 32    4551 CRM                          3
 45   16554 HR                          36
119    9812 KHANR                    36522
```

MPYLE and KHANR are the two potentially bothersome accounts in this example. The LAST_CALL_ET column output data has the number of seconds since there was any activity. MPYLE has been inactive for over eight days! KHANR is a little less alarming at about 10 hours, but nonetheless, that would most likely require some explanation.

Note that the command uses the WHERE clause USERNAME IS NOT NULL. Oracle internal processes show up in this list as unnamed users, and you don't want those getting in the way of evaluation. Also, this example includes identification columns SID and SERIAL#. Together, these two columns uniquely identify a session within the database.

If you see a session you want to get rid of, type the following:

```
<alter system kill session '65,23451';>
```

You should see this:

```
System altered.
```

Releasing the bug

We had a client system that had over 3,000 connected sessions regularly. While evaluating the sessions, we discovered that 1,200 sessions had never issued a single command after logging in and setting a date format. It turned out to be an application bug that created multiple sessions for each application operation — one of them a session to set the date format. Of course, it did no good to set a session date format and log in to another session to do the work. Regardless, the client fixed the bug. The fix released nearly 6GB of memory from the OS!

Before you go killing sessions that have long periods of inactivity, check with application folks to determine whether a connection is part of a connection pool that just hasn't been used for a while. Usually, removal is safe if it isn't an application ID or if you can identify the user. Do your research!

Policing for login abuse and unauthorized logins

People everywhere are abusing their login privileges, and such abuse is a significant security problem. Unfortunately, it's usually people higher up in the application chain of command who tend to have more privileges giving out their login ID to subordinates to help with work. In other cases, co-workers decide to share a login ID because an account became locked or someone forgot his or her password.

Track this abuse down by comparing the database login ID with the OS login ID. Oracle tracks both. Type the following to see all the users connected with both IDs:

```
<select sid, serial#, username, osuser, program
from v$session
where username is not null;>
```

You might see something like this:

```
       SID    SERIAL# USERNAME   OSUSER      PROGRAM
---------- ---------- ---------- ---------- ----------------
       112       3741 MPYLE      MPYLE       sqlplusw.exe
       122       3763 MPYLE      RKHAN       sqlplusw.exe
       115       9853 SYSMAN     oracle      OMS
       122      35878 HR         HRAPP       sqlplus@classroom
       124          4 DBSNMP     oracle      emagent@classroom
```

MPYLE has given his login ID to RKHAN (or at least the evidence suggests that). Evaluate this information carefully and do a thorough investigation. Take appropriate measures if there's been a violation of your security policy.

Checking backups

Checking your backups should be a regular part of your daily routine.
Checking backups includes these things:

- Ensuring the database backups completed successfully and without errors.

  From an Oracle DBA's standpoint, you need to make sure the entire backup process is logged and no errors were detected. A common mistake is for the DBA to setup a database backup, but not monitor the output logs to confirm it was successful.

- Following up occasionally with appropriate personal about OS backups.

- Checking regularly to ensure the system admin is moving the database backup from disk to tape.

Too many environments put system backups on the back burner because they were scheduled jobs; no alerting was in place. If you subscribe to this methodology, you could be signing up for a heap of trouble. Be sure to verify that your backups are running without errors. It would be extremely embarrassing and potentially career-limiting to discover you've "lost" a database because, as the DBA, you ignored e-mailed error messages for months.

Keep these backup tips in mind:

- **Oracle Recovery Manager has a LOG option that you can pass in with your backup script.** This option forces RMAN to log the details for every step of the backup as it runs. This shell script example logs the output of your RMAN backup on Linux/UNIX:

```ksh
#/usr/bin/ksh

# Environment Settings
export ORACLE_BASE=/u01/app/oracle
export ORACLE_HOME=$ORACLE_BASE/product/12.1.0
export ORACLE_SID=dev12c
export BAK_DATE=`date '+%d%b%Y_%H_%M'`
export PATH=$ORACLE_HOME/bin:$PATH

# Run Backup
rman target / cmdfile=full_hot_backup.rmn
log=full_hot_backup_${ORACLE_SID}_${BAK_DATE}.log

# Check Error Code
Export ECODE=$?

if [ $ECODE -gt 0 ]; then
          mailx -s "RMAN BACKUP FAILED!" dba@yourcompany.com
else echo "RMAN BACKUP SUCCESSFUL"
fi
```

The simple script, which you might schedule in cron, runs a backup script of your choice (called full_hot_backup.rmn) and logs the output to a file with the database name and date attached.

After the backup completes, the script checks whether RMAN exited cleanly. It does this by checking a mechanism called an *error code*. Well-written programs have this mechanism. If the environment variable $? has a value of non-zero, something failed.

I have an if-then section that sends an e-mail if that backup failed. Of course, if there's a failure, you have to find out why and fix it. Either way, implementing a notification similar to the example helps you tighten your backup and recovery planning.

✔ **Make sure the backup is usable.** This task is important for all backups but is especially important if you store any backups to tape. Make sure those backups can be restored from tape and then actively recovered to a database. For obvious reasons, you don't necessarily have to do this with your production database. You can do the restore to a differ-ent database. A common DBA task is to refresh test database images with production backup copies; this process is a good way to test your production backups. Either way, as reliable as you would like to think tapes can be, you need to test them. What if one of the tape's heads is going bad and writing corrupt blocks? Silent corruption of backups is a rare but serious problem encountered by DBAs. Testing your backups helps you to practice your recovery strategies and validate your overall backup and recovery posture.

✔ **At the very least, date and save this backup log in a directory on the system.** If you want to go one step further, have it e-mailed to you every day when the backup completes. If you need to use a backup from a spe-cific date, saving the log files for those backups helps you confirm the backup is valid.

✔ **Look at the backup log for errors.** Imagine how you'd feel if you experi-enced a failure and had to tell your boss that you can't recover because the backup's been failing for six months. It's surprising how often we run into situations like this while helping clients with their backup and recovery strategies.

Checking batch jobs

Almost all companies we have worked for have some sort of nightly batch jobs that run against the database. They range from loading data to generat-ing reports to some sort of data processing. They might be scheduled by you or someone else. Either way, we find it common that the DBA is the one responsible for monitoring them and ensuring their success. If you think about it, they're on your turf because you're in charge of the database.

Whether you or someone else developed the scripts, the scripts, like RMAN, should have some sort of logging and notification system in place. Such a system makes it easier for you to identify a problem when it occurs. By having status e-mails generated and sent out, you're all but forced to keep up with the results. If your e-mail program allows filtering, you can send the notifications to separate folders for each batch job. Just remember to check them. Again, we're trying to help you cover all the bases that an Oracle DBA might commonly have on his or her plate.

Reviewing audit logs

What's the use of auditing in the database if you aren't doing anything with the information? You should develop some ideas on what types of information you're looking for. Additionally, regularly back up and purge the audit logs (whether they're in the database or the OS). This way, they aren't taking up space and they are easier to search when looking for potential problems.

Many companies are required to comply with various auditing and compliance laws, policies, and guidelines. These requirements specify what activities are logged, how often the logs are reviewed and by whom, and how long the logs are retained. Be sure you're aware of the requirements for your company and can prove to an auditor that you're in compliance.

Maintaining logs

Oracle generates all kinds of logs for various components. Depending on what features you enabled in the database, there may be more or fewer. Some logs (alert and listener, for example) should be regularly:

- ✔ Checked to identify errors
- ✔ Renamed with a timestamp added
- ✔ Trimmed down in size so they do not grow excessively large
- ✔ Backed up so they can be reviewed later if necessary

If certain logs grow too large, they can cause problems in the database where either the database suspends or activity is not logged.

Oracle database logs contain valuable information that frequently helps identify problems. When a problem is encountered, one of the first things a DBA does is review the appropriate database logs for errors and background information. In addition to Oracle's logs, don't hesitate to look at items such as Windows Event view or the message logs on Linux/UNIX systems. They also contain valuable information for the operating system and server hardware which support the Oracle database.

Automating Chores with the Oracle Scheduler

With the use of the Oracle Scheduler, you can run almost any type of program with a robust resource-management and scheduling system. The Scheduler is intended to help you create and automatically run many of your administrative tasks managed from within the database. Oracle Scheduler is implemented via the DBMS_SCHEDULER database package and is a replacement for the old DMBS_JOB package.

The Scheduler can run these programs:

- PL/SQL stored procedures
- PL/SQL anonymous blocks
- Java stored programs
- Local and remote external programs such as shell scripts and executables

You can schedule jobs that are

- **Timed-based:** A job can run simply from wall-clock time. It can repeat on a schedule based on hours, days, months, and so on.
- **Event-based:** The results of certain conditions or events in the environment can cause a job to run. This trigger is useful when you have to wait for other processes to finish before a job is run.
- **Dependency-based:** You can set up dependency such as success or failure. Depending on the outcome of one job, one or more dependant scenarios can be executed.

Scheduler objects

The Scheduler can use a number of objects to run jobs. Not all of them are mandatory. These objects specify job parameters, timing, execution windows, and resource limits.

- **Programs:** Programs are the actual code that the Scheduler will run. They identify the execution code, arguments, and job type.
- **Schedules:** The job schedules are just what you think. They contain parameters such as when and how often. A schedule should be created by the DBA and then shared for many jobs.

✔ **Jobs:** When a job object is created, it contains the executable and the schedule required to run the job. You can enable the job for it to begin the task based on the parameters. Jobs are categorized as any of the following:

- *Database* jobs run out of the database from PL/SQL commands.

- *External* jobs run off the operating system from external executables.

- *Chain (Dependency)* jobs run based on status of other jobs.

- *Detached* jobs run to simply kick off another job in a new process.

- *Lightweight* are simple jobs that exist only for their immediate execution. They aren't stored as schema objects. They're used for quick, low-overhead applications.

✔ **Windows:** Helps schedule jobs for certain times, which can help control resource usage. When a window becomes active, certain resource directives are enabled that might restrict a job from overwhelming the system.

Creating your first Scheduler job

The Oracle Scheduler example in this section creates a simple job that runs a stored PL/SQL procedure. The procedure selects a count of the number of users on the system and inserts that number into a table with a timestamp. It runs every five minutes.

Follow these steps to schedule a job for the first time:

1. **Log in to SQL*Plus as the SYS user.**

2. **Give the intended job creator the ability to create jobs:**

   ```
   <grant create job to hr;>
   ```

   You should see this:

   ```
   Grant succeeded.
   ```

   This example job is created and run by HR.

3. **Let HR see the V$SESSION table:**

   ```
   <grant select on v_$session to hr;>
   ```

   You should see this:

   ```
   Grant succeeded.
   ```

   The _ in V_$SESSION isn't a typo! V$SESSION is a synonym for V_$SESSION. For the grant to work, you have to give the view name.

4. **Log in to SQL*Plus as the job creator and make a table to hold the data:**

```
< create table user_count (
number_of_users NUMBER(4),
time_of_day     TIMESTAMP
)
TABLESPACE users;>
```

You see this:

```
Table created.
```

5. **Create a stored procedure:**

```
< CREATE OR REPLACE PROCEDURE insert_user_count AS
   v_user_count NUMBER(4);
BEGIN
  SELECT count(*)
           INTO v_user_count
    FROM v$session
    WHERE username IS NOT NULL;

    INSERT INTO user_count
       VALUES (v_user_count, systimestamp);
    commit;

END insert_user_count;
/ >
```

The stored procedure gathers the number of users and inserts them into the table with a timestamp. You should see this:

```
Procedure created.
```

6. **Create a program for the job:**

```
< BEGIN
DBMS_SCHEDULER.CREATE_PROGRAM (
    program_name          => 'PROG_INSERT_USER_COUNT',
program_action       => 'INSERT_USER_COUNT',
program_type         => 'STORED_PROCEDURE');
END;
/>
```

You see this:

```
PL/SQL procedure successfully completed.
```

7. **Enable the program:**

```
<exec dbms_scheduler.enable('PROG_INSERT_USER_COUNT')>
```

You see this:

```
PL/SQL procedure successfully completed.
```

8. **Create a schedule for the job to run:**

```
< BEGIN
DBMS_SCHEDULER.CREATE_SCHEDULE (
   schedule_name      => 'my_weekend_5min_schedule',
   start_date         => SYSTIMESTAMP,
   repeat_interval    => 'FREQ=MINUTELY; INTERVAL=5; BYDAY=SAT,SUN',
   end_date           => SYSTIMESTAMP + INTERVAL '30' day,
   comments           => 'Every 5 minutes');
END;
/>
```

This example job runs every five minutes. You see this:

```
PL/SQL procedure successfully completed.
```

9. **Create your job with the program and schedule you defined:**

```
< BEGIN
DBMS_SCHEDULER.CREATE_JOB (
   job_name           => 'my_user_count_job',
   program_name       => 'prog_insert_user_count',
   schedule_name      => 'my_weekend_5min_schedule');
END;
/>
```

You see this:

```
PL/SQL procedure successfully completed.
```

10. **Enable your job so it runs within the defined schedule:**

```
< exec dbms_scheduler.enable('my_user_count_job')>
```

You see this:

```
PL/SQL procedure successfully completed.
```

The job runs at the specified start time (at SYSTIMESTAMP). If you choose a calendar date in the future, it doesn't start until then.

11. **After the job's been running for 17 minutes, type the following to see your USER_COUNT table:**

```
< select *
from user_count;>
```

You see this:

```
NUMBER_OF_USERS TIME_OF_DAY
--------------- ----------------------------------
             14 09-AUG-13 02.15.14.118495 PM
             14 09-AUG-13 02.00.14.137300 PM
             13 09-AUG-13 02.05.14.120116 PM
             13 09-AUG-13 02.10.14.120680 PM
```

TIP

When you have the job running, you can get details about the success or failure by querying the following views:

```
USER_SCHEDULER_JOB_RUN_DETAILS
USER_SCHEDULER_JOB_LOG
```

These views show information only about your jobs. To get information on the recent runs of our job, log in as the job creator and type

```
< select job_name, status, run_duration, cpu_used
from USER_SCHEDULER_JOB_RUN_DETAILS
where job_name = 'MY_USER_COUNT_JOB';>
```

You see this:

```
JOB_NAME               STATUS       RUN_DURATION      CPU_USED
--------------------   ----------   ---------------   -------------------
MY_USER_COUNT_JOB      SUCCEEDED    +000 00:00:00     +000 00:00:00.01
MY_USER_COUNT_JOB      SUCCEEDED    +000 00:00:00     +000 00:00:00.01
MY_USER_COUNT_JOB      SUCCEEDED    +000 00:00:00     +000 00:00:00.00
MY_USER_COUNT_JOB      SUCCEEDED    +000 00:00:00     +000 00:00:00.01
```

Disabling a job

You can disable a job after it's completed. That way, if necessary, you can easily re-enable it later. To disable your job, type the following:

```
<exec dbms_scheduler.disable('my_user_count_job')>
```

You should see this:

```
PL/SQL procedure successfully completed.
```

Removing the job

If your job is no longer needed, you can remove just the job and leave the program out there, or you can remove both. Same goes for the schedule you created.

If you no longer need this particular job, you can remove it by typing

```
<exec dbms_scheduler.drop_job('my_user_count_job')>
```

You should see this:

```
PL/SQL procedure successfully completed.
```

If you no longer need your program, you can remove it by typing

```
<exec dbms_scheduler.drop_program('prog_insert_user_count')>
```

You should see this:

```
PL/SQL procedure successfully completed.
```

If you no longer need a particular schedule, remove it by typing

```
<exec dbms_scheduler.drop_schedule('my_weekend_5min_schedule')>
```

You should see this:

```
PL/SQL procedure successfully completed.
```

The job schedule you created can be used for multiple jobs; be careful when removing your schedule to ensure you aren't impacting more than what you expect.

Using Oracle Data Pump

Oracle Data Pump is one tool we use constantly to move data within databases and between databases.

Data Pump is modeled after Oracle's Export/Import tools that were available prior to Oracle 10g. Export/Import is still available, but Data Pump has taken the tasks traditionally done by Export/Import and added a lot more options and flexibility.

Data Pump is useful for

- ✔ Moving data from one **schema** to another
- ✔ Moving data from one **version** of Oracle to another
- ✔ Moving data from one **OS** to another
- ✔ Creating logical backups

You can use Data Pump to transport an entire database from one instance to another. This capability includes new Oracle 12c pluggable databases as well as older nonpluggable databases. You can use this to move a database to a new server environment or to upgrade to a higher database version.

Like the older Export/Import utilities, you must run Data Pump from the command line. That makes it easy to script and schedule automated jobs. Data Pump is controlled by a series of parameters and files.

You should be familiar with these files:

- **Dump file:** This file is created during a Data Pump Export. It's the import file when you do a Data Pump Import. It's binary so you can't open it to see anything useful.

- **Parfile:** This optional file lists the parameters that control the Data Pump Import or Export. You create this text-based file yourself.

- **Log file:** This output is for all Data Pump Import and Export jobs unless you specify otherwise. You can name it yourself or let it have a default name. It's useful for getting jobs statistics and for troubleshooting.

You can interactively do these things with Data Pump jobs:

- Start
- Stop
- Pause
- Restart
- Kill

The result is that you can start a job from the command line, detach from it to do something else (while it's still running), and re-attach later to check progress or make changes. When a Data Pump job runs into a problem, it automatically suspends itself; that way you have a chance to fix the problem before the job fails altogether. This can be a real time-saver. Prior to Data Pump, if an Export/Import job ran into a problem, it would fail immediately, sometimes wasting hours of time.

In our experience, Data Pump Export is significantly faster than traditional exports on large jobs. If you have a small job, like one or two small tables or a small schema, it doesn't really seem to make a difference. But on large jobs, the difference is phenomenal.

In one example, a job took around 12 hours to dump out about 200GB with the old Export tool. When we upgraded from 9i to 11g and converted to Data Pump, it took only 45 minutes. Part of the reason is that Data Pump can be easily parallelized. *Parallelizing* Data Pump means starting multiple processes that run simultaneously to split up the job. The only way to parallelize traditional exports is to manually split the workload into multiple jobs. That manual splitting was tedious and time-consuming.

Data Pump Export

The command-line program expdb launches Data Pump Export. All Data Pump Export jobs are estimated at the beginning so you see the estimate before it runs the actual export. Remember that estimates may not always be completely accurate.

From the OS command line, launch Data Pump Export and have it show a list of the parameter:

```
<expdp help=y>
```

You see something like this:

```
Export: Release 12.1.0.1.0 - Production on Sat Jul 20 06:56:47 2013

Copyright (c) 1982, 2013, Oracle and/or its affiliates.  All rights reserved.


The Data Pump export utility provides a mechanism for transferring data objects
between Oracle databases. The utility is invoked with the following command:

    Example: expdp scott/tiger DIRECTORY=dmpdir DUMPFILE=scott.dmp

You can control how Export runs by entering the 'expdp' command followed
by various parameters. To specify parameters, you use keywords:

    Format:  expdp KEYWORD=value or KEYWORD=(value1,value2,...,valueN)
    Example: expdp scott/tiger DUMPFILE=scott.dmp DIRECTORY=dmpdir SCHEMAS=scott
            or TABLES=(T1:P1,T1:P2), if T1 is partitioned table
...output snipped...
```

You can see that Data Pump lists all the parameters you have to choose from and gives a brief explanation of each.

You can specify parameters at two locations:

- ✔ On the command line
- ✔ In a parameter file

Go over some of the more useful parameters in detail:

- ✔ **COMPRESSION:** This parameter allows you to compress the output of Data Pump while the job is running. This trick is handy when space is at a premium. This parameter degrades the performance of the export, but that's to be expected.

✔ **CONTENT:** This specifies what type of data you want to get. Do you want just object definitions? Do you want just the data? Both? Determine what you want to export and specify accordingly.

✔ **DIRECTORY:** This specifies the directory where you want the dump file to go. This is an Oracle Object directory, not a simple path on the OS. We show you how to create a directory later in this chapter.

✔ **DUMPFILE:** This parameter names the dump file to be output. You can also have Data Pump number the files if you like. This numbering is handy when you use parallelism or have Data Pump break the job into multiple files of manageable size. To have Data Pump number the files, use the %U argument:

```
DUMPFILE=my_dp_exp_%U.dmp
```

Data Pump starts with 1 and numbers the files to 99. What if you need more than 99 files? Try something like this:

```
DUMPFILE= my_dp_exp_seta_%U.dmp, my_dp_exp_set_b_%U.dmp
```

You can have it dump to multiple files, which is especially useful when you're parallelizing the output.

✔ **ESTIMATE:** This parameter estimates your job size but won't run it. Very handy when space is at a premium. This parameter stops the job after estimating.

✔ **EXCLUDE:** You can exclude certain objects from the export. For example, say you want everything but the HR and OE schemas as well as all views and functions. EXCLUDE can have multiple entries. You can say this:

```
EXCLUDE=SCHEMAS:"'HR','OE'"
EXCLUDE=VIEW,FUNCTION
```

✔ **INCLUDE:** Mutually exclusive with EXCLUDE, use this parameter if you want to get a specific type of object. When the list is small, this can be very useful:

```
INCLUDE=VIEWS, TRIGGERS
```

✔ **FILESIZE:** You can break your Data Pump Export into multiple files, which aids file management. For example, if you have a 200GB export to do, you might not want a 200GB dump file to manage afterward. Instead, use this parameter to break it into 4GB chunks or something similar.

✔ **FLASHBACK_TIME:** If you want to dump the data from a time other than the present, you can use this parameter to specify a date and time. As long as your database still has the old data in its undo retention space, this parameter can be very useful.

✔ **NETWORK_LINK:** You can connect from one database to export to another by setting up a database link and specifying it with this parameter.

✔ **PARALLEL:** To help speed up your dump, you can parallelize it. Try different values to find the most efficient number of processes across different systems. At the very least, you should be able to parallelize by the number of CPUs you have while recalling the capabilities of the storage media to which you're writing.

✔ **SCHEMAS:** This parameter gives a list of schemas to Data Pump and tells it what to get. By default, Data Pump exports the schema that's logging in to do the job.

✔ **TABLES:** This restricts the export to a list of tables.

✔ **TABLESPACES:** This parameter restricts the export to a list of tablespaces only.

Data Pump Import

The command-line program impdb launches Data Pump Import. From the OS command line, launch Data Pump Import and have it show a list of the parameters:

```
<impdp help=y>
```

You see something like this:

```
Import: Release 12.1.0.1.0 - Production on Sat Jul 20 06:54:52 2013

Copyright (c) 1982, 2013, Oracle and/or its affiliates.  All rights reserved.


The Data Pump Import utility provides a mechanism for transferring data objects
between Oracle databases. The utility is invoked with the following command:

    Example: impdp scott/tiger DIRECTORY=dmpdir DUMPFILE=scott.dmp

You can control how Import runs by entering the 'impdp' command followed
by various parameters. To specify parameters, you use keywords:

    Format:  impdp KEYWORD=value or KEYWORD=(value1,value2,...,valueN)
    Example: impdp scott/tiger DIRECTORY=dmpdir DUMPFILE=scott.dmp
...output snipped...
```

Like Data Pump Export, Import lists the parameters that can be used with the import portion of Data Pump. Many of these parameters behave the same way they do when you're using Data Pump Export.

Take a closer look at some the Data Pump Import parameters:

- **CONTENT:** If you have a full content export file, you can choose to import only the metadata. For example, you might want to create all the tables with no rows. Obviously, if you didn't include the rows in the export dump file, you can't tell Data Pump Import to put them in!

- **ESTIMATE:** This parameter estimates the size of the Data Pump Import.

- **DIRECTORY:** This one tells Data Pump Import where it can find the dump file. It doesn't have to be the same place it was dumped, but you must move the file to the new location. This parameter might be useful when moving the file to another machine or OS.

- **DUMPFILE:** A complete listing of all the files created by Data Pump Export.

- **EXCLUDE:** This works much like Data Pump Export but tells Data Pump Import what to leave from the dump file.

- **INCLUDE:** This parameter is another way of controlling what objects are put into the target database.

- **FLASHBACK_SCN, FLASHBACK_TIME:** Use these parameters with the Data Pump Import tool only when connecting through a NETWORK_LINK. Data Pump Import can connect directly to a remote database across a database link and write the data directly into the target system. Use these parameters to pull data from the past.

- **NETWORK_LINK:** You can connect from one database and import into another by setting up a database link and specifying it with this parameter. No files are created when this method is used. This parameter is very handy for logical recovery and cloning.

- **PARALLEL:** This helps speed up your import.

- **REMAP_SCHEMA:** This parameter is handy for copying the objects/data from one schema to another.

- **REMAP_TABLESPACE:** Moves the objects into a new tablespace. By default, they go into the same tablespace they came from. This parameter is useful when used in conjunction with remap_schema and while moving data from one database to another.

- **SCHEMAS:** This parameter gives a list of schemas to Data Pump to tell it what to import. By default, Data Pump imports everything in the file. In essence, you can have a full export but then pick and choose what you want to import.

- **TABLES:** As with SCHEMAS, you can choose from your dump file what to import.

- **TABLESPACES:** You can choose what tablespaces you want import from the dump file.

Creating Oracle Directories

An Oracle directory is required for Data Pump. A *directory* is basically a portal to a location on the operating system.

Directories are controlled by both system and object privileges. You need a system privilege, CREATE DIRECTORY, to create one. If your user doesn't own the directory, you need READ and/or WRITE object privileges on the directory to use it.

To create a directory, log in to the database as a user with appropriate privileges and type the following:

```
create directory my_data_pump_dir as '/u01/app/oracle/dumpfiles';
```

You should see this:

```
Directory created.
```

Using Data Pump with a Parameter File

A *parameter file* is a text file listing the parameters for the Data Pump Export or Import and setting the chosen values. Data Pump Export and Import parameter files are constructed the same way.

Follow these steps to run a Data Pump Export with this parameter file:

1. **Type the parameter file into a text editor and save it to a directory.**

   This example is a parameter file that exports the DEPARTMENTS and EMPLOYEES tables of the HR schema:

   ```
   # File: /u01/app/oracle/scripts/datapump/my_data_pump_parfile.par
   DIRECTORY=my_data_pump_dir
   DUMPFILE=my_data_pump_dumpfile.dmp
   LOGFILE=my_data_pump_logfile.log
   SCHEMAS=HR
   TABLES=EMPLOYEES, DEPARTMENTS
   COMPRESSION=ALL
   ```

2. **Open a command-line prompt and go to the directory where your parameter file is saved.**

3. **Launch Data Pump Export with your parameter file:**

```
<expdp parfile=my_data_pump_parfile.par>
```

You should see this:

```
Export: Release 12.1.0.1.0 - Production on Sat Jul 20 06:51:40 2013

Copyright (c) 1982, 2013, Oracle and/or its affiliates.  All rights
        reserved.

Username:
```

4. **Enter the username and give the password for the user you want to export with.**

You should see something like this:

```
Connected to: Oracle Database 12c Enterprise Edition Release 12.1.0.1.0 -
        64bit Production
With the Partitioning, OLAP, Advanced Analytics and Real Application
        Testing options
Starting "SYS"."SYS_EXPORT_SCHEMA_01":  /******** AS SYSDBA parfile=my_
        data_pump_parfile.par
Estimate in progress using BLOCKS method...
Processing object type SCHEMA_EXPORT/TABLE/TABLE_DATA
Total estimation using BLOCKS method: 128 KB
...output snipped...
. . exported "HR"."DEPARTMENTS"                     5.437 KB      27 rows
. . exported "HR"."EMPLOYEES"                       8.726 KB     107 rows
Master table "SYS"."SYS_EXPORT_SCHEMA_01" successfully loaded/unloaded
**************************************************************************
Dump file set for SYS.SYS_EXPORT_SCHEMA_01 is:
  /u01/app/oracle/dumpfiles/MY_DATA_PUMP_FILE.DMP
Job "SYS"."SYS_EXPORT_SCHEMA_01" successfully completed at 06:52:25
```

5. **Create the user and the tablespace.**

Make sure both users have the same privileges.

6. **Create a parameter file that imports the data into a new user in its own tablespace.**

In this example, HR2 is imported to its own tablespace, HR2_DATA.

Because this export is only a partial piece of the HR data model, you exclude constraints and triggers; they have dependent objects that aren't in the export dump file. You don't have to exclude them, but you get an error in the log file as Data Pump tries to create them.

Such a parameter file might look like this:

```
# File: /u01/app/oracle/scripts/datapump/my_HR2_data_pump_parfile.par
DIRECTORY=my_data_pump_dir
DUMPFILE=my_data_pump_file.dmp
LOGFILE=my_HR2_data_pump_logfile.log
EXCLUDE=CONSTRAINT
EXCLUDE=TRIGGER
REMAP_SCHEMA=HR:HR2
REMAP_TABLESPACE=EXAMPLE:HR2_DATA
```

7. **Run the import:**

```
<impdp parfile=my_hr2_data_pump_parfile.par>
```

You should see something like this:

```
Import: Release 12.1.0.1.0 - Production on Sat Jul 20 07:00:17 2013

Copyright (c) 1982, 2013, Oracle and/or its affiliates.  All rights
          reserved.

Username: / as sysdba

Connected to: Oracle Database 12c Enterprise Edition Release 12.1.0.1.0 -
          64bit Production
With the Partitioning, OLAP, Advanced Analytics and Real Application
          Testing options
Master table "SYS"."SYS_IMPORT_FULL_01" successfully loaded/unloaded
Starting "SYS"."SYS_IMPORT_FULL_01":  /******** AS SYSDBA parfile=my_hr2_
          data_pump_parfile.par
Processing object type SCHEMA_EXPORT/USER
Processing object type SCHEMA_EXPORT/TABLE/TABLE
Processing object type SCHEMA_EXPORT/TABLE/TABLE_DATA
. . imported "HR2"."DEPARTMENTS"                      5.437 KB      27 rows
. . imported "HR2"."EMPLOYEES"                        8.726 KB     107 rows
...output snipped...
Job "SYS"."SYS_IMPORT_FULL_01" successfully completed at 07:02:53
```

By default, the log file is created in the same directory as your dump file. The log file is a text file that any text editor can read.

If the user is someone other than the schema you're exporting or importing, you need one of these two things:

✔ DBA privileges

✔ The DATAPUMP_EXP_FULL_DATABASE and DATAPUMP_IMP_FULL_ DATABASE roles

If you're working as an administrator in a container database (CDB), you also need the CDB_DBA role.

Chapter 9

Tuning an Oracle Database for Performance

. . . .

In This Chapter

▶ Knowing the tuning tools and techniques

▶ Tuning before a problem occurs

▶ Tuning after a problem occurs

▶ Tuning SQL

▶ Tuning the database

. . . .

Tuning an Oracle database is one of the most challenging activities you encounter as a database administrator. Heck, we could probably write an entire book on the tools Oracle provides and the methodologies you can use when tackling a database performance issue. Knowing the tools and techniques will get you a long way, but the problems DBAs uncover also require an understanding of basic computer functionality and cooperation with other members of the infrastructure management team within your organization.

In this chapter, we explore the tuning methods an experienced database administrator might employ. We introduce you to concepts of performance tuning and provide some fundamental techniques that will allow you to take advantage of what Oracle has to offer before you even begin to install and configure the software. We also review the features within the Oracle software designed to help you tackle performance-related problems in the database.

However, tuning a database doesn't come naturally for a lot of people, and the process can take some time to master. The information in this chapter is helpful when you begin your career as an Oracle database administrator, but you'll want to seek out more information to perfect your performance-tuning skills. Practice and further education both help you become more adept and efficient. A number of tools that are available from third-party vendors can also help you.

Many aspects of performance tuning contribute to its difficulty, but the tools and techniques discussed here help make the process less painful and, when successful, quite rewarding.

Tuning Costs

There's a saying in the motor racing industry that goes something like, "Speed costs, so how fast do you want to spend?" This saying might also apply to database tuning. Don't despair though. We focus mostly on the tools that Oracle offers as standard features within its software stack. However, we also discuss the "for pay" features. If you can get your company to spring for them, paid tools can sometimes make up the expense quickly. Rather than have a performance problem costing your company revenue, it might be worth your while to spend some money up front to have the right tools in your hands to make performance problems go away.

Are we saying that a good database administrator should be able to tune a database with just the free stuff? Well, to an extent, yes. The more experience you have, the better you can take advantage of what is at hand. An experienced carpenter can probably build a deck by using a rock instead of a hammer, but having an actual hammer would make the job go faster and reduce the fatigue he or she would experience. See Table 9-1 for a cost-comparative list of resources that you can use when tuning your database.

Table 9-1	Cost Comparison of Tuning Resources	
Tuning Resource	*Example or Where to Find This Resource*	*Cost*
Oracle Documentation	docs.oracle.com	Free
Oracle Non-Licensed Tools	STATSPACK	Free
Oracle Support	support.oracle.com	$ (The cost is normally included with license.)
Oracle Training	Oracle University	$
Third-Party Tools	Quest TOAD	$
Oracle Licensed Tools	Tuning pack	$$
Specialized Consultants	Outside Contractor	$$$

There's a saying that claims, "Time is money." It's good to keep in mind when considering which database-tuning resources to have on hand.

Also, keep in mind that hearing someone say, "The database is slow. Can you fix it?" can be frustrating when the person reporting the problem has no idea whether the issue lies in the database or in one of the other layers of the complex software stack. No one wants to spend hours looking for a problem that doesn't exist, but many tuning efforts are spent proving that the problem is indeed not within the database. This fact goes for newbies and experienced administrators alike. We have a combined 30+ years of experience working in the Oracle software stack, and we still dread hearing the proclamation that the database is slow.

The good news is that, as you practice the tuning techniques, you get better and faster at finding the cause of performance issues — even those not within the database.

Tuning Basics

Having the right approach and a good plan helps reduce the time spent identifying and fixing a database performance problem. Just like tackling any kind of problem in life, learning from the experience of others and furthering your education make you more successful. Valuable practices can save you time and effort tackling your database performance problems.

Asking questions

When a performance problem is brought to your attention (by self-discovery or by others), you need an accurate scope of the issue. Understanding the issue might involve talking to different people within the application stack. Some questions you might ask are

- How is this problem presenting itself to you or others?

- When did the problem start? Did it begin suddenly, or has it been worsening over time?

- What is the impact of this problem for you or the company? Is the issue isolated or company-wide?

- Has anything changed in the environment recently?

- Is there a workaround to use while the problem is researched?

Knowing the answers to these questions helps you prioritize the issue and possibly engage others to help find the cause. (Remember: The problem might not be in the database.) Issues can be very impactful of a company's bottom line; therefore, scramble all resources that can contribute to the solution.

 Don't try to do all the work by yourself — while you look for the issue on the database, make sure others are searching for it outside of the database. If you focus on the database while no one is seeking the issue elsewhere and you then discover the database is not the problem, valuable time is lost.

Pinpointing the problem

Familiarize yourself with the entire technology stack that supports the application to help you pinpoint where bottlenecks exist. A problem related to the database could be many things:

- ✔ High CPU consumption
- ✔ High IO consumption
- ✔ Poorly performing SQL commands
- ✔ Database design issues
- ✔ Hardware problems
- ✔ Application problems
- ✔ Software bug

Unfortunately, the list goes on.

Tuning Tools

Knowing what tools are available and how to use them will greatly improve your tuning proficiency. Have you ever tried to turn a screw with a pair of pliers? Using the wrong tool or not knowing the proper tool for the job can make any task difficult or impossible. You have a variety of tools at your disposal when tuning an Oracle database.

Oracle documentation

Oracle provides a vast and comprehensive set of documentation for the database. If you visit the Oracle documentation website (`http://docs.oracle.com`), you see documentation for versions going back to 8.1.7 (last time we checked). This documentation, organized into books and sections according to topic, is free to anyone on the Internet. You also see an entire book dedicated to tuning. Some sections of the documentation are dedicated to helping you use specific Oracle-provided tools.

Just because you see a tool in the free documentation set, that doesn't mean you're licensed to use it. Check with your Oracle sales rep to find out what your license covers.

At first, navigating the documentation site can be intimidating. However, with practice, you will get to know the locations of your favorite sections, including SQL tuning, instance tuning, recovery tuning, and everything else in between.

On the home page of the documentation set for each specific version is a Master Book List link. Use this link to jump to entire books on such topics as performance tuning or backup and recovery.

Oracle Support

Oracle Support isn't an anonymous group that meets Tuesday nights in a local church basement. Rather, it's a website (support.oracle.com) that contains a vast amount of resources. Knowing how to efficiently search through all the information available is half the battle. The search bar allows you to input search strings just like any website. You can type descriptions of specific problems, the names of features, error messages, and so on. The list is lengthy.

Articles and documents written (and for the most part tested) by the Oracle technical staff are available. Because there are so many Oracle software users in this world, you'll rarely encounter a problem that hasn't already been encountered by someone else.

To use official Oracle Support, you need a customer service identifier, commonly referred to as a CSI number. Without this number, you can't use the support website. When you purchase the Oracle software you intend to use, you should also consider paying for support. Last we checked, this is not a requirement, but we cannot stress how important having Oracle Support is. Even the most seasoned and respected Oracle professionals in the industry can't overcome every problem encountered. And, if the problem you encounter is a bug, you can't obtain a patch for your bug without Oracle Support.

Oracle user groups

You've certainly heard someone say, "There's no sense in reinventing the wheel." It's true; many of the problems you encounter have already been encountered by someone else. Getting help or advice from other like-minded individuals can be a very cost-effective and expedient way to solve a problem.

We're active participants in both local and national Oracle user groups. User groups are Oracle clubs. Depending on your locality, they may be large or small. Some user groups are regional; they might be associated with a city, a town, or a particular part of the country. You can join national and international groups. There are even virtual groups (such as forums on the web) that can be valuable resources if you're a member. Some user groups are free, some are cheap, and some may cost hundreds of dollars to join.

Beyond hobnobbing with your Oracle buddies, often these user groups have regularly scheduled technical sessions. These sessions can range from how to use a new feature to how to solve a particular performance problem. The best example is Oracle's annual bash, Oracle Open World. You can sit in on literally thousands of sessions, many delivered by the foremost experts in the industry.

If you need to pay to become a member of a particular user group, ask your supervisor at work whether the cost is covered under training expenses.

Training classes

Although not always cheap, training classes can be some of the most valuable methods to gain proficiency in database tuning. We categorize this as *active tuning*. Understanding the fundamentals of setting up your database and using the tools provided is key to being a successful Oracle professional.

Training classes can be free if provided by your local user group. However, they may not be as comprehensive and hands-on as attending a full, multi-day course. Sometimes these can seem expensive up front. The average cost is probably in the $2,000–$4,000 range, and you may need to cover travel expenses as well if the class is not local. However, dollar for dollar, getting your hands dirty with actual classroom exercises and labs is often the most bang for your buck when you're a new database administrator.

Before you attend a class, ask your peers or those you know from your local user groups about the course instructor. Unfortunately, not all classes and instructors are created equal. Although getting any experience when you're a new DBA can be valuable, having a top-notch and well-established instructor can be worthwhile.

Licensed tools

Oracle offers a wide variety of licensable tools that you can use to tune your database. Of the available tuning tools, foremost are the Diagnostic and Tuning packs for Oracle Enterprise Manager. These packs contain all kinds of devices and advisories for tuning your database.

Most of the licensed tools are built around data that is readily available in the database, and a very experienced database administrator can make quick use of the metadata to gather the information for tuning a particular problem. However, that isn't necessarily the quickest approach to solving every pending issue. Although Oracle internally provides most, if not all, of the information to help you fix a performance problem, compiling and analyzing the information can take a considerable amount of time — even for the most seasoned database administrators.

Table 9-2 lists some of the tools included with the Oracle Diagnostic and Tuning packs for Oracle 12c Enterprise Manager Cloud Control.

Table 9-2   Tools Available with Diagnostic and Tuning Packs

Name	Pack	Description
Automatic Database Diagnostics Monitor (ADDM)	Diagnostic	This tool provides focused analysis of activities the database is spending most time on to determine the root causes of problems.
Automatic Workload Repository (AWR)	Diagnostic	At regular intervals, the database takes a snapshot of its workload information and stores it for analysis of past activity.
Active Session History (ASH)	Diagnostic	Similar to AWR, this tool stores information specific to sessions, such as past SQL executed and performance metric history.
Monitoring and Alerting	Diagnostic	You get a comprehensive set of monitoring and notification features.
Real Time Monitoring	Tuning	This tool enables graphical analysis of real-time performance database activity within Enterprise Manager. (A picture really is worth a thousand words.)
SQL Tuning Advisor	Tuning	This advisor automates the SQL tuning process by comprehensively exploring all the possible ways of tuning SQL statements. This tool also provides action plans to remediate issues.
SQL Access Advisor	Tuning	This advisor recommends design and parameter changes to emphasize more throughput and better performance.

Although they come with the database, you are not allowed to use the tools without a license. If you do, you run the risk of being in violation of your license agreement with Oracle. You can talk to your Oracle Sales rep about getting licensed to use these tools. Licensed tools allow you to reduce the time it takes to find and solve problems. They are pieces of software, just like the database, therefore, Oracle charges you for them.

Tuning the Database before Something Goes Wrong

Benjamin Franklin thought an ounce of prevention was worth a pound of cure. At today's prices, a pound of cure comes with a pretty hefty price tag, so preparation and planning are paramount to any software installation. A properly executed Oracle database installation and configuration lay the groundwork for an environment that is void of underlying systemic issues that can contribute to performance-related problems.

Pre-installation planning and preparation

Planning the installation of your database software or a new database is an important step in performance tuning. Poor planning can lead to problems that can't be surmounted easily by the tools at your disposal. For example, if you're going to have a database that has a very high IO requirement, you need a solid storage foundation underneath the database that can handle the workload. If you don't, no amount of SQL tuning can overcome the physical shortage of resources needed.

Table 9-3 provides a short list of details to consider before beginning an Oracle installation.

Table 9-3	Planning Your Oracle Installation
Item	*Considerations*
Number of users	Concurrency, CPU/cores, memory
High transaction workload type	CPU, memory, database parameters, recovery time
High read workload type	Parallelism, SSDs, SAN, spindles, file organization
High availability	Clustering, redundancy
Ad hoc querying	Reporting tools, materializing data, indexing, ETL/batch jobs

The answers you gain by understanding what the application and database are going to support can help you design a system capable of handling your workload. These concepts are not new. Apply what you've experienced in any major undertaking to the Oracle-related task at hand.

Selecting software

Another area that can help you put your best foot forward when preparing and planning an Oracle installation is careful selection of the software version. The best guideline is to go with the latest version available. However, here are a couple of caveats to consider:

- ✔ **Latest is not always greatest.** Some people say you should never buy the first year of a new model of car. As with anything super-new, you can sometimes fall victim to undiscovered glitches and bugs. With Oracle, our approach is simply be wary of using brand-new versions of Oracle without at least one patch set update (PSU). PSUs from Oracle come out every three months. Therefore, you won't have to wait long before fixes become available.

- ✔ **If you have third-party packaged software, make sure you're using an approved or certified version of Oracle.** Even though Oracle 12c patchset "X" might be available, make sure that if your database is going to support another software vendor's packaged application, it's certified by the vendor to work with Oracle. Unfortunately, it is common for software vendors' certification to fall behind the latest software version of Oracle. This can be frustrating. However, more frustrating is when you're trying to make a software package work on one version of the database when it has been tuned for another.

After you settle on a version of the Oracle software to use, make sure you have the latest maintenance packs, Patch Set Updates (PSU), or Security Patch Updates (SPU) applied. Each update can contain fixes that improve the performance of the database engine.

The hard part

As you can probably imagine, the hardware is an important part of any software installation. Everyone has different backgrounds and familiarity with computer hardware. Your experience may be simply using your computer at home or your laptop at work. Or, you may have a background in system administration.

Because the hardware selection is such an important part of the configuration, be sure to assess your ability to make hardware recommendations. If you aren't up to speed on the latest hardware trends or how to appropriately size a server or system, make sure you have someone available who is.

There is no shame in asking for help with hardware selection. Many companies these days have experts on staff whose job it is to help make these decisions. It's better to do the job right the first time by asking for help than having to go back and do it again.

There is no shortage of vendors wanting to sell hardware to your company. In our experience, most hardware vendors also have experts on staff who are well-versed in helping spec out an Oracle system. These experts can talk to you about the features and differences of the gear they can provide.

Make sure that you understand the budget as well. Most often, Oracle licensing is calculated by CPU socket/core. Although a hardware vendor may want to set you up with 64 CPUs of processing power, make sure you can afford to run Oracle on that configuration. With that said, don't let budget alone determine your hardware. That's a sure-fire way to head down the road to failure.

Server and storage vendors want to spend your money. However, they also want you to be happy with the product you're getting. Talk to a technical expert from the vendor (or someone within your company) about the purpose of the system. Aspects of the hardware selection may gravitate from one configuration to another depending on whether you're supporting something like a data warehouse or a system that needs to process transactions quickly. Configurations can affect CPU, disk, memory, and network resources. Also discuss high availability, scalability, and redundancy. To get answers to all these questions, you also may have to coordinate with the project owners and application experts. The sooner you, as a database administrator, get included in the project planning the better off you'll be in the long run.

Often, database administrators are left out in the cold when a project kicks off. Many people see a database as a black box data store. That is absolutely not the case. Despite the performance-related issues that can arise, failing to use all the other features Oracle offers de-values the investment you're making.

Lastly, and this is often an overlooked part of the hardware selection process, don't forget about lower region systems that will support the production application environment:

- **Development:** This region is where all the initial coding and new or updated coding should take place. It's where the application developers get to try out new things. You want an isolated system that's as close to identical as possible to production in terms of software configuration. Often, the hardware for this environment is of lesser capability to save costs.

- **Testing:** This region should be closer to prod in configuration. (We explain the prod region in the upcoming Table 9-4.) It really should not be used for developing new code. It should have realistic volumes of data and have an identical configuration for hardware and software, from the database to the application servers.

The two preceding suggestions are the very minimum you should employ. In fact, some companies have many more levels of lower regions before they get to the production environment. Table 9-4 lists some of the other regions you may come across or have to configure in your environment.

Table 9-4	Database Regions
Name	*Use*
Development	Develop new code and features.
UAT (User Acceptance Testing)	This testing is done by the end user and software design team.
IAT (Integration Acceptance Testing)	Test to make sure changes don't break anything in the rest of the software stack
Pre-prod	The environment is an exact copy of production. This is the final stop before code is deployed.
Prod	This is the production operating environment.
Failover	This is a copy of production to support high availability or disaster recovery.
Demo	It acts as a subset of dummy data for demonstrating application feature to customers.
Training	This is a subset of dummy data used for training purposes.

Tuning after a Problem Arises

Unfortunately, no matter how much preparation and configuration you do before you deploy your database, someday a performance problem will arise. Performance tuning is one of the more difficult tasks for DBAs whether they're new or seasoned. Entire books, week-long training classes, and large pieces of software have been written to help you deal with the inevitable performance problems that will arise.

In the following sections, we focus primarily on what you have available out of the box from Oracle after you've installed the database. Heck, we don't even have enough pages to cover that in its entirety. However, we get you started in the right direction so you have the correct fundamentals on which to build your tuning resume.

Tell me, what is your problem?

Even though it's not funny, the running joke about a database performance problem always seems to start with, "A guy walks into a bar and says, 'My database is slow. . . .'"

When a guy, I mean a user, comes up to the DBA and makes a comment like that, what exactly does that mean? Often, the database is blamed for issues that could be related to something else entirely. The database always seems to get a bad rap. As a DBA, your first task is to see whether the database actually has a problem.

First, collect some basic information from the user:

- ✔ When did this problem start?
- ✔ Are you the only one experiencing it?
- ✔ Can you replicate the problem at will, or is it intermittent?
- ✔ Can you show me how to replicate the problem?
- ✔ Does it happen only during certain times of the day?
- ✔ What is the impact of this problem to the business?

After you get some of the above questions answered, see whether you can verify the problem. If you can't verify it at your desk, it may be something that would make a trip to the user's desk worthwhile to see the problem in person. After all, you may find that he has 100 programs open on his machine, which is slowing down everything he does. Or, you may note that he is operating in a different building, on a different part of the WAN, or off of a wireless connection, which could explain a perceived problem with the database.

If you can't replicate the problem in person or explain why he is experiencing the problem, one of the next steps to take is to ask for some help. We don't necessarily mean from other DBAs (although that never hurts); we mean from other infrastructure teams. For example, you might engage the system administrators to check the database server or the application servers for overloading, or you might engage the storage team to look at the filers or SAN (Storage Area Network) where the data resides.

The reason you want to engage these other teams early is often times a performance problem can be crippling to the business. It's better to involve them now to start working on the issue rather than after two hours trying to solve it yourself. They may come back and say everything looks like business as usual or they may see some increase in resource consumption. Sometimes, they can trace resource hogs to individual user processes on the system. If that sort of red flag can be identified, you'll head in the right direction sooner. When you have something to focus on, you can start employing some of the tools at your disposal to fix the problem.

Tuning SQL

The biggest bang you are going to get in terms of performance tuning is by having good SQL. Badly written SQL is predominantly the cause for most performance problems in a database. Writing good SQL from the get go when a new application is being developed can save you buckets of money and time later on. Unfortunately, as a DBA, most of the situations you find yourself in are on pre-existing systems where the SQL is already in place.

Generating an Explain Plan

Say you have narrowed a performance problem down to a specific SQL statement in the database. Through questioning the user and testing the problem yourself, you've been able to replicate the issue with a specific SQL statement. One of the tools provided with the database that you first want to become familiar with is Explain Plan. Explain Plan does just what it says. It shows you the execution of the SQL statement and explains what each step of the plan is doing.

The Explain Plan is generated by using the SQL command EXPLAIN PLAN FOR. As a simple example, say you have the following SQL statement, which is taking a long time to execute:

```
SELECT first_name, last_name
FROM emp
WHERE last_name = 'Hopkins';
```

Here is how you generate an Explain Plan for the preceding statement:

```
EXPLAIN PLAN FOR
SELECT first_name, last_name
FROM emp
WHERE last_name = 'Hopkins';
```

You see this output after generating the Explain Plan:

```
Explained.
```

After the SQL statement is explained, by default the plan is stored in the data dictionary table called the PLAN_TABLE$. There is a public synonym, PLAN_TABLE, that allows all users to have access to this internal table. We were specific to say "by default" because there are other methods to store execution plans, but for the purposes of this book we use the default method.

Displaying and reading the SQL statement output

You can pull out the information in the PLAN_TABLE in a number of ways. There is a lot of information to be displayed. Displaying all of it is not always useful. One simple method is to run an Oracle-supplied script to read and format the information. This method displays only the most recent Explain Plan. The script is stored in the $ORACLE_HOME/rdbms/admin directory. The script is named utlxpls. From SQL in the same session where you ran the EXPLAIN, type this:

```
SQL> @?\rdbms\admin\utlxpls
```

A shortcut to specifying ORACLE_HOME is the "?" as shown in the preceding statement.

The explained output of your SQL statement looks similar to this:

```
PLAN_TABLE_OUTPUT
-----------------------------------------------------------------------
Plan hash value: 3956160932
-----------------------------------------------------------------------
| Id  | Operation         | Name | Rows  | Bytes | Cost (%CPU)| Time     |
-----------------------------------------------------------------------
|   0 | SELECT STATEMENT  |      |     1 |    15 | 40335   (2)| 00:00:02 |
|*  1 |  TABLE ACCESS FULL| EMP  |     1 |    15 | 40335   (2)| 00:00:02 |
-----------------------------------------------------------------------

Predicate Information (identified by operation id):
---------------------------------------------------
   1 - filter("LAST_NAME"='Hopkins')
```

Although it takes some experience to read the fine details in the EXPLAIN PLAN output, a few things jump out:

- The use of a full table scan (TABLE ACCESS FULL EMP)
- The Predicate Information (1 – filter("LAST_NAME"='Hopkins'). This is your where clause.
- The number 1 matching the Predicate Information back to the operation. The number indexes this back to the step in the section above. In this example, it seems simple, but, if you have an Explain Plan with dozens of lines, this can be very helpful.

Another bit of information you may note is the value for COST. In the preceding case, the COST is 40335. Although the cost in and of itself doesn't necessarily mean anything at face value, you can use it to compare the changes that you make to the execution plan. Typically, the lower the cost is, the better your plan is. Statements with many different operations have costs associated with each step. By looking at the cost of each step, you can determine what stage of the execution is the most expensive (resource-wise, not money-wise). Then you can focus your tuning on that stage. Most of the time, as you make changes and lower the cost, you're making moves in the right direction.

Here's a more complex example of an execution plan:

```
explain plan for
SELECT first_name, last_name, department_name
FROM emp join departments using (department_id)
WHERE last_name = 'Hopkins';

Explained.

Elapsed: 00:00:00.09
SQL> @?\rdbms\admin\utlxpls

PLAN_TABLE_OUTPUT
-----------------------------------------------------------------------------

Plan hash value: 3338584009


-----------------------------------------------------------------------------
| Id  | Operation                    | Name         | Rows | Bytes | Cost (%CPU)| Time     |
-----------------------------------------------------------------------------
|   0 | SELECT STATEMENT             |              |    1 |    34 | 40336   (2)| 00:00:02 |
|   1 |  NESTED LOOPS                |              |      |       |            |          |
|   2 |   NESTED LOOPS               |              |    1 |    34 | 40336   (2)| 00:00:02 |
|*  3 |    TABLE ACCESS FULL         | EMP          |    1 |    18 | 40335   (2)| 00:00:02 |
|*  4 |    INDEX UNIQUE SCAN         | DEPT_ID_PK   |    1 |       |     0   (0)| 00:00:01 |
|   5 |   TABLE ACCESS BY INDEX ROWID| DEPARTMENTS  |    1 |    16 |     1   (0)| 00:00:01 |
-----------------------------------------------------------------------------

Predicate Information (identified by operation id):
---------------------------------------------------

   3 - filter("EMP"."LAST_NAME"='Hopkins')
   4 - access("EMP"."DEPARTMENT_ID"="DEPARTMENTS"."DEPARTMENT_ID")
```

Are indexes always the answer?

Are indexes always going to fix performance problems? In short, no. For example, a seasoned DBA will look at the nearby example and see that the full table scan is causing the performance issue. An index can often fix a full table scan. Because you're searching on last_name, indexing last_name may help. However, your task isn't always that simple. In this case, because this is a list of employees for the company, you can be pretty confident that last_name is fairly unique. Therefore, an index might be preferable. However, what if instead of last_name, the search was on department_id? That may not be very unique, and an index wouldn't be desirable. (We don't index the word *oracle* in this book, for example, because it occurs too many times.)

In this example, you see five operations. By looking at the height operation (Step 5) and working back, you can see that the cost looks like this:

Step 5 = 1

Step 4 = 0

Step 3 = 40335

Step 2 = 40336

Step 1 = 40336

Total = 40336

Notice how the cost of all the steps adds up. Also notice how the cost of Step 3 is by far the most expensive. With that said, a DBA would want to focus his tuning efforts on Step 3.

If you don't have the Explain Plan information at your fingertips or people to consult about making the correct tuning decisions, you can try using the Oracle utility called the SQL Tuning Advisor. You can use this built-in tool to provide suggestions or recommendations about certain SQL statements. Although it may not always give perfect advice, just like anything else, having it in your toolbox of tuning techniques is beneficial.

In Chapter 6, we talk about how it can be useful for the DBA to have an understanding of PL/SQL; this is where it can help. Running the SQL Tuning Advisor requires several steps:

1. **Use PL/SQL and the internal package DBMS_SQL_TUNE to create a tuning task. Type this:**

```
DECLARE
  l_sql             VARCHAR2(500);
  l_sql_tune_task_id  VARCHAR2(100);

BEGIN

  l_sql := 'SELECT first_name, last_name, department_name ' ||
           'FROM emp JOIN departments USING (department_id) ' ||
           'WHERE last_name = ''Hopkins''';

  l_sql_tune_task_id := DBMS_SQLTUNE.create_tuning_task (
                    sql_text    => l_sql,
                    user_name   => 'HR',
                    scope       => DBMS_SQLTUNE.scope_comprehensive,
                    time_limit  => 60,
                    task_name   => 'emp_dept_tuning_task',
                    description => 'Tuning task for an EMP to
         DEPARTMENT join query.');
  DBMS_OUTPUT.put_line('l_sql_tune_task_id: ' || l_sql_tune_task_id);
END;
/
```

You should see the following:

```
PL/SQL procedure successfully completed.
```

In the preceding command, note the TIME_LIMIT of 60. That limits the processing time to 60 seconds. You may not always want to run something like this for long periods in your database, because it incurs system overhead. This is a good example of where it can be useful to have a copy of your production system elsewhere for testing and tuning — if you use that little trick, you won't have to be as concerned about over-head. Either way, pay attention to this limit, you may have to adjust it up if you don't have enough time to tune a complex statement. For a statement such as the preceding one, which is pretty simple, this limit should suffice.

2. **Execute the tuning advisor with your task by typing this:**

```
EXEC DBMS_SQLTUNE.execute_tuning_task(task_name => 'emp_dept_tuning_task');
```

Because of the limit of 60 seconds provided in the task creation, this step may take up to 60 seconds to complete. During this time, your prompt won't come back.

When it completes, you should see this:

```
PL/SQL procedure successfully completed.
```

If you've set a longer time and are getting impatient, you can open another SQL window to make sure that the task is still executing by typing

```
SELECT task_name, status, execution_start
FROM dba_advisor_log WHERE owner = 'HR';
```

You see something like the following:

```
TASK_NAME                        STATUS            EXECUTION_START
-------------------------------  ---------------   --------------------
emp_dept_tuning_task             EXECUTING         19-JUL-2013 15:35:42
```

3. **When the execution is complete, you can view the results by running the BMS_SQLTUNE.report_tuning_task procedure. Type the following:**

```
SELECT
DBMS_SQLTUNE.report_tuning_task('emp_dept_tuning_task') AS recommendations
FROM dual;
```

For the sake of space, we've snipped some sections from the output that follows, but you see something like this:

```
RECOMMENDATIONS
----------------------------------------------------------------------
GENERAL INFORMATION SECTION
----------------------------------------------------------------------
Tuning Task Name      : emp_dept_tuning_task
Tuning Task Owner     : HR
Workload Type         : Single SQL Statement
Scope                 : COMPREHENSIVE
Time Limit(seconds):  60
Completion Status     : INTERRUPTED
Started at            : 07/19/2013 15:21:39
Completed at          : 07/19/2013 15:22:43


----------------------------------------------------------------------
Error: ORA-13639: The current operation was interrupted because it timed
       out.
----------------------------------------------------------------------


----------------------------------------------------------------------
Schema Name: HR
SQL ID       : 47uvvzcuu5mdg
SQL Text     : SELECT first_name, last_name, department_name FROM emp JOIN
               departments USING (department_id) WHERE last_name = 'Hopkins'


RECOMMENDATIONS
----------------------------------------------------------------------
----------------------------------------------------------------------
```

```
FINDINGS SECTION (1 finding)
------------------------------------------------------------------------


1- Index Finding (see explain plans section below)
--------------------------------------------------

  The execution plan of this statement can be improved by creating one or
          more indices.

  Recommendation (estimated benefit: 99.98%)
  ------------------------------------------

  - Consider running the Access Advisor to improve the physical schema
          design or creating the recommended index.
    create index HR.IDX$$_03170001 on HR.EMP("LAST_NAME");


  Rationale
  ---------

    Creating the recommended indices significantly improves the execution
          plan of this statement.
    However, it might be preferable to run Access Advisor using a
          representative SQL workload as opposed to a single statement.
    This will allow you to get comprehensive index recommendations, which
          takes into account index maintenance overhead and additional
          space consumption.
...output snipped...
```

The latter part of the report shows the *before* and *after* execution plans. In this case, you've seen the before when you were generating execution plans. Go ahead and add the index, regenerate the execution plan, and see whether you've made an improvement.

Before you add the index, note that the recommendations give the SQL to add the index:

```
  Recommendation (estimated benefit: 99.98%)
  ------------------------------------------
  - Consider running the Access Advisor to improve the physical schema
          design
    or creating the recommended index.
    create index HR.IDX$$_03170001 on HR.EMP("LAST_NAME");
```

You don't have to follow the exact naming conventions Oracle chooses. Sometimes they're a little awkward. We use some that are more readable and relevant to us, and you can too.

Also note that Oracle gives a warning:

```
RECOMMENDATIONS
------------------------------------------------------------------------
    account index maintenance overhead and additional space consumption.
```

As we mention earlier, adding an index isn't always a perfect solution. Here Oracle is warning you that even though adding the index may help performance, it also has overhead associated with it in the form of space and maintenance (inserts, updates, deletes). This is the sort of thing that over time a seasoned DBA becomes keen to notice.

4. Add the index with your own name by typing this:

```
CREATE INDEX emp_last_name_idx ON emp(last_name);
```

You should see something like the following:

```
Index created.
```

5. Take a look at the execution plan. Type the following:

```
explain plan for
SELECT first_name, last_name, department_name
FROM emp join departments using (department_id)
WHERE last_name = 'Hopkins';

Explained.

Elapsed: 00:00:00.09
```

And then type

```
@?\rdbms\admin\utlxpls
```

You should see output like this:

```
PLAN_TABLE_OUTPUT
----------------------------------------------------------------------------
Plan hash value: 1505300146


----------------------------------------------------------------------------
| Id  | Operation | Name       | Rows | Bytes | Cost (%CPU)|    Time |
----------------------------------------------------------------------------
|   0 | SELECT STATEMENT|      | 1    | 34    |   5 (0)    | 00:00:01|
|   1 |  NESTED LOOPS  |       |      |       |            |         |
|   2 |   NESTED L     |       | 1    | 34    |   5 (0)    | 00:00:01|
|   3 |    TABLE ACCESS BY INDEX ROWID BATCHED|EMP|1|18|4 (0)| 00:00:01|
|*  4 |     INDEX RANGE SCAN  | EMP_LAST_NAME_IDX | 1 | | 3 (0)| 00:00:01|
|*  5 |    INDEX UNIQUE SCAN  | DEPT_ID_PK      | 1 | | 0 (0)| 00:00:01|
|   6 |   TABLE ACCESS BY INDEX ROWID|DEPARTMENTS| 1 |16|1 (0)| 00:00:01|
----------------------------------------------------------------------------

Predicate Information (identified by operation id):
---------------------------------------------------

   4 - access("EMP"."LAST_NAME"='Hopkins')
   5 - access("EMP"."DEPARTMENT_ID"="DEPARTMENTS"."DEPARTMENT_ID")
```

Now that you've added the index, a few things are evident:

✔ The cost of the plan dropped from 40336 to 5.

✔ There are now six steps.

✔ The full table scan is gone. Instead you see the use of your new index.

Although each system performs differently, we found that after making the index change in our test system, the execution time dropped from eight seconds to less than one second.

Often one of the tough parts about tuning a database is having a solid understanding of the application and the data. The issue might not always be obvious. Sometimes engaging other application and data experts helps. Explain to them your findings and what you propose. They may be able to help you come to a conclusion. Also, if the data is part of a packaged third-party application, sometimes opening a ticket with the vendor is the way to go.

Tuning the Database

Tuning SQL is just one aspect of Oracle performance management. The database itself can also be configured and tuned for better performance. It is typical that SQL tuning will give you the best performance advantages out of the gate, but it isn't always possible. For example, you may run a packaged vendor application in which you cannot change SQL. Although you may submit performance Service Requests to the vendor in order to receive new code, what can you do in the meantime to alleviate performance overhead?

To tune the database, you can employ various methods:

✔ **Oracle Instance Parameters:** You can adjust these parameters to influence how the instance and the optimizer are configured to handle memory, parallelism, and execution plan generation.

✔ **Oracle Infrastructure Features:** Different editions of the database come with features that can be implemented to overcome certain types of performance problems. Some examples of these features are partitioning, materialized views, object and system statistics, and SQL profiles.

✔ **Infrastructure Enhancements:** These sorts of changes often require interaction with other professionals in your organization to make improvements to the underlying infrastructure that runs the database (for example, server upgrades, SAN improvements, or network transmission speeds).

One of the challenges you'll encounter when coming up with methods to tune the database is of course identifying the problems. Oracle and other software vendors provide various tools that will holistically examine the database software and configuration to make recommendations. As mentioned earlier in this chapter, these sorts of tools can be expensive.

The following sections provide you with some examples of bare-bones, no-cost approaches from which you can start building your skills. When you're comfortable with the fundamentals of tuning, you can better evaluate some of the more expensive options on the market. We want to be careful and not discourage you from considering some of the other licensed options. Sometimes, no matter how experienced a DBA is, a tool can do the job better and faster, which translates into money saved. However, before you go requisitioning purchases, you should understand how tuning the database works.

Installing STATSPACK

STATSPACK is an Oracle supplied group of programs that allows you to slice up the Oracle operating metrics into sections of time or periods for focused analysis. You then look at the operational statistics and SQL captured during these periods to identify bottlenecks and wait times. After you identify these problems, you can then begin to research methods for tuning them out of the database.

For some reason, as of Oracle 12c, Oracle no longer provides STATSPACK documentation as part of the main Oracle documentation website. However, Oracle still provides text-based documentation in the software install directory. We urge you to review this documentation if you have the desire for more information. You can find the Oracle STATSPACK documentation here:

$ORACLE_HOME/rdbms/admin/spcdoc.txt

To install STATSPACK on a Linux server running Oracle, follow these steps:

1. **From the server command prompt, start SQL*Plus and log in as SYSDBA by typing**

   ```
   sqlplus / as sysdba
   ```

   You see something like this:

   ```
   SQL*Plus: Release 12.1.0.1.0 Production on Fri Jul 19 17:14:30 2013
   Copyright (c) 1982, 2013, Oracle.  All rights reserved.
   Connected to:
   Oracle Database 12c Enterprise Edition Release 12.1.0.1.0 - 64bit
               Production
   With the Partitioning, OLAP, Advanced Analytics and Real Application
               Testing options
   ```

2. Run the creation utility, which requires some inputs, by typing

```
SQL> @?/rdbms/admin/spcreate
```

You see something like this:

```
Choose the PERFSTAT user's password
-----------------------------------
Not specifying a password will result in the installation FAILING

Enter value for perfstat_password:
```

For testing purposes, type the following password:

```
Perf$tat
```

You see something like the following:

```
Choose the Default tablespace for the PERFSTAT user
---------------------------------------------------
Below is the list of online tablespaces in this database which can
store user data.  Specifying the SYSTEM tablespace for the user's
default tablespace will result in the installation FAILING, as
using SYSTEM for performance data is not supported.

Choose the PERFSTAT users's default tablespace.  This is the tablespace
in which the STATSPACK tables and indexes will be created.

TABLESPACE_NAME                 CONTENTS  STATSPACK DEFAULT TABLESPACE
------------------------------  --------  ---------------------------
MY_DATA                         PERMANENT
MY_INDEX                        PERMANENT
RMAN_DATA                       PERMANENT
SYSAUX                          PERMANENT *
USERS                           PERMANENT

Pressing <return> will result in STATSPACK's recommended default
tablespace (identified by *) being used.

Enter value for default_tablespace:
```

Oracle recommends SYSAUX as the default tablespace for STATSPACK
objects. Type

```
SYSAUX
```

You see something like this:

```
Choose the Temporary tablespace for the PERFSTAT user
-----------------------------------------------------
Below is the list of online tablespaces in this database which can
store temporary data (e.g. for sort workareas).  Specifying the SYSTEM
tablespace for the user's temporary tablespace will result in the
installation FAILING, as using SYSTEM for workareas is not supported.

Choose the PERFSTAT user's Temporary tablespace.

TABLESPACE_NAME                      CONTENTS  DB DEFAULT TEMP TABLESPACE
-----------------------------------  --------- --------------------------
TEMP                                 TEMPORARY *

Pressing <return> will result in the database's default Temporary
tablespace (identified by *) being used.

Enter value for temporary_tablespace:
```

3. **Accept the default TEMP tablespace by pressing Enter.**

You see something like this:

```
... Creating PERFSTAT user

... Installing required packages

... Creating views

... Granting privileges
... output snipped...
Creating Package STATSPACK...

Package created.

No errors.
Creating Package Body STATSPACK...

Package body created.

No errors.

NOTE:
SPCPKG complete. Please check spcpkg.lis for any errors.
```

STATSPACK is very similar to a tool called the Automatic Workload Repository (AWR). However, the AWR requires a license to the Diagnostic pack.

Taking snapshots with STATSPACK

The way to use STATSPACK is to bracket the performance problem by getting a snapshot before the issue begins and after the issue ends. This task can be tricky. You may not be able to predict when the performance problem occurs. Or, perhaps the problem already occurred, and you can't repeat it because you're concerned about adding further overhead to the system or the problem happens only on a pre-scheduled time, such as with a batch job.

First assume that the problem is something for which you can easily create snapshots. For example, there is a report that runs at 3 p.m. every day. Normally, the report runs in five minutes. However, the last few days, the report has taken over an hour.

To get snapshots that bracket the report, you must take a snapshot right before the report starts and another snapshot right after the report ends. This effort ensures that the statistics the snapshot collects are specific to the time period and any major operations that were occurring.

Here's how to bracket an issue by using STATSPACK:

1. **Log in to SQL*Plus from the operating system as the new PERFSTAT user with the password you chose during installation and type**

   ```
   sqlplus perfstat
   ```

   You see this:

   ```
   SQL*Plus: Release 12.1.0.1.0 Production on Fri Jul 19 17:33:22 2013

   Copyright (c) 1982, 2013, Oracle.  All rights reserved.
   Enter password:
   Connected to:
   Oracle Database 12c Enterprise Edition Release 12.1.0.1.0 - 64bit
             Production
   With the Partitioning, OLAP, Advanced Analytics and Real Application
             Testing options
   ```

2. **To take your beginning snapshot, type**

   ```
   exec statspack.snap
   ```

   You see the following:

   ```
   PL/SQL procedure successfully completed.
   ```

3. **After the report finishes running, take another snapshot the same way you did before by typing**

   ```
   exec statspack.snap
   ```

You see this:

```
PL/SQL procedure successfully completed.
```

Next, you need to generate your STATSPACK report. The STATSPACK report generates all the operational statistics during the time period between the two snapshots so you can see where the system focused its time.

To generate your STATSPACK report:

1. **Log in to SQL*Plus from the operating system as the new PERFSTAT user with the password you chose during installation and type**

```
sqlplus perfstat
```

You see this:

```
SQL*Plus: Release 12.1.0.1.0 Production on Fri Jul 19 17:37:41 2013

Copyright (c) 1982, 2013, Oracle.  All rights reserved.
Enter password:
Connected to:
Oracle Database 12c Enterprise Edition Release 12.1.0.1.0 - 64bit
          Production
With the Partitioning, OLAP, Advanced Analytics and Real Application
          Testing options
```

2. **Type**

```
@?/rdbms/admin/spreport
```

You see something like the following:

```
~~~~~~~~~~~~~~~~~

  DB Id     DB Name      Inst Num Instance
---------- ------------ -------- ------------
3615982967 DEV12C              1 dev12c


Instances in this Statspack schema
~~~~~~~~~~~~~~~~~~~~~~~~~~~~~~~~~~~

  DB Id    Inst Num DB Name      Instance     Host
---------- -------- ------------ ------------ ------------
3615982967        1 DEV12C       dev12c       orasvr01

Using 3615982967 for database Id
Using           1 for instance number
```

```
Specify the number of days of snapshots to choose from
~~~~~~~~~~~~~~~~~~~~~~~~~~~~~~~~~~~~~~~~~~~~~~~~~~~~~~~~~
Entering the number of days (n) will result in the most recent
(n) days of snapshots being listed.  Pressing <return> without
specifying a number lists all completed snapshots.


Listing all Completed Snapshots
                                                   Snap
Instance     DB Name        Snap Id  Snap Started  Level Comment
------------ ------------   --------- ---------------- ----- ---------------
dev12c       DEV12C             1 19 Jul 2013 17:34     5
                                11 19 Jul 2013 17:38     5


Specify the Begin and End Snapshot Ids
~~~~~~~~~~~~~~~~~~~~~~~~~~~~~~~~~~~~~~~~~
Enter value for begin_snap:
Enter number 1 for the begin snap from the list shown above.
```

You see something like this:

```
Begin Snapshot Id specified: 1

Enter value for end_snap:
```

3. Enter number 11 from the preceding list.

Because you have only two snapshots at this time, this step is fairly straightforward.

You see this:

```
Specify the Report Name
~~~~~~~~~~~~~~~~~~~~~~~~~
The default report file name is sp_1_11.  To use this name,
press <return> to continue, otherwise enter an alternative.

Enter value for report_name:
```

4. Enter a name for the report. For this example, type

```
test_report_snaps_1_11
```

After pressing Enter, your screen scrolls through a lot of information. Don't worry about reading it at this time; it's all going into the report you specified.

Interpreting STATSPACK output

The report you get from running spreport will most likely be more than 50 pages, in text format, and saved in the directory you were in when you created the report. Believe us when we say there is more information in there than most people will use. However, understanding a few key sections can give you a leg up on making use of the results.

Here are some of the key sections you should focus on when looking at the report output:

- **The First Page:** This section contains all the relevant information about the state of the database for which the snapshot period applies. It contains the length of time between snapshots, the number of logged in users, memory component sizes, and the database and instance names. It also includes some high-level metrics such as the instance memory efficiency percentages, number of physical reads and writes, and SQL parsing information. This section gives you a good overview of what was going on when the snapshots were taken in case you're just the interpreter of the report and were not involved with the taking of the snapshots.

- **Top 5 Timed Events:** This section is one of our favorites. It boils down to where the database spent most of its time and puts the information into five buckets. If you see any buckets that consume the lion's share of the time, it can lead you down the first path for focused tuning. For example, if IO or CPU were in the 90 percent range, you may want to look at the SQL section, the file sections, or the memory-tuning sections and start looking for items to tune that fit those buckets.

- **SQL Sections:** The SQL sections break down the top SQL statements by CPU, elapsed time, physical IO, buffer gets, reads, executions, parses, and shareable memory. These sections can help identify problem SQL that's responsible for heavy use of resources during the snap period. A DBA or application developer can also look for specific SQL to identify that is part of the application. You can then attack and tune the SQL.

- **Tablespace and Datafile IO Stats:** Finding what tablespaces and data files comprise most of your reads and writes can help you identify hot (heavily used) files and devices that may benefit from striping or other storage adjustments. You can also use this information to decide whether certain tablespaces may benefit from more separation of objects that may be getting concurrently accessed.

- **Memory Advisory Sections:** The memory advisory sections contain Oracle's self-evaluation of the different memory pools for things like the shared pool, buffer cache, and PGA. By looking at the findings Oracle has come up with, you can increase the memory areas to tune things such as IO, parsing, or sorting.

- **Init Parameter Section:** This section lists the initialization parameters that were set to non-default values during the report period. You can look for anything which represents an anomaly or a value which can explain certain performance characteristics. When you're comparing different reports over time, this section can also help identify instance configuration parameters that may have taken place. For example, if you have a report from a week ago when performance was good and a report from today where performance was poor, a good way to start would be comparing the initialization parameters. Finding a difference is what we would call "low-hanging fruit" or "easy pickings" as a potential cause for bad performance.

Scheduling snapshots

The method for taking snapshots and generating reports is handy when you have a predictive performance issue or a situation where the problem is easily repeatable. You can take the snapshots and interpret the results. However, this method doesn't let you look at the past or compare time periods easily. Say you have a weekend batch job take ten times longer than normal. You can't wait until next weekend to take the snapshots. You would be better off to have these snapshots on Monday when you return to work.

To take advantage of snapshots and reports in this way, Oracle offers the built-in ability to schedule the snapshots to be taken at specific intervals. That is, you can keep a history of snapshots so you can go back a day, a week, or even a year (depending on your snap retention period) to analyze performance.

By default, the interval for automatic snapshots that Oracle provides is one hour. You can change this if you want by editing the job scheduler or the script that sets up the automatic snapshots.

To use the default time of one hour to automatically schedule snapshots to be taken:

 1. **Log in to SQL*Plus from the operating system as the new PERFSTAT user with the password you chose during installation and type**

```
sqlplus perfstat
```

You see this:

```
SQL*Plus: Release 12.1.0.1.0 Production on Fri Jul 19 17:37:41 2013

Copyright (c) 1982, 2013, Oracle.  All rights reserved.
Enter password:
Connected to:
Oracle Database 12c Enterprise Edition Release 12.1.0.1.0 - 64bit
          Production
With the Partitioning, OLAP, Advanced Analytics and Real Application
          Testing options
```

2. **Type**

```
@?/rdbms/admin/spauto
```

You see something like the following:

```
PL/SQL procedure successfully completed.

Job number for automated statistics collection for this instance
~~~~~~~~~~~~~~~~~~~~~~~~~~~~~~~~~~~~~~~~~~~~~~~~~~~~~~~~~~~~~~~~~~~~
Note that this job number is needed when modifying or removing
the job:

    JOBNO
----------
        1
Job queue process
~~~~~~~~~~~~~~~~~~
Below is the current setting of the job_queue_processes init.ora
parameter - the value for this parameter must be greater
than 0 to use automatic statistics gathering:

NAME                                 TYPE        VALUE
------------------------------------ ----------- ---------------------------
job_queue_processes                  integer     1000

Next scheduled run
~~~~~~~~~~~~~~~~~~
The next scheduled run for this job is:

       JOB NEXT_DATE NEXT_SEC
---------- --------- --------
         1 19-JUL-13 19:00:00
```

This output shows that the next execution of an automatic snapshot will occur at 19:00 hours and every hour thereafter.

One thing to consider when automatically creating snapshots is your retention interval. You need to think about how long you will reasonably ever look back. One month? One year? Longer? We've had instances where going back one year was not uncommon. This is especially evident when looking at batch jobs that might run yearly.

If you have a retention schedule, eventually you'll need to remove snapshots that exceed this time period. Oracle provides a script for that called ?/rdbms/admin/spurge.

Running this script does three things: It lists all your snapshots, asks for a beginning snapshot and ending snapshot, and deletes the range you specify. Out of the box, there is no way to automate this. If you upgrade to the Diagnostic pack, you can use AWR, which automatically schedules and purges snapshots based on preconfigured settings.

Chapter 10

Securing and Auditing Your Database

....

In This Chapter

▶ Verifying identities through authentication

▶ Granting privileges to users

▶ Creating roles

▶ Auditing the database

....

Security is an especially important concern when dealing with anything relating to computers and the Internet. As an administrator of software applications such as the Oracle database, you are concerned with security because you want to protect your data. Security is vital because you don't want the wrong people looking at the data and because you need to protect the data from being altered or corrupted. Being able to restrict and monitor the users in the system helps you provide a safe and secure operating environment for you and your customers or clients.

Staying Authentic with Authentication

Authentication is all about making sure your users are who they say they are. This process begins well before users even try to access the database. You need to set up a system or process that allows you to verify users' identity. You also need a method for users to access the system that both identifies them and restricts their privileges to their required needs. Finally, we recommend using a security mechanism such as a password or operating system account so access isn't open to anyone who tries.

User authentication

After you set up your databases, the next step is to allow users access to the data. You may have all sorts of users in your environment, from people who need full access to the data and database (such as a DBA) to an application that runs on a machine for users connecting from the Internet.

User authentication, the first step to protecting your data, means verifying that a resource (user, program, another machine) trying to connect to your database is authorized to do so.

You can establish the following by authenticating users:

- ✔ **Accountability:** Having an accountability system forces users to take responsibility for their actions. It helps track down the culprits when problems occur.

- ✔ **Trust:** A system of authentication allows you to operate within a realm of trust. Make sure a potential user is qualified before she's given data access. Qualifications can be as simple as a one-hour training class or as detailed as a full-blown, government-sponsored background investigation.

- ✔ **Proper privileges:** You must restrict and grant access according to a resource's identity and qualifications. Different resources have different types of access to accomplish different jobs. You can manage such restricting and granting of access through a system of varying roles and privileges.

- ✔ **Tracking mechanisms:** Many databases need a Big Brother. When something goes wrong, a tracking mechanism can help you hunt down and plug any security holes. It can also help you make sure resources in your environment aren't snooping.

Password authentication

Password protection is the most common way to protect data in computer systems. This truth applies to bank ATMs, websites, and of course your Oracle database. Password protection helps establish identity. Passing this verification is the first step in showing you're a trusted member of the club.

Nowadays when you create the database

- ✔ Default accounts are locked.
- ✔ SYS and SYSTEM passwords are chosen and set during database creation.
- ✔ Password security is enhanced by forcing complex passwords.

With these measures, the database is fairly secure as soon as it's created. Chapter 5 covers user creation; this chapter expands on password security options.

Security past

In the past, Oracle has given you tools to implement very secure password authentication methods, but Oracle has left the implementation up to you almost entirely. With each release of the database, Oracle has increased default security in the system. Oracle *has* been non-secure in the past. However, administrators had to deal with access being nearly wide open when software was installed and a database was created. DBAs had to set and manage authentication. Unfortunately, not all database users knew what to configure and lock down. Many internal accounts were created with high levels of access with default passwords that were easily found anywhere on the Internet.

Enforcing password security with profiles

A *password profile* is a mechanism in the database that forces a user to follow guidelines when creating or changing passwords. The guidelines help provide stronger security in the system by not allowing weak passwords.

The following are bad ideas for creating passwords, and neither you nor your users should do any of these things. Otherwise, you're opening the door to uninvited guests. So don't consider

- ✔ Making the password the same as the username
- ✔ Making *password* your password
- ✔ Reusing the same password when the system asks you to change

Having to remember complex passwords is sometimes inconvenient, but accept it as part of your responsibility. Otherwise, you may at some point have to take the blame for someone guessing your password.

Password profiles prevent each of the problems in the preceding list. Password profiles are a DBA tool, and they let you do the following:

- ✔ **Limit the number of times a password can be reused.** If you want to give your users a break, let them reuse the password twice — but that's it.

- ✔ **Limit the amount of time before a password can be reused.** Maybe you let them reuse the password, but they have to wait 90 days to do so.

- ✔ **Limit failed login attempts.** If this number is met, you can lock the account until a security administrator unlocks it or for a certain period of time.

✔ **Assign a password lock time.** If someone (or some*thing*) reaches the limit you set for the failed login attempts setting, you can force a waiting period before the user can try again. This setting can help against *brute force* attacks, where a machine bombards your database with a password cracker.

✔ **Give passwords a time limit (or in Oracles terminology, a limited life time).** When this life time is met, the system asks the user to change his password.

✔ **Have a password grace time.** When the life time is reached, the user is prompted with "You have *X* number of days to change your password."

✔ **Check password complexity.** A verification function

- Makes sure the password and username are different.

- Makes sure the new password differs from the previous by three characters.

- Ensures the password is made up of alphabetical, numeric, and special characters.

You can create your own password verify function and attach it to a profile. A *password verify function* is a program written in PL/SQL that examines passwords when they're chosen and accepts or rejects them based on criteria. If you have special password requirements, you can write your own password verify function and assign it to your password profile by using the PASSWORD_VERIFY_FUNCTION attribute of the profile.

Oracle supplies a standard password verify function with the database. By default, it ensures the following:

✔ The password is not the same as the username (forward and backward).

✔ The password is more than seven characters.

✔ The password is not the same as the server name.

✔ The password is not a common poor choice, such as welcome1, password, database, abcdefg.

To use Oracle's provided password verify function, follow these steps:

1. **Log in to the database using SQL*Plus as SYS.**

2. **Run the following:**

```
$ORACLE_HOME/rdbms/admin/utlpwdmg.sql
```

This step creates the default password verify function and assigns it to the DEFAULT profile. If you're comfortable with PL/SQL, you can even take Oracle's example file and modify it to fit your needs.

Creating a password profile

To create a password profile, follow these steps:

1. **Log in to the database via SQL*Plus as SYSTEM.**

2. **Create the profile and limit the failed login attempts, password lock time, and password life time:**

```
<CREATE PROFILE report_writer LIMIT
FAILED_LOGIN_ATTEMPTS 3
PASSWORD_LOCK_TIME 1/96
PASSWORD_LIFE_TIME 90;>
```

In this example, failed login attempts are limited to three, password lock time is limited to 15 minutes, and password life time is limited to 90 days.

You see this:

```
Profile created.
```

The password lock time in the preceding code is 1/96. In Oracle time, that is 15 minutes. The whole number 1 is 1 day, and 1/24 is one hour. Divide 1/24 by 4 and you get 1/96 (or 15 minutes).

3. **Assign the report writer user profile to a user:**

```
<ALTER USER hr PROFILE report_writer;>
```

This example assigns the new profile to the HR user. You see this in return:

```
User altered.
```

DEFAULT profile

What if you don't give your users a profile? In that case, all users have the DEFAULT profile.

By default in Oracle 12c, the DEFAULT profile limits the following:

- ✔ FAILED_LOGIN_ATTEMPT = 10
- ✔ PASSWORD_GRACE_TIME 7 (DAYS)
- ✔ PASSWORD_LIFE_TIME 180 (DAYS)
- ✔ PASSWORD_LOCK_TIME 1 (DAY)
- ✔ PASSWORD_REUSE_MAX UNLIMITED
- ✔ PASSWORD_VERIFY_FUNCTION NULL (no complexity enforced)
- ✔ PASSWORD_REUSE_TIME UNLIMITED

You can edit your profile or the DEFAULT profile. For example, to change the failed login attempts setting to 3 on the DEFAULT profile, type the following:

```
<ALTER PROFILE default LIMIT
    FAILED_LOGIN_ATTEMPTS 3;>
```

You see this:

```
Profile altered.
```

Operating system authentication

You may not always want to require a user password. In those cases, operating system authentication can be useful and, if set up properly, offer some security advantage over using a password. Use operating system authentication with caution though.

Operating system authentication recognizes a user as logged in to the OS and waives the password requirement. Operating system authentication can be especially useful when you have an application that requires a log in to the database to run a program. Say a job runs every night to generate reports and deposit them into a directory.

How will the user inside your batch job connect? You could embed a password in the program, but that isn't secure. Instead, create an account in the database that links to the OS user and configure it with OS authentication. That way, you protect the OS user's password and avoid a traditional username/password combination for the user to log in to run the reports.

You're safe as long as only authorized personnel know the OS user password.

Type this code to create an OS-authenticated user in Oracle for someone named REPORTS:

```
<CREATE USER OPS$REPORTS IDENTIFIED EXTERNALLY;>
```

You see this:

```
User created.
```

Notice how the OS user is called REPORTS and the Oracle user is called OPS$REPORTS.

The user prefix OPS$ must precede the OS username for the username to be identified externally.

External identification means that instead of the user requiring a password in the database, Oracle looks to the OS and matches the username (minus the OPS$) to a user on the operating system. Oracle assumes that because the user is logged in to the OS, the user must be authenticated. You can change that prefix, OPS$, by revising the Oracle parameter OS_AUTHEN_PREFIX.

After setting up all the necessary privileges for that user (detailed later in this chapter), the user can log in from the OS command line without a password:

```
<sqlplus />
```

Granting Privileges

After you create a user, you have to decide what types of things the user can do in the database. You probably want to allow the user to be able to log in, but you may need to limit whether the user can do any of the following tasks:

- ✔ Accessing certain data
- ✔ Starting and stopping the database
- ✔ Creating tables, indexes, and views
- ✔ Deleting data
- ✔ Performing backups

You determine what a user can do via *privileges*. The database has two types of privileges:

- ✔ **System privileges** control what a user can do in the database. For example, can they create tables, create users, and drop tablespaces? These privileges apply mainly to adding or changing structures in the database.

- ✔ **Object privileges** control how a user can access the actual data in the database. For example, what data can he see, change, or delete? These privileges apply primarily to rows in a table or view.

You manage all privileges with the GRANT and REVOKE commands. It's pretty clear from their names which one giveth and which one taketh away. However, you form the commands depending on the type of privilege. For example, when you give, you GRANT TO and when you take you REVOKE FROM.

Granting and revoking system privileges

System privileges are the first privileges any user needs. There are literally hundreds of system privileges. This chapter lists the common ones that provide about 90 percent of the access that users need.

Before any user can do anything with the database, they need to be able to connect, The CREATE SESSION privilege gives users access to the database. Without this privilege, no other privileges matter.

Follow these steps to grant CREATE SESSION privileges to the user DTITILAH:

1. **Log in to the database as the user SYSTEM.**

2. **Type the following:**

```
<GRANT CREATE SESSION TO dtitilah;>
```

You see the following, which means DTITILAH can connect to the database:

```
Grant succeeded.
```

What if the password for the user DTITILAH has been compromised? A quick way to make sure that a user can no longer access the database, externally or not, is to revoke the CREATE SESSION privilege from that user.

Revoke the CREATE SESSION from DTITILAH with these steps:

1. **Log in to the database as SYSTEM.**

2. **Type the following:**

```
<REVOKE CREATE SESSION FROM dtitilah;>
```

You see this:

```
Revoke succeeded.
```

When that user tries to connect, he sees this:

```
ERROR:
ORA-01045: user DTITILAH lacks CREATE SESSION privilege; logon denied
```

3. **Address the security breach by finding out why the password was compromised.**

4. **Re-grant the privilege by following the steps earlier in this section.**

Processing continues as normal.

A user might also have these system privileges that allow them to create objects in the database:

- ✔ RESUMABLE allows jobs to be suspended and resumed when space restrictions are met.
- ✔ FLASHBACK ARCHIVE allows users to retrieve data from the past. See Chapter 14 for more about flashback archiving.
- ✔ CREATE JOB allows users to create jobs that can be run in the Oracle Scheduler.
- ✔ CREATE SYNONYM allows users to be able to create alias for objects for easier access.

The following privileges apply commonly to developers:

- ✔ CREATE TABLE
- ✔ CREATE VIEW
- ✔ CREATE SEQUENCE
- ✔ CREATE PROCEDURE
- ✔ CREATE TRIGGER

DBAs commonly have these privileges:

- ✔ CREATE ANY TABLE creates tables in any user's schema.
- ✔ DROP ANY TABLE drops tables from any user's schema.
- ✔ CREATE TABLESPACE creates tablespace storage areas.
- ✔ ALTER USER changes user characteristics.
- ✔ DROP USER . . . uh, drops a user.
- ✔ ALTER SYSTEM changes system operation parameters.
- ✔ GRANT ANY OBJECT allows grantee to manage any object privilege against any object in the database. Very powerful!

WITH ADMIN OPTION is another feature associated with system privileges. You can use this option when granting a system privilege to allow the user to grant the privilege to someone else. For example, say you've hired a new DBA with the username RPLEW. You want the user MJAUST to connect to the database with the CREATE SESSION privilege, but you also want him to be able to grant that privilege to someone else.

To grant a system privilege WITH ADMIN OPTION, take these steps:

1. Log in to SQL*Plus as SYSTEM.

2. **Type the following:**

```
<GRANT CREATE SESSION TO maust WITH ADMIN OPTION;>
```

You see this:

```
Grant succeeded.
```

Now MAUST can administer CREATE SESSION as well.

If WITH ADMIN OPTION is revoked, all users given that privilege by that person retain the privileges. Act accordingly. It is not a cascading revoke like the WITH GRANT OPTION.

Object privileges

Object privileges control data access and modification.

Understanding object privileges

You can grant only eight object privileges:

- ✔ **SELECT** lets the recipient select rows from tables. See Chapter 7 for more info.
- ✔ **INSERT** lets the recipient insert rows into tables.
- ✔ **UPDATE** lets the recipient change existing rows in tables.
- ✔ **DELETE** lets the recipient remove existing rows from tables.
- ✔ **REFERENCES** lets a user create a view on, or a foreign key to, another user's table. We share more details on foreign keys in Chapter 7.
- ✔ **INDEX** lets one user create an index on another user's table. You can find more on indexes in Chapter 7.
- ✔ **ALTER** lets one user change or add to the structure of another user's table.
- ✔ **EXECUTE** lets the recipient run procedures owned by another user.

Keep these privilege tidbits in mind:

- ✔ When you own an object, you automatically have all the privileges on that object. In other words, you don't have to be granted SELECT on your own table.
- ✔ Object privileges cannot be revoked from the owner of an object.
- ✔ Whatever schema owns the object ultimately controls that object's privileges.

✔ Without express permission, no one else can manage the object privileges of said object — well, no one except a user who might have the system privilege GRANT ANY OBJECT (usually reserved for DBAs).

✔ Object privilege cannot be revoked by anyone but the person who granted it except for someone with the GRANT ANY OBJECT privilege. Not even the owner can revoke a privilege on her own object unless she was the grantor.

Managing object privileges

In the following steps, the users MAGGIE, JASON, and MATT work in a database that contains recipes. This example uses object privileges to allow them to view and add more recipes.

1. Maggie logs in.

2. Maggie types the following:

```
<GRANT SELECT ON vegetarian_recipes TO jason;>
```

This lets user MAGGIE allow JASON to select from her VEGETARIAN_ RECIPES table. She sees this:

```
Grant succeeded.
```

Similar to WITH ADMIN OPTION of system privileges, object privileges have something called WITH GRANT OPTION.

✔ MAGGIE can allow JASON to be able to INSERT into her table and allow JASON to pass on that privilege:

```
<GRANT SELECT ON vegetarian_recipes TO jason WITH GRANT OPTION;>
```

✔ JASON can pass on that INSERT privilege to MATT:

```
<GRANT SELECT ON maggie.vegetarian_recipes TO matt;>
```

✔ MAGGIE cannot revoke the INSERT privilege from MATT. She has to ask JASON to do so.

✔ If JASON refuses to revoke INSERT privileges for MATT, MAGGIE can revoke the privilege from JASON and, in turn, revoke it from MATT. It's called a *cascading revoke.* Note that this is different from system privileges.

✔ MAGGIE can revoke the INSERT privilege from JASON and in the meantime automatically revoke them from MATT:

```
<REVOKE INSERT ON vegetarian_recipes FROM jason;>
```

She sees this:

```
Revoke succeeded.
```

If a user wants to see what object privilege they have given out, she can query the view USER_TAB_PRIVS.

For example, MAGGIE can see what privileges JASON has left on her objects:

```
<SELECT * FROM USER_TAB_PRIVS
WHERE GRANTEE = 'JASON';>
```

She sees something like this:

```
GRANTEE     OWNER       TABLE_NAME          GRANTOR     PRIVILEGE
----------  ----------  ------------------  ----------  ----------
JASON       MAGGIE      VEGETARIAN_RECIPES  MAGGIE      SELECT
```

Creating Roles

You can group privileges with database roles for ease of management. Instead of an object owner individually granting privileges to one or more users with similar job descriptions, the object owner can create a role and grant the role instead.

For example, say you're a DBA for a major retailer. Every day, new store clerks are hired. The application allows them to do dozens of requirements, including

✔ INSERT into the SALES table

✔ UPDATE the INVENTORY table

✔ DELETE from the ORDERS table

Follow these steps to use a role to grant privileges:

1. **Log in to SQL*Plus as HR.**

2. **Type the following:**

   ```
   <CREATE ROLE sales_clerk;>
   ```

   This role is called SALES_CLERK, and you see this:

   ```
   Role created.
   ```

3. **Grant system and object privileges to the role:**

   ```
   <GRANT INSERT ON sales TO sales_clerk;>
   <GRANT UPDATE ON inventory TO sales_clerk;>
   <GRANT DELETE ON orders TO sales_clerk;>
   ```

   And so on.

4. **Grant the role to the employees:**

   ```
   <GRANT sales_clerk TO rob, nora, dan;>
   ```

The role is granted to new clerks ROB, NORA, and DAN. You see this:

```
Grant Succeeded.
```

Another nice thing about roles is *dynamic privilege management,* where adding and removing privileges from a role immediately affects all users who have the role.

All users need special access during a certain time (a few months, for example), to be able to SELECT from the INVENTORY table. Instead of granting it to possibly hundreds of clerks, grant the role and they will automatically have it. It makes managing privileges much easier.

Oracle-supplied roles

Some roles come already created and set up by the database, making it easier to manage certain tasks.

Here are some of the many roles supplied by Oracle when the database is installed:

- ✔ **CONNECT** includes the privileges needed to connect to the database.
- ✔ **RESOURCE** includes many of the roles a developer might use to create and manage an application, such as creating and altering many types of objects including tables, view, and sequences.
- ✔ **EXP_FULL_DATABASE/IMP_FULL_DATABASE** allows the grantee to do logical backups of the database.
- ✔ **RECOVERY_CATALOG_OWNER** allows grantee to administer Oracle Recovery Manager catalog.
- ✔ **SCHEDULER_ADMIN** allows the grantee to manage the Oracle job scheduler.

- ✔ **DBA** gives a user most of the major privileges required to administer a database. These privileges can manage users, security, space, system parameters, and backups.

The SYSDBA role

SYSDBA is the top dog of all roles. Anyone with this role can do anything they want in the database. Obviously you want to be careful with some of these. For example, be very particular about whom, if anyone, you give the SYSDBA role. Those users should be fully trained, qualified Oracle administrators. If they are not, they could irreparably damage your database. Also, if too many people have this role, it destroys the chain of accountability in the database.

Oracle-supplied roles are managed just like the roles you create.

Auditing: Oracle's Big Brother

Just when users think it's safe to do whatever they want in the database, along comes auditing. No, really . . . being able to audit what happens in the database is like having police on the streets. Auditing can

- Protect you from people with prying eyes or malicious intentions.
- Help you track down who's responsible for certain actions in the database.
- Help analyze access data.

You can choose from many auditing options:

- **Users:** Auditing can be turned on for everything a user does, from logging in to what SQL statements he's running.
- **Objects:** Every action against an object can be audited.
- **System privileges:** Specific SQL statements such as ALTER, DROP, CONNECT, and CREATE can be audited.
- **Combination:** Most likely, you will choose a combination of users, objects, and system privileges to accomplish your auditing needs.

You will rarely audit everything in the database. Some overhead is involved. Auditing can cost you in terms of the following:

- **CPU:** Audit operations execute inside the database with each SQL statement or connection you run. The more you audit, the more work there is in the background for Oracle to do.
- **Storage:** Oracle audits generate an *audit trail* for you to look at later. Again, the more data being audited, the more information is generated.
- **Personnel:** Viewing and analyzing the auditing information could be a job in and of itself if you have a very large database with lots of users and lots of auditing. Someone has to interpret the audit trail and determine how the data will be used. The audit trail itself has to be managed. How long are you going to keep the info? Where will it go for long-term storage? Who will clean it up when it is no longer needed?

Find out what your auditing requirements are. Sometimes companies are bound by corporate guidelines. Or, you may be under the gun for industry certifications such as Sarbanes-Oxley, which require a fair amount of auditing.

Although Oracle auditing can cover a lot of the bases, it may not meet all your requirements. Make sure you can equate each one of your auditing requirements with Oracle auditing capability. In most cases, the database will have you covered.

Getting ready to audit

Oracle 11g changed the amount of auditing turned on by default. In 12c, all the following database actions are automatically audited by default:

ADMINISTER KEY MANAGEMENT

ALTER ANY PROCEDURE

ALTER ANY SQL TRANSLATION PROFILE

ALTER ANY TABLE

ALTER DATABASE

ALTER DATABASE LINK

ALTER PROFILE

ALTER ROLE

ALTER SYSTEM

ALTER USER

AUDIT SYSTEM

CREATE ANY JOB

CREATE ANY LIBRARY

CREATE ANY PROCEDURE

CREATE ANY SQL TRANSLATION PROFILE

CREATE ANY TABLE

CREATE DATABASE LINK

CREATE DIRECTORY

CREATE EXTERNAL JOB

CREATE PROFILE

CREATE PUBLIC SYNONYM

CREATE ROLE

CREATE SQL TRANSLATION PROFILE

CREATE USER

DROP ANY PROCEDURE

DROP ANY SQL TRANSLATION PROFILE

DROP ANY TABLE

DROP DATABASE LINK

DROP DIRECTORY

DROP PROFILE

DROP PUBLIC SYNONYM

DROP ROLE

DROP USER

EXEMPT ACCESS POLICY

EXEMPT REDACTION POLICY

GRANT ANY OBJECT PRIVILEGE

GRANT ANY PRIVILEGE

GRANT ANY ROLE	PURGE DBA_RECYCLEBIN
LOGMINING	SET ROLE
LOGOFF	TRANSLATE ANY SQL
LOGON	

Furthermore, in 11g the database parameter AUDIT_TRAIL was set to DB. This was a significant change over previous versions. Before, it was set to NONE, meaning auditing was not turned on. Turning it on required restarting the database; a tall order in a production system. Having the default parameter set to DB was convenient in case you forgot when you created the database. However, in 12c, this parameter no longer has any effect for newly created databases. It applies only to databases that are migrated from 11g to 12c.

Oracle 12c also changes the way default auditing is done in the database. Prior to 12c, each user had to have his or her auditing enabled in a very granular fashion. In 12c, a new feature called Unified Auditing greatly simplifies setting up and managing auditing in the database. It allows you to group not only users and roles but also features, parameters, and applications in such a way that configuring proper auditing can be done quickly and efficiently.

By default, in 12c the database is delivered with a basic policy that covers some of the main audits that most DBAs would be concerned about. These audits, however, are constrained to SYSTEM privileges primarily. If you think about it, Oracle doesn't have the intrinsic knowledge of your application. Therefore, it is up to you to configure object level auditing if required in your environment.

The AUDIT_TRAIL parameter no longer applies in newly created 12c databases. If you migrated from 11g, all your audit entries go into the table SYS. AUD$. Keep an eye on this internal table. Depending on your level of auditing, it can grow very quickly. Consider creating a maintenance plan that has directives for either purging the table or moving the audit rows to more permanent long-term storage (depending on your organization).

Enabling and disabling audits with unified audit policies

You can do all the setup you want, but nothing is audited (except for defaults) until you choose to do so. This benefits you because you can set up, create, and configure your application and objects before you have to manage an audit trail. You turn auditing on and off with the AUDIT or NOAUDIT command.

Because Oracle 12c does a fair amount of default auditing, consider turning off some before setting up your application. Then you can enable all the auditing you want right before your application goes to production. Make that decision based on your own business needs.

A unified audit policy is a named group of audit settings that audit a particular aspect of user behavior. The CREATE AUDIT POLICY statement creates the policies. The policy can be as simple as auditing the activities of a single user or an organized set of complex audit policies that use conditions to affect specific audits.

You can also have more than one audit policy enabled in the database. Policies can include both system-wide and object-specific audit options. Most of the auditing that you will do for general activities (including standard auditing) should use audit policies.

Auditing system privileges

With security being so important, Oracle 12c ships with some auditing turned on automatically via the ORA_SECURECONFIG policy. Furthermore, it's not always users' actions you want to audit but what they are *trying* to do. An audit can be generated even when someone tries to do something he isn't allowed to do.

Auditing defaults

Default, preconfigured audits in 12c include the system privilege or statement audits, including commands and actions such as CONNECT, ALTER, DROP, CREATE, and so on.

For example, you might want to track who is creating tables in the database or how often tables are created. This simple policy turns on auditing for any CREATE TABLE statement, which generates an audit entry every time someone creates a table. Type the following:

```
CREATE AUDIT POLICY table_cre_policy
PRIVILEGES CREATE TABLE;
```

You see this:

```
Operation 229 succeeded.
```

To enable this policy for the user SHARDIN, type

```
<AUDIT POLICY table_cre_policy BY shardin;>
```

You see this:

```
Audit succeeded.
```

To disable the policy for SHARDIN, type this:

```
<NOAUDIT POLICY table_cre_policy BY shardin;>
```

Auditing successful and unsuccessful attempts

The default is to audit both successful and unsuccessful attempts. You can audit the statement if the user successfully executes the command; the audit doesn't happen if the command fails. This approach can be useful two ways:

- ✔ If you audit only successful commands, you don't have to sift through a bunch of audit entries that show a user trying to get the correct syntax.

- ✔ If you audit specifically the unsuccessful commands, you can catch users trying to do things that they aren't supposed to. For example, suppose users are forbidden to drop tables that they don't own. First, you can prevent inappropriate drops by not giving them the DROP ANY TABLE system privilege. Second, if they try to do it anyway, it generates an error and audit the unsuccessful attempt.

This policy audits the DROP ANY TABLE command. Type the following:

```
<CREATE AUDIT POLICY drop_any_table_policy
PRIVILEGES DROP ANY TABLE;>
```

You see this:

```
Operation 229 succeeded.
```

To audit only unsuccessful attempts for the user JKOTAN, execute the following:

```
<AUDIT POLICY drop_any_table_policy BY jkotan WHENEVER NOT SUCCESSFUL;>
```

You see this:

```
Audit succeeded.
```

Auditing objects

Consider object auditing if you want to audit statements, such as SELECT, INSERT, UPDATE, and DELETE. Object auditing can track

✔ Actions against specific objects

✔ Privileges on all or specific tables

Sifting through an audit trail of a database with thousands of audited objects can be daunting. It's also likely that some objects simply don't need auditing. If so, restrict your auditing to specific objects.

Furthermore, you can audit objects with these parameters:

✔ When the operation is successful or when it fails

✔ Just once per session or every time it is executed

If you audit an object just once per session, it is audited the first time the user issues the statement. Every time after that, it is ignored. This cuts down your audit trail but also keeps you from being 100 percent sure if said user is responsible for later operations against a specific object in a session.

For example, if a user deletes a row from EMPLOYEES, the statement is audited. If the user goes back later and deletes another row within the same session, it will not be audited. You know what they say though: Where there's smoke, there's fire!

To create an audit policy on SELECT against the HR.EMPLOYEES table, type the following:

```
<CREATE AUDIT POLICY hr_emp_select
ACTIONS SELECT ON hr.employees;>
```

You see this:

```
Operation 229 succeeded.
```

To then audit each statement for the user DCOLLINS, type

```
<AUDIT POLICY hr_emp_select BY dcollins;>
```

You see this:

```
Audit succeeded.
```

Verifying an audit

After you turn on auditing in the database, keep track of the audits that you enact so you know what you have done.

Luckily, Oracle provides a few views in the database to help you keep track of your actions:

- ✔ To verify what system privileges you configured for auditing, use the view AUDIT_UNIFIED_POLICIES.

- ✔ To see what privileges are being audited by default for specific policies, type

```
< SELECT POLICY_NAME, AUDIT_OPTION, AUDIT_OPTION_TYPE
FROM AUDIT_UNIFIED_POLICIES
where policy_name = 'ORA_SECURECONFIG'
order by policy_name, AUDIT_OPTION;>
```

You see something like this:

```
POLICY_NAME          AUDIT_OPTION                        AUDIT_OPTION_TYPE
-------------------- ----------------------------------- -----------------
ORA_SECURECONFIG     ADMINISTER KEY MANAGEMENT           SYSTEM PRIVILEGE
ORA_SECURECONFIG     ALTER ANY PROCEDURE                 SYSTEM PRIVILEGE
ORA_SECURECONFIG     ALTER ANY SQL TRANSLATION PROFILE   SYSTEM PRIVILEGE
ORA_SECURECONFIG     ALTER ANY TABLE                     SYSTEM PRIVILEGE
ORA_SECURECONFIG     ALTER DATABASE                      SYSTEM PRIVILEGE
ORA_SECURECONFIG     ALTER DATABASE LINK                 STANDARD ACTION
ORA_SECURECONFIG     ALTER PROFILE                       STANDARD ACTION
ORA_SECURECONFIG     ALTER ROLE                          STANDARD ACTION
ORA_SECURECONFIG     ALTER SYSTEM                        SYSTEM PRIVILEGE
ORA_SECURECONFIG     ALTER USER                          STANDARD ACTION
<output truncated for space...>
```

- ✔ To see which users or roles have been enabled to be audited by policies in the database, type

```
< SELECT *
FROM AUDIT_UNIFIED_ENABLED_POLICIES;>
```

You should see something like this:

```
USER_NAME POLICY_NAME                     ENABLED_ SUC FAI
--------- ------------------------------- -------- --- ---
HR        TABLE_POLICY                    BY       YES YES
HR        DROP_ANY_TABLE_FAIL_POLICY BY            NO  YES
OE        HR_EMP_SELECT                   BY       YES YES
ALL USERS ORA_SECURECONFIG                BY       YES YES
```

The last two columns, SUC and FAI, stand for SUCCESS or FAILURE. You can capture an audit for SUCCESS or FAILURE or both. The policy you created, DROP_ANY_TABLE_FAIL_POLICY, captures only the times when a drop table fails.

Viewing audit information

After configuring for and turning on auditing, see what audit data is being collected.

- ✔ **DBA_AUDIT_TRAIL** shows all audit entries in the system.
- ✔ **DBA_AUDIT_OBJECT** shows all audit entries in the system for objects.
- ✔ **DBA_AUDIT_STATEMENT** shows audit entries for the statements GRANT, REVOKE, AUDIT, NOAUDIT, and ALTER SYSTEM.
- ✔ **DBA_AUDIT_SESSION** shows audit entries for the CONNECT and DISCONNECT actions.

In 12c the unified audit trail simplifies viewing and reporting audit information.

To see all the audits captured for the HR user, type

```
<SELECT EVENT_TIMESTAMP, CLIENT_PROGRAM_NAME, ACTION_NAME,
UNIFIED_AUDIT_POLICIES
FROM UNIFIED_AUDIT_TRAIL
WHERE DBUSERNAME = 'HR'
ORDER BY EVENT_TIMESTAMP DESC;>
```

You might see something like this:

```
EVENT_TIMESTAMP              CLIENT_PROG ACTION_NAME     UNIFIED_AUDIT_POLICY
--------------------------- ----------- --------------- --------------------
29-JUN-13 04.11.08.472263 PM sqlplus.exe CREATE TABLE    TABLE_POLICY
29-JUN-13 04.10.23.333411 PM sqlplus.exe LOGON           ORA_SECURECONFIG
29-JUN-13 04.06.03.025363 PM sqlplus.exe LOGOFF          ORA_SECURECONFIG
29-JUN-13 04.01.04.588854 PM sqlplus.exe LOGON           ORA_SECURECONFIG
29-JUN-13 01.58.25.908652 PM sqlplus.exe LOGOFF          ORA_SECURECONFIG
```

Specific columns are selected. (There is so much information in this table that we can't possibly fit the whole table into this chapter.) This output shows that the HR user created a table as well as the logon and logoff activity. Try your own queries to see what kind of information you can get.

Turning off audits

Turning off auditing is as easy at turning it on. You may have to use the audit options to help remember what you have turned on.

After you identify the audits you no longer need, use the NOAUDIT command to turn off the audits for the users or roles.

Earlier, you turned on auditing for SELECT on the HR.EMPLOYEES table by the user DCOLLINS. To turn off this audit, type the following:

```
<NOAUDIT POLICY hr_emp_select BY dcollins;>
```

You see this:

```
Noaudit succeeded.
```

Chapter 11

Facilitating Backup and Recovery

In This Chapter

▶ Knowing data integrity threats

▶ Protecting and backing up files

▶ Viewing backup information

▶ Understanding and maintaining archives

▶ Recovering your database

Forget the Boy Scouts. DBAs need to be prepared for anything. In addition to handling the database's security, DBAs must protect the data. All kinds of threats are out there waiting to destroy or damage your information. A database can experience loss and corruption from hardware crashes, software bugs, failed processes, and, of course, human error. Depending on the severity of the issue, failure to protect the data can cause you a bit of pain and suffering at times. That's not hyperbole: A lack of data integrity (or no data integrity at all!) can lead to several problems, including the loss of business revenue or even the loss of your job.

To safeguard your information (and to stay employed as a DBA), you need a backup and recovery plan. However, there's no singular button you can push to make everything okay. Rather, creating a backup and recovery strategy that addresses threats and minimizes data loss and corruption involves many steps and tools, as we explain in this chapter.

Understanding Threats to Your Database

Before you can create guidelines to lower the risk of data loss and corruption or take the steps to recover your information quickly, you have to understand what you're up against. A good backup and recovery plan can help guard against the following threats.

Instance failure

Instance failure occurs when Oracle, as a running program, crashes. The good news here is Oracle has provided a recovery mechanism and can automatically recover from instance failure. All you have to do is restart the database instance. However, you might want to investigate what caused the instance failure so you can prevent it from happening again.

Losing files

Losing files within the Oracle *code tree* can result in your database crashing. The code tree has the files that you install when you put Oracle on your system, including the database files, the patch sets and patches you apply, and any other tools required to make your application run.

Make sure the code tree is part of the OS backup; it's an often-overlooked portion of a solid backup and recovery strategy. Sometimes the loss of a file in the Oracle code tree can be restored quickly out of the OS backup instead of doing an entire reinstallation.

Keep all the Oracle installation software handy in case you need to reinstall it. Keeping it handy means having a hard copy of it ready to go rather than storing it on the network. In the event of a disaster, you may not have access to those network resources. Don't rely on being able to download it from the Oracle website. That could take hours depending on how busy the site is.

Dropped objects

Objects in the database are dropped by humans. Problems occur when someone drops an object that she either didn't mean to drop or that she later decides she wants back.

Unless DBAs are involved with application design, many times they're simply told what and when to remove something from the database. Always take a Data Pump export of that object before you drop it. (See Chapter 8 for more on Data Pump.)

Media failure

Media failure occurs when a file or log required for the database to operate is lost, including

- ✔ **Data files,** which store the bulk of your data. Data files typically have an extension of .dbf.

- ✔ **Control files,** which store information about how your database is configured. For example, are you in ARCHIVELOG mode? How many data files are you allowed to have? You can find control files by checking the initialization parameter control_files. Typically, these files have an extension of .ctl or .con.

- ✔ **Parameter files,** such as PFILE or SPFILE. If your database uses an SPFILE, check the initialization parameter for spfile. Otherwise, by default, the file is in $ORACLE_HOME/dbs for Linux/UNIX or $ORACLE_HOME/database for Windows.

- ✔ **Archive logs,** which are created when you turn on archiving in the database. You can find the logs by checking the initialization parameter log_archive_dest_n (with n being a number from 1–10). Else, look in at the parameter db_recovery_file_dest to find them in the Fast Recovery Area. Typically, archive logs have an extension of .arc.

We show you methods to recover these file types (which we also discuss in Chapter 2) in the "Recovering Your Oracle Database" section, later in this chapter.

Corruption

Corruption is one of the most elusive and difficult types of failure to deal with. Figuring out why it occurred is often a considerable challenge. When things are *corrupted,* rows become unreadable in the database and the rows can report errors.

Corruption can be

- ✔ **Physical:** Actual sectors on the disk are physically damaged.

- ✔ **Logical:** Not physical damage, but data somehow went missing or is unreadable.

- ✔ **Your data:** The data itself is just wrong. For example, all your last_ names were updated to be the same as the first names.

- ✔ **In the data dictionary:** This is corruption in the metadata that Oracle uses to manage the database.

You can use RMAN, Block Media Recovery, and Data Pump to help recover from corruption problems. Fortunately, this type of failure is rare.

If you're having corruption troubles in your database, consider contacting Oracle Support for help. This is the type of issue where Oracle earns those hefty support contracts.

User error

User error isn't actually a type of failure, but it's probably the most common cause for recoveries. We mention it because you can protect against user error (even your own in case you're fallible).

Proper training, including training your users, can help reduce the chances of user error.

Finding Files with Recovery Manager

Recovery Manager (RMAN, as we lovingly refer to it) is Oracle's backup and recovery solution to protect the files in your database. It can recover from things like lost rows or lost objects, but its primary purpose is to restore and recover lost files.

RMAN is Oracle's replacement to Enterprise Backup Utility (EBU) from Oracle 7. RMAN first reared its head in Oracle 8.0.*x,* but it was not well received in its earliest versions. It was difficult to configure and use. RMAN came of age with the release of Oracle 9.*x.* Further improvements in 10g and 11g have led it to become almost the *de facto* standard now for backup of Oracle files. This trend has continued in 12c. The commands are more concise and meaningful than in previous versions of RMAN. Repeated operations and options can be preconfigured instead of being coded into every script. It's fast, efficient, and reliable. Most of all, it's easy to learn and implement.

Starting RMAN

You have a number of ways to launch RMAN:

- Launch the tool and then log in.
- Launch the tool and login all at once.
- Launch the tool and have all the output go to a log file. This option is typically used when running RMAN as a scheduled task.

Here is an example of probably the simplest way to get RMAN going:

1. **Set your ORACLE_SID from the OS command line:**

   Windows:

   ```
   <set ORACLE_SID=dev12c>
   ```

   Linux/UNIX:

   ```
   <. oraenv>
   <dev12c>
   ```

   This example uses dev12c for the ORACLE_SID. There will be no output for setting your ORACLE_SID.

2. **Launch RMAN:**

   ```
   <rman>
   ```

   RMAN launches, as shown in Figure 11-1.

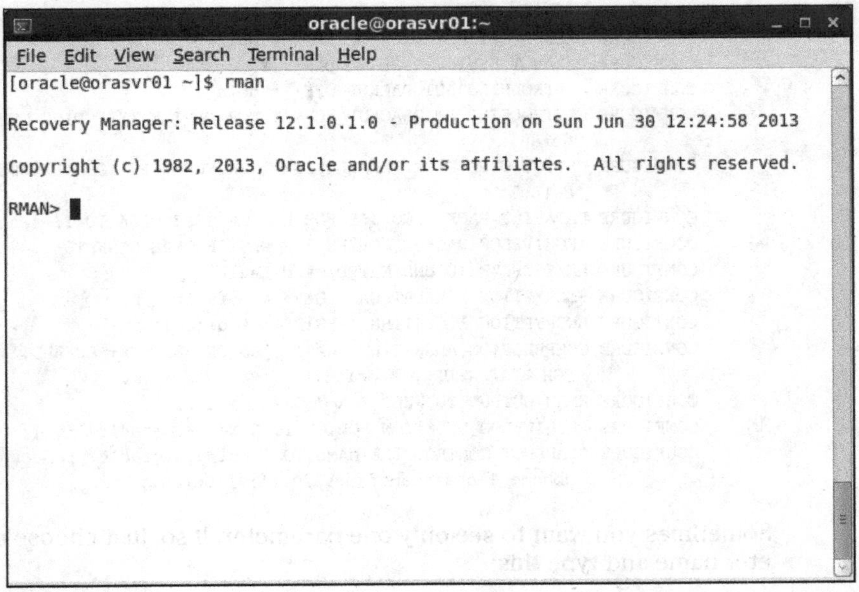

```
oracle@orasvr01:~                                    _ □ ×

File  Edit  View  Search  Terminal  Help
[oracle@orasvr01 ~]$ rman

Recovery Manager: Release 12.1.0.1.0 - Production on Sun Jun 30 12:24:58 2013

Copyright (c) 1982, 2013, Oracle and/or its affiliates.  All rights reserved.

RMAN> █
```

Figure 11-1:
Use
Recovery
Manager
to back up
and recover
files.

3. **Connect to the database you want to back up:**

   ```
   RMAN> connect target /
   ```

   You see something like this:

   ```
   connected to target database: DEV12C (DBID=3615982967)
   RMAN>
   ```

You have to connect to RMAN as SYSDBA. However, don't specify it. It is included by default.

Configuring RMAN

You can preconfigure some parameters for RMAN. These parameters are primarily for options that you want to use for all your backups and recoveries. They can be overridden inside your scripts for one-off operations.

1. **Launch RMAN.**

2. **View a list of these parameters by typing the following:**

   ```
   <show all;>
   ```

   You see this:

   ```
   using target database control file instead of recovery catalog
   RMAN configuration parameters for database with db_unique_name DEV12C are:
   CONFIGURE RETENTION POLICY TO REDUNDANCY 1; # default
   CONFIGURE BACKUP OPTIMIZATION OFF; # default
   CONFIGURE DEFAULT DEVICE TYPE TO DISK; # default
   CONFIGURE CONTROLFILE AUTOBACKUP OFF; # default
   CONFIGURE CONTROLFILE AUTOBACKUP FORMAT FOR DEVICE TYPE DISK TO '%F'; #
            default
   CONFIGURE DEVICE TYPE DISK PARALLELISM 1 BACKUP TYPE TO BACKUPSET; #
            default
   CONFIGURE DATAFILE BACKUP COPIES FOR DEVICE TYPE DISK TO 1; # default
   CONFIGURE ARCHIVELOG BACKUP COPIES FOR DEVICE TYPE DISK TO 1; # default
   CONFIGURE MAXSETSIZE TO UNLIMITED; # default
   CONFIGURE ENCRYPTION FOR DATABASE OFF; # default
   CONFIGURE ENCRYPTION ALGORITHM 'AES128'; # default
   CONFIGURE COMPRESSION ALGORITHM 'BASIC' AS OF RELEASE 'DEFAULT' OPTIMIZE
            FOR LOAD TRUE ; # default
   CONFIGURE RMAN OUTPUT TO KEEP FOR 7 DAYS; # default
   CONFIGURE ARCHIVELOG DELETION POLICY TO NONE; # default
   CONFIGURE SNAPSHOT CONTROLFILE NAME TO '/u01/app/oracle/product/12.1.0/
            dbhome_1/dbs/snapcf_dev12c.f'; # default
   ```

Sometimes you want to see only one parameter. If so, just choose one parameter name and type this:

```
<show retention policy;>
```

You see this:

```
RMAN configuration parameters for database with db_unique_name DEV12C are:
CONFIGURE RETENTION POLICY TO REDUNDANCY 1; # default
```

To change a parameter, copy what you see from the SHOW command and change the value accordingly. For example, type

```
<CONFIGURE RETENTION POLICY TO recovery window of 3 days;>
```

And you see this:

```
new RMAN configuration parameters:
CONFIGURE RETENTION POLICY TO RECOVERY WINDOW OF 3 DAYS;
new RMAN configuration parameters are successfully stored
```

Take a closer look at some of the configuration parameters:

✔ **Retention Policy:** Configuring a retention policy tells RMAN how long you want to keep your backup information. For example, if you reuse your backup tapes every two weeks, you can set your retention policy to expire those backups after 14 days. That way, you can purge them from RMAN to avoid cluttering the catalog of backup information that RMAN stores. Retention policies can be set two ways:

- *Recovery Window* specifies that after so many days the backup information will expire.

- *Redundancy* tells RMAN that after you get so many backups of your files, they will expire. For example, if you set redundancy to 3, the first one becomes obsolete after you take the fourth backup.

✔ **Backup Optimization:** If you turn on backup optimization and a backup fails halfway through, RMAN picks up where it left off when you restart the backup. If this option is turned off, RMAN starts from the beginning.

✔ **Default Device Type:** You can have RMAN back up files to disk or tape. This parameter configures what the default method is when the option is omitted from the backup command.

✔ **Control File Autobackup:** You can configure RMAN to take a backup of the control file and the spfile every time a backup runs. Also, if the database is in archive log mode, it will take a backup of the control file any time the database file structure changes, such as renaming or adding a data file.

✔ **Control File Autobackup Format:** This feature tells RMAN the name and location you would like control file auto backups to take on.

✔ **Parallelism:** On a machine with many backup devices, such as tapes or disks as well as multiple CPUs, you can set this parameter to use more resources in hopes of speeding up the backup. You can experiment with this to find the optimal setting.

✓ **Data File Backup Copies:** This parameter tells RMAN how many copies to make when backing up files. The more you have the safer you are from losing a backup file. However, backups will take longer and require more space.

✓ **Archive Log Backup Copies:** This parameter is similar to data file backup copies, but it applies to archive logs.

✓ **MAXSETSIZE:** Use this parameter when backing up to tape to make sure that the backup files don't span multiple tapes. This way, losing one tape won't nullify an entire backup. Typically, this parameter is left to unlimited when you're backing up to disk.

✓ **Encryption for Database:** Typically, the backup files created will contain the character strings of data that reside in your data files. A clever hacker can extract this data and perhaps make sense out of it. By turning on this parameter, all the data in the backup file will be garbled.

✓ **Encryption Algorithm:** You can choose the level of encryption in Oracle. The higher the encryption level, the longer it can take to back up the database. Here are your choices:

- AES128 AES 128-bit key

- AES192 AES 192-bit key

- AES256 AES 256-bit key

✓ **Compression Algorithm:** As of Oracle version 11g, you can choose the compression algorithm that RMAN uses to compress backups. You can choose between these two:

- High compression (BZIP2)

- CPU efficiency (ZLIB)

✓ **Snapshot Control File Name:** Tell RMAN where to put the control file and what to name it when a snapshot of the control file is taken.

RMAN catalog

When setting up your RMAN environment, consider the recovery catalog. A *recovery catalog* is a repository for all your RMAN configuration parameters, backup operations, and metadata. The catalog can store backup information indefinitely.

Selecting a catalog mode

RMAN provides two options for storing backup data:

✔ NOCATALOG mode stores backup data only in the control file for each individual database. This is the default.

✔ CATALOG mode stores backup data in both the control file and the catalog.

Storing backup data in only the control file has some limitations:

✔ By default, Oracle stores seven days of backup data in the control file. The database parameter control file_record_keep_time can change the length of time. Still, it isn't recommended that you use your control file for long backup retention periods. It causes control file growth, and if you ever lose your control files, you've lost all your recovery information. It's doesn't make recovery impossible, but it's a real pain.

✔ Limits the type of reporting you can do on your backups. You can query only one database at a time, after which you have to manually aggregate all the reports for multiple databases together.

Consider using a catalog if

✔ You have a lot of databases to back up.

✔ All the databases you back up are different versions of Oracle.

✔ You want to save your backups more than 60 days.

✔ You know what kind of reporting you want to do.

✔ You can afford the resources it requires to keep and maintain a catalog database.

Suppose that at the end of every week you want a report that sums up all the backup information for 50 databases ranging from Oracle 8i to 12c. You want that report to include things such as elapsed time, average piece size, compression info, and backup type. A recovery catalog can easily generate that report.

The recovery catalog has a set of views you can query, with SQL, to get backup information. Getting historical backup information for multiple databases is next to impossible to do without a recovery catalog because all the backup information is stored separately in each database.

If you have only one or two databases to back up and want simple reports and short retention policy, perhaps the recovery catalog is overkill. After all, it has to go into its own database, be backed up, and be maintained just like any other application. However, Oracle helps by providing a limited use license for having an RMAN recovery catalog. That means you don't have to have an Oracle database license for the catalog on a separate machine as long as you use the catalog only for RMAN.

Creating the catalog

If you decide to create a catalog, it's easy. Follow these steps for a Linux environment (they'll be almost identical for Windows):

1. **Create a tablespace to hold the RMAN data by typing in SQL*Plus:**

   ```
   <create tablespace rman_data datafile
   '/u01/app/oracle/oradata/dev12c/rman_data01.dbf' size 100M
   autoextend on next 100M maxsize 2G;>
   ```

   You see this:

   ```
   Tablespace created.
   ```

2. **Type the following to create the catalog owner:**

   ```
   <create user rmancat identified by rmancat
   default tablespace rman_data
   quota unlimited on rman_data;>
   ```

   You see this:

   ```
   User created.
   ```

3. **Grant appropriate privileges:**

   ```
   <grant connect, recovery_catalog_owner to rmancat;>
   ```

   You see this:

   ```
   Grant succeeded.
   ```

4. **From a terminal window, log in to the recovery catalog with the owner and create the catalog:**

   ```
   <rman catalog rmancat@rcvcat>
   ```

   You see output like this:

   ```
   Recovery Manager: Release 12.1.0.1.0 - Production on Sun Jun 30 10:13:59
           2013
   Copyright (c) 1982, 2013, Oracle and/or its affiliates.  All rights
           reserved.
   recovery catalog database Password:
   connected to recovery catalog database
   ```

5. **When you're connected to the catalog database, create the catalog repository:**

   ```
   <create catalog;>
   ```

   You see this:

   ```
   recovery catalog created
   ```

6. **Type the following to connect to both the target database and the catalog:**

```
<rman target / catalog rmancat@rcvcat >
```

Every time you back up a database, you need to connect to both the target and the catalog.

You see this:

```
Recovery Manager: Release 12.1.0.1.0 - Production on Sun Jun 30 10:17:30
        2013
Copyright (c) 1982, 2013, Oracle and/or its affiliates.  All rights
        reserved.
connected to target database: DEV12C (DBID=3615982967)
recovery catalog database Password:
connected to recovery catalog database
```

Don't specify the password on the command line when you launch RMAN. It is not a secure way to log in, because it can expose your password to other people on the system.

7. **Connect to both the target and the catalog and type this:**

```
<register database;>
```

Register any database that you will back up within the recovery catalog.

You see this:

```
database registered in recovery catalog
starting full resync of recovery catalog
full resync complete
```

Everything else in RMAN functions exactly the same whether or not you use a catalog.

Backup File Types with RMAN

You can create backups with RMAN in two ways:

- ✔ **Backup sets** are a special type of RMAN file.

- ✔ **Copies** are block-for-block replicas of the files you're backing up. Although they're made within RMAN via the COPY command, the end result is the same as if you used an OS command.

Table 8-1 lists some key points of both.

Table 8-1	Backup Sets versus Copies
Backup Sets	*Copies*
Must be restored with RMAN before use	Block-for-block exact images of source file
Can be any part of an incremental strategy	Don't have to be restored to be used
Can be compressed during the backup	Can't be compressed during the backup
Can be streamed to multiple devices for parallelism (including tape)	Can be rolled forward by applying incremental backups of source files
Can be into multiple, more manageable pieces	Can't be split into multiple pieces
Can contain more than one data file	Can be only the first level (0) of an incremental strategy
Can be encrypted	Can't be streamed directly to tape or to multiple devices

We tend to use backup sets. Being able to compress and stream directly to tape while at the same time encrypting is a very good quality. However, using copies can significantly reduce recovery time because they don't have to be restored. They can be used from disk in place. All you have to do is roll them forward with whatever archive log files were generated between when the copy was made and when the failure occurred.

Backing up with backup sets

RMAN makes backing up your database a breeze. The examples in this section are hot backups to the Fast Recovery Area.

A *hot backup* is simply a backup while the database is running. You can do it at any time, but you should usually pick a time when there is less activity. That way, the hot backup won't compete for resources.

Of course, figuring out what needs to be backed up is one of the first steps. You need to know what files are out there and whether they've been backed up.

1. **Launch RMAN as described in the "Finding Files with Recovery Manager" section.**

These examples don't use a recovery catalog because it is discussed earlier in this chapter. Just remember to connect to it if you choose to use one. After you connect, the commands to do all the various types of backups remain the same whether you're connected to a catalog or not.

2. **Set your database to automatically back up the control file and spfile:**

```
RMAN> show CONTROLFILE AUTOBACKUP;
```

3. **If you see something like this, skip to Step 5:**

```
RMAN configuration parameters for database with db_unique_name DEV12C are:
CONFIGURE CONTROLFILE AUTOBACKUP ON;
```

If your response reads as follows, go to Step 4.

```
CONFIGURE CONTROLFILE AUTOBACKUP OFF;
```

4. **Type the following:**

```
CONFIGURE CONTROLFILE AUTOBACKUP ON;
```

You should see this:

```
new RMAN configuration parameters:
CONFIGURE CONTROLFILE AUTOBACKUP ON;
new RMAN configuration parameters are successfully stored
```

5. **Get a list of the data files in your database:**

```
<report schema;>
```

You should see something like Figure 11-2.

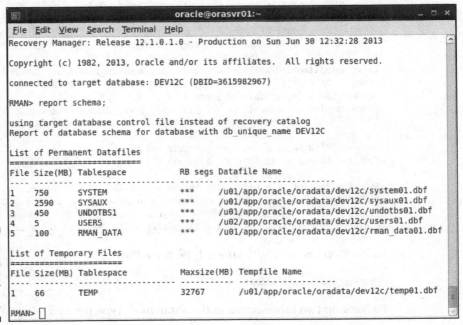

Figure 11-2: Running the RMAN REPORT command.

Backing up the database or tablespaces

You can back up the database and tablespaces in several ways:

- Back up the whole database.
- Back up one or more tablespaces.
- Back up one or more data files.

To back up the whole database, type the following:

```
<backup database;>
```

The output should look something like this:

```
Starting backup at 30-JUN-2013 10:45:10
using target database control file instead of recovery catalog
allocated channel: ORA_DISK_1
channel ORA_DISK_1: SID=48 device type=DISK
channel ORA_DISK_1: starting full datafile backup set
channel ORA_DISK_1: specifying datafile(s) in backup set
input datafile file number=00002 name=/u01/app/oracle/oradata/dev12c/sysaux01.
        dbf
input datafile file number=00001 name=/u01/app/oracle/oradata/dev12c/system01.
        dbf
input datafile file number=00003 name=/u01/app/oracle/oradata/dev12c/undotbs01.
        dbf
input datafile file number=00005 name=/u01/app/oracle/oradata/dev12c/rman_
        data01.dbf
input datafile file number=00004 name=/u01/app/oracle/oradata/dev12c/users01.dbf
channel ORA_DISK_1: starting piece 1 at 30-JUN-2013 10:45:12
channel ORA_DISK_1: finished piece 1 at 30-JUN-2013 10:48:18
piece handle=/u01/app/oracle/fast_recovery_area/DEV12C/backupset/2013_06_30/o1_
        mf_nnndf_TAG20130630T104511_8x0k3rlq_.bkp tag=TAG20130630T104511
        comment=NONE
channel ORA_DISK_1: backup set complete, elapsed time: 00:03:06
Finished backup at 30-JUN-2013 10:48:18

Starting Control File and SPFILE Autobackup at 30-JUN-2013 10:48:18
piece handle=/u01/app/oracle/fast_recovery_area/DEV12C/autobackup/2013_06_30/
        o1_mf_s_819456498_8x0k9lq1_.bkp comment=NONE
Finished Control File and SPFILE Autobackup at 30-JUN-2013 10:48:19
```

To back up just one tablespace, type the following:

```
<backup tablespace users;>
```

To back up two tablespaces at the same time, type the following:

```
<backup tablespace system, users;>
```

Naming your backups

You can give your backup a name. It's called a *tag*. We name backups because it is easy to see which is which when looking at a list. A tag can be an alphanumeric string up to 30 characters.

Type the following to back up your database and give it a name (database_full_backup in this case):

```
<backup database tag=database_full_backup;>
```

Compressing your backups

As of Oracle 10g, you can compress your backups as they run. Compression usually shows a significant reduction in space usage.

As of Oracle 11g, you can change your compression algorithm (discussed earlier in the chapter) to help tune backup compression. Doing so can save time or resources.

Our experience shows that any kind of compression can make the backup take two to three times as long. To find out what works best for you, try different compressions and note the times.

Take a compressed backup of your entire database with this code:

```
<backup as compressed backupset database tag=compressed_full_bak;>
```

Incremental backups

You may want to consider an *incremental backup*, which copies only some of the blocks based on when the last incremental was done and what blocks have changed. Incremental backups come in three levels (0 and 1 differential and 1 cumulative) published in Oracle 12c:

- **Differential** copies only blocks that have changed since the last incremental backup of any type. For example, if you do a level-1 differential on Monday and a level-1 differential on Tuesday, the Tuesday backup gets only the blocks changed since the level 1 on Monday.

- **Cumulative** gets all blocks that were changed since the last level-0 backup, even if several level-1 differentials were taken since then.

Incremental backups conserve time and space when you're designing a backup strategy. You might consider an incremental strategy if your database is extremely large and takes hours to go through a full backup.

Because backups incur overhead on the system, if at all possible, don't run them when users are trying to access data. If your database is getting large and the backup has run for five hours and is cutting into core business hours, look at an incremental approach to your backups and/or increasing backup job parallelism.

These are typical solutions that use incremental backups:

- ✔ You schedule your full weekly backup for Sunday at 3:00 a.m. This backup takes five hours to complete during the least amount of user activity on the system. Your database is 400GB, and even though you compress the backup it still takes 50GB of space.

- ✔ You schedule a differential level-1 backup to run daily at 3:00 a.m., Monday through Saturday. This backup takes only 15 minutes and is 2GB in size after compression.

If your database is small, if it doesn't take long to back up, and if the backup doesn't interfere with your operations, consider doing full backups every day to reduce the complexity of your backup strategy. Keep things simple when you can.

Block change tracking

Block change tracking just tracks what blocks have changed; when it comes time to do an incremental backup, you can get the blocks that you need instead of reading every single one. This technique speeds up incremental backups tremendously.

Check to see whether your database has block change tracking enabled:

```
<select *
from v$block_change_tracking;>
```

If it does not, enable block change tracking:

```
<alter database enable block change tracking
 Using file <specify a file name here>;>
```

Put the file with the rest of your data files and name it something like block_change_tracking.dbf. This feature has little overhead. The block change tracking file is, on average, 1/30,000 the size of the data blocks to be tracked. You can have a very large database before worrying about this file taking up much space.

To do the weekly level-0 backup on Sunday, type the following:

```
<backup incremental level 0 as compressed backupset database tag=weekly_
          level_0;>
```

To do the daily level-1 backup, type the following:

```
<backup incremental level 1 as compressed backupset database tag=daily_level_1;>
```

Do the daily backup every day besides Sunday if you're doing a weekly level 0 on Sunday. If you're doing a monthly level 0 (for example, on the first of the month), run the daily level 1 *every other day* of the month. Basically, if you're doing a level 0 on a given day, there's no need to do a level 1.

To make sure you start your incremental backup strategy correctly, specify a level 0. If you do not, RMAN will do a *full* backup, which won't record the necessary information to do incremental backups from there forward.

Making copies

If you want to incorporate copies into your backup strategy, the commands are slightly different than with backup sets.

Copies are block or block images of the files in your database. Their main advantage is that they don't have to be restored and can immediately be ready for action (making for quick database failure recovery). However, don't forget that they come at the cost of speed and space.

Make a copy of your entire database:

```
<backup as copy database;>
```

Many commands discussed in the backup sets sections are also available with copies.

Make a copy of just one tablespace:

```
<backup as copy tablespace users;>
```

Make a backup of your tablespace users and give it a tag (users_copy in this example):

```
<backup as copy tablespace users tag=users_copy;>
```

You can use copies as the level 0 of an incremental strategy. However, copies can be only for the level-0 portion of the incremental strategy.

To make a level-0 copy for the first stage of an incremental backup strategy, type the following:

```
<backup incremental level 0 as copy database tag=level0_copy;>
```

Viewing Backup Information

Use the LIST command to see what backups you have stored. You can list the following:

- ✔ All your backups
- ✔ Backups for certain tablespaces
- ✔ Backups of certain data files as well as archive logs and copies

You have different outputs to choose from:

- ✔ See a short listing called a summary.
- ✔ See a fully detailed listing with the VERBOSE option.

The LIST command is very powerful. Use it to show small bits of information about your backups, or all the information stored about your backups. Try some of the following examples to get a feel for how the command works:

- ✔ To see a summary list of the backups that contain the tablespace users, type this:

  ```
  < list backup of tablespace users summary;>
  ```

- ✔ To see a summary of all your backups, type this:

  ```
  <list backup summary;>
  ```

- ✔ To see a verbose list of all your backups with the tag database_full_ backup, type this:

  ```
  <list backup tag=database_full_backup;>
  ```

The LIST command is a little different if you want to see copies: You use the COPY keyword.

- ✔ To see copies of your database, type this:

  ```
  <list copy of database;>
  ```

- ✔ To see what data files copies you have for tablespace users, type this:

  ```
  <list copy of tablespace users;>
  ```

You can find a lot of information in a VERBOSE listing. Figure 11-3 shows what the output may look like if you list the backups of the tablespace users.

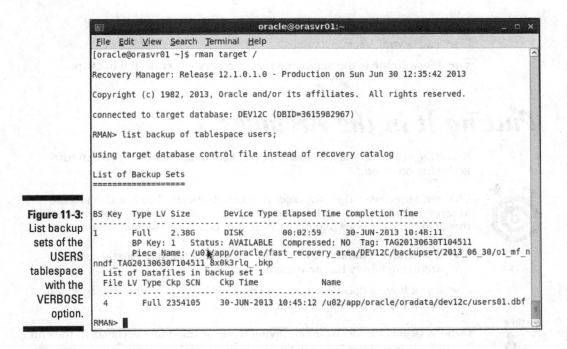

Figure 11-3:
List backup
sets of the
USERS
tablespace
with the
VERBOSE
option.

If you take a closer look at Figure 11-3, you discover the following:

- **BS Key** is a backup set key. Every backup must have a backup set key, an ever-increasing unique identifier for each backup.

- **Type** tells you more about what type of backup was taken, such as a full or an incremental backup.

- **LV** is short for *level*. When you're doing incremental backups, they can have multiple levels.

- **Size** is the size for that particular backup.

- **Device Type** indicates disk or tape for each backup set.

- **Elapsed Time** is how long the backup set took to run.

- **Completion Time** pretty much explains itself.

- **BP Key** is the backup piece key. If you break the backup into multiple pieces, each piece gets a unique identifier.

- **Status** tells you if a backup is available for RMAN to immediately use. You can make a backup unavailable if you remove the backup files (for example, if you take the tape out of the drive and put in storage).

- ✔ **Compressed** tells whether or not the backup was compressed.
- ✔ **Tag** is your backup's name.
- ✔ **Piece Name** is the actual file that is created to store the backup.

Putting It in the Archives

Archiving is the database's ability to track all data changes. You can turn archiving on or off.

Chapter 2 discusses the processes and files associated with archiving and asserts that running in archive mode has processing and storage overhead. Is this going to slow your database? Well, it depends on the following:

- ✔ If you have a database with very few changes and is mostly read, archiving barely has an impact.
- ✔ If you have a database under a constant barrage of data changes and batch loads, you might feel it a little.

Luckily, Oracle has designed archiving to cause minimal overhead. In the end, the price is worth the peace of mind you have of having a 24/7 operation with darn-near-guaranteed zero data loss.

Turning archiving on and off

With archiving off, you can take backups of the database only when it's closed (also called *consistent* backups). You do so by shutting down that database and starting it in mount mode. As a result, no changes are allowed to the data. This method allows you to take a consistent copy of the data as it exists at that point in time. If you ever have to restore this backup, your database will look exactly as it did when the backup was taken . . . even if it was a year ago.

You might begin to see some inconveniences if you turn archiving off:

- ✔ Inconveniences are unacceptable if your database requires 24/7 availability. You can't just shut it down and disallow changes for as long as your backup takes.
- ✔ Even if you do consistent backups every day, what happens to the changes that occur between backups? They're lost if you have to restore from a previous backup.

With archiving turned on, you get the following benefits:

✔ All data changes are tracked.

✔ You can do backups with the database open and available to all users.

✔ If you ever have to restore a backup that was taken the night before, you can apply the archives that were tracked up until the point of failure.

In reality, archiving is a must for almost all live production databases. It's rare that you can afford to take the database offline for significant periods of time or afford to lose data in the event that a backup has to be restored.

Archive logs

Besides the impact of the archiving process, you have to consider what to do with all the archive log files being created. Again, your database size and number of changes determine how much archive data you will create.

You have two choices for where to store the archive logs:

✔ **Fast Recovery Area:** If you store the archive logs here, Oracle neatly organizes them by database and date. This solution results in less work and fewer parameters to configure.

✔ **LOG_ARCHIVE_DEST_*n* initialization parameter:** This is actually 30 parameters. The *n* represents a number from 1 to 30. That's right: You can store up to 30 copies of your archive logs (but doing so would be overkill). DBAs commonly have two, maybe three copies. Here's an example of how you might set the LOG_ARCHIVE_DEST_1 parameter in your spfile:

```
alter system set log_archive_dest_1='LOCATION=/u01/oradata/dev12c/archive';
```

The bottom line is that you need to monitor the creation, storage, and backup of the archive logs. It's a fact of DBA life.

The good news is you need to keep the archive logs only for recovery between backups. Does that mean if you back up every night, you can trash all archive logs created prior to that backup? No. *Do not* trash them every day. We can't tell you how long to keep them, but consider the following situation:

It's Wednesday. You're taking a full backup of your database every night and running in archive log mode. After the backup is complete, you delete all the archive logs created prior to that backup. At noon, you have a catastrophic disk failure and must restore backups from the previous night (Tuesday). You discover that the backup tape from the previous night had coffee spilled on it (tsk tsk) and is no longer good.

See where we're going with this?

- ✔ You have to go back to the backup tape from two nights ago (Monday).
- ✔ You restore that backup and find that you can't roll forward to the time that your disk failed today because you trashed all the archive logs after each nightly backup.

Again, we recommend not only keeping archive logs for some time but also including them as part of your backup.

With no other requirements, we tend to keep archive logs for at least 30 days. This system gives us plenty of time to go back in the event that daily or even weekly backups incur some sort of unfortunate mishap.

Look at it this way: If you back up archive logs, you can remove them from the system to conserve space. Another reason to keep archive log backups: It allows you to restore your database to periods from long ago.

Take this instance: We have a client who, in June, wanted a copy of the client's database restored to December 31 at 11:59:59 p.m. of the prior year. We knew, from client conversations, that these operations were possible. Therefore we keep all backups and all archive logs on tape and offsite indefinitely. We requested the files (from querying the recovery catalog) and retrieved them from long-term storage. We ended up restoring the database to a new server to avoid interfering with the client's current production database. Everyone lived happily ever after.

Enabling archiving

If you haven't already done so, enabling archiving is a simple process. However, keep these things in mind:

- ✔ You have to shut down and restart the database.
- ✔ You must have enough space to store your archive logs.

Before you turn on archiving, decide where to store the archive log files. Use the Fast Recovery Area (briefly mentioned in Chapter 4). We show you how to do it here from the command line.

The database-creation steps in Chapter 4 give you the option to enable archiving. If you haven't read Chapter 4 or recently created a database, we go through it here. Furthermore, in that chapter, we use the GUI *Database Configuration Assistant* (DBCA). Here we do it from the command line.

Enabling the Fast Recovery Area

Follow along to enable the Fast Recovery Area:

1. **Open a command prompt to your operating system.**

2. **Log in to SQL*Plus as SYSDBA:**

```
<sqlplus / as sysdba>
```

3. **Configure how much space you want to dedicate to your Fast Recovery Area:**

```
<alter system set db_recovery_file_dest_size = 100G;>
```

This example dedicates 100GB. You should see this:

```
System altered.
```

4. **Choose the destination:**

```
<alter system set db_recovery_file_dest=
'/u01/app/oracle/fast_recovery_area';>
```

You should see this:

```
System altered.
```

Now Oracle automatically creates your archive logs under the Fast Recovery Area. The archive process creates a folder for your database and the subfolder for the date the archives were created. It organizes them very nicely.

If you want to see how much of your Fast Recovery Area is used, log in to SQL*Plus and query the view V$FLASH_RECOVERY_AREA_USAGE. It's sort of a misnomer. Oracle still hasn't changed the name of this view from FLASH to FAST even though they made the change in the documentation two versions ago.

After determining where you want to keep the archive logs, you can turn on archiving. These steps walk you through the process:

1. **Open a command prompt to your operating system.**

2. **Log in to SQL*Plus as SYSDBA:**

```
<sqlplus / as sysdba>
```

3. **Shut down the database:**

```
<shutdown immediate>
```

You see this:

```
Database closed.
Database dismounted.
ORACLE instance shut down.
```

4. **Start the database in mount mode:**

```
<startup mount>
```

You see something like this:

```
ORACLE instance started.

Total System Global Area 1336176640 bytes
Fixed Size                   2287480 bytes
Variable Size             1258293384 bytes
Database Buffers            67108864 bytes
Redo Buffers                8486912 bytes
Database mounted.
```

5. **Issue the command to enable archive mode:**

```
<alter database archivelog;>
```

You should see this:

```
Database altered.
```

6. **Open the database:**

```
<alter database open;>
```

You should see this:

```
Database altered.
```

Now your database is in archive log mode, and archive log files should show up in your Fast Recovery Area.

If you're impatient and want to see them now, type the following:

```
<alter system archive log current;>
```

You see this:

```
System altered.
```

If you navigate to your Fast Recovery Area, you should see one of your archive logs under a subdirectory with today's date.

Maintaining the Archives

Archive logs are a fundamental part of your backup and recovery strategy. However, they can take up a lot of space and need to be backed up. Luckily, backing up your archive logs is no more difficult than backing up anything else in your database. Furthermore, RMAN has some features to help you reclaim that space the archives occupy.

Make a backup of all your archive logs with this:

```
<backup archivelog all tag=archive_bak;>
```

This command backs up all the archive logs in your archive destination, which can be a tall order depending on how often you issue this command.

Back up your archive logs at least once per day. Keep your archive logs for up to 30 days.

Instead of backing up all archive logs every time, you might try backing up only the ones created since the last backup. To do so, type this:

```
<backup archivelog all not backed up tag=archive_bak;>
```

You could issue that command every day as part of your backup strategy. You could even do it several times a day just to be sure you get all of your archive logs backed up as often as possible. When the archive logs are backed up, you may not want them in the archive destination; they take up space after all.

RMAN offers a convenient command to clean up any successfully backed-up archives. If you want to back up all your archive logs and then delete the files that were backed up, type this:

```
<backup archivelog all delete input tag=archive_bak;>
```

We favor the "delete input" clause of the command as part of an archive log backup strategy:

- ✔ It allows you to back up any archive logs that exist in your archive desti-nation while at the same time freeing up space.

- ✔ RMAN deletes the archive logs only if the backup was successful.

- ✔ You don't have to worry about coming up with a time formula that will back up the archives every so often. Because it deletes the ones it suc-cessfully backs up, you can specify "all" every time, ensuring that none are missed.

Run an archive log backup command every time you do any database backup. That way, you have everything you need to recover if there's a failure.

Recovering Your Oracle Database

Many types of failures can befall your database. Oracle Recovery Manager is a tool that can help you get back on your feet after many of these failures.

Sometimes it is the only option, sometimes it is the best approach of several, and sometimes it isn't the right approach at all. This section focuses on the times RMAN shines and helps you bring a dead or damaged database back to life.

RMAN can really help with two types of failures:

- ✔ **Media failure:** Loss of files
- ✔ **User error:** Mistakes that lead to damaged databases or data

Whether RMAN can always help you when it comes to user error depends on what type of problem has been created. For example, if a user accidentally removes a file or a tablespace, RMAN can help very easily. However, if a user accidentally drops a table or corrupts data, RMAN *can* help, but it might not be the quickest approach. If a user drops a table, it might be quicker to retrieve it from the database Recyclebin or Flashback Database.

However, if the user has purged the Recyclebin or the Flashback Database isn't configured, Recovery Manager is your only choice.

RMAN can do two types of recoveries:

- ✔ **Complete:** All files are brought back to the time the database failed. No data is lost.
- ✔ **Incomplete:** The database is recovered but stopped short of a full recovery. There may be data loss. Sometimes this is what you want. For example, if a user drops a table at 10:13 a.m. sharp, you do an *incomplete* recovery to 10:12 a.m. to get the database back before the drop occurs.

Complete recovery is what usually happens. However, be prepared for anything.

Verifying the problem

Finding out what went wrong with your database isn't always an easy task. Sometimes you get lucky (if you want to use the term *lucky* in the face of a broken database). For example, maybe you know what happened:

- ✔ A system administrator told you a disk croaked.
- ✔ A user told you they dropped a table.
- ✔ You caused the error and you know what happened and why.

These might not be the problem, however. Sometimes you're presented with sneaky problems, in which case you take on the role of a detective. Say you start the database or access the data while the database is still open and get an error similar to this one:

```
ORA-01157: cannot identify/lock data file 4 - see DBWR trace file
ORA-01110: data file 4: '/u01/app/oracle/oradata/dev12c/users01.dbf'
```

You look for the file in the location that it gives. Lo and behold, it is gone (or maybe the whole disk is gone). You had more than one file on that disk. Why is Oracle telling you only that it can't find one of your files? Because when you start the database, Oracle reads the data file list in the control file. As soon as it can't find one in the list, it stops opening and presents the error. Or, if the database is already open, Oracle tells you only about the error that you're experiencing as a result of your specific action. Unfortunately, this is a little misleading; you might restore and recover the file only to find another error just like it for a different data file.

You can do a couple of things when you see the error:

✔ Query the dynamic performance view V$RECOVER_FILE to see a list of all files that Oracle is having trouble with, the error, and the file number(s) in question. Take that file number and plug it into the view V$DATAFILE to get a list of the filenames that need recovery.

✔ Oracle has a fancy tool called the Data Recovery Advisor. This tool won't work in all situations. It works when you have missing media, such as loss of files.

Complete recovery

Complete recovery (as opposed to incomplete recovery) is always what you want to shoot for. It means you recover every block and every transaction that was ever committed into the database. You let Oracle take over and do the recovery until the end of all the backup files and archive logs; don't manually intervene and stop it before it's finished.

Complete recovery: One or more data files

If you see the "unable to identify/lock datafile" error, you need to do a couple of things:

✔ Know the extent of the damage. This knowledge helps so you only have to do one recovery instead of two.

✔ Determine whether the lost file is required for the instance to run (or if it is an application data file). Required data files are SYSTEM, SYSAUX, and UNDO. This is important for reducing your overall *mean time to recovery* (MTTR). Oracle crashes only if you lose a required data file.

If you determine that the lost files aren't important to basic operation, you can open the database (if it even went down) before you begin recovery. That allows at least partial data access to some users. You may prefer that users remain out of the system until you're done.

What's the first thing to do if Oracle 12c crashes? Go to the Data Recovery Advisor (DRA). For the DRA to work, the database has to, at the very least, be in NOMOUNT state. The database can't be completely shut down. The DRA can also be run with the database open, minimizing downtime.

In the following exercise, the USERS tablespace data file was lost while the database was running. Because that data file is not a required data file (system, sysaux, undo), you can do the recovery without even shutting down the database.

1. **Log in to your target with RMAN.**

2. **Type this:**

   ```
   <list failure;>
   ```

   You see something like this:

   ```
   List of Database Failures
   ===========================

   Failure ID Priority Status    Time Detected        Summary
   ---------- -------- --------- -------------------- -------
   722        HIGH     OPEN      30-JUN-2013 11:25:20 One or more non-system
                       datafiles are missing
   ```

   A non-system (critical) file is missing. What to do?

3. **Ask the DRA what to do:**

   ```
   <advise failure;>
   ```

   You see something like this:

   ```
   Database Role: PRIMARY

   List of Database Failures
   ===========================

   Failure ID Priority Status    Time Detected        Summary
   ---------- -------- --------- -------------------- -------
   722        HIGH     OPEN      30-JUN-2013 11:25:20 One or more non-system
                       datafiles are missing

   analyzing automatic repair options; this may take some time
   allocated channel: ORA_DISK_1
   channel ORA_DISK_1: SID=56 device type=DISK
   ```

```
analyzing automatic repair options complete
Mandatory Manual Actions
========================
no manual actions available

Optional Manual Actions
=======================
1. If file /u01/app/oracle/oradata/dev12c/users01.dbf was unintentionally
          renamed or moved, restore it

Automated Repair Options
========================
Option Repair Description
------ ------------------

1      Restore and recover datafile 4
  Strategy: The repair includes complete media recovery with no data loss
  Repair script: /u01/app/oracle/diag/rdbms/dev12c/dev12c/hm/
          reco_3875560744.hm
```

Get a load of that! Not only does the DRA tell you exactly what you need
to do, but it also provides a script so you don't have to write a single
line of code. If you open that script, it looks something like this:

```
# restore and recover datafile
sql 'alter database datafile 4 offline';
restore ( datafile 4 );
recover datafile 4;
sql 'alter database datafile 4 online';
```

4. **Type the following to have the DRA fix the problem:**

```
<repair failure;>
```

You see something like this:

```
RMAN> repair failure;

Strategy: The repair includes complete media recovery with no data loss
Repair script: /u01/app/oracle/diag/rdbms/dev12c/dev12c/hm/reco_
          3875560744.hm

contents of repair script:
   # restore and recover datafile
   sql 'alter database datafile 4 offline';
   restore ( datafile 4 );
   recover datafile 4;
   sql 'alter database datafile 4 online';

Do you really want to execute the above repair (enter YES or NO)? YES
repair failure complete
```

At the very end of an Advisor-based recovery, if the database was closed, it asks whether you want to open the database. Most of the time you will choose Yes. You might choose No if you want to spend more time going over what happened before you release the database back to the users.

If we had to nitpick about the DRA, here is what we'd say:

- ✔ The DRA doesn't say you can take data files offline and then open the database for everyone else if the database is closed. It tells you that the files can be offline and recovered if the database is already open. At least it told you that they were non-system files.

- ✔ If you have to restore the files to a new location, the DRA can't take over and do the whole recovery for you. Say you lost a disk and it ain't coming back. The DRA isn't smart enough to choose a new location for you and incorporate that into a repair script. It tells you what's wrong and what it suggests doing, which may help get you going in the right direction, but it falls short after that.

Be realistic. How can you expect it to have every situation indexed for all types of systems and environments?

Complete recovery: One or more control files

What if you manage to lose all your control files and your database crashes?

Control files are critical system files.

DRA to the rescue:

1. **Log in to RMAN.**
2. **List failure.**
3. **Advise failure.**
4. **Repair failure.**

If you're lost, go to the earlier "Complete recovery: One or more data files" section for the full steps.

But wait a minute . . . Why didn't these steps open the database? Recovery from losing all your control files is a little more involved than standard data file recovery. (We suppose the DRA doesn't want to continue with the recovery without you getting a chance to check things out.)

Complete recovery without the DRA

We don't want you to rest on your laurels too much, so we're showing you a recovery without the DRA. The DRA won't help you in every situation. What if the file you need to restore has to go somewhere else? The DRA won't know where to put it.

Plus, it's good to understand how to recover without the DRA. You might find yourself in a non-12c database someday. The following method works all the way back to the dawn of Recovery Manager (as far as we know).

This example has you losing a data file but being unable to put it back in the same place. (By *you*, we mean *RMAN*.) You have to tell RMAN where to put the file; then RMAN will restore it to the proper location.

- ✔ You lost a disk with a data file on it.
- ✔ The disk won't be replaced, and you have to restore the data file elsewhere.
- ✔ You tell RMAN where to put the data file.
- ✔ You tell RMAN to restore the data file.
- ✔ You tell RMAN to recover the data file.
- ✔ If the database was closed, you open it. If the database was open, you online the data file.

This example using Oracle on Linux starts with the database closed; you open it and then fix the error. To create this error, we simply renamed the users01.dbf data file while the database was down.

1. **Start the database and read this error:**

   ```
   ORA-01157: cannot identify/lock data file 4 - see DBWR trace file
   ORA-01110: data file 4: '/u01/app/oracle/oradata/dev12c/users01.dbf'
   ```

2. **See if that is the only missing file:**

   ```
   <select * from v$recover_file;>
   ```

3. **Determine whether this is the only file affected and whether it is a critical file.**

   You also determine that it must be restored to a different disk.

4. **Launch RMAN and take the data file offline:**

   ```
   <alter database datafile 4 offline;>
   ```

   You see this:

   ```
   using target database control file instead of recovery catalog
   Statement processed
   ```

5. **Open the database:**

   ```
   <alter database open;>
   ```

6. **Tell RMAN to restore to the correct location:**

```
<run {
set newname for datafile 4 to '/u02/app/oracle/oradata/dev12c/users01.dbf';
restore tablespace users;
switch datafile all;
recover tablespace users;
}>
```

In this case, it is disk u02, a different location. The output indicates that the file is being restored and recovered in the new location:

```
executing command: SET NEWNAME

Starting restore at 30-JUN-2013 11:48:46
using target database control file instead of recovery catalog
channel ORA_DISK_1: SID=7 device type=DISK
channel ORA_DISK_1: restoring datafile 00004
input datafile copy RECID=12 STAMP=819457925 file name=/u01/app/oracle/
          fast_recovery_area/DEV12C/datafile/o1_mf_users_8x0lp5mo_.dbf
destination for restore of datafile 00004: /u02/app/oracle/oradata/dev12c/
          users01.dbf
channel ORA_DISK_1: copied datafile copy of datafile 00004
output file name=/u02/app/oracle/oradata/dev12c/users01.dbf RECID=13
          STAMP=819460128
Finished restore at 30-JUN-2013 11:48:49
datafile 4 switched to datafile copy
Starting recover at 30-JUN-2013 11:48:49
using channel ORA_DISK_1
starting media recovery
...output snipped...
media recovery complete, elapsed time: 00:00:01
Finished recover at 30-JUN-2013 11:48:52
```

7. **When the recovery finishes, alter the tablespace to put it back online:**

```
<alter tablespace users online;>
```

Quite a few more steps without the DRA, isn't it? Either way, it's not too difficult. If you haven't already, make sure you set up a test database and practice these and other scenarios. You'll be a recovery expert in no time at all.

Incomplete recovery

Incomplete recovery is usually a very unfortunate position to be in. Typically, it means you will be losing data (hence *incomplete*). Also, the DRA cannot help at all in this situation. In an incomplete recovery scenario, the database has not actually failed. Someone has done something to put the database in a state that requires you to go back in time.

Here's a situation where incomplete recovery may apply:

It is Sunday morning. You have taken a backup of your database last night. You are in archive log mode.

At 1:00 p.m., Barry tells you he accidentally dropped a major table out of the accounting schema around 11:45 a.m. Not only did he drop it, but he purged it from the Recyclebin because he "knew it was the right one." It wasn't. Assuming you have no other way to retrieve the table from a logical backup or re-create it, you decide incomplete recovery is your only choice. You will take the database down to restore the backup from last night. Then you will roll the database forward to 11:44 a.m. and open it.

Any transactions that occurred between 11:45 and 1:00 p.m. will be lost and have to be manually re-entered.

A key piece of information is that Barry told you he dropped the table at 11:45 a.m.

Spend a few minutes doing some research to verify that the reported time is truthful. If you roll forward too far, the table will be dropped again during the recovery process, and you will have to start over.

Here are the steps to incomplete recovery:

1. **Shut down the database.**
2. **Start up the database in mount mode.**
3. **Set the time for the restore to work from.**
4. **Restore the database.**
5. **Recover the database.**
6. **Open the database with RESETLOGS.**

   The control files won't match the data files. You have to re-sync the control files with the data files.

7. **Open a prompt to your OS command line.**
8. **Log in to your database with RMAN:**

   ```
   <rman target /
   ```

9. **Put the database in mount mode:**

   ```
   <shutdown immediate>
   <startup mount>
   ```

10. **Use the following RMAN command to recover your database to the appropriate time (11:44 a.m. in this case):**

```
RMAN> run {
set until time =
"to_date('30-JUN-2013:11:44:00','DD-MON-YYYY:HH24:MI:SS')";
restore database;
recover database;
sql "alter database open resetlogs";
}
```

When the command completes, you should see something like this:

```
executing command: SET until clause

Starting restore at 30-JUN-2013 11:58:52
allocated channel: ORA_DISK_1
channel ORA_DISK_1: SID=20 device type=DISK
…output snipped…
Finished recover at 30-JUN-2013 12:02:56
sql statement: alter database open resetlogs
```

11. **Make sure the table you were trying to recover has indeed been recovered.**

There's nothing more embarrassing than telling everybody you recovered data only to have someone else discover that the data still isn't there. If you discover it isn't there, do the recovery again, going back a little farther in time.

After any type of recovery, take a fresh, full backup immediately — just in case. We recommend it as a best practice — especially for a RESETLOGS recovery.

Recovering your database with copies

Copies allow for superfast recovery and fewer technical recoveries when you've lost a disk and the file has to go to a different location.

Some DBAs would argue that it's incorrect to use the copy in the place you backed it up. Good DBAs subscribe to the mantra "Everything has its place; everything in its place." However, times are changing. For example, the popularity of large *storage area networks* (SANs), where all your files go to the same place, is growing. DBAs don't have as much responsibility to organize, separate, stripe, and label data, nor do they have as much time. The SAN does all the protection and striping for you. Furthermore, Oracle has even released, in essence, its own volume manager: *Automatic Storage Management* (ASM). ASM can help you:

✔ Relax your regimented file and naming conventions.

✔ Find more time to make better use of the features that Oracle has to protect and manage data.

You get a call from a user who is getting the following error:

```
SQL> select *
 2 from emp;
from emp
     *
ERROR at line 2:
ORA-01116: error in opening database file 4
ORA-01110: data file 4: '/u02/app/oracle/oradata/dev12c/users01.dbf'
ORA-27041: unable to open file
Linux-x86_64 Error: 2: No such file or directory
Additional information: 3
```

After some investigation, you see that someone has removed the data file from the USERS tablespace. This tablespace is critical and must be recovered immediately. You decide to recover with RMAN using a COPY of the data file.

1. **Log in to your target with RMAN.**

2. **Make sure you have a copy of your USERS tablespace data file:**

```
<list copy of tablespace users;>
```

You should see something like this:

```
List of Datafile Copies
=========================

Key     File S Completion Time        Ckp SCN    Ckp Time
------- ---- - -------------------- ---------- --------------------
19      4    A 30-JUN-2013 12:11:31 2365031    30-JUN-2013 12:11:30
        Name: /u01/app/oracle/fast_recovery_area/DEV12C/datafile/o1_mf_
             users_8x0p5lyh_.dbf
        Tag: LEVEL0_COPY

12      4    A 30-JUN-2013 11:12:05 2356203    30-JUN-2013 11:12:05
        Name: /u01/app/oracle/fast_recovery_area/DEV12C/datafile/o1_mf_
             users_8x0lp5mo_.dbf
        Tag: LEVEL0_COPY

7       4    A 30-JUN-2013 11:08:20 2355686    30-JUN-2013 11:08:20
        Name: /u01/app/oracle/fast_recovery_area/DEV12C/datafile/o1_mf_
             users_8x0lh47j_.dbf
        Tag: USERS_COPY

6       4    A 30-JUN-2013 11:08:08 2355658    30-JUN-2013 11:08:08
        Name: /u01/app/oracle/fast_recovery_area/DEV12C/datafile/o1_mf_
             users_8x0lgrkr_.dbf
        Tag: TAG20130630T110808
```

```
5       4   A 30-JUN-2013 11:08:04 2355632     30-JUN-2013 11:08:03
        Name: /u01/app/oracle/fast_recovery_area/DEV12C/datafile/o1_mf_
             users_8x01gmrf_.dbf
        Tag: TAG20130630T110430
```

3. **Take the tablespace offline (because the database is open):**

```
< sql "alter tablespace users offline";>
```

You see this:

```
sql statement: alter tablespace users offline
```

4. **Switch to the copy:**

```
<switch tablespace users to copy;>
```

You see something like this:

```
datafile 4 switched to datafile copy "/u01/app/oracle/fast_recovery_area/
           DEV12C/datafile/o1_mf_users_8x0p5lyh_.dbf"
```

5. **Recover the copy that was taken earlier:**

```
<recover tablespace users;>
```

You see something like this:

```
Starting recover at 30-JUN-2013 12:21:52
allocated channel: ORA_DISK_1
channel ORA_DISK_1: SID=48 device type=DISK

starting media recovery
media recovery complete, elapsed time: 00:00:00

Finished recover at 30-JUN-2013 12:21:53
```

6. **Alter the tablespace to put it back online:**

```
<alter tablespace users online;>
```

You see this:

```
Statement processed
```

All done! Do you see how quick that was without having to restore the file? Of course, you have to come to terms with it being in your Fast Recovery Area. If that really bugs you, you can do one of the following:

✔ You can rename the file and move it later when you have a maintenance window.

✔ When you take the copy, you can copy the file to an auxiliary area outside your Fast Recovery Area (where you don't mind it being) in case you have to use it.

Chapter 12

Troubleshooting an Oracle Database

In This Chapter

▶ Using a system-level troubleshooting methodology

▶ Troubleshooting with Oracle database logs

▶ Employing other diagnostic utilities

*N*o matter what the salespeople claim, any system made by mortal beings will have issues and sometimes even break; that's reality. Worse yet, those same salespeople who claimed their system was perfect aren't around to fix it when it does break; that's *your* job. Fortunately, this chapter provides the information you need when problems arise.

Before jumping into database-specific diagnostic techniques, we give you a method for troubleshooting at the system level. Remember: Oracle exists as part of an overall information *system*. Here you explore the methods and tools you need to operate at system level.

Oracle provides a wealth of information, almost an overload, in its multiple log and trace files. Between the different files and tracing levels, odds are good that the information you need to solve the problem is there somewhere . . . if you know where to look for it. We provide that knowledge.

Just when you thought you couldn't get any more information about your Oracle database, we do just that via Oracle diagnostic tools and scripts. We're not showing tools that provide pointless data; rather, we explain tools that provide fast, actionable information.

Troubleshooting with System Methodology

If an Oracle crash hasn't happened to you yet, it will happen sometime. When it does, it won't be at a convenient time.

The problem is that people assume that because they have an Oracle-based system, the problem must be with Oracle. It could be, but you don't know just yet. Oracle is simply a component of a larger system, and the root cause and solution may not be Oracle-based. Even if you get an Oracle database error message, the cause may be something outside of Oracle. We often see people become so focused on the specific error message that they lose awareness of the overall system environment hosting the database. Be sure to look at the overall *system* supporting the database, not just the database itself.

Don't react to a problem report on face level. Apply a structured, repeatable pattern when addressing problems. We can't stress this next statement enough: *Yours is a technical profession, and you're paid to solve problems, not simply to react and hope for a quick fix.*

Everyone has a troubleshooting methodology tailored for their unique environment, but we suggest the following as a start:

1. **Identify the real problem.** Determine and confirm what's happening in the system.

2. **Perform basic system checks.** Check the server, operating environment, and connectivity for outright errors and performance degradation.

3. **Perform basic database checks.** Confirm that the database is running and see whether you can log in to it.

4. **Determine what your error messages mean.**

5. **Develop a solution and apply it.** Confirm that the fix works and that there aren't unintended consequences.

With experience and time, you will modify these steps for your environment. Depending on the situation, you may process some steps very fast — but they're still processed, not skipped.

Identifying the real problem

Before doing anything to fix the perceived problem, you need to *know* what the *real* problem is. You can't guess or assume. It's far better to treat the real cause of a problem, not just the symptoms.

People reporting problems get excited, miss key details, make assumptions, and often inaccurately state the nature and severity of a problem; that's simply human nature. If you think otherwise, ask any cop or ER doctor about the quality of the initial witness reports they receive. This is exacerbated in computer work because many people who are reporting problems aren't technical and can't articulate their problems very well.

You need to determine what system component has the problem and what is specifically happening before you can develop and apply a fix. Ask the following questions:

- ✔ **What:** What specifically is happening? Have the user walk through what he's doing when the error occurs. Work directly with the person having problems and monitor the issue in real time rather than getting second- or third-hand information. Get screen shots or the error messages themselves.

- ✔ **Who:** Who's being impacted? Is it one or two users? Is it a specific subclassification of users? Is it everyone? Also, is it your production, test, or development system? Never assume that because someone is excited, it must be production. Trying to fix the wrong database will leave you blushing with embarrassment.

- ✔ **Where:** Are affected users spread over a wide geographic location, or are they in a specific city or building?

- ✔ **When:** How long has this been occurring, and has it occurred before? Also, does it happen every time or just sometimes? If it happens only occasionally, drill down into what's being done prior to the error. If it occurred only since a recent system change (such as a patch, an upgrade, or a reboot), that can be a valuable clue. The question "What has recently changed in the system?" is a *great* one to ask!

- ✔ **How bad:** Is this a total loss of service where the company is stopped, or is it just an annoyance on a seldom-used development system?

After asking these questions, you should know what's happening, who it's happening to, how bad it is, and when it started. You should also have a rough idea of what subsystem or components to start checking.

Keep a cool head when troubleshooting hot issues; be methodical and work in a logical manner until the problem is fixed (and confirmed to be fixed). Other people may become excited, stressed, or unprofessional, but you need to keep your wits and professionalism as you work toward a solution. Don't let yourself be intimidated by irate users or management standing over your shoulder.

Performing basic system checks

You need to perform basic system checks to ensure the system is in a state that can support a database. If the network is down, server is overloaded, or disk system has run out of space, your database may be impacted and display database errors, but the root problem is system related.

Investigate these key areas:

✔ **Network:** Can you connect to the server or application?

✔ **Server utilization:** What are the top processes on the server?

✔ **CPU utilization:** Is the CPU maxed out?

✔ **Memory:** How much memory is available?

✔ **Available disk space:** Is there disk space available?

✔ **System event logs:** Is anything being reported to the system?

You don't need to be a system administrator to perform these checks.

Network

If you can't connect to the database server, odds are good that your users can't either. You have two easy ways to check this:

✔ Ping to test server connectivity.

✔ Log in to the server as the Oracle user.

From the DOS or Linux command prompt, type **ping SERVER NAME** to see whether the target server can be reached.

```
$ ping oralinux1
PING oralinux1 (192.168.2.121) 56(84) bytes of data.
64 bytes from oralinux1 (192.168.2.121): icmp_seq=1 ttl=64 time=0.020 ms
64 bytes from oralinux1 (192.168.2.121): icmp_seq=2 ttl=64 time=0.007 ms
64 bytes from oralinux1 (192.168.2.121): icmp_seq=3 ttl=64 time=0.007 ms

--- oralinux1 ping statistics ---
3 packets transmitted, 3 received, 0% packet loss, time 1999ms
rtt min/avg/max/mdev = 0.007/0.011/0.020/0.006 ms
```

In the preceding code, three ping packets were sent, and all three arrived successfully. Depending on the ping version, you get back slightly different output, but all outputs specify whether the server was reachable.

If the server comes back as unavailable, the problem is one of these things:

✔ The server is shut down.

✔ The network is down.

✔ You're prevented from pinging servers.

Sometimes security blocks the ping utility, so check whether it works before problems occur so you know the test is valid.

After you confirm the server can be reached, try actually logging in as the owner of the Oracle software if possible. Note that on some systems you have to log in as yourself (for security-auditing purposes) and then switch users to the Oracle software owner. This action confirms the server is not only running but also able to support a login attempt.

Server utilization

If a program, process, or job is consuming all the resources on a server and has been doing so for a long enough time, a database can

- Slow down
- Be rendered unusable
- Be killed (in rare cases)

The processes themselves may be one of three things: valid, a competing database (multiple databases can be on the same server), or an out-of-control, runaway process.

You must identify the programs that are running before you can determine whether they're valid or hurting the system. There are several graphical tools to do this.

- On **Windows,** use Windows Task Manager to see which applications are running (under the Applications tab). For more detail, use the Processes tab shown in Figure 12-1.

- For **Linux/UNIX,** use the command top to display the top processes on a server and their *process ID* (PID), as shown in Figure 12-2. The output is text based and refreshed every few seconds.

Additionally, at the top of the screen is the machine's *load average*. This derived value reflects relative load on the server.

- Values up to 3 are light and shouldn't reflect performance problems.
- Values in the teens reflect higher use of a busy system, and performance may suffer.
- Values above 20 indicate a busy system where performance is likely impacted.

For **Linux/UNIX**, the uptime command helps you see system load:

```
$ uptime
 23:13:03 up 4 days, 10:27,  1 user,  load average: 0.00, 0.00, 0.00
```

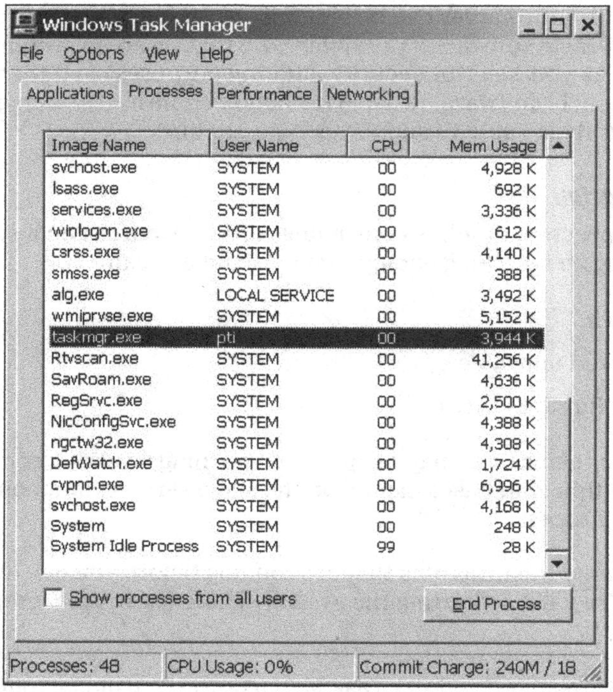

Figure 12-1:
Windows
Task
Manager
has multiple
processes
executing
as multiple
users via the
Processes
tab.

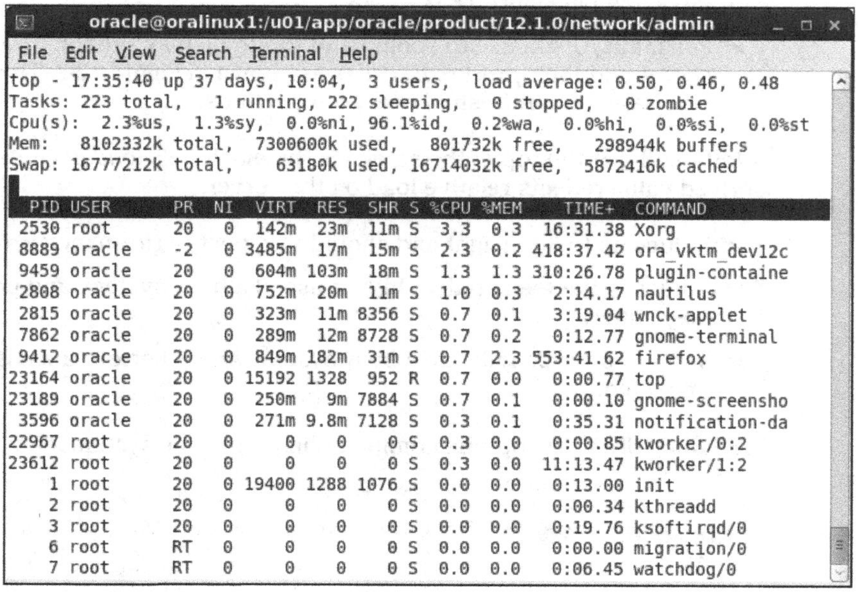

Figure 12-2:
The top util-
ity shows
the top
processes.

Moonlighting

Have you ever noticed that the system time examples in many technical books are often late at night or very early in the morning, like the 11:13 p.m. example regarding the uptime command? Many, if not most, technical authors are primarily consultants or otherwise actively working in their field full time. The benefit to you, the reader, is you get good, practical, and current information. The negative for us, the writers, is we don't get a lot of sleep during these projects!

System load values are the same as with the top command:

- ✔ The leftmost value is the current load.
- ✔ The middle value is the load 5 minutes previous.
- ✔ The rightmost value is the load 15 minutes prior.

Another useful value is the time since the last server restart. Obviously if users reported problems and you see the server recently rebooted a few minutes prior, the server reboot (or crash) is the likely culprit.

- ✔ On **UNIX Oracle Solaris** systems, prstat is an alternative to top.
- ✔ On **HP-UX** systems, the glance command is extremely useful.

CPU utilization

Servers may have single or multiple CPUs. Regardless, processing needs to be available for the server to process application requests.

If a machine has a very high or complete CPU use, performance issues will occur.

- ✔ On **Windows,** the previously mentioned Windows Task Manager has a Performance tab. That tab displays CPU use as a percentage and as recent spikes; see Figure 12-3.
- ✔ For **Linux/UNIX** systems, the previously described top command displays CPU utilization at the top of the screen.

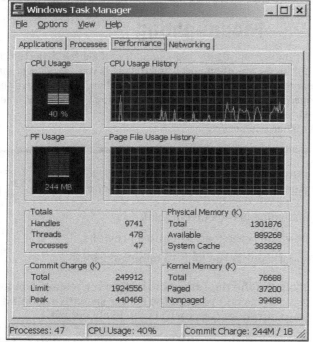

Memory

If the server is lacking memory, system performance suffers or even stands still. It isn't desirable to run a server with little or no memory available. If you find the server is consistently memory starved, either add more memory or reduce the amount of memory allocated for programs.

- ✔ To check memory on **Windows**, the Windows Task Manager Performance tab provides the total memory on the machine and amount available.

- ✔ **Linux/UNIX** systems have multiple tools to check memory, but the top utility provides this information rapidly.

Available disk space

Disk space is different than *disk utilization*. The frequency of reads and writes on a disk is utilization and can be a major performance factor. Running out of available disk space can bring your system to a halt and is the focus here because you, as the DBA, can do something about it.

However, poor disk utilization won't often bring your system to a complete standstill without warning. Measuring and accurately interpreting disk utilization, especially in large SAN environments, is outside the scope of this book. You should work with your storage engineers to address that topic.

What can happen when a disk fills up? It depends on what's writing to that disk. At minimum, log files can't be written to and tablespaces can't be expanded. At worst, archive log files can't be successfully written, and the database hangs. With other software, processes can spin high amounts of CPU, and Java Virtual Machines can crash. Any one of these problems is likely to generate a panicked call to your desk.

The quickest way to check for disk space is to see if any file systems are 100 percent full.

- ✔ For **Windows** systems, the fastest way is to go to My Computer and look at free space for each disk drive. Be sure to have the Details option selected on the View tab to get the full information.

- ✔ The df -m command helps **Linux** and Oracle Solaris users:

```
$ df -m
Filesystem           1M-blocks     Used Available Use% Mounted on
/dev/sda3                 8064     3587      4068  47% /
tmpfs                     3957     1885      2072  48% /dev/shm
/dev/sda5                 8064      208      7447   3% /home
/dev/sda6                 8064      147      7508   2% /tmp
/dev/sda1                64310    17016     44028  28% /u01
/dev/sr0                  2367     2367         0 100% /media/
                                                       Oracle12cBeta
```

This code shows the file systems, their percentage used, percentage free (available), and the actual amounts in megabytes. The df -k command can show the same info but listed in kilobytes. The –k flag is useful because some versions of UNIX don't support the -m flag.

- ✔ On **HP-UX UNIX** systems, use bdf.

System event logs

If all else fails, listen to what the computer is telling you. As a DBA, you should have at least read access to the system event logs on your server and hopefully all servers that are part of the application. System event logs record routine events on the server but also may list special error events that could be the cause of your system problems. Sometimes the event logs clearly list hardware issues, or that the file systems are full, or that the machine just rebooted or crashed. All of these are good things to know when you're trying to track down a problem.

The location of the event logs can vary, and often additional logs are beyond the OS logs to review when you learn your system.

✔ On **Windows** systems, go to Control Panel➪Administrative Tools➪Event Viewer to see the system and application logs.

✔ On **Linux/UNIX** systems, /var/adm/messages and /var/log/syslog are quite valuable. The dmesg command can see the end of the most recent system log file.

Much of this information may not make sense to a DBA who isn't OS savvy; however, seeing errors can be enough to seek the opinion of the system administrator.

Performing basic database checks

If you've confirmed you can get to the server and that it should be able to support an application database, perform three basic database checks:

✔ Verify the database is running.

✔ Verify Oracle Net functionality.

✔ Perform a database connection.

Running database instance

You should check whether the database is actually running because, sometimes, databases crash, fail to startup, or for whatever reason are not running when they should be running. Automated monitoring tools to detect if a database is not running are plentiful, but every DBA should know how to check if their database is indeed running.

Oracle database instances execute with different mandatory processes, such as PMON.

✔ On **Windows** systems, go to Control Panel➪Administrative Tools➪ Services to see whether the Oracle service has started. You can also look under Windows Task Manager to find similar information.

✔ On **Linux/UNIX** systems, simply check for the PMON process. Without PMON, there's no Oracle database instance running.

```
$ ps -ef|grep pmon
oracle    8885      1  0 Jul20 ?        00:04:51 ora_pmon_dev12c
```

The PMON process is for dev12c, which is a running Oracle database. You could search for additional database processes, but if you know PMON is, you can safely assume the rest of the database instance is running too.

After you confirm a working basic network infrastructure and a connectable database server, you have to confirm the Oracle Net infrastructure is working so users can connect to the database.

Oracle Net functionality

Execute tnsping from the DOS or Linux command prompt. It uses the Oracle Net protocol to see whether it can connect to the database.

```
$ tnsping dev12c

TNS Ping Utility for Linux: Version 12.1.0.1.0 - Production on 02-AUG-2013
          17:37:36

Copyright (c) 1997, 2013, Oracle.  All rights reserved.

Used parameter files:
/u01/app/grid/12.1.0/network/admin/sqlnet.ora


Used TNSNAMES adapter to resolve the alias
Attempting to contact (DESCRIPTION = (ADDRESS_LIST = (ADDRESS = (PROTOCOL = TCP)
          (HOST = oralinux1)(PORT = 1521))) (CONNECT_DATA = (SERVICE_NAME =
          dev12c)))
OK (40 msec)
```

Note how the output from a tnsping specifies the host, port, and SID information for that database. This information is valuable when troubleshooting errors.

- ✔ If the output for host, port, or SID doesn't match what you know to be correct, it is a clue.
- ✔ If output for the tnsping doesn't come back at all, it may be a network or server failure.
- ✔ Depending on the Oracle error returned, a tnsping test may suggest an error with the database listener process.

Database connection

When you know the database is up and you can establish an Oracle Net communications handshake, log in to see whether you can establish a database session.

1. **Identify the problem tier that users are reporting.**

   In a client-server application, this tier is the workstation.

   In a multi-tier architecture, this tier is likely the web application server.

2. From the tier where the problem exists, try logging in to the database via SQL*Plus, preferably as a typical user, to mimic the connection which is failing.

Here's connecting as an application user to a remote database dev12c:

```
$ sqlplus dwilson@dev12c

SQL*Plus: Release 12.1.0.1.0 Production on Fri Aug 2 17:38:32 2013

Copyright (c) 1982, 2013, Oracle.  All rights reserved.

Enter password:
Last Successful login time: Sat Jul 20 2013 11:05:24 -04:00

Connected to:
Oracle Database 12c Enterprise Edition Release 12.1.0.1.0 - 64bit
          Production
With the Partitioning, OLAP, Advanced Analytics and Real Application
          Testing options

SQL> show user
USER is "DWILSON"
```

The SQL*Plus attempt shows a successful connection to a remote database as an application user. You want to force the use of the Oracle Net infrastructure in this test. The @dev12c denotes that you'll use Oracle Net to connect to the remote database rather than directly logging in if you're already on the same server.

If you logged in, you're done with your basic database checks; you confirmed a user can connect to the database. On the other hand, you may have encountered any of the following common errors:

✔ **You cannot archive the log file.** If the archive dump destination is full, or for any other reason the archiver processes can't properly write the archive log file, your login attempt fails. Oracle does this because even a login generates archive log information and Oracle guarantees it will track that information or it won't perform the action.

Fix: Resolve that archiver problem.

You can always log in on the server itself with / as sysdba to perform maintenance.

✔ **The database is in a restricted session.** The database may be running, but if it's in a restricted session, then only users with RESTRICTED SESSION system privilege can log in. Generally, the database is in the state because some form of database maintenance is occurring and the DBA doesn't want normal users in the system.

Fix: Determine why the database is in restricted session mode and take it out of that mode if appropriate. Or you can grant RESTRICTED SESSION to the user(s), but that usually defeats the purpose of having restricted session.

✔ **The login simply hangs.** Sometimes the login attempt hangs and doesn't immediately generate an error message. These can be tough to diagnose because you're not getting any feedback.

Fix: Try connecting from a different tier. Also try logging in from the database server itself; see whether you can find where you can connect from and generate an actionable log message. Also revalidate your network, server, and system checks to confirm that they're valid and then search for error messages.

Performing basic database checks is a way to confirm there's nothing obviously wrong with the database, such as it isn't running or you can't connect to it. After you perform those checks, you can begin the more detailed problem and error log analysis.

Analyzing error messages

Ever hear the expression "hiding in plain sight"? That phrase often applies when people see an Oracle error message. They see the message, but they don't actually read it and think about what it says. As a result, the most valuable clue you have isn't fully maximized.

Avoid falling into that trap. Make the most of your error messages:

✔ **Slow down and read the error message — several times if necessary.** Think about what it's saying. Don't just rattle off ORA-1234 and the description. Ask yourself what specific action is failing based on the context of the error message and what is going on at the time of the message.

✔ **Pretend you're the application and ask what you were doing when the error occurred.** Then apply the text of the message to see which piece or action is failing. Breaking down a larger process into individual steps and performing each step to see where something breaks is an effective troubleshooting technique.

✔ **Apply most of your focus on the *first* error message you receive.** Often a series of error messages occurs related to one event, but typically that first message is the cause of the other messages.

✔ **Know the types of error messages and which components they relate to:**

• ORA denotes database or SQL errors.

• TNS denotes database listener or Oracle Net communication issues.

- HTTP is web related.

- LDAP denotes details with your directory server, perhaps Oracle Internet Directory.

The architecture of your system determines what components may generate errors. Know what components exist within the system and the process flow so you can tell what part of the system is failing based on the type of message.

✔ **Become familiar with normal messages versus extraordinary error messages.** Many harmless informational messages crop up for events that aren't errors — particularly when working with log files. Know what your system logs look like during normal operations so that when real errors occur, you can identify them easily.

✔ **Plug the error message into My Oracle Support (formerly Oracle Metalink) and your favorite Internet search utilities to get more detailed descriptions and possible fixes.** Expect lots of irrelevant information and false leads. But odds are good that your search results will also include information that helps identify and fix the problem.

Knowing database and system anatomy

A firm understanding of Oracle database architecture and processes is key to your ability to understand error messages and diagnostic output. Think of it as database anatomy. You would flee if your doctor said "I don't really understand that heart stuff," right? Similarly, what kind of DBA is clueless about the SYSTEM tablespace? Even if you think you know it, a periodic review of Chapter 2 is time well spent for any DBA.

Where in the overall system does your database fit, and what are the components? If people are reporting an HTTP-404 error, you probably want to get the web administrator involved because the problem may be a web server or content. But if your database generates the HTML content via mod_plsql Web Toolkit, it may actually be your database having issues. Not knowing that would result in the problem being routed to the wrong people, further delaying the fix. There simply is no substitute for knowing the specifics of how your system works and being able to apply that knowledge.

Error system example

Look at this example of a common message that confuses people. Upon analysis, the cause is simple to identify.

```
ORA-01034: ORACLE not available.
```

ORA denotes a database message (versus TNS for a listener or HTTP for a web error). What does *Instance not available* mean in terms of databases? If you know database architecture, you know that an *instance* is the memory and background processes for a database. Thus, the database instance may not be running; you need to confirm that.

A quick `ps -ef | grep pmon` on the server shows no PMON process running, so now you have confirmed the database instance is down. A further check using the uptime command shows the server was restarted 15 minutes ago; you can assume the database didn't restart after a server crash or reboot. At this point, you can check database logs to see whether the instance tried to restart and failed or no attempt was made to restart. Based on that, you can manually restart the database and get users back to work.

oerr utility

The oerr utility gets more information about an error message. This command-line utility is where you specify an error number and the oerr utility provides the most likely problem causes and possible solutions. Although it isn't in-depth troubleshooting, it is very handy:

```
$ oerr ora 1034
01034, 00000, "ORACLE not available"
// *Cause: Oracle was not started up. Possible causes include the following:
//          - The SGA requires more space than was allocated for it.
//          - The operating-system variable pointing to the instance is
//            improperly defined.
// *Action: Refer to accompanying messages for possible causes and correct
//          the problem mentioned in the other messages.
//          If Oracle has been initialized, then on some operating systems,
//          verify that Oracle was linked correctly. See the platform
//          specific Oracle documentation.
```

Developing and applying a solution

How do you fix a problem? Sometimes it is a simple command that is obvious even to the most inexperienced administrator. More commonly it is a multi-step operation that may span both database and non-database areas. Consider these guidelines as you develop and implement your plan.

For very simple and obvious fixes, you clearly aren't going to apply every step listed in the following exhaustive detail. However, you should review the guidelines and see how they apply to what you're doing.

Technical fixes and software patches don't always work, which is outside your control. However, planning the repair process is something you can control, and it will better the odds of your success greatly.

Researching

You should *understand* what is happening and *why*. What is causing the problem and how is that best remedied?

- Review the error messages.
- Read the documentation.
- Search the Internet.
- Talk to other administrators.
- Get Oracle Support assistance.

It's dangerous to apply a fix when you don't know why something is occurring. Only through understanding will you have the confidence that whatever fix you apply is the right one and won't cause further damage.

Develop the pseudo-code list of steps that you will need to perform based on your research. This task may bring up more questions as it is developed, but that's good. The end product is a high-level plan for fixing the problem.

Planning

How will you specifically fix the problem? After creating your high-level plan, make it technically detailed:

- Identify the technical substeps for each high-level pseudo-code step.
- Know what commands need to be issued and by which account.
- Know the time necessary for each step to occur and dependencies between steps.
- If additional software or patches are required, make sure those needs are addressed.

Have another administrator review your fix-planning steps to make sure you haven't skipped anything.

Ramifications

If you perform the fix, what are the side effects?

- Will you have to restart and place the system in restricted session for a complex fix, kicking off system users?
- How long will the system be unavailable? Remember to leave yourself a margin for error and unexpected issues.
- When is the best downtime to impose a reduced impact on end users while still having outside support if needed?
- Can you perform the fix solo, from end to end, or do you need help from other groups (such as networking or the system administrator)?
- Does the fix void your software warranty or break other components?

Unfortunately, not all solutions are easy decisions and sometimes there are downsides to a fix. Carefully weigh the benefits of a fix and the negatives of the existing problem against the downsides of implementing the fix. Be sure to include input from all affected parties to allow a more informed decision.

Coordinating with other groups and the user community for a fix is often a big hurdle when working on large, distributed, and complex systems. It's helpful to have management support as well as documented policies and procedures to support coordination efforts.

Testing

Don't tell me you're trying something in production before testing it first! If at all possible, re-create the problem in a test environment and apply the fix there before doing it in production.

Testing accomplishes these things:

✔ Ensures your steps are complete

✔ Provides accurate timeframes for the total fix

✔ Verifies your syntax with the opportunity to make mistakes

✔ Confirms the problem is actually fixed

✔ Verifies there are no unintended consequences

Many organizations are under mandate to test changes before going into production, and that is generally a good policy. When you're troubleshooting complex problems or operating on large amounts of data, testing is even more important.

We've seen many ill-advised attempts at applying untested fixes that ended in disastrous results. Don't let that happen to you.

Fallback options

The fix doesn't work and things go from bad to worse. You do have a fallback plan, right? A good administrator always has a workable fallback plan for when things go wrong. Those who don't, sooner or later, end up seeking other employment opportunities.

Before performing nearly any technical fix, do these things:

✔ Take another database backup or verify that your most recent backups are valid and accessible.

✔ If backups are stored offsite for disaster recovery, recall those backups. You may need them before you start your maintenance operation.

✔ Consider taking multiple backup copies too, in case one copy is bad. Parachutists jump with a backup chute; shouldn't you?

After large amounts of data have been modified, can it be undone without a backup? You may need to work with the application developers on data changes. Also consider other items that need to be undone outside the database. For example, a network change with DNS may require several hours to take effect. If you push a change to thousands of client workstations, how do you roll that back if necessary?

Support

Odds are good that you'll be performing your maintenance over a weekend or late at night. If so, are the other people available to perform their parts of the fix?

✔ Do you have everyone's phone numbers?

✔ Are they willing and able to help you at 3 a.m. when you discover a problem? Be sure to let them know you may require their assistance *before* you start your work.

✔ Are they authorized to make the change?

Verification

Who is going to test and confirm the fix actually worked? A test plan with testers or knowledgeable users is a good idea, particularly if data or application changes are necessary.

✔ Run through the plan first; otherwise you may discover broken parts of the application unrelated to the problem you're attempting to fix.

✔ Make sure these testers are available when you're done with your work.

Backup

After you've developed, tested, applied, and verified your technical fix, what's the final step before turning it over to the users? Often the final step is performing a full database or system backup. The benefit is that if something unrelated occurs and you need to restore, you don't need to go through the previous fix.

Troubleshooting Using Oracle Database Logs

You need to dive into the Oracle logs themselves. Each database has a set of directories where key log, trace, and dump files are stored.

Database log infrastructure

Using log files to diagnose a problem is often a daily task for the DBA so knowing how Oracle manages this critical resource is important. Oracle log file structure and management are referred to as the *Automatic Diagnostic Repository* (ADR). ADR provides these log management capabilities:

- ✔ **Integrated log management** not just for the database but other Oracle products. Currently, Automatic Storage Management and listener also write to the new log infrastructure.
- ✔ **Event logging** in terms of incidents with included diagnostic data and stored in zip files that can be reviewed and sent to Oracle Support. The idea is to better compartmentalize error events and neatly package them so they can be sent directly to Oracle Support.
- ✔ **Incident flood control** to intelligently limit the creation and size of trace files. If an event repeats at an extreme rate above a defined threshold, only the occurrence of the event is logged.

It's important to know where the key diagnostic files are located:

- ✔ The location for the diagnostic subdirectories (diag) is the ADR_BASE and is typically under the ORACLE_BASE.
- ✔ The location of the base for the log subdirectories is the ADR_HOME and is defined by database parameter DIAGNOSTIC_DEST.
- ✔ The ADR_HOME is beneath the ADR_BASE location and is under the database SID directory.

The structure for ADR_HOME for databases follows:

```
$ADR_BASE/diag/rdbms/DATABASE NAME/DATABASE SID
```

For example, here's the following structure for the dev12c database:

```
$ ls $ORACLE_BASE/diag/rdbms/dev12c/dev12c
alert  hm        incpkg lck metadata      metadata_pv sweep
cdump  incident  ir     log metadata_dgif stage       trace
```

The ADR_HOME location is the full path up to and including the second reference to dev12c.

You see this same information neatly stored within the database and can be queried via V$DIAG_INFO:

```
SQL> select name, value from v$diag_info;

NAME            VALUE
-----------     ----------------------------------

Diag Enabled          TRUE
ADR Base              /u01/app/oracle
ADR Home              /u01/app/oracle/diag/rdbms/dev12c/dev12c
Diag Trace            /u01/app/oracle/diag/rdbms/dev12c/dev12c/trace
Diag Alert            /u01/app/oracle/diag/rdbms/dev12c/dev12c/alert
Diag Incident         /u01/app/oracle/diag/rdbms/dev12c/dev12c/incident
Diag Cdump            /u01/app/oracle/diag/rdbms/dev12c/dev12c1/cdump
Health Monitor        /u01/app/oracle/diag/rdbms/dev12c/dev12c/hm
Default Trace File
    /u01/app/oracle/diag/rdbms/dev12c/dev12c/trace/dev12c_ora_23293.trc
Active Problem Count  0
Active Incident Count 0

11 rows selected.
```

Within each database directory are subdirectories where different files are
stored. Table 12-1 lists each primary directory and its purpose.

Table 12-1 **Database Trace and Log Directories**

Directory	Purpose
alert	Stores very important XML-formatted alert log for database
cdump	Core dump location of memory stack when a process fails
incident	Subdirectories relating to individual events or incidents
trace	Trace and dump files for background and user processes; also contains text formatted alert log

This is a listing of each directory:

```
$ ls $ORACLE_BASE/diag/rdbms/dev12c/dev12c
alert   hm        incpkg lck metadata      metadata_pv  sweep
cdump   incident  ir     log metadata_dgif stage        trace
oralinux1> ls $ORACLE_BASE/diag/rdbms/dev12c/dev12c/alert
log.xml
$ ls $ORACLE_BASE/diag/rdbms/dev12c/dev12c/cdump
$ ls $ORACLE_BASE/diag/rdbms/dev12c/dev12c/incident
$ ls $ORACLE_BASE/diag/rdbms/dev12c/dev12c/trace
alert_dev12c.log        dev12c_m000_23037.trc dev12c_ora_6593.trm
dev12c_aqpc_24310.trc   dev12c_m000_23037.trm dev12c_ora_760.trc
```

These directories can get cluttered with many files and eat up disk space.

Have a process to clean up the trace, cdump, and incident directories so they don't fill up your disk and are easier to manage.

Database alert log

By far the most important file to review for a database is the alert log. This file is where database-level errors are written and operations such as startup, shutdown, and other events are logged. Oracle writes to this text-based file in a chronological order when the database is running.

The alert log is in the alert subdirectory and is named log.xml.

✔ Whenever a problem occurs, review the alert log file.

✔ Review the alert log file daily (if you're the DBA) to ensure errors are not occurring undetected.

Many DBAs even write scripts to scan the alert log for errors and have e-mail messages sent to them if key events are detected. Also, many DBAs copy off their alert log weekly to prevent it from becoming excessively large.

Here's a sample of an alert log file in XML format:

```
<msg time='2013-07-19T13:22:18.955-04:00' org_id='oracle' comp_id='rdbms'
 msg_id='opiexe:3292:2802784106' type='NOTIFICATION' group='admin_ddl'
 level='16' host_id='oralinux1' host_addr='192.168.1.66'
 module='sqlplus@oralinux1 (TNS V1-V3)' pid='24286'>
 <txt>Completed: CREATE DATABASE &quot;dev12c&quot;
MAXINSTANCES 8
MAXLOGHISTORY 1
MAXLOGFILES 16
MAXLOGMEMBERS 3
MAXDATAFILES 100
DATAFILE &apos;/u01/app/oracle/oradata/dev12c/system01.dbf&apos; SIZE 700M REUSE
 AUTOEXTEND ON NEXT  10240K MAXSIZE UNLIMITED
EXTENT MANAGEMENT LOCAL
SYSAUX DATAFILE &apos;/u01/app/oracle/oradata/dev12c/sysaux01.dbf&apos;
SIZE 550M REUSE AUTOEXTEND ON NEXT  10240K MAXSIZE UNLIMITED
SMALLFILE DEFAULT TEMPORARY TABLESPACE TEMP TEMPFILE &apos;/u01/app/oracle/orada
ta/dev12c/temp01.dbf&apos; SIZE 20M REUSE AUTOEXTEND ON NEXT  640K
MAXSIZE UNLIMITED
SMALLFILE UNDO TABLESPACE &quot;UNDOTBS1&quot; DATAFILE  &apos;
/u01/app/oracle/o
radata/dev12c/undotbs01.dbf&apos; SIZE 200M REUSE AUTOEXTEND ON NEXT  5120K
MAXSIZE UNLIMITED
CHARACTER SET WE8MSWIN1252
NATIONAL CHARACTER SET AL16UTF16
```

```
LOGFILE GROUP 1 (&apos;/u01/app/oracle/oradata/dev12c/redo01.log&apos;) SIZE
          50M,
GROUP 2 (&apos;/u01/app/oracle/oradata/dev12c/redo02.log&apos;) SIZE 50M,
GROUP 3 (&apos;/u01/app/oracle/oradata/dev12c/redo03.log&apos;) SIZE 50M
USER SYS IDENTIFIED BY  USER SYSTEM IDENTIFIED BY
  </txt>
</msg>
<msg time='2013-07-19T13:22:19.033-04:00' org_id='oracle' comp_id='rdbms'
 msg_id='opiexe:3209:4222364190' type='NOTIFICATION' group='admin_ddl'
 level='16' host_id='oralinux1' host_addr='192.168.1.66'
 module='sqlplus@oralinux1 (TNS V1-V3)' pid='24311'>
  <txt>CREATE SMALLFILE TABLESPACE &quot;USERS&quot; LOGGING  DATAFILE  &apos;/u0
1/app/oracle/oradata/dev12c/users01.dbf&apos; SIZE 5M REUSE AUTOEXTEND ON NEXT
1280K MAXSIZE UNLIMITED  EXTENT MANAGEMENT LOCAL  SEGMENT SPACE MANAGEMENT  AUTO
  </txt>
</msg>
```

This code shows routine messages for a database creation.

A text-formatted version is still available for people using command-line editors like vi or Notepad. It is in the trace subdirectory and has the standard name format alert_*SID*.log (which is alert_dev12c.log in this example). Without the XML tags, you can easily read it via a command-line utility.

Here's the same information as the XML file, but without the tags:

```
Fri Jul 19 13:21:21 2013
CREATE DATABASE "dev12c"
MAXINSTANCES 8
MAXLOGHISTORY 1
MAXLOGFILES 16
MAXLOGMEMBERS 3
MAXDATAFILES 100
DATAFILE '/u01/app/oracle/oradata/dev12c/system01.dbf' SIZE 700M REUSE
             AUTOEXTEND ON NEXT  10240K MAXSIZE UNLIMITED
EXTENT MANAGEMENT LOCAL
SYSAUX DATAFILE '/u01/app/oracle/oradata/dev12c/sysaux01.dbf' SIZE 550M REUSE
             AUTOEXTEND ON NEXT  10240K MAXSIZE UNLIMITED
SMALLFILE DEFAULT TEMPORARY TABLESPACE TEMP TEMPFILE '/u01/app/oracle/oradata/
             dev12c/temp01.dbf' SIZE 20M REUSE AUTOEXTEND ON NEXT  640K MAXSIZE
             UNLIMITED
SMALLFILE UNDO TABLESPACE "UNDOTBS1" DATAFILE  '/u01/app/oracle/oradata/dev12c/
             undotbs01.dbf' SIZE 200M REUSE AUTOEXTEND ON NEXT  5120K MAXSIZE
             UNLIMITED
CHARACTER SET WE8MSWIN1252
NATIONAL CHARACTER SET AL16UTF16
LOGFILE GROUP 1 ('/u01/app/oracle/oradata/dev12c/redo01.log') SIZE 50M,
GROUP 2 ('/u01/app/oracle/oradata/dev12c/redo02.log') SIZE 50M,
GROUP 3 ('/u01/app/oracle/oradata/dev12c/redo03.log') SIZE 50M
USER SYS IDENTIFIED BY  USER SYSTEM IDENTIFIED BY
Database mounted in Exclusive Mode
```

```
Lost write protection disabled
Ping without log force is disabled.
Using default pga_aggregate_limit of 2560 MB
Fri Jul 19 13:21:28 2013
db_recovery_file_dest_size of 4815 MB is 0.00% used. This is a
user-specified limit on the amount of space that will be used by this
database for recovery-related files, and does not reflect the amount of
space available in the underlying filesystem or ASM diskgroup.
Successful mount of redo thread 1, with mount id 3622234653
Using SCN growth rate of 16384 per second
Assigning activation ID 3622234653 (0xd7e6ea1d)
Starting background process TMON
Fri Jul 19 13:21:28 2013
TMON started with pid=24, OS id=24298
Thread 1 opened at log sequence 1
  Current log# 1 seq# 1 mem# 0: /u01/app/oracle/oradata/dev12c/redo01.log
Successful open of redo thread 1
```

Here's what an Oracle error looks like from a trace file:

```
*** KEWROCISTMTEXEC - encountered error: (ORA-06525: Length Mismatch for CHAR or
            RAW data
ORA-06512: at "SYS.DBMS_STATS", line 40111
```

Review and manage the alert log regularly so you can catch small issues before they grow into large problems.

Trace and dump files

When a problem event occurs (such as a failed process or failed memory allocation), log files for that event are written into the *trace directory*.

The format for the log filename is *SID_process name_process ID*.trc:

```
$ ls $ORACLE_BASE/diag/rdbms/dev12c/dev12c/trace
alert_dev12c.log        dev12c_m000_23037.trc  dev12c_ora_6593.trm
dev12c_aqpc_24310.trc  dev12c_m000_23037.trm  dev12c_ora_760.trc
```

Here are the contents of a trace file:

```
Trace file /u01/app/oracle/diag/rdbms/dev12c/dev12c/trace/dev12c_dbw0_24263.trc
Oracle Database 12c Enterprise Edition Release 12.1.0.1.0 - 64bit Production
With the Partitioning, OLAP, Advanced Analytics and Real Application Testing opt
ions
ORACLE_HOME = /u01/app/oracle/product/12.1.0
System name:    Linux
Node name:      oralinux1
Release:        2.6.39-400.17.2.el6uek.x86_64
Version:        #1 SMP Wed Mar 13 12:31:05 PDT 2013
```

```
Machine:         x86_64
Instance name: dev12c
Redo thread mounted by this instance: 0 <none>
Oracle process number: 11
Unix process pid: 24263, image: oracle@oralinux1 (DBW0)


*** 2013-07-19 13:21:21.458
*** CLIENT ID:() 2013-07-19 13:21:21.458
*** SERVICE NAME:() 2013-07-19 13:21:21.458
*** MODULE NAME:() 2013-07-19 13:21:21.458
*** ACTION NAME:() 2013-07-19 13:21:21.458


2013-07-19 13:21:21.458540 :kjcipctxinit(): (pid|psn)=(11|1): initialised and
linked pctx 0x125d93038 into process list
```

The difference between a dump and a trace file: A *trace* is an ongoing log of a problem event. The *dump* is the one-time dumping of information into a file for a problem event. As a DBA, you should review these text files to diagnose what is occurring.

If a process crashes, a core dump can be created in the cdump directory. This is a binary trace file of the memory process and its contents at the time of the crash. Although many people consider these to be "hands-off" for a DBA to review, that isn't necessarily the case. The Linux and UNIX strings command can show the printable text of a binary file. If you opt to upload the core file to any support organization, you may want to review it first for username and password combinations because they are sometimes present in clear text in these files.

Listener log

You may have to track connections into the database via the listener. Every time a connection to the database occurs, that event (or failure) is stored in the *listener log*. Chapter 5 goes into greater detail about the database listener architecture.

Knowing where listener logs are generated is important to troubleshooting. You can find the listener log under the ADR_BASE/diag/tnslsnr directory tree. (In this example, it's /u01/app/oracle/diag/tnslsnr/oralinux1/listener/trace/listener.log.)

Here's a sample log entry:

```
02-AUG-2013 17:38:48 * (CONNECT_DATA=(SERVICE_NAME=dev12c)
  (CID=(PROGRAM=sqlplus)(HOST=oralinux1)(USER=oracle))) *
  (ADDRESS=(PROTOCOL=tcp)(HOST=192.168.2.121)(PORT=21165))
  * establish * dev12c * 0
```

Key information is the time, host, and program for the incoming connections.

Here's a Dell TOAD software utility user connecting, most likely from a user's workstation:

```
02-AUG-2013  11:57:45 * (CONNECT_DATA=(SERVICE_NAME=192.168.2.121)
   (CID=(PROGRAM=C:\Program?Files\Quest?Software\TOAD\TOAD.exe)
   (HOST=LPT-MPYLE)(USER=mpyle))) * (ADDRESS=(PROTOCOL=tcp)
   (HOST=192.168.2.170) (PORT=3108))
   * establish * 192.168.2.121 * 12514
```

Finally, an error is occurring:

```
TNS-12514: TNS:listener does not currently know of service
            requested in connect descriptor
```

 You can search for the *Transport Network Substrate* (TNS) error code in the listener log to see what errors are occurring. This search is useful because there will (hopefully) be far more connections than errors and, like the alert logs, the listener log can grow large.

Benefiting from Other Diagnostic Utilities

As a DBA, you should be grounded in the fundamentals of how your database works and where files are located.

Sometimes you'll have only a command-line interface into your database server and have to manually review log files. However, you also should know several easier, faster methods:

- ✔ Oracle Enterprise Manager and Database Express 12c
- ✔ Remote Diagnostic Assistant (RDA)
- ✔ Database diagnostic scripts

Oracle Enterprise Manager and Database Express 12c

Graphical tools, such as Oracle Enterprise Manager and Database Express 12c, let you review alert messages and view incidents. These easy methods of checking for critical errors let you avoid manually sifting through text files. Depending on the graphical tools used, you can upload files to Oracle Support in the form of a Service Request (SR). Some versions of Oracle GUI software also combine log files in a central location for easier viewing and management.

The capabilities of each GUI tool and the location of each utility change from release to release. Although these changes are a little frustrating at first, Enterprise Manager and Database Express 12c are very intuitive, so you can find what you need very quickly. For detailed information on these tools, see Chapter 13.

Remote Diagnostic Agent

Oracle *Remote Diagnostic Agent* (RDA) is an Oracle Support utility that captures Oracle-related information on an entire server and stores the results in a series of HTML files. RDA can be integrated with *Oracle Configuration Manager* (OCM) and can query a myriad of Oracle components outside the database, such as Oracle WebLogic or Enterprise Manager, in addition to your database. The utility asks you a series of simple questions about your environment and what components you want to investigate. Don't worry if you don't know the answer to a question; you can accept the provided default answer.

The intent is to capture data about the operating system, hardware, Oracle software versions, database instances, listeners, and activities within the database environment in an automated manner. You can view that information as a series of static HTML pages to get fast graphical access to all Oracle-related information for a given server.

Not only is graphical information useful to DBAs, but when you provide an RDA to Oracle Support it gives an accurate picture of your database environment. In fact, one of the first things many Oracle Support analysts request is an RDA of your server.

Oracle RDA comes as a tar or zip file available for download via the My Oracle Support network. When downloaded, it executes on the server as either a Perl or shell script. The output is a zip file that you can

✔ Upload to Oracle Support as part of a Service Request

✔ Unzip into a series of HTML files that you can navigate to find key information

In Figure 12-4, you see the main index page of the RDA output where you can drill down into multiple useful areas.

RDAs are a great way to get a quick snapshot of a system even when there are no problems (per se). For example, if you are consulting and need a quick overview of a client's system, the RDA is very handy. Or if you're taking over an existing database server, the RDA tells you exactly what's on that server and how it's configured.

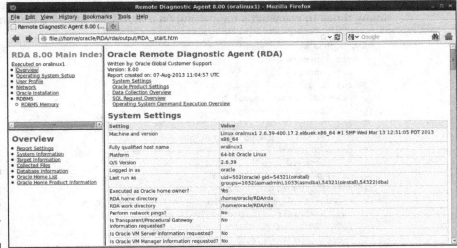

Figure 12-4:
The RDA
initial RDA_
Start page.

Database diagnostic scripts

Most old-school DBAs from the Oracle 7 days lived and died by their toolbox of database scripts — and for good reason. Database scripts based on internal database views and tables provided the raw information for what was going on in a database. That raw data, coupled with a real understanding of how the database and application worked, often made for a very skilled administrator who could solve most problems. Toward that end, entire books are dedicated to database scripts, and many websites make scripts available for download.

Oracle provides a set of database scripts in every $ORACLE_HOME/rdbms/ admin directory. In it are core scripts necessary to create a database, build the data dictionary, and other maintenance operations that aren't very useful for troubleshooting.

However, the $ORACLE_HOME/rdbms/admin directory also has useful scripts such as utllockt.sql and utlrp.sql. Use them to search for database locks and compile invalid database objects. We encourage you to become familiar with the scripts in this directory and identify the ones that fit into your toolbox.

Many good third-party scripts exist both from books and Internet downloads. We can't validate everything out there, so use your own best judgment and don't run anything you don't understand or trust. However, some good scripts are available, so don't be afraid to seek out good sources and test them first on your *development* database.

And if all else fails, write your own. Here's one of our favorites we've used many times to see what's happening on a database and who is doing it:

```
SQL>get show_session_short.sql
  1  set linesize 180
  2  set pagesize 20
  3  col "Logon Time" format a11
  4  col "UNIX Proc" format a9
  5  col username format a15
  6  col osuser format a13
  7  col "Program Running" format a20
  8  col sid format 9999
  9  col "Connect Type" format a12
 10  col serial# format 9999999
 11  select s.username, osuser, status,
 12  to_char(logon_time,'fmHH:MI:SS AM') as "Logon Time",
 13  sid, s.serial#,  p.spid as "UNIX Proc"
 14  from v$session s, v$process p
 15  where s.paddr = p.addr
 16  and s.username is not null
 17* order by status, s.username, logon_time
SQL>@show_session_short

USERNAME         OSUSER        STATUS    Logon Time    SID  SERIAL# UNIX Proc
---------------  ------------  --------  -----------  ----- -------- ---------
SYSTEM           oracle        ACTIVE    11:39:11 PM   125       12     29062
SYS              oracle        ACTIVE    12:18:25 AM   119      829     31376
MWESSLER         oracle        ACTIVE    11:40:39 PM   124       54     29264
CRUEL            oracle        ACTIVE    11:41:19 PM   138       35     29359
MPYLE            oracle        INACTIVE  11:37:51 PM   135       13     28749
MWESSLER         oracle        INACTIVE  11:40:26 PM   129       24     29258
DWILSON          oracle        INACTIVE  11:40:49 PM   155       32     29273
CSARJENT         oracle        INACTIVE  11:40:59 PM   126       54     29275
DBSNMP           oracle        INACTIVE  11:41:29 PM   132       19     29357
APEX_WEB         oracle        INACTIVE  11:41:39 PM   131       55     29355
RMAN             oracle        INACTIVE  11:41:49 PM   127      323     29361

11 rows selected.
```

Although the script is useful, the actual point is to show you the power of a simple script and what it can provide quickly.

Despite all the wiz-bang GUI tools and wonderful database advisors, many folks still use database scripts for some, if not all, of their administrative work.

A toolbox of useful scripts coupled with modern Enterprise Manager tools provides DBAs with the best capability to manage their databases.

Chapter 13

Managing Your Database with Enterprise Manager

You probably know lots of ways to manage your Oracle database. This book offers a few ideas. You may have been approached by various software companies with their own solutions. The most popular database management approaches follow:

✔ Command line SQL and OS commands

✔ Oracle Enterprise Manager (Database Express/Cloud Control)

✔ Third-party software vendor tools

✔ Any combination of these

What works best for you? Whatever you're most comfortable with. Some methods are better than others for specific tasks. Most people end up with some sort of hybrid approach.

This chapter focuses on the Oracle Enterprise Manager method, gives you an overview of the tool's unique features, and navigates many of its management pages.

Getting to Know the Enterprise Manager Family

Oracle Enterprise Manager (EM) became available in Oracle 7 and has gone through numerous changes since then. EM basically started as a desktop client and evolved into the web-based application it is today.

Oracle supports several current flavors of Enterprise Manager. We discuss EM Database Express, but you should know the differences between these tools.

EM Database Express

Oracle Enterprise Manager Database Express is a web-based database management tool that is built inside each Oracle database. All the SQL commands you normally type have been translated into a graphical point-and-click interface. EM Database Express even supports RAC database management.

EM Database Express started shipping in Oracle 12c and above and serves as the replacement for EM Database Control that shipped with 10g and 11g. This lighter weight tool for just Oracle database management is the second major shift in graphical-based management options that Oracle has offered since Oracle 8i.

Some users find this method easier than learning SQL and typing commands. However, if you have many databases, you might find this method tedious and resource-consuming.

EM Cloud Control

EM Cloud Control offers everything in EM Database Express and much more. Cloud Control is truly an enterprise level management suite, covering the Oracle database plus server, network, and storage management. It can even be used to manage non-Oracle databases. Covering Cloud Control would take an entire book. We mention it because it is the source from which Database Express has sprouted. The interface is similar when you're working on individual databases; it also acts as a central console for managing your entire environment, including the following:

- ✔ Oracle Software stacks
- ✔ Windows and Linux operating systems
- ✔ Microsoft SQL Server
- ✔ Other software products

With regard to databases, EM Cloud Control can register and maintain Oracle versions from 9i through 12c. As of this writing, Oracle has shipped 12c Cloud Control Release 3. EM Cloud Control is installed on its own centralized server in your enterprise. You can deploy the Oracle Management Agent to all the hosts with software you want EM Cloud Control to manage. The install and setup can be a little intimidating at first, but if you have a diverse environment with many servers and versions of Oracle, it can be a lifesaver in the long run.

Configuring EM Database Express with the DBCA

The easiest way to set up EM Database Express is to configure it during database creation with the *Database Configuration Assistant* (DBCA). Chapter 4 briefly describes this option. Figure 13-1 shows the DBCA asking whether you want to configure your database with EM Database Express (for local management).

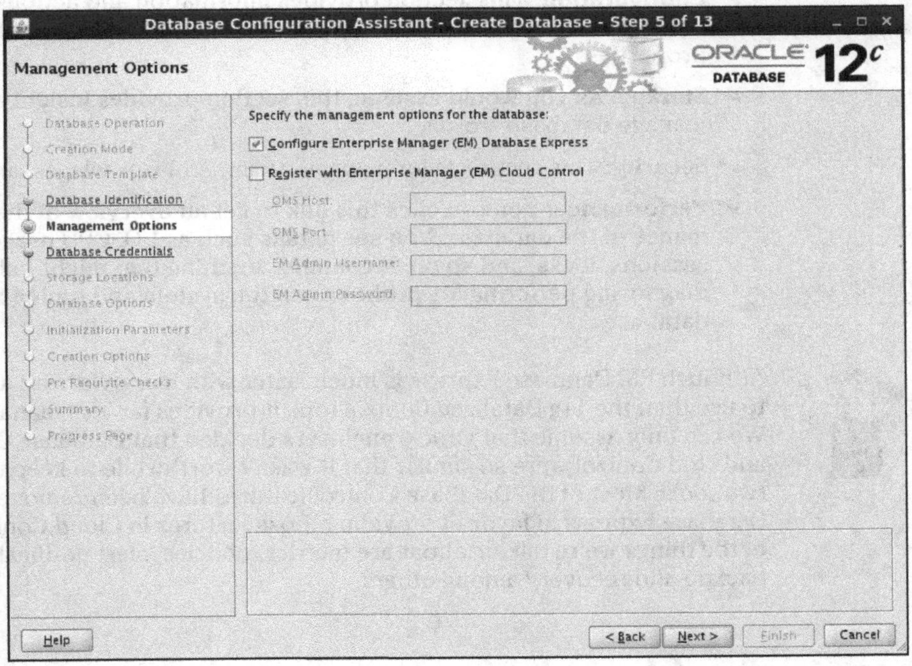

Figure 13-1:
The Database Configuration Assistant offers its Enterprise Manager Options screen.

We recommend EM Database Express because it is the easiest approach when learning to be a DBA. When you let the DBCA set up the database for you, it gathers the required answers for the installation while it takes you through different steps.

When your database creation is complete, open a browser and log in to EM Database Express to begin managing your database. Typically, this URL is most common: `https://hostname:5500/em`.

You can log in with any username that has DBA, EM_EXPRESS_ALL, or EM_EXPRESS_BASIC roles. Check the SYSDBA option if you want to do advanced DBA activities. Just make sure your user has the SYSDBA privilege.

Navigating EM Database Express

The EM Database Express main page, or the *dashboard,* gives you an idea of your database's overall health. Figure 13-2 shows the way it looks when you first log in.

All the major sections are listed and separated on the menu bar at the top according to task. As shown is Figure 13-2, the sections are

- ✔ **Database name:** Clicking this link always takes you to the main dashboard of the database.

- ✔ **Configuration:** This section provides information and actions against initialization parameters, memory, database feature usage, and database properties.

- ✔ **Storage:** As you would assume, this section provides insight and tools to manage database storage.

- ✔ **Security:** This section is for managing users, role, privileges, and profiles.

- ✔ **Performance:** You can click this link to get an overview of the performance of the database. You see details such as I/O, CPU usage, top sessions, locks, and so on. It contains anything that might help when diagnosing performance problems on the system and tuning SQL in the database.

Although EM Database Express is much faster with less overhead and is easier to use than the 11g Database Control tool, it provides far less manageability. We can only assume that Oracle engineers decided that Database Control and Grid Control were so similar that it wasn't worthwhile to keep updating two tools. Most of the Database Control features have been removed from EM Database Express in favor of providing those features in Cloud Control. Some of the things we're talking about are metrics, policies, alert notification, and backup and recovery among others.

Dashboard

The dashboard is the landing page of EM Database Express when you first log in. This page gives you a general overview of what is going on in your database. It is also the gateway for the rest of the actions that can be launched within EM Database Express.

One of the nice things about Oracle 12c is that the new EM Database Express tool is much more lightweight and faster than the older Database Control because it no longer requires an Oracle Application Server running in the background to support it. It runs directly out of the database as opposed to running in a separate Oracle Application Server container. This consumes far fewer resources. The old iAS Container was always difficult to manage and keep running at times.

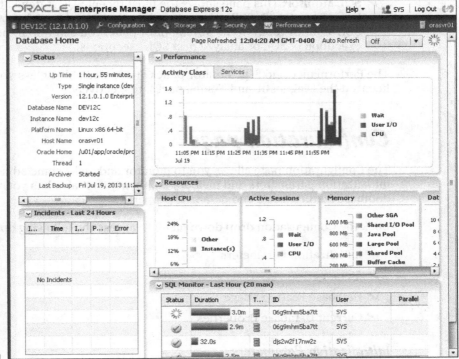

Figure 13-2:
The EM
Database
Express
main page is
chock-full
of data.

The dashboard offers many panes of information (refer to Figure 13-2):

✓ **Status:** This pane gives you an overview of the main characteristics of the database, such as Version, Database Name, Oracle Home, Last Backup, and so on.

✓ **Performance:** In this pane, you find a simplified breakdown of resource consumption between IO and CPU as well as time spent waiting. We say "simplified" because if you choose Performance from the menu bar and go to the performance hub, you get much more detailed information. The dashboard just gives you a quick glance.

✓ **Incidents:** If any problems have been detected and stored in the Automatic Diagnostic Repository, you see them here.

✓ **Resources:** This pane gives you an overview of the database/server resource consumption for things like CPU, memory, or storage.

✓ **Running Jobs:** Aptly named, this portlet gives you information about currently executing jobs in the database. These are named jobs, not run of the mill SQL execution. Named jobs, which run from the Oracle scheduler, can include statistics collection, backups, or application batch processes.

✔ **SQL Monitor:** This pane shows the most recent SQL statement executions. The statement IDs are active links that you can click to access the SQL Monitor tool. On the SQL Monitor pane, you can watch the real-time execution of SQL or analyze past SQL executions.

The Performance and SQL Monitor panes aren't available unless you have licensed the Diagnostic and Tuning packs, respectively.

Configuration page

The Configuration page allows you to monitor and make some adjustments to initialization parameters and memory components. It also lets you view the database feature usage and database properties.

Click the Configuration drop-down menu to access the following options:

✔ Initialization Parameters

✔ Memory

✔ Database Feature Usage

✔ Current Database Properties

Initialization Parameters

The Initialization Parameters page lets you make adjustments to the hundreds of initialization parameters discussed in Chapter 4. To make a change, you simply highlight the parameter and click the Set button at the top of the page. This action opens the Set Initialization Parameter dialog box, as shown in Figure 13-3.

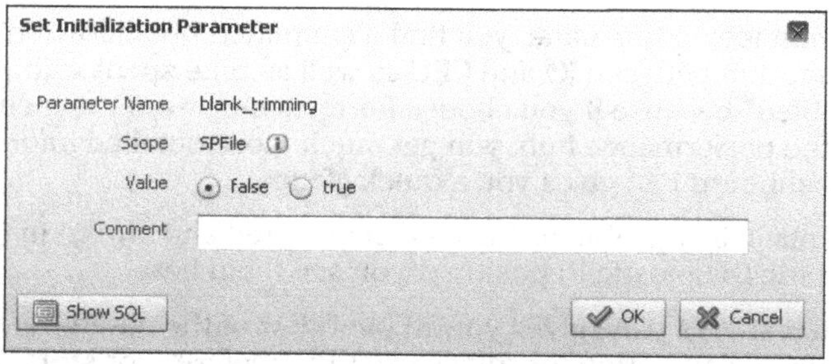

Figure 13-3:
The Set
Initialization
Parameter
dialog box.

> **Set Initialization Parameter** ☒
>
> Parameter Name   blank_trimming
>
> Scope   SPFile ⓘ
>
> Value   ● false   ○ true
>
> Comment   [   ]
>
> 🖳 Show SQL   ✔ OK   ✖ Cancel

Note the exclamation point bubble next to the Scope line. If clicked, this bubble warns you that changing this parameter requires a bounce of the database. You can also tell by looking at the main initialization parameter page. There is a column labeled Dynamic. If this column has a check mark, you can change the parameter on the fly. If it does not have a check mark, you have to restart the database if you want to change the parameter.

As we mention earlier, there are hundreds of parameters. On the Initialization Parameter page, you can easily search and filter the list. On the upper right, you see check boxes for the following:

- ✔ **Modified** displays only parameters that are changed from default.

- ✔ **Basic** displays only a subset of the database parameters that Oracle deems as basic.

You can also enter parameter names, or even partial names, in the search box to actively reduce and refine the list.

Memory

By choosing Memory from the Configuration drop-down menu, you're taken to the Memory Management page. This page breaks down all the memory components and provides not only an overview of the current settings but also some tuning advice. You can click the Configure Memory button at the upper left to make changes. You may not be able to make all the changes that you want without restarting the database. Notice that when you click the Configure Memory button, all that happens is that EM Database Express takes you back to the Initialization Parameter page with a filtered list of memory related parameters!

Database Feature Usage

The Database Feature Usage pane gives you an overview of all the features that are available in the database and whether Oracle has detected a use of them. This information can be important to you as a DBA for a few reasons:

- ✔ By seeing what has run, you can know whether you or your colleagues are using any unlicensed features.

- ✔ You can detect whether you're using all the features you're paying for. Maybe the next time you renew your license, any unused features can be dropped.

- ✔ Knowing dates and times certain features were used can be useful when auditing activities in the database.

Current Database Properties

The Current Database Properties pane gives you a quick overview of the options that were chosen (or left at Default) during database creation. (See Chapter 4.) Having a quick list of these can be handy to help answer questions about your environment. For example, if you ever have to open a support ticket with Oracle, this information will be relevant for them. Or, if you are installing a third-party software package into your database, the vendor might have certain properties that must be set, or other requirements. You can quickly look through this section to see how the database has been configured.

Storage page

The Storage page lets you manage objects like tablespaces and data files which are the backbone of the database storage. The page's Storage drop-down menu has the following options:

- ✔ **Tablespaces:** Some of the features on this pane are covered in Chapter 7, where we talk about creating tablespaces. To manage your seg-ments, you have to manage your storage containers, called tablespaces. Management includes such tasks as growing by extending or adding data files. It also includes shrinking. You can also perform other actions, such as taking tablespaces offline (for recovery) or making them read only.

- ✔ **Undo Management:** When working with transactions and flashback tech-nology in the database, undo management can be an important task. The undo space is important to make sure you can roll back transactions and use in the flashback features covered in Chapter 14. Although this section in EM Database Express is more of an overview than a way of making changes, it allows you to quickly see what kind of space you're using for undo and how far back your undo lets you go. It also incorpo-rates the Undo Advisor for keeping on top of storage when you're lever-aging the flashback retention.

- ✔ **Redo Log Groups:** Managing redo logs is done in this section. You can create or drop groups, add members, see details about the log sequences, and archive the status of the redo logs.

- ✔ **Archive Logs:** This section lets you see the archive logs that have been created along with their size and location. You can't make any changes in this section. Almost all archive log changes are done with initializa-tion parameters.

Click the Configuration Button and choose the Initialization Parameters option. Then, type **archive** in the search box on the right to bring up the editable archive log parameters.

- ✔ **Control Files:** This section lets you view the control file properties. You also find a Backup to Trace button for backing up the control file to a trace file.

Backing up the control file to a trace file creates the backup in the diagnostic destination. You can view this location by looking at the DIAGNOSTIC_DEST parameter. The name of the file is also displayed after the backup completes.

Security page

The Security page allows you to create, drop, and alter users. It also allows you to create and drop roles. Not only can you manage users and roles, but you can also control the security and permissions of these users, as described in Chapter 10.

We describe user management in more detail in the next section, "Creating and Managing EM Database Express Users." Even though the description suggests these are users specific to EM Database Express, Database Express users are all the same as normal database users.

The Security page also allows you to manage profiles. *Profiles* are attributes that manage resource consumption and password protection in the database. For example, profile settings determine how many times a password can be reused and how long a password takes to expire. You can create different types of profiles in your database for different classes of users. You might have one profile for web-based application users and another for batch job users. Profiles allow you to control how resources are consumed and passwords are managed by grouping users together.

Performance page

Although Chapter 9 gets you started with performance tuning, we purposefully left out the EM Database Express component. The main reason is because we want you to learn the fundamentals of performance tuning before you jump into using the available tools. Understanding the fundamentals takes you much further with such a difficult subject. Also, because this page isn't available unless you license the Diagnostic and Tuning packs, we don't want to provide you with a bunch of techniques you may not be able to use.

The Performance page is made up of two sections:

✔ Performance hub (part of the Diagnostic pack)

✔ SQL Tuning Advisor (part of the Tuning pack)

Performance hub

The performance hub is just want it sounds like: a central hub to give you a 360 degree view of what resource consumption is like on your system. Not only does it display information about database resource consumption, but it also contains some information about the operating system resource usage. The performance of the overall operating system is every bit as important as that of the database because on many systems you will have more than one database. If the operating system itself has nothing more to give, trying to tune at the database level may just be an exercise in futility.

In any case, because this is a separately licensed option, we don't get into the nitty-gritty. If you have a strong understanding of the concepts in Chapter 9, you can easily view and navigate the sections of the performance hub to facilitate quicker performance problem diagnosis and resolution.

SQL Tuning Advisor

The SQL Tuning Advisor gives you real-time access to both running and past SQL statements. It's a graphical interface that paints pictures of the different activities within the execution of a SQL statement. Like the performance hub, this is a separately licensed tool. What it can do is help speed up the problem diagnosis. It isn't required to be a strong DBA. Again, however, sometimes speed is worth paying for. The SQL Advisor lets you see execution plans at the click of a button. It also lets you tune the statement like we do with the internal package DBMS_SQLTUNE in Chapter 9. Again, speed is the name of the game here. If you're fortunate enough to have your company purchase the licensing for this tool, it can certainly pay for itself.

Creating and Managing EM Database Express Users

When you first create your database, two users are allowed to log in:

- ✔ SYS
- ✔ SYSTEM

However, creating your own users is the best practice. This way each person can set up her own tasks and notifications, and you can more easily identify who has made changes.

In Enterprise Manager Database Express, *all* users with the DBA or EM_EXPRESS_ALL roles are super users. This means that they can do almost anything in the tool including causing damage to the database. Therefore, be very careful to whom you grant these roles and allow to access EM Database Express.

1. **Choose Security from the menu bar at the top of any page within Enterprise Manager.**

2. **From the drop-down menu, choose Users.**

   Figure 13-4 shows the Users configuration page. You can see a Create User button on top of that list.

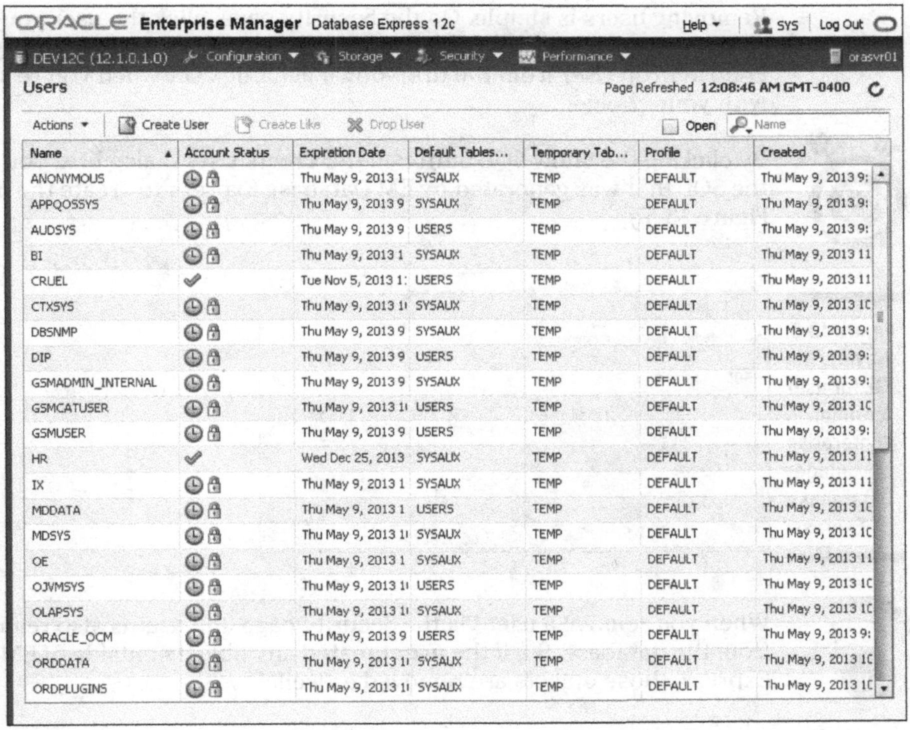

Figure 13-4: The Users configuration page in EM Database Express.

3. **Click the Create User button.**

   The Create User dialog box opens.

4. **Fill in these fields:**

   • Name

   • Password

   • Confirm Password

   Leave everything else as default.

5. **Click the Next arrow.**

6. **Leave the DEFAULT and TEMPORARY tablespaces with the default values.**

7. **Click the Next arrow to complete your selection of privileges.**

8. **Choose the EM_EXPRESS_ALL role and move it to the right by clicking the right arrow. Then click OK.**

   The user is created.

Removing users is simple. On the Security page, click the user you want to remove, click Actions in the upper-left corner of the Security page, and choose Drop User from the drop-down list. Click OK when you're satisfied with your choice.

By clicking the Show SQL button in the Create User dialog box, you can see the SQL that was generated by EM Database Express to create the user. (See Figure 13-5.)

Figure 13-5:
Review the
SQL for user
creation in
Enterprise
Manager
Database
Express.

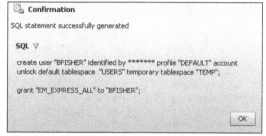

> 🗐 **Confirmation**
>
> SQL statement successfully generated
>
> **SQL** ▽
>
> create user "BFISHER" identified by ******* profile "DEFAULT" account
> unlock default tablespace "USERS" temporary tablespace "TEMP";
>
> grant "EM_EXPRESS_ALL" to "BFISHER";
>
> OK

When you remove a user via the Security page, the user is also removed from the database. So, if the user created any objects outside of EM Database Express, those objects are removed as well.

Part IV
Advanced Oracle Technologies

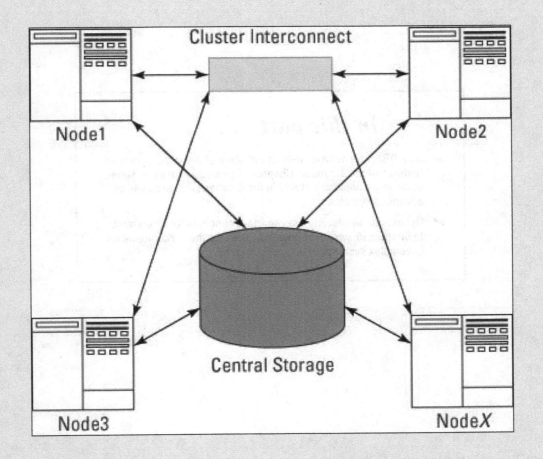

In this part . . .

✔ As a DBA, you need to understand some of the more advanced features of the database. Chapter 14 gets you started on some of the more popular features in the database that are used by advanced systems.

✔ Uptime and availability are important concepts to understand. In Chapter 15, we cover how Oracle meets these requirements in complex systems.

Chapter 14

Advanced Features

· ·

· ·

*O*racle RDBMS is an extremely large software package. What makes Oracle one of the best database platforms out there is its rich feature content. This chapter details features that you don't use on most Oracle enterprises from day to day. Regardless, most DBAs who are new to the sport probably won't start here; these features are for more advanced administration. We categorize some features as "advanced" because they're used less frequently and sometimes require a little extra knowledge to configure and use than the day-to-day features.

Also, though not the case with all features in this chapter, advanced components sometimes require extra licensing. We point out where that's the case — after all, you don't want to be caught with your pants down in an Oracle audit only to feel we've misled you. With that said, if you're unsure about licensing, you can always call your friendly local Oracle sales rep to ask questions. Furthermore, there are also companies out there that can help you do your own audit to identify the features you use.

In this chapter, we cover just few of the advanced features that we find particularly interesting. There are probably a hundred additional features we would have liked to include, but we weren't allowed to make this chapter hundreds of pages long. We hope you find our choices useful.

Flashing Back

Have you ever wanted a time machine? No such thing exists. Or does it? The Oracle time machine known as *Flashback* lets you rewind, fast forward, and recover from situations with ease. *Flashback* can sound intimidating, but the feature is simple. The following sections cover several types of Flashback:

- ✔ Flashback Query
- ✔ Flashback Table
- ✔ Flashback Database

Flashing your query back

A feature called Flashback Query is one of the simplest and easiest to use variations of the Oracle Flashback technology. Simply put, it allows you to query a table at a point in the past. This means that, despite any updates, inserts, and deletes that may have happened, you see the table as it existed at the point in time you choose.

Here's a quick demo with the example schema, HR:

1. **Log in to SQL*Plus as the HR user.**

2. **Look at the data in your departments table.**

3. **Restrict the query to both minimize output and make the demo more obvious. Type the following:**

```
<select department_id, department_name
from departments where manager_id is null;>
```

You should see something like this:

```
DEPARTMENT_ID DEPARTMENT_NAME
------------- ------------------------------
          120 Treasury
          130 Corporate Tax
          140 Control And Credit
          150 Shareholder Services
          160 Benefits
          170 Manufacturing
          180 Construction
          190 Contracting
          200 Operations
          210 IT Support
          220 NOC
          230 IT Helpdesk
          240 Government Sales
```

```
        250 Retail Sales
        260 Recruiting
        270 Payroll

16 rows selected.
```

4. **Modify the table by removing the rows selected in the preceding output. To remove the rows, type**

```
<delete from departments
where manager_id is null;>
```

You should see this:

```
16 rows deleted.
```

5. **Commit your changes by typing**

```
<commit;>
```

You should see this:

```
Commit complete.
```

6. **Run the original query again.**

You should see this:

```
no rows selected
```

The next step is where you use the magic of Flashback Query. Think of the time before the delete occurred. In this example case, it was five minutes ago.

7. **Type something similar to the following to see the data as it existed five minutes ago:**

```
<select department_id, department_name
from departments
AS OF TIMESTAMP SYSDATE - 1/288
where manager_id is null;>
```

You see the rows as they existed in Step 2. The key is the AS OF TIMESTAMP clause. For the target of the timestamp, you can see that the example uses math on the SYSDATE function. SYSDATE represents the current time, right now. Subtracting 1 from SYSDATE means yesterday. The example subtracts the fraction 1/288, which means five minutes, from SYSDATE. To get that fraction, the example uses the following formula:

24 (hours in a days) × 60 (minutes in an hour) = 1440 (minutes) in a day

So, 5 over 1440 is equal to 1 over 288.

You can also use an explicit timestamp instead of a SYSDATE function. For example:

```
select department_id, department_name
from departments
AS OF TIMESTAMP TO_DATE('16-AUG-2013 20:04:00','DD-MON-YYYY HH24:MI:SS')
where manager_id is null;
```

Here's a neat trick. Suppose you accidentally deleted those rows and want to insert them back into your table. You can use Flashback Query to do such a thing. This is going to be *much* faster than doing an RMAN recovery to a point in time.

To insert your deleted rows back into your table, type

```
< insert into departments
select *
from departments
AS OF TIMESTAMP TO_DATE('16-AUG-2013 20:04:00','DD-MON-YYYY HH24:MI:SS')
where manager_id is null;>
```

You should see this:

```
16 rows created.
```

Query the table and, when you're satisfied, commit your changes.

You can only flash back as far as your setting for the instance parameter undo_retention. By default, this parameter is set to 15 minutes (900 seconds). If the time you wish to go back to is further than your undo_retention, you may not be able to see your data and will receive an error instead.

Before you take the previous tip and set your undo_retention to reflect a month's worth of time, consider that this will cause your UNDO tablespace to grow because it has to store images of your old data. You should carefully balance a realistic undo_retention setting with space consumption.

Flashing your table back

Very similar to Flashback Query is Flashback Table. In fact, both are built on the same underlying technology. Flashback Table is capable of flashing back row changes or the entire table if it was accidentally dropped.

Keep the following requirements in mind:

✔ Just like in the previous section, the UNDO_RETENTION parameter is going to control how far back you can flash the table.

✔ You need to use a feature called row movement that must be enabled on any table you want to flash back rows. (The upcoming steps show you how to enable row movement.)

✔ If you want to be able to flash back a table from a drop, you need to have your parameter RECYCLEBIN set to ON. This parameter is turned on by default, but note that if it has been turned off it requires a database bounce to turn it back on.

Consider the earlier example where we accidentally deleted some rows from our table. They were very easy to recover because identifying them wasn't difficult. However, suppose you want to recover from an accidental update. Updates are harder to recover from with Flashback Query. You can do it, but you may be able to make it easier on yourself by flashing back the entire table.

Flashback Table works on the entire table, not just certain rows, so make sure that bringing the entire table back in time is not going to cause other problems.

To use Flashback Table, follow these steps:

1. **You must have row movement enabled; to enable it, type**

   ```
   <alter table departments enable row movement;>
   ```

   You should see this:

   ```
   Table altered.
   ```

   As a side note, you don't have to enable row movement before you change your data. You can do it after the fact.

2. **See what your data looks like by typing**

   ```
   <select department_name, manager_id
   from departments
   where manager_id is not null;>
   ```

   You should see something like this:

   ```
   DEPARTMENT_NAME                      MANAGER_ID
   ------------------------------      ----------
   Administration                             200
   Marketing                                  201
   Purchasing                                 114
   Human Resources                            203
   Shipping                                   121
   IT                                         103
   Public Relations                           204
   Sales                                      145
   Executive                                  100
   Finance                                    108
   Accounting                                 205

   11 rows selected.
   ```

To "mess up" the data, type the following:

```
< update departments
set manager_id = 205
where manager_id is not null;
commit;>
```

You shoud see something like this:

```
11 rows updated.
Commit complete.
```

3. **Look at your data again by typing**

```
<select department_name, manager_id
from departments
where manager_id is not null;>
```

You should see something like this:

```
DEPARTMENT_NAME                         MANAGER_ID
------------------------------- ----------
Administration                             205
Marketing                                  205
Purchasing                                 205
Human Resources                            205
Shipping                                   205
IT                                         205
Public Relations                           205
Sales                                      205
Executive                                  205
Finance                                    205
Accounting                                 205

11 rows selected.
```

4. **To flashback all the changes on the rows, type**

```
<flashback table departments
to timestamp TO_DATE('16-AUG-2013 20:40:00','DD-MON-YYYY HH24:MI:SS');>
```

You should see something like this:

```
Flashback complete.
```

5. **Check your data again by typing**

```
<select department_name, manager_id
from departments
where manager_id is not null;>
```

You should see something like this:

```
DEPARTMENT_NAME                 MANAGER_ID
------------------------------- ----------
Administration                         200
Marketing                              201
Purchasing                             114
Human Resources                        203
Shipping                               121
IT                                     103
Public Relations                       204
Sales                                  145
Executive                              100
Finance                                108
Accounting                             205

11 rows selected.
```

The data is back where it was at the timestamp specified.

The next exercise helps you if you accidentally dropped your table. It utilizes the feature we mentioned above called the Recyclebin. It functions much like the Recycle Bin on a Windows desktop. You can restore an object to what it looked like before it was dropped.

For this next example, you start by making a copy of the employees table to work with. The reason you're making a copy is that in the demo schema provided with the database there is a lot of referential integrity, which prevents you from dropping tables in the first place (one of the many reasons referential integrity is such a good idea!).

1. **To make a copy of your employees table, type**

   ```
   <create table emp as select * from employees;>
   ```

   You see something like this:

   ```
   Table created.
   ```

2. **"Accidentally" drop the new emp table by typing**

   ```
   <drop table emp>;
   ```

   You see something like this:

   ```
   Table dropped.
   ```

3. **Query your Recyclebin to see what you can recover — type**

   ```
   < select object_name, original_name, operation, droptime
   from user_recyclebin;>
   ```

You see something like this:

```
OBJECT_NAME                          ORIGINAL_NAME   OPERATION DROPTIME
-----------------------------------  --------------- --------- -----------------
BIN$5BtB5dF6GmXgQ1ABqMC8yg==$0 EMP                   DROP      2013-08-
                                                               16:21:02:12
```

Notice the funny name starting with BIN$. With the Recyclebin turned on, what's actually happening during a drop is the object is being renamed. You can still query the original table by using this name! This might be useful if you want to restore just a few rows rather than the entire table. You can query those rows or do a "create table as select" to store them in a new table altogether.

4. **To undrop your table, type**

```
< flashback table emp to before drop;>
```

You see this:

```
Flashback complete.
```

You can now query your table again.

Although flashing back the table to before a drop does put back all privileges and indexes, the indexes keep the BIN$ name. We aren't sure why Oracle does this. You can give your indexes back the original name with a rename command if you want.

Flashing your database back

You could argue that moving the database forward and back with Oracle Recovery Manager with good backups is possible. However, restoring a large database to a previous point is time-consuming and tedious. Also, if you don't go back far enough, you have to start over from the beginning.

You might want to flash back the database for these reasons:

- ✔ **Repeated testing scenarios:** Say you have an application that you're testing in your development environment. Every time you run the application, it changes your data. You want to reset the data to its original values before the next test. Flashback is an excellent tool for this.

- ✔ **Logical Data Corruption:** Perhaps someone accidentally ran the wrong program in your production environment; you need to return to a point before the mistake occurred. You could do this with a data recovery, but Flashback is quicker and easier.

- ✔ **Deployment procedures:** Perhaps you're releasing a new version of your code that updates all sorts of objects in your production schema with both DDL and DML. You can easily roll it back if the application isn't working properly in target performance parameters.

Flashback Database works by recording extra information that allows you to roll back transactions without doing a full database recovery. Not only that, but it works very quickly. The Flashback Database has these quick features, among others:

- ✔ You can open the database in read only mode to see whether you went back far enough.
- ✔ Not far enough? Quickly roll back farther.
- ✔ Too far? Roll forward again.

You can perform all these tasks with simple commands inside SQL*Plus or Oracle Enterprise Manager. To do them with RMAN, you're talking multiple full restores and lots of time in between.

Configuring and enabling Flashback Database

Flashback Database works differently than the Flashback features we explore earlier in the chapter. With Flashback Database, Oracle stores a file called a flashback log. *Flashback logs* have the data to roll back blocks to a previous time. Flashback logs are stored in the flash_recovery_area. Chapter 11 shows how to configure the Flash Recovery Area.

Two variables come into play here:

- ✔ How far back do you want to go?
- ✔ How much data is changed in your database within that time period?

The farther back you go and the more changes you have, the more flashback logs you generate. Be sure you have enough space to store those logs, or you won't be flashing anywhere.

If you're considering implementing Flashback Database, you may need to enlarge the parameter db_recovery_file_dest_size. How much you enlarge it depends on the two variables: how far back and how much data? If you want a good starting point, use this formula:

New Flash Recovery Area Size = Current Flash Recovery Area Size + Total Database Size × 0.3

In essence, you're trying to reserve roughly 30 percent of your total database size in the Flash Recovery Area for flashback logs.

From then on, you can monitor how much space the flashback logs are consuming. We show you how to do that shortly.

After you configure the Flash Recovery Area, turn on the Flashback feature in the database by following these steps:

1. **Consider how far back you want to be able to flash back.**

   The default value is 24 hours (or 1,440 minutes). Say you want to be able to flash back up to 48 hours.

2. **Configure how far back you want to go with the parameter db_flashback_retention_target; to do so, log in to SQL as SYSDBA and type**

   ```
   <alter system set db_flashback_retention_target =2880;>
   ```

   In this example, the time is set for 2,880 minutes (48 hours).

   You should see the following for any amount of time you choose.

   ```
   System altered.
   ```

3. **Shut down your database and restart it in mount mode.**

4. **Put the database in flashback mode by typing this:**

   ```
   <alter database flashback on;>
   ```

   You should see this:

   ```
   Database altered.
   ```

5. **Open the database by typing this:**

   ```
   <alter database open;>
   ```

   You should see this:

   ```
   Database altered.
   ```

   Now that the database is in flashback mode, you can flash back to any time within your Flashback window.

Rolling your database back

When the database must be flashed back, don't worry. The process is relatively easy.

Flashing back a database removes any change that occurred after the point in time chosen to return. Don't take this consideration lightly.

To see how far back you can go, type this:

```
< select oldest_flashback_time
from v$flashback_database_log;>
```

You should see something like this:

```
OLDEST_FLASHBACK_TIM
--------------------
14-AUG-2013 06:34:03
```

db_flashback_retention_target should be about the limit of that time frame. You may find it to be longer if space isn't a concern and the database hasn't yet purged old flashback logs.

Say a user accidentally dropped the HR schema from your database about an hour ago.

1. **Shut down your database.**

2. **Restart it in mount mode.**

3. **Type the following, where 1 is the number of hours you want to flash back:**

   ```
   < flashback database to timestamp sysdate - 1/24;>
   ```

   You should see this:

   ```
   Flashback complete.
   ```

4. **Check the flashback before making it permanent:**

   ```
   < alter database open read only;>
   ```

   You should see this:

   ```
   Database altered.
   ```

5. **If you're satisfied with the result, go to Step 6. If you're not satisfied with the time, skip to Step 9.**

6. **Shut down the database.**

7. **Start the database in mount mode.**

8. **Open the database with Resetlogs:**

   ```
   < alter database open resetlogs;>
   ```

   You should see this:

   ```
   Database altered.
   ```

9. **Restart the database in mount mode.**

10. **Type the following:**

    ```
    <recover database;>
    ```

    You should see this:

    ```
    Media recovery complete.
    ```

11. **Start your database in mount mode.**

    If you want to flash back to a timestamp, go to Step 12. If you want to flash back to a previously created restore point, go to Step 13.

For more on restore points, see the nearby "Using restore points" sidebar.

12. **Type the following:**

```
<flashback database to timestamp
to_timestamp('14-AUG-2013 13:00:00','DD-MON-YYYY HH24:MI:SS');>
```

You should see this:

```
Flashback complete.
```

13. **Type the following if you want to flash back to a restore point:**

```
<flashback database to restore point pre_deploy_15AUG2013;>
```

You should see this:

```
Flashback complete.
```

Using restore points

Flashing back a database is time based. Normally, you select a time and tell the database to go back to that time within the Flashback window. However, another convenient feature is a *restore point* — a named, easily identified point for locating a specific instance in the past.

Say you're doing a code deployment and want to mark the time to which the database will be returned if you have to back out the change. You could record the time, but Oracle may not get it exact when you flash back. Buck the margin of error, which is plus or minus a few seconds, and create a restore point — an exact time.

To create and name a restore point, follow these steps:

1. **Log in to the database as SYS.**

2. **Type the following with your restore point name:**

```
<create restore point pre_deploy_15AUG2013;
```

In this example, the restore point is called pre_deploy_15AUG2013. You should see this:

```
Restore point created.
```

Restore points come with a few other handy options:

- **Get a list of all the restore points you created:**

```
< select scn, time, name
From v$restore_point;>
```

You should see this:

```
     SCN TIME                                       NAME
---------- ----------------------------------- ---------------------
22783928 155-AUG-13 01.15.01.000000000 PM       PRE_DEPLOY_15AUG2013
```

- **Create a restore point that's guaranteed forever.**

  Be careful using this method: Your flashback logs grow until the restore point is dropped.

  ```
  <create restore point pre_deploy_15AUG2013_g guarantee flashback
      database;>
  ```

  You should see this:

  ```
  Restore point created.
  ```

- **Drop the restore point when your code release succeeds:**

  ```
  drop restore point PRE_DEPLOY_15AUG2013;
  ```

  You should see this:

  ```
  Restore point dropped.
  ```

Compressing Data for Purging, Retention, and Archiving

DBAs spend a lot of their time and effort compressing data for retention and archiving. *Compression* is the act of taking data in your database and applying processes that reduce its storage footprint. Because each year that goes by results in more and more data in your database, without specific processes in place, a database can quickly grow out of control, consuming all sorts of resources and hindering performance. As a first-class database, Oracle gives the DBA compression tools to make the jobs of removing data (purging) and keeping data (retention and archiving) quicker and more efficient.

Basic compression

Basic compression in the database has been around since Oracle 9i. It is called *basic compression* because it is very simple in what it does. However, it is also limited in its uses. Basic compression works much like using a zipping tool to compress a file on your operating system. In the database, objects can be compressed.

Using basic compression to reduce your table sizes can afford you efficiencies in using of space (obviously), CPU (table scanning), and memory (buffer cache usage). The greater efficiency means that tablespaces and backups take up less space. Backups run more quickly as well.

Be aware, though, that basic compression is primarily recommended for objects with a low frequency of DML. It is preferred that the objects are practically read only. We say *practically* because some data isn't 100 percent black and white. For example, a person's name rarely changes, so a list of employee names is practically read only. A change may occur once in a while, but, it so infrequently that compressing the data and incurring the overhead of a change is negligible. Think of it this way, if you want to edit a compressed file on your OS, what do you have to do first? You have to uncompress it. The same is true with Oracle basic compression. DML on compressed files suffers in terms of performance.

Here's a compression example.

1. **Log in to SQL*Plus as the user HR and make a copy of the demo table employees called emp by typing**

   ```
   <create table emp as select * from employees;>
   ```

2. **Check the size of this table by typing**

   ```
   < select segment_name, bytes
   from user_segments
   where segment_name = 'EMP';>
   ```

   You see something like this:

   ```
   SEGMENT_NAME                    BYTES
   --------------- ---------------------
   EMP                            65,536
   ```

3. **Insert rows into emp by running the following statement until you see "109568 rows created":**

   ```
   < insert into emp select * from emp;>
   ```

4. **Check the size of the emp table again by typing**

   ```
   < select segment_name, bytes
   from user_segments
   where segment_name = 'EMP';>
   ```

   You see something like this:

   ```
   SEGMENT_NAME                    BYTES
   --------------- ---------------------
   EMP                        18,874,368
   ```

5. **Compress the rows by typing**

   ```
   <alter table emp move compress;>
   ```

   You see this:

   ```
   Table altered.
   ```

6. Check the size one more time by typing

```
< select segment_name, bytes
from user_segments
where segment_name = 'EMP';>
```

You see something like this:

```
SEGMENT_NAME                        BYTES
--------------    --------------------

EMP                             9,437,184
```

As you can see, the table has reduced to about 50 percent of the original size. Depending on the type and organization of your data, you may see varying degrees of compression.

To see your tables compression details in the data dictionary, type

```
<select table_name, COMPRESSION, COMPRESS_FOR
from user_tables
where table_name = 'EMP';>
```

You see something like this:

```
TABLE_NAME                         COMPRESS COMPRESS_FOR
------------------------------    --------  ------------
EMP                                ENABLED   BASIC
```

To remove compression from a table in case you need to update a lot of data, type

```
<alter table emp move nocompress;>
```

You see this:

```
Table altered.
```

Advanced compression

After reading the preceding section about basic compression, the primary thing to understand about advanced compression is it uses more highly developed compression algorithms and data access policies so that the over-head of issuing DML against your compressed objects is all but eliminated. Well, the other important thing you need to be aware of is that advanced compression is a licensed feature. Yes, that means you must pay extra for it. Your Oracle sales rep can help you figure out what it will cost. One thing you should consider, though, is the return on investment you can get from advanced compression. You'll require less storage, and many operations will be improved. Calculating these returns will be an important part of your decision process.

Using advanced compression is very simple. If you followed the demo in the preceding section, you have an emp table in noncompressed format. You use that emp table in the following steps to apply advanced compression:

1. **To compress your emp table with advanced compression, type**

   ```
   <alter table emp move compress for all operations;>
   ```

   You see something like this:

   ```
   Table altered.
   ```

2. **To check the new size of your emp table, type**

   ```
   <select segment_name, bytes
   from user_segments
   where segment_name = 'EMP';>
   ```

   You see something like this:

   ```
   SEGMENT_NAME                     BYTES
   --------------- --------------------
   EMP                          9,437,184
   ```

3. **Check the compression details in the data dictionary by typing**

   ```
   <select table_name, COMPRESSION, COMPRESS_FOR
   from user_tables
   where table_name = 'EMP';>
   ```

   You see something like this:

   ```
   TABLE_NAME                         COMPRESS COMPRESS_FOR
   ------------------------------ -------- ------------
   EMP                                ENABLED  ADVANCED.
   ```

   Your table is enabled for all operations including DML with minimal performance loss.

You may have noticed in the examples for both basic and advanced compression that we use the keyword MOVE in the commands. If you don't use the keyword MOVE, the table is not compressed, but all future data inserted into the table will be compressed.

If you use the keyword MOVE and there are indexes on the table, those indexes will become corrupt. This corruption occurs because you're changing the row location in the table when you proactively compress the data. To fix this problem, after a MOVE compression action, rebuild the indexes. This is one reason you may choose to compress the data for future operations now and then move it later when you can incur downtime to rebuild the indexes.

Flashback Data Archive

Flashback Data Archive is a database mechanism that allows you to periodically or indefinitely store all row versions in a table over its lifetime. You can then choose a time to view the data as it existed at a specific point in time.

Be aware that Flashback Data Archive is a licensed feature. The good news: It is included with advanced compression, which makes the advanced compression cost an even better value.

You don't need to code complex triggers to move rows to history tables. You also don't need to code complex application logic to retrieve the data. The archiving is completely transparent to developers and end users. Oracle has sometimes referred to this feature as *Oracle Total Recall*. (No, that's not a reference to some cheesy 1990s movie.)

When you enable Flashback Data Archive, the row versions are automatically compressed to conserve space. You can also specify the retention period.

You can't do certain operations (such as DROP or TRUNCATE) on tables where you've enabled Flashback Data Archive. Furthermore, you can't modify historical data; this ensures the validity and consistency of the archive data.

Flashback Data Archive is a totally online operation. No downtime is required to enable or use this feature. It's enabled on a table-by-table basis. You can also group objects according to retention periods for easier management. Indexes aren't maintained, but you can create your own index to facilitate searching.

After the specified retention period expires, data is automatically purged to conserve space. If space is a concern, you can set quotas to limit archive growth. Also, to best organize your Flashback data, create tablespaces to store Flashback data for specific retention periods.

If an archive quota is exceeded, new transactions are blocked. Keep an eye on space usage and periodically check the alert log for space warnings.

Here's how you might use a Flashback Data Archive:

1. **Create a tablespace that holds data for a one-year retention period:**

```
<create tablespace fbda_1yr datafile
'/opt/oracle/oradata/dev12c/fdba_1yr_01.dbf' size 100M
Autoextend on next 100M maxsize 10g;>
```

   The tablespace in this example is named for documentation purposes. You see this:

```
Tablespace created.
```

2. **Create a Flashback Data Archive object in your tablespace with a one-year retention and a 10GB space limit:**

```
<create flashback archive FBDA1
Tablespace fbda_1yr quota 10G retention 1 year;>
```

3. **Enable Flashback data archiving on the table to keep row history:**

```
<alter table emp flashback archive FBDA1;>
```

You see this:

```
Table altered.
```

4. **Query the table to see what it looked like:**

```
<select *
From emp
As of timestamp sysdate - 180;>
```

In this case, you're searching for emp 6 months prior. You see the row images as they existed 180 days ago.

You can't drop, truncate, or modify any historical rows in this table as long as Flashback Data Archive is enabled.

To remove the Flashback Data Archive status, deleting all historical data, type this:

```
<alter table EMP no flashback archive;>
```

You see this:

```
Table altered.
```

Oracle Database Replay

The Oracle Database Replay feature evolved as a solution for the need to be able to do realistic application testing. Before Database Replay, if you wanted to test any kind of changes against performance or workload, you had to buy a third-party tool or do massive amounts of coding to fake a workload. In most cases, neither method was truly representative of your real workload. Also, making changes to a production environment without testing them can be risky.

Database Replay is one more tool in your shed to cover all the bases.

In essence, Database Replay allows you to record your workload in real time and then play it back. Furthermore, you could play it against

- ✔ Another database
- ✔ A different version of Oracle
- ✔ A different OS

Database Replay captures the workload at below the SQL level. The workload is stored in binary files. You can then transfer these files to a test environment, run the workload, analyze problems, fix problems, and test again. The same workload is repeatable. In conjunction with a tool like Flashback Database, you can repeatedly test changes in quick succession. Ultimately, it helps reduce the chances of something breaking when environments are changed.

Database Replay provides a mechanism to help with these kinds of situations:

- ✔ Testing
- ✔ Configuration changes
- ✔ Upgrades
- ✔ Downgrades
- ✔ Application changes
- ✔ Debugging
- ✔ Storage, network, and interconnect changes
- ✔ Platform changes
- ✔ OS changes
- ✔ Conversion to Real Application Clusters (RAC)

Using Database Replay

Here's how to use Database Replay:

1. **Log in to SQL*Plus as a user with the SYSDBA privilege.**

   Oracle requires a directory in which to write the replay files.

2. **Create a directory to a location on the OS with plenty of space:**

   ```
   <create or replace directory capture_dir as
   '/u01/app/oracle/admin/devcdb/capture';>
   ```

You see this:

```
Directory created.
```

3. **Start a capture:**

```
<exec dbms_workload_capture.start_capture ('CAPTURE_DEMO','CAPTURE_DIR');>
```

This example uses the name CAPTURE_DEMO.

Ideally, you restart the database before the capture begins so that you can avoid catching any transactions in the middle. Of course, doing so isn't always an option when dealing with a production system.

You see this:

```
PL/SQL procedure successfully completed.
```

4. **Execute your workload.**

If it's just normal application behavior, let it run for the amount of time you want.

5. **When the workload is complete or your time target has passed, stop the capture process:**

```
<exec dbms_workload_capture.finish_capture;>
```

You see this:

```
PL/SQL procedure successfully completed.
```

According to Oracle documentation, capturing a workload can add up to 4.5 percent of processing overhead to the system as well as 64K of memory overhead for each session. Futhermore, if space runs out in the capture directory, the capture will stop. All the captured data up to that point will still be useful.

The idea is we will use our capture to "replay" the workload. In our experience, the workload is usually replayed against a different database, such as a test environment. However, this is not always the case.

If your database environment is one where lengthy maintenance windows can occur (such as over a weekend), you might find yourself doing these things:

- ✔ Enabling Flashback Database
- ✔ Creating a restore point on Friday morning
- ✔ Starting a workload capture for four hours from 8 a.m. to noon
- ✔ Restricting the system and creating another restore point after the employees go home on Friday evening
- ✔ Restoring the database to the restore point Friday morning
- ✔ Deploying database or application changes
- ✔ Replaying your workload to test the changes

✔ Flashing back the workload to Friday evening

✔ Deploying database or application changes to take effect when the workers come back Monday morning

Replaying the workload

Follow these steps to replay the workload:

1. **Create a directory for the replay capture files:**

```
<create or replace directory capture_dir as
'/u01/app/oracle/admin/devcdb/capture';>
```

You see this:

```
Directory created.
```

This example assumes the replay is taking place on another database. If it's on the same database, there is no need to create a directory and move the capture files because they will already be in the correct location.

2. **Move the files from the capture directory on the source system to the directory on the replay system.**

3. **Begin the replay process on the database:**

```
<exec dbms_workload_replay.process_capture ('CAPTURE_DIR');>
```

You see this:

```
PL/SQL procedure successfully completed.
```

4. **Initialize a replay session called REPLAY_DEMO:**

```
<exec dbms_workload_replay.initialize_replay
('REPLAY_DEMO_4','CAPTURE_DIR');>
```

You see this:

```
PL/SQL procedure successfully completed.
```

5. **Tell Oracle to prepare the replay files:**

```
<exec dbms_workload_replay.prepare_replay ;>
```

You see this:

```
PL/SQL procedure successfully completed.
```

Start *replay clients,* which are processes that execute and manage the workload. These processes are launched from the OS's command line.

6. **The following example starts a replay client with oracle as the password:**

```
<wrc system/oracle>
```

You see this:

```
Workload Replay Client: Release 12.1.0.1.0 - Production on Fri Aug 16
        22:24:44 2013

Copyright (c) 1982, 2013, Oracle and/or its affiliates.  All rights
        reserved.

Wait for the replay to start (22:24:44)
```

7. **Tell the database to start the replay:**

```
<exec dbms_workload_replay.start_replay;>
```

You see this:

```
PL/SQL procedure successfully completed.
```

8. **Check on the status while the replay runs:**

```
<select id, name, status, duration_secs
  from dba_workload_replays;>
```

Basically, you're querying the DBA_WORKLOAD_REPLAYS table. You see this (or something like it):

```
ID NAME                       STATUS        DURATION_SECS
---------- -------------------- ----------- -------------
10 REPLAY_DEMO                 IN PROGRESS       369
```

When everything is done, you should clean up the replay metadata.

1. **Capture ID info on the source system:**

```
<select id, name
  from dba_workload_captures;>
```

You might see something like this:

```
ID NAME
---------- ------------------------------------
4 CAPTURE_DEMO
```

2. **Delete the capture information:**

```
<exec dbms_workload_capture.delete_capture_info(4);>
```

You see this:

```
PL/SQL procedure successfully completed.
```

3. **Find the replay id on the replay system:**

```
<select id, name
  from dba_workload_replays;>
```

You might see something like this:

```
        ID NAME
---------- -----------------------------------
        10 REPLAY_DEMO
```

4. **Delete the replay information:**

```
<exec dbms_workload_capture.delete_replay_info(10);>
```

Multitenant Architecture and Pluggable Databases

One of the most talked about new features of Oracle 12c is *multitenant databases*. They have also come to be known as *pluggable databases*. If you haven't heard about the cloud, you must have been living under a rock for the past several years. As you know by now, the *c* in 12c stands for *cloud*. Serving up computing resources and applications in the cloud is all the rage these days. Doing so reduces capital expenditures for corporations and has immediate tax benefits as well. Therefore, companies have a lot of incentive to take advantage of cloud computing.

One of the technologies that has really taken off with the cloud computing revolution is *virtualization*. Using virtual machines carved out of larger physical machines and leveraging fractional licensing further reduces costs for corporations. Oracle multitenant databases were developed to help companies take advantage of all these technologies and cost savings.

The Multitenant option of Oracle 12c is licensed. As usual, check with your Oracle sales rep for costs. Again, though, make sure you're aware of the return on investment that this feature can bring you.

You need to be aware of the new types of databases that are now part of a multitenant architecture:

- ✔ **Container Database (CDB):** The primary database that contains multiple plugged-in databases. Many operations can be performed at the container level to reduce management costs. A database is created as either a CDB or a non-CDB.

- ✔ **Pluggable Database (PDB):** A set of schemas, objects, and non-schema objects that can be plugged and unplugged from a container database. The PDB appears to OracleNet and end users as a database in and of itself but is actually managed within a container that may have many PDBs.

- ✔ **Seed Database (Seed PDB):** A default PDB that the system uses as a template to quickly provision other user-created PDBs. Internally, it's called PDB$SEED.

The Multitenant option helps you accomplish the following:

- **High consolidation density:** Many databases can share memory and background processes.

- **Provisioning:** A database can be unplugged from one environment and plugged into another or cloned with SQL commands in just a few seconds. They can even be plugged across operating systems and chipsets.

- **Patching and upgrades:** You can patch a database simply by unplugging from one unpatched container and plugging it into another patched container.

- **Manage many databases as one:** You can do tasks such as backing up and patching on the primary container database instead of the individual pluggable databases.

- **Resource management:** The Oracle Resource Manager feature can work at the pluggable database level for you to manage resource competition among the databases in your environment.

One other thing worth mentioning is that a pluggable database is fully compatible with a non-CDB. In fact, Oracle has something it is calling the *PDB/non-CDB compatibility guarantee,* which states that anything you would do in a non-CDB would also work in a PDB. This compatibility guarantee is important when it comes to certifying things like third-party vendor products to work in a multitenant architecture.

Creating a multitenant database environment

When creating a database, you must designate it as a CDB or non-CDB for it to be able to support the multitenant architecture. The next set of examples walks you through the steps to create a container database with the DBCA. There is only one step that differentiates a CDB from a non-CDB when using the DBCA.

Following the advanced path of creating a database, the first thing you may notice is a check box for Create As Container Database on Step 4 of 13, as shown in Figure 14-1.

You also can choose the number of PDBs created at this time. We choose only one because we plan to show you how to add more at a later time. You can also choose to create an empty container database with no pluggable databases at the onset. The rest of the steps are pretty much the same as when you create a non-CDB.

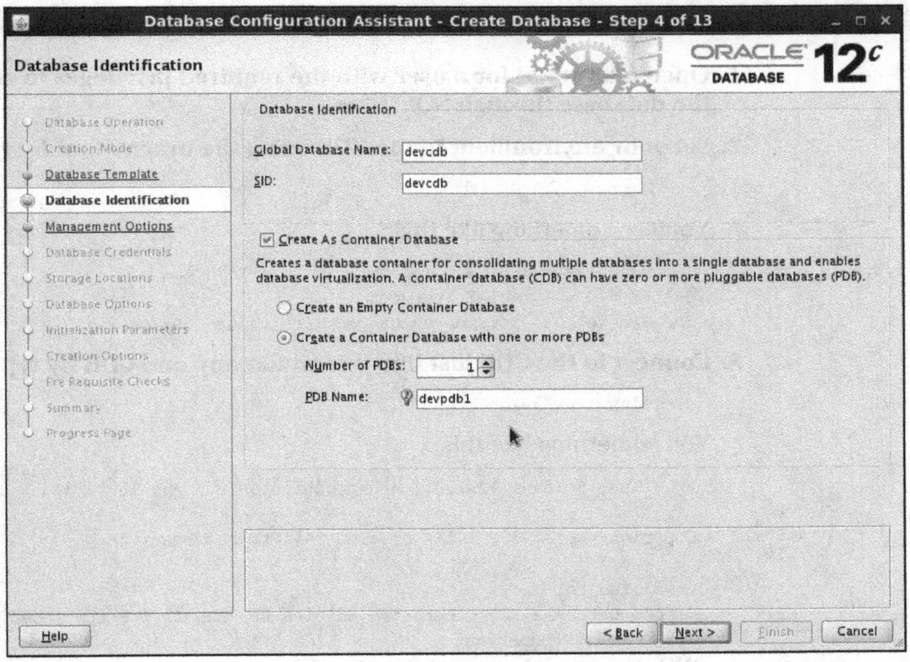

Figure 14-1:
Filling in the
information
for creating
a CDB.

Navigating a multitenant architecture

A big difference with working in a multitenant architecture is how you connect to your databases. Because there is only one SGA and one set of background processes, simply connecting to an instance like you have been taught for non-CDBs does not apply in quite the same way. You're going to want to be aware of some key new commands and data dictionary views.

First of all, how do you connect to the CDB and or PDBs? You connect to the CDB the same way you used to do in the past. You can set your ORACLE_SID and connect with SQL*Plus or RMAN as SYSDBA. Connecting to the pluggable databases is where things differ. You can connect to a PDB in two ways:

✔ You can connect to the CDB and then alter your session to set your environment to a PDB.

✔ You can set up Oracle Net to route you to a PDB through a service name by using the TNSNAMES.ORA file.

To connect to a PDB through the CDB on Linux, follow these steps:

1. **Open a terminal for a user with the required privileges to connect to the database through SQL*Plus.**

2. **Set your environment to the CDB using the oraenv tool by typing**

   ```
   <. oraenv>
   ```

   You see something like this:

   ```
   [oracle@orasvr01 ~]$ . oraenv
   ORACLE_SID = [oracle] ? devcdb
   The Oracle base remains unchanged with value /u01/app/oracle
   ```

3. **Connect to the CDB just like you would any non-CDB by typing**

   ```
   <sqlplus / as sysdba>
   ```

   You something like this:

   ```
   SQL*Plus: Release 12.1.0.1.0 Production on Fri Aug 16 23:34:59 2013

   Copyright (c) 1982, 2013, Oracle.  All rights reserved.

   Connected to:
   Oracle Database 12c Enterprise Edition Release 12.1.0.1.0 - 64bit
             Production
   With the Partitioning, OLAP, Advanced Analytics and Real Application
             Testing options
   ```

4. **To see where in the multitenant architecture you're connected, type the new 12c command:**

   ```
   <show con_name>
   ```

   You see something like this:

   ```
   CON_NAME
   ------------------------------
   CDB$ROOT
   ```

5. **Get a list of your PDBs by querying one of the new data dictionary views for supporting a multitenant environment by typing**

   ```
   <select name, open_mode
   from v$pdbs;>
   ```

   Alternatively, you can use this shortcut to get the same output:

   ```
   SQL> show pdbs
   ```

   You see something like this:

   ```
   NAME       OPEN_MODE
   ---------- ----------
   PDB$SEED   READ ONLY
   DEVPDB1    READ WRITE
   ```

Note that the PDB$SEED is visible in read only mode. It is rare that you would ever need to connect to this database — it is used primarily internally for optimization purposes when creating PDBs.

6. **To connect to your PDB DEVPDB1 from within your CBD, type:**

```
< alter session set container=devpdb1;>
```

You see something like this:

```
Session altered.
```

7. **To show that you are now in the PDB container, type**

```
<show con_name>
```

You see something like this:

```
CON_NAME
------------------------------
DEVPDB1
```

As we mention earlier, the other way to connect to your containers is directly through Oracle Net. This method supports the guarantee that the multitenant environment will be entirely compatible with non-CDB environments.

1. **Make sure that the databases are listed with the listener on the server. To do this, log in to the OS as the oracle software owner and type**

```
<lsnrctl status>
```

You see something like this:

```
Service "devcdb" has 1 instance(s).
  Instance "devcdb", status READY, has 1 handler(s) for this service...
Service "devpdb1" has 1 instance(s).
  Instance "devcdb", status READY, has 1 handler(s) for this service...
```

This output shows that the CDB and PDB have service registered with the listener.

2. **Make sure there are TNS entries on the clients from which you want to connect.**

For example, you should have entries modeled after this example:

```
DEVPDB1 =
  (DESCRIPTION =
    (ADDRESS = (PROTOCOL = TCP)(HOST = orasvr01)(PORT = 1521))
    (CONNECT_DATA =
      (SERVER = DEDICATED)
      (SERVICE_NAME = devpdb1)
    )
  )
```

3. **After you confirm the preceding configurations, you can connect from your Oracle SQL*Plus client by typing**

```
<sqlplus system@devpdb1>
```

You see something like this:

```
Last Successful login time: Fri Feb 01 2013 09:48:20 -04:00
Connected to:
Oracle Database 12c Enterprise Edition Release 12.1.0.1.0 - 64bit
          Production
With the Partitioning, OLAP, Advanced Analytics and Real Application
          Testing options
SQL>
```

Starting and stopping pluggable databases

Because the instance architecture of pluggable databases is entirely different from a non-container database, one would imagine that managing their state of readiness is also different. Well, it's true. We start by looking at the CDB itself.

The first thing to remember is that because the CDB maintains the instance for which all PDBs share, that instance must be up and open for people to be able to connect to the PDBs. Starting and stopping the CDB is not different from non-CDBs.

The next thing to remember is that when you start a CDB, all of its associated PDBs are left in MOUNT state, which means that, by default, they are not opened with the CDB. As of this writing, 12cR1 doesn't offer an option to change this behavior. However, 12c does provide a new type of trigger that will fire if it detects a CDB opening and will then open specified PDBs. See the Oracle documentation for further information on setting this up.

After starting and opening a CDB, you can open any corresponding PDBs like so:

```
SQL> alter pluggable database devpdb1 open;
Pluggable database altered.
```

Or:

```
SQL> alter pluggable database all open;
Pluggable database altered.
```

To close PDBs, you can essentially do the opposite of the preceding commands:

```
SQL> alter pluggable database devpdb1 close;
Pluggable database altered.
```

Or:

```
SQL> alter pluggable database all close;
Pluggable database altered.
```

As we mention earlier, you can use the V$PDBS data dictionary view to get information on the readiness of the PDBs.

Creating new PDBs

You can create new PDBs with traditional SQL or with the DBCA. You may note that when launching the DBCA now, a new option appears on the main screen: Manage Pluggable Databases. When you select this option, the DBCA walks you through many different activities that you can exercise against a PDB, such as

- ✔ Create
- ✔ Unplug
- ✔ Delete
- ✔ Configure

Because earlier steps show you how to do some of the CDB activity in the DBCA, the next two activities walk you through how to create a new PDB by using SQL from the SQL*Plus. We could say that it's up to you to choose which method you choose. However, using SQL offers one important benefit. To use the DBCA, you must be on the server itself to launch the tool from OS that houses the CDB. Using SQL from SQL*Plus, you can manage the PDBs from anywhere on the network with simple SQL commands that you are familiar with. You can also set up privileges to allow some user communities to have a level of self-service access for provisioning PDB environments.

Create a new PDB by using the seed on Linux

This method copies the files for the seed to a new location and associates the copied files with the new PDB, which we will call DEVPDB2. Although you have many options for creating PDBs, this example is one of the simplest ways to get up and running. Consult Oracle documentation for different options. Using this method leaves you with a "virgin" PDB with no customizations.

1. **Log in to your CDB using SQL*Plus as SYSDBA. To make sure you're in the correct location, type**

   ```
   <show con_name>
   ```

   You should see something like this:

   ```
   CON_NAME
   ------------------------------
   CDB$ROOT
   ```

   The out-of-the box file location for PDBs is in a subdirectory under the oradata directory for the CDB. For this example, we follow that approach.

2. **Create a subdirectory for the new PDB under the CDB file location from the OS oracle software owner by typing**

   ```
   <mkdir /u01/app/oracle/oradata/devcdb/devpdb2>
   ```

   If this command succeeds, you get no output. You can list the new directory by typing

   ```
   <ls -l /u01/app/oracle/oradata/devcdb |grep devpdb2>
   ```

   You should see something like this:

   ```
   drwxr-xr-x. 2 oracle oinstall      4096 Aug 17 01:56 devpdb2
   ```

3. **Back in SQL*Plus as SYSDBA, create pluggable database command by typing**

   ```
   <CREATE PLUGGABLE DATABASE devpdb2 ADMIN USER pdb2dba identified by
               "oracle"
   DEFAULT TABLESPACE USERS
   DATAFILE '/u01/app/oracle/oradata/devcdb/devpdb2/users01.dbf'
   SIZE 250M AUTOEXTEND ON
   FILE_NAME_CONVERT=(
   '/u01/app/oracle/oradata/devcdb/pdbseed/',
   '/u01/app/oracle/oradata/devcdb/devpdb2/');>
   ```

   You should see this:

   ```
   Pluggable database created.
   ```

   The new PDB is left in a mount state.

4. **Show the new PDB and open it by typing**

   ```
   <show pdbs>
   <alter pluggable database devpdb2 open;>
   ```

   You should see this:

   ```
   CON_ID CON_NAME                        OPEN MODE  RESTRICTED
   ------- ------------------------------ ---------- ----------
        2 PDB$SEED                        READ ONLY  NO
        3 DEVPDB1                         READ WRITE NO
        4 DEVPDB2                         MOUNTED
   Pluggable database altered.
   ```

5. **Verify the status by typing**

```
<show pdbs>
```

You should see this:

```
CON_ID CON_NAME                          OPEN MODE  RESTRICTED
------ ------------------------------    ---------- ----------
     2 PDB$SEED                          READ ONLY  NO
     3 DEVPDB1                           READ WRITE NO
     4 DEVPDB2                           READ WRITE NO
```

Create a new PDB by cloning an existing PDB on Linux

This method copies the files for the new PDB from the existing DEVPDB1 to a new location. We call the new PDB DEVPDB3. Again, you have many options for creating PDBs, but this example is one of the simplest ways to get up and running. Consult Oracle documentation for different options. Using this method leaves you with a PDB with all customizations of the source PDB.

DEVPDB1 has been customized with a unique tablespace MY_DATA, within which there is a table HR.EMP. These customizations carry over to the new DEVPDB3.

1. **Log in to your CDB using SQL*Plus as SYSDBA. To make sure you're in the correct location, type**

```
<show con_name>
```

You should see something like this:

```
CON_NAME
------------------------------
CDB$ROOT
```

The out-of-the box file location for PDBs is in a subdirectory under the oradata directory for the CDB. For this example, we follow that approach.

2. **Create a subdirectory for the new PDB under the CDB file location from the OS oracle software owner by typing**

```
<mkdir /u01/app/oracle/oradata/devcdb/devpdb3>
```

If this command succeeds, you get no output. You can list the new directory by typing

```
<ls -l /u01/app/oracle/oradata/devcdb |grep devpdb3>
```

You should see something like this:

```
drwxr-xr-x. 2 oracle oinstall     4096 Aug 17 02:18 devpdb3
```

3. **The source PDB needs to be put into read only mode. Do this by typing**

```
<alter pluggable database devpdb1 close immediate;>
```

You should see this:

```
Pluggable database altered.
```

Then type

```
< alter pluggable database devpdb1 open read only;>
```

You should see this:

```
Pluggable database altered.
```

4. **Run the clone command by typing**

```
< CREATE PLUGGABLE DATABASE devpdb3 FROM devpdb1
FILE_NAME_CONVERT=(
'/u01/app/oracle/oradata/devcdb/devpdb1/',
'/u01/app/oracle/oradata/devcdb/devpdb3/');>
```

You should see this:

```
Pluggable database created.
```

The new PDB is left in a mount state.

5. **Show all the PDBs and their status by typing**

```
<show pdbs>
```

You should see this:

```
CON_ID CON_NAME                           OPEN MODE  RESTRICTED
------ ----------------------------------  ---------- ----------
     2 PDB$SEED                           READ ONLY  NO
     3 DEVPDB1                            READ ONLY  NO
     4 DEVPDB2                            READ WRITE NO
     5 DEVPDB3                            MOUNTED
```

6. **Open the source DEVPDB1 read write and open the new DEVPDB3 by typing**

```
<alter pluggable database devpdb1 close immediate;>
<alter pluggable database devpdb1 open;>
<alter pluggable database devpdb3 open;>
```

You see something like this for each command:

```
Pluggable database altered.
```

7. **Show the new status of the PDBs by typing**

```
<show pdbs>
```

You should see this:

```
CON_ID CON_NAME                           OPEN MODE  RESTRICTED
------ ----------------------------------  ---------- ----------
     2 PDB$SEED                           READ ONLY  NO
     3 DEVPDB1                            READ WRITE NO
     4 DEVPDB2                            READ WRITE NO
     5 DEVPDB3                            READ WRITE NO
```

The final check is to see that the custom tablespace and table are in the new PDB.

8. **Connect to the container database. One way to do this is through the root CDB by typing**

   ```
   < alter session set container = devpdb3;>
   ```

   You see this:

   ```
   Session altered.
   ```

   You can double-check your container by typing

   ```
   <show con_name>
   ```

   You see this:

   ```
   CON_NAME
   --------------
   DEVPDB3
   ```

9. **Check your tablespaces by typing**

   ```
   <select tablespace_name, file_name
   from dba_data_files;>
   ```

   You should see something like this:

   ```
   TABLESPACE_NAME FILE_NAME
   --------------- --------------------------------------------------------------
   SYSTEM          /u01/app/oracle/oradata/devcdb/devpdb3/system01.dbf
   SYSAUX          /u01/app/oracle/oradata/devcdb/devpdb3/sysaux01.dbf
   USERS           /u01/app/oracle/oradata/devcdb/devpdb3/SAMPLE_SCHEMA_
                   users01.dbf
   EXAMPLE         /u01/app/oracle/oradata/devcdb/devpdb3/example01.dbf
   MY_DATA         /u01/app/oracle/oradata/devcdb/devpdb3/my_data01.dbf
   ```

10. **Check the HR.EMP table by typing**

    ```
    < select owner, table_name, tablespace_name
    from dba_tables
    where owner = 'HR'
    and table_name = 'EMP';>
    ```

    You see something like this:

    ```
    OWNER           TABLE_NAME                     TABLESPACE_NAME
    --------------- ------------------------------ ---------------
    HR              EMP                            MY_DATA
    ```

Unplugging and plugging in your PDBs

The activity we cover here focuses on the actual pluggable part of the PDBs. You may want to move your PDBs around for a number of reasons. For example:

- Upgrades
- Patching
- Relocation to a different CDB
- Testing
- The sky's the limit!

Unplugging your PDB

A PDB is unplugged by connecting to the root CDB and issuing the ALTER PLUGGABLE DATABASE statement to specify an XML file that will contain metadata about the PDB after it is unplugged. The XML file contains the required information to enable a CREATE PLUGGABLE DATABASE statement on a target CDB to plug in the PDB.

1. **Log in to your CDB using SQL*Plus as SYSDBA. To make sure you're in the correct location, type**

   ```
   <show con_name>
   ```

   You should see something like this:

   ```
   CON_NAME
   -------------------------------
   CDB$ROOT
   ```

2. **Get a list of your PDBs by typing**

   ```
   <show pdbs>
   ```

   You should see this:

   ```
   CON_ID CON_NAME                        OPEN MODE   RESTRICTED
   ------ ------------------------------- ----------- ----------
        2 PDB$SEED                        READ ONLY   NO
        3 DEVPDB1                         READ WRITE  NO
        4 DEVPDB2                         READ WRITE  NO
        5 DEVPDB3                         READ WRITE  NO
   ```

   Next you need to unplug DEVPDB3.

3. **Close DEVPDB3 by typing**

   ```
   <alter pluggable database devpdb3 close immediate;>
   ```

You should see this:

```
Pluggable database altered.
```

4. **Run the ALTER PLUGGABLE DATABASE statement with the UNPLUG INTO clause and specify the PDB to unplug and the name and location of the PDB's XML metadata file by typing**

```
<ALTER PLUGGABLE DATABASE devpdb3 UNPLUG INTO '/home/oracle/devpdb3.xml';>
```

You should see this:

```
Pluggable database altered.
```

Plugging in your PDB

Before you plug in a PDB, you must meet some requirements:

- ✔ The CDB must have the same endianness.
- ✔ The CDB must have the same set of options installed.
- ✔ The source CDB and the target CDB must have compatible character sets and national character sets.

For simplicity purposes, we show you how to unplug and replug the DEVPDB3 database into the same CDB root database:

1. **Log in to your CDB using SQL*Plus as SYSDBA.**

   To make sure you are in the correct location, type

   ```
   <show con_name>
   ```

   You should see something like this:

   ```
   CON_NAME
   ------------------------------
   CDB$ROOT
   ```

   Next you need to drop the existing DEVPDB3 database.

2. **To drop DEVPDB3 in a manner that preserves the data files (because they're needed to plug in database), type**

   ```
   <drop pluggable database devpdb3 keep datafiles;>
   ```

   You should see this:

   ```
   Pluggable database dropped.
   ```

3. **Run the DBMS_PDB.CHECK_PLUG_COMPATIBILITY function to determine whether the unplugged PDB is compatible with the CDB.** Type

```
SET SERVEROUTPUT ON
DECLARE
   compatible CONSTANT VARCHAR2(3) :=
     CASE DBMS_PDB.CHECK_PLUG_COMPATIBILITY(
             pdb_descr_file => '/home/oracle/devpdb3.xml')
     WHEN TRUE THEN 'YES'
     ELSE 'NO'
END;
BEGIN
   DBMS_OUTPUT.PUT_LINE(compatible);
END;
/
```

If all requirements are met, you see this:

```
YES
```

4. **Check the existing PDBs by typing**

```
<show pdbs>
```

You should see something like this:

```
CON_ID CON_NAME                         OPEN MODE  RESTRICTED
------ -------------------------------- ---------- ----------
     2 PDB$SEED                         READ ONLY  NO
     3 DEVPDB1                          READ WRITE NO
     4 DEVPDB2                          READ WRITE NO
```

5. **Plug in the database using the metadata file by typing**

```
<create pluggable database DEVPDB3 using
'/home/oracle/devpdb3.xml' NOCOPY TEMPFILE REUSE;>
```

You should see this:

```
Pluggable database created.
```

6. **Check the status of your PDBs again by typing**

```
<show pdbs>
```

You should see something like this:

```
CON_ID CON_NAME                         OPEN MODE  RESTRICTED
------ -------------------------------- ---------- ----------
     2 PDB$SEED                         READ ONLY  NO
     3 DEVPDB1                          READ WRITE NO
     4 DEVPDB2                          READ WRITE NO
     5 DEVPDB3                          MOUNTED
```

7. **Open your newly plugged in PDB by typing**

```
<alter pluggable database devpdb3 open;>
```

You should see this:

```
Pluggable database altered.
```

Chapter 15

Using High-Availability Options

A high-availability architecture combines hardware and software solutions to help reduce the impact of outages during planned and unplanned downtime. Your data's availability is of utmost importance. However, the level of availability varies by business. Some can deal with a little downtime here and there with minor business interruptions. A minute of downtime for others can cost tens of thousands of dollars. Luckily, Oracle helps you harden against the forces out there that want to make your database unavailable. Hardening your database means protecting it against unplanned downtime. Unplanned downtime can be caused by hardware failure or events like fires, floods, user errors, etc.

Implementing a high-availability architecture may not be cost effective for everyone. It can be expensive in terms of hardware and software licenses. However, if downtime costs you thousands of dollars in short intervals, look at some of Oracle's high-availability options.

This chapter is about a couple of Oracle features that you can configure for high availability. Each feature has its strengths and weaknesses. You sometimes can combine features to get the best result. And because licensing Oracle options seems to change constantly and varies from site to site and version to version, we're deferring any questions about the licensing of these features to your friendly Oracle sales rep.

Lastly, entire books and weeklong classes deal with these technologies. We give an overview within this chapter. Unfortunately, we can't prepare you for an enterprise installation and configuration of these options. Consider this a guide with tools that help you investigate.

Gathering Real Application Clusters

If you've visited Oracle's websites in the last 12 years, you've seen the marketing byline: "Unbreakable." That tag line refers to the feature *Real Application Clusters* (RAC). Of course, a lot of elements are involved, but RAC has the spotlight.

RAC is Oracle's database clustering solution. In a sense, it works on the theory that there is strength in numbers. RAC lets you have parallel database instance operating environments. These instances cooperate to share work and back each other up in case one of them fails. RAC can help with both planned and unplanned outages. It allows you to shift your processing from server to server with little to no interruption to your end users and applications.

Determining whether RAC is right for you is a big decision. Implementing RAC requires lots of resources and money. However, sometimes spending a little more up front can save you later.

Consider what RAC can offer:

- ✔ **Scalability:** The technology is based on computers and resources that team up as one. With RAC, you can purchase and license hardware as you need it. Furthermore, you can plug in the new hardware as you go without taking down your database. If you've exceeded your computing capabilities for the server, seamlessly add one to your configuration.

- ✔ **Uptime:** RAC can harden your computing environment against planned and unplanned downtime. You can transparently remove portions of the application for planned downtime (such as maintenance, patches, and upgrades) with little to no interruption to end users. Furthermore, if one of your environment's computing resources fails, RAC automatically transfers application connections to other resources in the framework.

- ✔ **Performance:** Some might argue with this point, but you have to carefully define RAC's performance capabilities:

  - • Because RAC is a complicated environment, your application has to be designed to best take advantage. If you ignore this fact, RAC can actually hurt performance. Keep that in mind.

  - • RAC can offer performance benefits when it comes to the divide-and-conquer methodology. You can split large jobs across computers. If you know an underpowered machine is limiting your company, reconfiguring the job to run on multiple machines can offer great benefits. It's called *parallel processing,* and it's part of RAC fundamentals. RAC is a *scaling out* (horizontal) solution. This means you add nodes to the cluster rather than having one server replaced with another more powerful server, or *scaling up* (vertical).

TECHNICAL STUFF

RAC versus OPS

RAC, which has been around for many years, was previously known as the *parallel server option*. Before we get flamed about when RAC was RAC, we're perfectly happy to admit that before the RAC moniker, Oracle Parallel Server (OPS) was far from the capabilities that RAC has to offer. Oracle significantly hardened the architecture, making it more accessible and easier to set up. Oracle also focused on the components of the environment that minimize downtime. So, you could say that RAC is a new breed of OPS that far surpasses prior capabilities in usability and performance.

Exploring RAC Architecture

RAC works through a complex organization of hardware and software configurations. Mostly throughout this book we talk of Oracle databases as a single set of files (the database) and a single set of memory and process components (the instance) that work together for you to access and maintain your data. That is the most typical configuration for an Oracle installation. In this configuration, the database files can be mounted and accessed by only one machine and one Oracle instance at a time.

With RAC, those files are sharable so many machines and instances can access the same files. You can have (depending on certification and versions) 100 database instances accessing the same shared database. Just like you might have two DBAs in your office:

- ✔ One can vacation while the other works (read: high availability).
- ✔ Both can work together on a large project to split the workload and meet an aggressive timeline (read: performance).
- ✔ Add a third person to meet workload requirements as the Oracle responsibilities grow (read: scalability).

Many components are required in a RAC setup. To get a general idea of what the architecture looks like, see Figure 15-1.

Hardware considerations for RAC

RAC has some special hardware requirements that single instance or non-RAC database don't have.

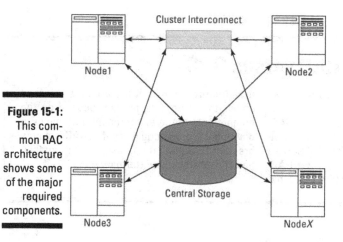

Figure 15-1:
This com-
mon RAC
architecture
shows some
of the major
required
components.

Nodes

A *node* is a server that runs an Oracle instance. A true RAC configuration has at least two nodes.

The number of nodes in your RAC configuration depends on hardware and software limitations. According to Oracle's documentation and support websites, Oracle software itself can support upwards of 100 nodes, but other forces may limit you to fewer.

If you're getting into lots of nodes (more than eight), check with all your hardware and software vendors to see what your limit is.

Add nodes as you scale your cluster. You can add and remove them with minimal or no service interruption to your application. This ensures high availability. Typically, each node will have its own installation of the Oracle software.

You can have one central, shared software directory for each node to use. However, a configuration like this limits your high-availability capabilities.

For example, one advantage to installing the Oracle software on each node is the ability to individually patch the nodes by taking them down one at a time. This *rolling patch* avoids a complete application outage. You can't apply all patches this way. Check with patch documentation to be sure. On the other hand, one central installation requires you to shut down the entire cluster to apply the patch.

Each node should have its own Oracle software code tree if you want high availability.

Central storage

The following are some RAC configuration central storage requirements:

- ✔ **All your database files, control files, redo logs, archive logs, and spfile should be on shared storage.** This way, each of the nodes has access to all the required files for data access, recovery, and configuration.

- ✔ **Attach the central storage to each node in the form of some high-speed media.** Lots of high-speed connections (fiber channel or iSCSI, for example) are available from different storage vendors. Make sure the storage and attachments are approved for Oracle RAC before making your decisions. (For example, NFS mounting drives to each server isn't typically a certified configuration.) You can use almost any shared storage configuration with decent education and testing results.

- ✔ **When choosing a storage vendor, consider your applications' performance needs.** Your disk subsystem should be able to scale as easily as your RAC nodes. As you add nodes, you may need to add physical disks to support the increased demand on the storage subsystem. You should be able to do this with little or no downtime.

- ✔ **The disk on the shared storage subsystem must be configured for shared access.** You may have up to four choices for this:
  - Raw file system (unformatted disks)
  - Oracle Cluster File System (OCFS) (available on Windows and Linux only)
  - Oracle Automatic Storage Management (ASM) (an Oracle-supplied volume manager of sorts for database-related files)
  - Third-party solution (such as Veritas)

You may have to combine options. For example, you might use Oracle ASM for your database files, but you might want something other than ASM for RMAN backup files.

Cluster interconnect

The *cluster interconnect* is a dedicated piece of hardware that manages all the inter-instance communication. A lot of communication across instances occurs in a RAC configuration: maintaining consistency, sharing lock information, and transferring data blocks.

Oracle uses Cache Fusion for managing data transfer between nodes. Cache Fusion requires an extremely reliable, private, high-speed network connecting all the nodes.

Cache Fusion is a critical component for getting RAC to perform well. The interconnect needs to be gigabit speeds or better.

When you have cluster communication performance issues, the interconnect's ability to provide the required bandwidth is questioned. It's a necessary expense to set up an RAC environment appropriately. Would you spend thousands of dollars on a race car and then put street tires on it?

Network interfaces

Make sure you have the right network interfaces on the server for proper communication. This includes multiple network interface cards:

- One for the public or user connections to the machine
- One for the private interconnect for the cluster to share information across the nodes

At the very least, a RAC configuration should have two network interface cards:

- One for the private network for cluster interconnect traffic
- One for the public network

The public network is the connection for all cluster connections, from your applications and end users (including you and the sys admin).

Software considerations for RAC

Before you set up RAC, investigate the software it needs to run smoothly. Consider the following areas of software.

Operating system

Though nearly all popular OSs run an RAC installation, you need to

- Verify that the OS is certified.
- Make sure the right release and patchsets are confirmed as RAC certified.
- Ensure that your Oracle version is certified with your OS configuration.

The Oracles Support website (http://myoraclesupport.com) provides a matrix to help you identify certified combinations.

Furthermore, an uncertified OS may be certified later. It can be complicated at first, but getting this right to start with helps you a long way down the line.

Clustering software

Arguably, clustering software is the most important piece of software. Without clustering software, there is no cluster.

The software tracks cluster members such as databases, instances, listeners, and nodes. Lots of other cluster components run on each of the nodes and require maintenance for the clusterware to work properly. The clustering software tracks these components and facilitates internode communication and health.

Depending on your experience level with different types of clustering software, you might choose one over the other. Oracle provides clustering software in the form of Oracle Grid Infrastructure. Since Oracle 10g, Oracle Clusterware is available for almost all the major operating systems. Grid Infrastructure is the preferred software to use for clustering Oracle databases.

Prior to Oracle 11gR2, Grid Infrastructure was referred to as Oracle Clusterware.

If you go with third-party clustering software, make sure it's certified by Oracle for RAC. Veritas and Sun Cluster are examples of certified third-party clustering software. However, make sure they're certified for your OS.

Oracle database

The Oracle database software is nothing special when it comes to RAC. You don't need to download any special components or anything else to make an Oracle database RAC ready. RAC is built into the database software. When you go to install Oracle RDBMS on a cluster, it recognizes that a cluster exists and asks whether you would like to do a cluster install. It's as simple as that.

Optional software

You might want to use some optional pieces of software:

- ✔ **Oracle Agent:** If you manage your database with Oracle Grid Control, you need to install an agent on the cluster. Like the database software, the agent recognizes that it's being installed on a cluster and configures itself appropriately.

- ✔ **Oracle ASM:** This is the preferred storage mechanism for Oracle database files in a RAC database. As of Oracle 11gR2, it is integrated with the Grid Infrastructure software stack. It is required for the Oracle Grid Infrastructure OCR and Voting disks, which are used for cluster node management and consistency. For database files, you can continue to use other shared file systems, such as raw or NFS.

Preparing for a RAC Install

Each OS has its own configuration for an RAC install. It's virtually impossible to cover everything here.

However, we can offer a few pieces of advice:

✔ **Thoroughly read the Oracle Grid Infrastructure installation and deployment guide for your specific OS.** What applies on one OS may not fly on another.

✔ **Be consistent across all nodes when naming users, groups, group IDs, and user IDs.** Make sure the same user owns all the Oracle software components.

For example, on Linux, *oracle* is typically an account that owns the Oracle software installation. Create this user exactly the same way as you go to all the nodes. Linux has at least two OS groups for Oracle (dba and oinstall). These must be identical. For the users and groups, this goes for the group ID (gid) and user ID (uid) as well. The gid and uid maintain permissions at the OS level. If they're not identical across nodes, permissions won't be maintained correctly, and the cluster won't function.

✔ **Set up the hosts file correctly.** This goes for all RAC installations. The clustering software uses the *hosts file* to install the software and maintain communications. The domain name server, or DNS, doesn't substitute for this. You can add the host configuration to the DNS if you want, but make sure the hosts file is properly configured.

Here's an example of what a two-node RAC host file may look like:

```
127.0.0.1 localhost.localdomain localhost

192.168.100.11 node1-priv.perptech.com node1-priv # node1 private
192.168.100.12 node2-priv.perptech.com node2-priv # node2 private

192.168.200.11 node1.perptech.com node1 # node1 public
192.168.200.12 node2.perptech.com node2 # node2 public

192.168.200.21 node1-vip.perptech.com node1-vip # node1 virtual
192.168.200.22 node2-vip.perptech.com node2-vip # node2 virtual
```

• Each cluster node connects to another through a *private* high-speed network *(cluster interconnect)*.

• The *public* IP used for all user communication to the nodes isn't related to the interconnect.

- Each cluster node also has a *virtual* IP address that binds to the public NIC. If a node fails, the failed node's IP address can be reassigned to another node so applications can keep accessing the database through the same IP address. As of Oracle 11gR2, this is done using a new cluster networking component called a SCAN. SCAN stands for single-client-access-name. Three VIPs are assigned on the network to a scan name (typically the name of your cluster), and that one SCAN name is then used for all communication. The three VIPs can float across the nodes to provide constant connectivity and failover capabilities.

✔ **When using Oracle Grid Infrastructure, install it in a directory that's *not* a subset of your Oracle base.** For example:

```
ORACLE_BASE=/u01/app/oracle
ORA_CRS_HOME=/u01/app/grid
```

You must set many permissions under the Grid Infrastructure home for special root access. You don't want those settings to interfere with the database software installation.

✔ **When using Oracle Grid Infrastructure, correctly set the permissions for the underlying storage devices that are used for the ASM disk groups.** If you don't get the permissions right, you can't complete the installation or a node reboot may either cause the clustering services to not rejoin the cluster or the node to continually reboot itself.

✔ **Configure the nodes in your cluster to be able to use the following:**

- rsh or ssh (ssh is recommend if you're on 10gR1 or greater.)
- rcp or scp (scp is recommend if you're on 10gR1 or greater.)
- User equivalence for nonpassword authentication

The communication and copying features are for software installation and patching. They aren't required for RAC to work after the fact if opening these things is against company security policies.

Tools for managing a RAC installation

Oracle supplies several tools for managing a RAC installation. Some of the tools are RAC specific, but others are also for non-RAC databases. All the tools for both RAC and non-RAC databases become *cluster aware* when you launch them in the presence of a clustered environment. This means that they will see the cluster and all the nodes in it.

Cluster awareness is extremely handy because a lot of the things you do in one node have to be done across many of the nodes. Cluster-aware tools help you accomplish those tasks more easily.

Oracle Universal Installer for Grid Infrastructure

If you choose Oracle Grid Infrastructure as your clustering software, right off the bat the Oracle Universal Installer (OUI) makes the software stack installation easy.

As long as you meet the following two criteria, the OUI begins by installing the software from one node, and then it replicates across the entire cluster:

✔ Correctly configure the hosts file across all the nodes.

✔ Enable user-equivalence, ssh/rsh, and scp/rcp for the Oracle user across all your nodes.

This way, you have to install the software only once. (You still have to run a couple of configuration scripts on the remaining nodes after the initial install on the primary node.)

Furthermore, if you ever want to add a node to the cluster, with OUI you can use the primary node to clone the software across the network to the new node.

Oracle Universal Installer for other software

After you configure the cluster, the OUI is cluster aware for all installs thereafter. That means every time you go to install Oracle software, it asks you to choose the nodes you want to do the install on. This option is very nice when you do your database and agent installations. Furthermore, all patchsets that you apply also give you the option of pushing out to all the nodes.

Of course, if you're patching in a rolling method, you can apply it one node at a time (hence, *roll* from one node to the next).

Database Configuration Assistant (DBCA)

You use the Database Configuration Assistant (DBCA) to create a database in Chapter 4. When the DBCA is launched from a node in a cluster, it too is automatically cluster aware. It begins the database creation and configuration by asking on what nodes you want to perform operations. To create a four-instance cluster across four nodes, you have to log on to only one of the servers and do it all from the DBCA. This huge timesaver automatically sets all the special initialization parameters for each node in each instance.

Network Configuration Assistant (NETCA)

When it comes to managing listeners and tnsnames files, NETCA is also cluster aware. If you need to add a listener or tnsnames entry, any action taken on one node is automatically propagated with appropriate settings across all the nodes. Configuring all the listener.ora and tnsnames.ora files across a multimode cluster would take a week by hand.

Server Control (srvctl)

Server Control is probably your day-to-day main command-line tool for managing your RAC environment.

To see an abbreviated list of all the things you can do with this tool, open a command-line prompt on your OS and type this:

```
<srvctl>
```

You see something like this:

```
Usage: srvctl <command> <object> [<options>]
    command: enable|disable|start|stop|relocate|status|add|remove|modify|getenv|
              setenv|unsetenv|config
    objects: database|instance|service|nodeapps|asm|listener
For detailed help on each command and object and its options use:
    srvctl <command> <object> -h
```

The server control utility lets you manage nearly all the resources across the entire cluster from one session. Say you're logged in to node1 and want to shut down the instance prod31 on node3 for the database prod3. This is what you'd type:

```
<srvctl stop instance -d prod3 -i prod31>
```

You should see this:

That's right: You see nothing if it works correctly. If you get errors, research appropriately.

You can use Server Control to do the following and any combination therein:

- ✔ Stop all instances of a database.
- ✔ Stop two of five instances for a database.
- ✔ Start all instances.
- ✔ Stop one or all listeners.

You can easily script Server Control into operating scripts. That's one of its big benefits. Tools such as SQL*Plus and the listener control utility (which require an execution on each node for multinode operations and multiline inputs) make for more complex scripts. With Server Control, everything is contained in one line for whatever operation you want to accomplish.

Cluster Control (crsctl)

Cluster Control is another command-line tool that controls the cluster-specific resources. It can start and stop the cluster components on individual nodes.

Type this to launch Cluster Control and get a list of the command options:

```
<crsctl>
```

You see something like this:

```
Usage: crsctl check crs - checks the viability of the Oracle Clusterware
          crsctl check cssd
                   - checks the viability of Cluster Synchronization Services
          crsctl check crsd - checks the viability of Cluster Ready Services
          crsctl check evmd - checks the viability of Event Manager
          crsctl check cluster [-node <nodename>]
                   - checks the viability of CSS across nodes
          crsctl set css <parameter> <value> - sets a parameter override
...output snipped...
          crsctl query crs activeversion - lists the Oracle Clusterware operating
If necessary any of these commands can be run with additional tracing by adding
             a 'trace' argument at the very front.
Example: crsctl trace check css
```

We cut a large portion of the output because this tool has a lot of options.

Patching the OS is one situation when Cluster Control is useful. These commands (which affect the operating state of the Grid Infrastructure) must be run as root. Commands that just report on the state of the Grid Infrastructure can be run as non-root users:

1. **Stop all the cluster resources on that particular node with Server Control.**

2. **Stop the cluster-specific components:**

   ```
   <crsctl stop crs>
   ```

   You see this:

```
Stopping resources.
Successfully stopped CRS resources
Stopping CSSD.
Shutting down CSS daemon.
Shutdown request successfully issued.
```

You might be required to reboot the node once or twice during the OS maintenance; you don't want the cluster to restart.

3. **Prevent the cluster services on this node from restarting:**

```
<crsctl disable crs>
```

4. **Do all the reboot you want.**

You don't have to worry about the cluster services interfering.

5. **Re-enable the cluster services:**

```
<crsctl enable crs>
```

6. **Restart the cluster services:**

```
<crsctl start crs>
```

All the cluster resources start, including the database-related resources on the node.

Oracle Interface Configuration Tool (OIFCFG)

If you need to change the cluster (changing server name or IP addresses, for instance), you must use the Oracle Interface Configuration Tool (OIFCFG) to reconfigure those changes in the internal cluster configuration.

Avoid making these types of changes. Put some thought into your network naming and IP choice ahead of time.

Oracle RAC application for high availability

RAC helps with *high availability* by providing redundancy in your environment — specifically, redundant Oracle instances. One instance in a multi-instance environment can be removed for OS, hardware, or Oracle software maintenance without disrupting the application.

Extended RAC

New developments are happening in a movement called Extended RAC. This RAC solution can protect against total site loss while providing all the other RAC features. As network transmission speeds increase over time, some people think that RAC is possible with instances in remote locations.

This configuration requires high-speed SAN mirroring and a network transmission media called dark fiber. *Dark fiber* is a private, direct connection between two remote sites that can handle multiple network transmissions at once over the same cable by using varying light frequencies.

At press time, Extended RAC appears to have distance limitations. The further apart the sites, the higher the latency. Latency turns into cluster performance degradation. We've been unable to find any definitive documentation on the distance limits. Degradation appears to factor heavily into your type of connection. Some sites use repeaters to extend even further.

In the meantime, if you need a remote site configured for disaster recovery, you may want to consider Data Guard. It can offer a lot of the features that Extended RAC does but at a fraction of the cost with no real distance limits.

However, make sure your expectations meet what RAC can deliver:

- ✔ RAC doesn't cover all points of failure. It definitely helps harden against node failure and instance failure. Unfortunately, it can't help with SAN, interconnect, or user error.

- ✔ RAC isn't typically considered a disaster-protection solution. If your entire site is compromised by wind, fire, or water, RAC is going with it.

Understanding Oracle Data Guard

Data Guard is Oracle's true disaster protection technology. In it, you have a minimum of two databases:

- ✔ A database called a *primary*
- ✔ A database called a *standby*

The two databases are connected by a network that ships all transactions from the primary and then applies them to the standby. In essence, you have one active database and one database in constant recovery.

Data Guard has options for multiple standby sites as well as an *active-active* configuration. By active-active, we mean both/all sites are up, running, and accessible. This is opposed to sites that have one active location and the others must be started up when they are needed. See Figure 15-2 for a general architectural layout.

Data Guard architecture

Start a description with the primary database is easy because it differs very little from any other database you might have. The only difference is what it does with its archived redo logs.

The primary database writes one set of archive redo logs to a Flash Recovery Area or a local disk. However, you may configure one or more other destinations in a Data Guard environment.

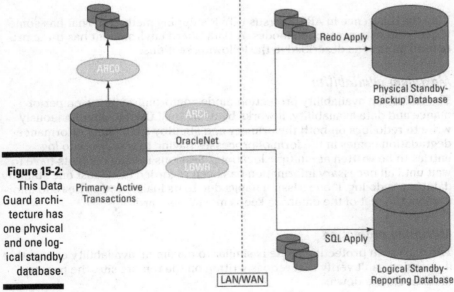

Figure 15-2:
This Data Guard architecture has one physical and one logical standby database.

The LOG_ARCHIVE_DEST_n parameter may look like this for the configuration in Figure 15-2:

```
LOG_ARCHIVE_DEST_10='LOCATION=USE_DB_RECOVERY_FILE_DEST'
LOG_ARCHIVE_DEST_1='SERVICE=PHYSDBY1 ARCH'
LOG_ARCHIVE_DEST_2='SERVICE=LOGSDBY1 LGWR'
```

- ✔ **LOG_ARCHIVE_DEST_10** is configured to send archive redo logs to the local Flash Recovery Area. One local destination is required for all archive log mode databases.

- ✔ **LOG_ARCHIVE_DEST_1** is configured to ship the archive logs via the archiver process (discussed in Chapter 2) to a remote site PHYSDBY1. The service name for this remote site has an entry in the tnsnames.ora file on the primary server.

- ✔ **LOG_ARCHIVE_DEST_2** is configured to ship the archive logs via the LGWR process to a remote site named LOGSDBY1. The service name for this remote site has an entry in the tnsnames.ora file on the primary server as well.

Why the difference in ARCn versus LGWR shipping methods? That has something to do with protection modes. A Data Guard environment has three protection modes, as described in the following sections.

Maximum availability

The maximum availability protection mode compromises between performance and data availability. It works by using the LGWR to simultaneously write to redo logs on both the primary and standby sites. The performance degradation comes in the form of processes having to wait for redo log entries to be written at multiple locations. Sessions issuing commits have to wait until all necessary information has been recorded in at least one standby database redo log. If one session hangs due to its inability to write redo information, the rest of the database keeps moving forward.

Maximum protection

The maximum protection mode is similar to maximum availability except that if a session can't verify that redo is written on the remote site, the primary database shuts down.

Configure at least two standby sites for maximum protection mode. That way, one standby site becoming unavailable won't disrupt service to the entire application.

This mode verifies that no data loss will occur in the event of a disaster at the cost of performance.

Maximum performance

The maximum performance protection mode detaches the log shipping process from the primary database by passing it to the archive log process (ARCn). By doing this, all operations on the primary site can continue without waiting for redo entries to be written to redo logs or redo shipping. This is opposed to log shipping modes that use the log writer to transfer transactions. Using the log writer can slow the processing of the transaction because it can be affected by the network availability or performance.

Maximum performance provides the highest level of performance on the primary site at the expense of *data divergence*. Data divergence occurs when the two sites' data starts to get out of sync. Archive redo data isn't shipped until an entire archive redo log is full. In a worst case scenario, an entire site loss could result in the loss of an entire archive redo log's worth of data.

Physical standby database

A *physical standby database* is a block-for-block copy of the primary site. It is built off a backup of the primary site and is maintained by shipping and applying archive logs to the standby site in the same way the transactions were committed on the primary site.

Physical standby databases can't be open for changes. You can stop recovery on the physical standby site and open it for read-only transactions. During this time, the standby site falls behind the primary site in terms of synchronicity. All the transactions are saved until the standby site's recovery is reactivated after reporting operations are done.

If you want a standby site available for reporting operations, consider setting up dual standby sites. That way, one can stay in recovery mode, and you perhaps can open the other for reporting operations during the day and then close it at night for catch-up. That way if you ever need to have a standby site activated, you won't have to wait for it to catch up first.

Here's a high-level overview of the steps to configure a physical standby database. In this example, the primary site name is prod_a and the standby site name is prod_b:

1. **Set various initialization parameters in the primary database to prepare it for redo log shipping:**

   instance_name (different on each site)

   ```
   instance_name = prod_a
   ```

db_name (same on each site)

```
db_name = prod
```

remote_archive_enable (enables sending of logs to remote site)

```
remote_archive_enable = true
```

log_archive_dest_1, 2

```
log_archive_dest_1 = 'LOCATION=/u01/arch/prod'
log_Archive_dest_2 = 'SERVICE=prod_b.world ARCH'
```

log_archive_format (tells primary how to name local and standby logs)

```
log_archive_format = arch_%S.arc
```

standby_file_management (makes adding data files easier)

```
standby_file_management = true
```

fal_client (tells primary where to re-ship "lost" archive logs)

```
fal_client = 'prod_b.world'
```

Regarding Steps 1 and 6: Set all the parameters on both sites to facilitate failover/switchover operations.

2. **Create a standby copy of your primary control file by logging in to SQL*Plus on the primary and typing the following:**

```
<alter database create standby controlfile as
'/u01/app/stdby_control.ctl';>
```

You should see this:

```
Database altered.
```

3. **Move this copy to the standby site and put it in the directory of your choice.**

4. **Modify the initialization parameters on the prod_b instance to point to the new control file.**

You can rename it however you want.

5. **Restore a backup of your primary site to the standby site.**

You can do this with RMAN or traditional hot/cold backup methods. To simplify things, put the files in the same locations on the standby site as the primary. If you can't do that, you have to rename the files after you mount the database, or you need to use the following initialization parameters on the standby site so the instance can convert the locations. Say the files were in /u01/app/oracle/oradata/prod on the primary and /disk1/app/oracle/oradata/prod on the standby:

```
DB_FILE_NAME_CONVERT = '/u01/', '/disk1/'
```

Oracle finds all instances of /u01 in your data filename and replaces them with /u02.

6. **Set the initialization parameters on the standby site:**

   instance_name (different on each site)

   ```
   instance_name = prod_b
   ```

   db_name (same on each site)

   ```
   db_name = prod
   ```

   remote_archive_enable (enables receiving of logs on remote site)

   ```
   remote_archive_enable = true
   ```

   standby_archive_dest (tells standby database where to find logs)

   ```
   standby_archive_dest = /disk1/arch/prod
   ```

   log_archive_format (tells standby how to interpret log names, set same as primary)

   ```
   log_archive_format = arch_%S.arc
   ```

   standby_file_management (makes adding data files easier)

   ```
   standby_file_management = true
   ```

   fal_server (tells standby where to search for "lost" archive logs)

   ```
   fal_server = 'prod_a.world'
   ```

7. **Mount the standby database:**

   ```
   <alter database mount standby database;>
   ```

   You should see this:

   ```
   Database altered.
   ```

8. **Start recovery on the standby database:**

   ```
   <recover managed standby database disconnect;>
   ```

   You see this:

   ```
   Media recovery complete.
   ```

9. **Log out of the standby site.**

   Let the recovery run in the background.

Logical standby database

A *logical standby database* works by copying your primary site with a backup. Then a process called SQL Apply takes the archive logs from the primary site and extracts the SQL statements from them to apply them to the logical standby database. During this time, the logical standby database is up and open. It's like having the best of both worlds. People can have updated data with the primary site for reporting purposes.

Because the standby database will be up and open, you must protect the data from being modified by anyone other than the SQL Apply services. If the data is modified outside of this procedure, the standby database will diverge from the primary. If you ever need to switch over to it for disaster recovery purposes, it won't match the primary.

To prevent replicated objects in the standby site from being modified, issue the following command in the standby environment:

```
ALTER DATABASE GUARD STANDBY;
```

Another unique feature of a logical standby database: the ability to replicate only certain objects. By default, all objects are replicated. However, you can force SQL Apply processes to skip certain objects. In addition, you can configure those skipped objects to allow modifications to them.

Performing switchover and failover operations

You can switch processing to your standby site two ways:

- ✔ **Switchover** is a planned switch that can occur if you want to do maintenance on the primary site that requires it to be unavailable. This operation may require a few minutes of downtime in the application, but if you have to do maintenance that lasts for an hour or more, the downtime could be worthwhile. This operation is called a *graceful* switchover because it turns the primary site into your standby and your standby site into your primary. Also, you can easily switch back to the original primary site without having to re-create it from scratch.

- ✔ **Failover** occurs when the primary site has been compromised in some way. Perhaps it was a total site loss, or maybe you discovered physical corruption in a data file. Not always, but usually after a failover, you have to either completely re-create the primary site or recover it from a backup and re-instate it. You usually perform a failover only when you've determined that fixing the primary site will take long enough that you prefer not to have an application outage for the entire time.

To perform a switchover, follow these steps:

1. On the current primary, log in to SQL*Plus and type the following:

```
<alter database commit to switchover to physical standby;>
```

You should see this:

```
Database altered.
```

2. **Shut down the primary database:**

```
<shutdown immediate>
```

You should see this:

```
Database closed.
Database dismounted.
ORACLE instance shut down.
```

3. **Start the primary database in nomount mode:**

```
<startup nomount>
```

You should see something like this:

```
ORACLE instance started.
Total System Global Area  789172224 bytes
Fixed Size                  2148552 bytes
Variable Size             578815800 bytes
Database Buffers          201326592 bytes
Redo Buffers                6881280 bytes
```

4. **Mount the database as a standby:**

```
<alter database mount standby database;>
```

You should see this:

```
Database altered.
```

5. **Start recovery:**

```
<recover managed standby database disconnect;>
```

You see this:

```
Media recovery complete.
```

6. **Log in to SQL*Plus on the current standby and type the following:**

```
<alter database commit to switchover to physical primary;>
```

You should see this:

```
Database altered.
```

7. **Shut down the standby database:**

```
<shutdown immediate>
```

You should see this:

```
Database closed.
Database dismounted.
ORACLE instance shut down.
```

8. **Make sure all appropriate initialization parameters are set for this database to behave properly as a primary.**

9. **Start it normally:**

   ```
   <startup>
   ```

   You should see something like this:

   ```
   ORACLE instance started.
   Total System Global Area  789172224 bytes
   Fixed Size                  2148552 bytes
   Variable Size             578815800 bytes
   Database Buffers          201326592 bytes
   Redo Buffers                6881280 bytes
   Database mounted.
   Database opened.
   ```

10. **Make sure the users and applications can connect to and use the new primary instance.**

Part V
The Part of Tens

Discover ten great Internet resources for Oracle information at www.dummies.com/extras/oracle12c.

In this part . . .

✔ Chapter 16 covers ten things you should definitely do when installing Oracle.

✔ Put your designer thinking cap on for Chapter 17, which covers ten things to do when designing your Oracle database.

Chapter 16

Ten Oracle Installation Do's

• •

*I*n this chapter, we describe ten things you shouldn't overlook when installing Oracle. Getting off to a good start with a solid, proper installation is key to success. By recognizing the common pitfalls up front, you experience less heartache and pain later on. As the saying goes, a house must be built on a solid foundation.

Know the Documentation

Every OS that runs Oracle has a corresponding documentation set. This documentation covers installation prerequisites such as operating system packages, kernel parameters, network configuration, and more.

Every operating system is different. Even if you think they're the same, you're wrong. UNIX is UNIX, right? Wrong. HP-UX, AIX, and Solaris each have very distinct prerequisites. Go to the Oracle documentation on the Internet and download the latest and greatest installation guide for your OS. Read it thoroughly before you begin. We even recommend listing all the little things that you have to check before you begin. For example:

✔ What is the default operating shell of the OS (Korn, BASH, or CSH)?

✔ What tools are used to view OS performance data?

✔ What commands are used to list the storage on the server?

If you make this a practice, you will find far fewer problems during and after installation.

Here's the quickest way to get to the Oracle documentation:

1. **Go to** `http://docs.oracle.com`.
2. **Select the version you're interested in.**

You see all the product offerings here, including the database. At this point, we're focused on the database, so find the appropriate section. Hint: It's usually at the top!

3. **When you enter the 12c documentation set, click the Installing and Upgrading link to go to a subset of the documentation that focuses on installation and upgrade topics.**

You can also click the + on the left side of the screen to get a list of more links for installing and upgrading.

4. **Click the OS of your choice to enter the OS-specific installation guide.**

Observe the Optimal Flexible Architecture

The *Optimal Flexible Architecture* (OFA) is an Oracle guideline that lays out how software and databases should be installed on a system. The OFA has these main purposes:

- ✔ Find Oracle files in explicit locations, even when on multiple devices.
- ✔ Set up a software tree that allows easy patching and upgrades.
- ✔ Mirror Oracle installations across all environments so they're the same or similar.
- ✔ Keep separate Oracle files and installation types.
- ✔ Facilitate routine management tasks.
- ✔ Facilitate backup and recovery.
- ✔ Manage and administer growth.
- ✔ Facilitate layout for best performance.

We recommend you fully read and understand the Oracle documentation to best implement the OFA.

There are many rules and guidelines for using Oracle — too many to cover here. The Oracle documentation gives explicit examples and suggestions for a variety of operating systems and storage. Furthermore, OFA has evolved over the years. The main ideas remain, but some have been tweaked. For each release of Oracle, don't hesitate to refresh yourself. The Oracle installation guide (which we mention earlier) has a section for each OS and its recommended OFA guidelines.

Configure Your Profile

The profile applies more to UNIX-type environments. However, by learning the key elements needed inside the profile, you can also see that they may apply to Windows.

The *profile* is the program (for lack of a better word) that runs every time you log in to your operating system. It is typically found in your home directory. Depending on the shell you use, it might be named any of the following ways:

- ✔ .profile
- ✔ .kshrc
- ✔ .bash_profile

By configuring this script, you can take better advantage of the operating environment and your Oracle software. Different types of users also may have different profiles. Furthermore, you may have multiple profiles depending on what you will do when you log in.

The profile sets up variables, execution paths, permissions, and sometimes limits in your session. The Oracle documentation recommends specific settings for your environment. Some are OS specific; others apply to almost all Oracle installations.

Definitely include these elements in your profile:

- ✔ Oracle base variable
- ✔ Oracle home variable
- ✔ Path variable
- ✔ Default file-permission settings
- ✔ Aliases
- ✔ Library variables

Without a properly configured profile, you have to change these every time you log in to the system. We want to say having a profile is a requirement, but technically it's not. However, you should make it part of your standard practice.

Write Your Own Documentation

Although plenty of documentation is available for you on the Internet and from Oracle itself, none of it is going to apply specifically to your installation. Every system has its little ins and outs and configuration customizations that differ slightly from what's out there. Even if you follow the Oracle documentation to the letter, wading through it to install the software a second time (say, on another machine) is sometimes tedious.

Call your documentation what you want:

- ✔ Playbook
- ✔ Cookbook
- ✔ Cheatsheet

Creating a document with all the concise steps needed for your installation (and patching, database creations, and backup strategies) and keeping it in a shared, accessible location will help all future activities be more consistent, efficient, and mistake free.

You may not always be at your company. You also may leave on good terms. Making sure your replacements have everything they need to understand what you did and why in the Oracle environment helps the transition go more smoothly. Plus, you can take your documentation with you to help on the next job!

Set umask

If you read and follow the Oracle documentation, setting the umask parameter should not be a problem. Linux/UNIX environments have an umask setting.

Forgetting to properly set the umask parameter means a difficult, if not impossible, Oracle installation. The result doesn't typically affect the Oracle software owner; instead, it affects the users who log in to the OS and try to use the system.

umask sets the default permission modes on files and directories that are added to the system. These permission modes can affect files copied to the system during installation, as well as things like log files, which are created as part of normal operation.

The Oracle-recommended umask is 022. This setting results in files being read+write for the owner and read for all others. If you put the umask setting in the profile, it sets each time you log in.

Become Oracle

On a production system, the Oracle database software should be installed by a user specifically created for the task. This user is typically named *oracle.* Imagine that. Now, this isn't a hard and fast rule, but we recommend that you seriously consider this — especially if you're a beginner. This is the setup that you find in most systems as well as training materials and documentation.

Naming the user *oracle* avoids this scenario: The Oracle software is installed as another named user or by a user associated with a different software package. You don't want John Smith installing the Oracle software stack under his own ID. He may leave the company someday, leaving you with a problem.

It's not best practice to let login IDs exist for people who no longer work at the company, which is a security concern, not to mention confusing.

Set up a dedicated ID (we recommend *oracle*) to install software with. This dedicated ID makes maintenance and training easier, and it eases personnel transitions. This recommendation also comes from Oracle.

Some people have multiple versions of the database installed on the same machine. This is okay. You can keep the versions separate by having separate oracle owners. For example, you might have ora11g, ora12c, and so on.

Stage It

If you download the software from the Oracle website, you don't need it on DVD for installation. We recommend keeping a hard copy somewhere for recovery reasons, but that's about it.

Even if you bought the installation DVDs, copy the material to the hard drive before the installation.

- ✔ The install is faster if the Oracle Universal Installer is reading from hard disk as opposed to DVD.
- ✔ You don't have to worry about someone else in the server room ejecting the disk and it disappearing forever.

✔ Having a copy of the software helps if you want to add a feature that you hadn't installed at first. It's easier to find the copy in a staging area than hunting down the disk.

✔ If the Oracle binary files are corrupt or lost due to some sort of disk failure and you need to reinstall a portion of the code tree, it's right there. Sometimes downloading it can take some time. Having it readily available is the best thing to do.

You can get software from Oracle two ways:

✔ Order it from the Oracle store.

✔ Download it from the Oracle website.

Both copies are identical. The downloadable software isn't a trial version. Anyone can download and use it, provided you contact an Oracle sales rep and pay for it.

Patch It

You just downloaded and installed your brand-new Oracle database. Now we're telling you it needs to be patched. What?! Whether you order the DVDs or download the software, you're probably not getting the most recent version. If you're licensed for Oracle — and you should be — log in to the Oracle Support website and search for the most recent patchsets to apply to your database.

1. **Go to the Oracle Support website at** `http://support.oracle.com.`

2. **Enter your login ID.**

   If you don't have one, click the Register button and follow those instructions.

3. **Enter your customer support identifier (CSI).**

   You get this when you purchase support from an Oracle sales representative.

   When you log in, you see tabs across the top of the page.

4. **Click the Patches and Updates tab.**

5. **Click Product or Family.**

6. **Enter the following information:**

   • Your product (RDBMS Server)

   • Your release

   • Your OS

   • On the left, options to customize your search

We recommend being on the latest, greatest maintenance release of the Oracle software — but make sure the software is compatible with or supported by your application.

Many times we've discovered a client with an older version of Oracle. When we recommend a patch, the client announces it has some third-party software vendor who certifies only on a certain patch level.

Despite the problems with third-party software, there are benefits to being on the latest Oracle patchset:

✔ Oracle keeps creating patches to fix bugs in the release as long as your patch level is supported. Otherwise, you're out of luck.

✔ Quarterly Oracle security patches are usually available for the most recent patchsets only.

✔ The patchsets are maintenance releases in essence. This means that bugs found in previous releases are fixed.

Despite all the good things about being on the latest Oracle patchset, read the patchset documentation before you apply the patch; specifically, check the known issues section. Unfortunately, sometimes bugs are introduced with a patchset. Make sure that any new issues don't affect the functionality your application works with.

Mind the User and Group IDs

This bit of advice pertains more to Linux/UNIX operating systems. When a group or user is created on Linux/UNIX, that group or user is assigned a user ID number. All file ownership and permissions are based on this number. By default, the OS chooses the first available number. This isn't where problems occur.

Problems occur when you install Oracle on multiple servers — especially systems using Oracle RAC or DataGuard. Due to file sharing, if the user and group IDs don't match across the systems, they're not going to function properly. Furthermore, if you're shipping Oracle files across the network (transportable tablespaces or cloning, for instance), you'll have problems reading these files when they arrive.

The best practice is to specifically assign a number to your Oracle user and its associated groups when they're created. Document this number in your company's Oracle operating procedures manual. If you have multiple DBAs or Oracle installers, use the same ID numbers across all systems.

Back It Up

You finally configured your OS, set up all the Oracle users and groups, configured your profile, staged the software (and its patches), installed Oracle, patched Oracle, and created your first database. Unlike the guidelines in Chapter 11, here we are specifically referring to the software binary directories . . . not your database.

Now back up your work! Also, test your backup to make sure it's usable. We have seen people lose jobs because they never tested a backup and were unable to recover something.

Besides just creating a backup at the end, you could do multiple backups as you go: after the OS prerequisites are done, after Oracle is installed, after the patch, and so on. That way, you can easily go back without completely starting over.

Chapter 17

Ten Database Design Do's

*I*n this chapter, we focus on some of the mistakes and shortcomings we've seen in Oracle databases over the years. Most of these are honest mistakes due to inexperience with Oracle or databases in general and can easily be overcome. After all, if it weren't for issues like these, DBAs like you wouldn't have anything to do!

Constrain Your Data

Constraints enforce rules against your data. Oracle offers some of these built-in constraints:

- **Primary keys** identify a column or columns in the table whose data for the values stored is unique and non-null.
- **Foreign keys** enforce something called *referential integrity*.
- **Check constraints** are customizable constraints that check the data entered into a column.
- **Not Null constraints** disallow an empty column to be empty.
- **Unique constraints** are a column or group of columns whose values together are unique for the row.

Constraints are a very useful and almost required feature in any database. Odd as it may seem, some software vendors don't natively include a system of constraints in the database software. This situation requires developers to code their own constraints in the application. This approach can be extremely difficult and a nightmare to maintain. Not to mention the fact that they will be enforced only through the application itself. Anybody gaining access via a tool such as SQL*Plus won't be required to obey the application constraints.

In some Oracle databases, the designer or primary developers came from a database that required the constraints to be created and managed in the application. Make sure you don't fall victim to this situation: Use the built-in Oracle constraints.

Spread Out Your IO

When laying the files down on your system, you should make sure to evenly balance the files across the available disks. Some people might argue that their hands are tied.

For systems using local storage inside the server, buy as many smaller disks as possible so you can balance your IO (input/output). These days, it seems that manufacturers are offering ever-larger devices for storage, which makes your job difficult. Keep in mind that when you work with the storage/server vendor, the machine is for storing and retrieving data. By having several locations to store your data, you get more tuning capabilities.

The rules for storing Oracle files can be broken down in an infinite number of ways. Here are some basics:

- ✔ Separate tables and indexes across different drives.
- ✔ Store your redo log groups and members separately.
- ✔ Store extraneous data unrelated to application data separately.
- ✔ Store table partitions separately.
- ✔ Store system files separately.
- ✔ Store the Oracle binaries on their own device.
- ✔ Store backups separately.
- ✔ Use storage performance tiering to separate your data (high-value data on the fast/expensive disks; low-value data on the slower/ cheaper disks).

You can break down your storage system even further depending on your data access behavior. By using the Oracle data dictionary and available monitoring tools, you can fine-tune the storage layout for your specific application.

Know Basic Data Modeling Skills

Data normalization is how you lay out your application storage needs in your tables. Before you begin designing a database from scratch, know the rules of normalization.

Some developers fall victim to data normalization shortcomings because of previous experience with other databases. For example, we've seen people design data models based on their experience with Microsoft Excel or Lotus Notes. These flat file-type databases have different rules for design. Normalization is a set of rules designed for relational type databases. Spend some quality time with an Oracle data-modeling book or class before you get too far in an application design project.

Use Naming Conventions

This topic boils down to good data-modeling skills. When you're creating objects in your system, it's important to follow rules. If you do your research or take a class on data modeling, you know the guidelines. Best practice is to adhere to those as best as possible. However, the most important thing is to follow some sort of documented, repeatable guidelines everyone can easily understand.

Avoid these common mistakes:

- ✔ **Don't use keywords.** Don't name your table *table*.

- ✔ **Don't let the system give default names.** This happens often with constraints. Take the time to come up with something descriptive.

- ✔ **Don't use quotes with column names and table names.** Many over-the-counter developer tools do this. The problem is that you can end up with objects that have mixed-case names. Next thing you know, you have different tables named EMP, emp, and emP.

Create a document that outlines the standard practices your company will use. This table will aid in the training of new hires and make sure the IT department is on the same page when working collaboratively on an application.

Watch Your Roles and Privileges

Make sure you don't fall to temptation and take the easy way out when configuring object access. Don't grant everything to everybody because the design team doesn't want to put a system of roles and privileges in place. Taking the easy way is especially tempting when you need to meet a project deadline and a developer is dead in the water.

Do your best to come up with different roles for your developers, application users, and application owners. This effort makes management and security much easier down the road. Chapter 10 deals with configuring roles and privileges in your database. That chapter is very important not only for security but manageability.

Always question people when they ask for privileges. Most of the time people ask for way more than they need.

Did you know that poor role and privilege design can also add to performance problems? It's true. Every time someone runs a SQL statement, all the privileges for the person and objects involved have to be examined. When people have more privileges than they need, more internal rows have to be examined when Oracle is figuring out what they're allowed to do. Examining these privileges may add only milliseconds to SQL execution, but as numbers of users executing SQL compound over time, the extra overhead of examining privileges takes away from memory and CPU resources.

Axe Ad Hoc Queries

Okay, getting rid of ad hoc queries is difficult advice to swallow. Dozens of companies offer tools that show managers how easy it is to go into a database and design all kinds of fancy reports with graphs and colors. They promise increased revenue and efficient information transfer. The problem is that these products are marketed to managers, not the technical team.

We aren't saying that there is no place for a tool like this. Quite the opposite. After all, the whole point of having a database is to serve up data. However, having some control over what type of reports are allowed is going to make the DBA, the system administrator, and the end users happier overall.

If you allow unsolicited ad hoc queries in your database to run any time, in any form, you're asking for trouble. Not only can they run slowly, but the entire database can become unusable during their execution.

In an ideal world, reports are designed, qualified, and approved before they're run. A team of developers can work with DBAs and managers to list information needs. Those can be skillfully and efficiently transformed into canned reports available at the click of a button. They can be scheduled to run at specific times to avoid impacting the system.

Enforce Password Security

When you create a user in Oracle, you're forced to set a password. This is good. However, not until 11g did Oracle force you to make sure that password was secure. During database creation, Oracle asks whether you want to revert to the pre-11g security requirements, which were minimal. Luckily, in 12c, Oracle doesn't ask you anymore. Instead, it forces you to use a more secure approach out of the gate. In any case, if you're new to a system, one of the first things we recommend is an overview of the password security system.

Oracle password profiles remedy the following common problems easily:

- ✔ Lack of password complexity
- ✔ No regular password expiration schedule
- ✔ Reusable passwords
- ✔ Shared logins
- ✔ Default passwords

Implementing password security through a user profile is extremely easy. Unfortunately, one of the side effects is that the users will hate you for it! People seem to hate having to remember a password that's something other than their username. However, don't let the moaning of your colleagues sway you. Strong passwords are critical. You don't want your company being the next one vilified on CNN because of a security breach.

Avoid Having Too Many Cooks in the Kitchen

Make sure that only company-approved people have access to the DBA role on the database. Not only does having unapproved DBAs threaten security, it also reduces accountability. Tracing problems is much easier when the source isn't a group of dozens of users. Most problems we encounter are due to user error because someone did something with a privilege without understanding all the consequences.

Again, expect resistant users. Every company has that person who's been with the team for 20 years and knows the business and application inside and out. He has always had DBA access. The problem is that he hasn't had any formal Oracle training or experience.

Do what you have to do to convince management that few people should have the keys to the kingdom. Also, make sure those people who *do* have the keys are trained and accountable for the actions they take. If you present your case correctly, people should be thanking you. You're removing untrained people from the pool of people who are going to have the finger pointed at them when problems occur. Think of it this way: As a DBA, you do not want root access. Sure, that is at times inconvenient, but, you also don't want your name in the hat when problems occur on the OS and blame is being assigned.

Package Code

SQL is the primary language for accessing and manipulating Oracle data. You can embed it in applications or store it in the database in the form of stored procedures.

Not all SQL needs to be stored in the database, but consider designing the application so the bulk of the business processes is made up of stored code.

Unless the developers are trained to take advantage of Oracle's stored procedure mechanisms, you don't have the best, most efficient database possible.

- ✔ **Stored code enforces security.** A stored procedure can be encrypted (*wrapped,* in Oracle terms). Users can run procedures without access to the base objects with which the code works. Stored procedures are executed with the owner's permissions, not the user who is calling it. When you store code, a user does not need a privilege to UPDATE or DELETE from a table. The user just needs access to the procedural code that does the UPDATE or DELETE for them. That way, he or she cannot access the table outside the program to modify the data. Heck, the user can't even see the table.

- ✔ **Stored code performs better.** It is precompiled in the database and can be stored in memory without parsing and compiling. This situation decreases CPU usage and increases system scalability. Stored code is easier to maintain because it's in one place. If you're adding functionality or changing business rules, the application can immediately take advantage of the changes without releasing a new version.

Test Recovery Strategies

With a little training, it's easy to design a backup process for your system. Testing is a key element to a robust backup and recovery strategy. However, running an error-free backup every night doesn't mean you can recover with it.

Now, we don't want to be doomsday preachers. Using RMAN and getting backups with no errors mean you have a significant chance of recovery. But what if you need those backups and they don't work? You could be, as they say, caught with your pants down. You might even be out of a job.

This advice about testing extends to training. Do you know what commands to issue for a recovery? Do you know the fastest way to recover given the specific type of failure? Will you use RMAN or Flashback Database?

Testing your recovery strategy checks the backup itself and lets you practice for situations where a speedy recovery is required. You don't want to spend an hour reading the Oracle documentation when you're in a pinch. Know how to reduce the liability of your skill set by testing and practice.

Also, harkening back to the preceding chapter, document your recovery process. You may not be the custodian of the databases forever. Someone will come along after you. Giving other people a leg up preserves your legacy. Or, you can think of it purely selfishly: What if you have to do a recovery and you haven't practiced for over a year? How much of your time is going to be spent figuring out the right commands to run? How will you get the backups from tape? If you have a playbook laid out, you can significantly reduce your mean time to recovery.

Installing Oracle 12c on Linux

* * *

* * *

To get you started, this appendix shows you how to install the Oracle 12c software on Linux, which is a readily available, free operating system. This chapter gives you the necessary steps to install Oracle on the many flavors of Linux, as well as some Unix systems. The examples in this appendix use Oracle Enterprise Linux 6 (OEL6.4).

This Oracle installation can test most of the features discussed in this book, with the exception of Oracle clustering covered in Chapter 15. We recommend having at least 2GB of memory and 10GB of free hard disk space.

Setting Up the Operating System

Linux environments have some stringent installation prerequisites. This appendix goes over the basic prerequisites as specified in the documentation set Oracle Database Quick Installation Guide for 12c Release 1 (12.1) for Linux x86.

To view this documentation set, follow these steps:

1. **Go to** http://docs.oracle.com.
2. **Click Oracle Database documentation, 12c Release 1 (12.1).**
3. **Click the + next to the Installing and Upgrading folder.**
4. **Click Linux Installation Guides.**

   The Quick Installation Guide for Linux x86, on the right, is the document you want.

The next section assumes you can complete the required tasks logged in as the user root.

Checking your operating system version

Oracle is certified to run on only particular versions of Linux. If you have trouble with your database and need Oracle support, those support folks may insist that you be on a certified version of Linux before they help you. Furthermore, running on a certified version of Oracle with the necessary set of patches eliminates many frustrating problems that can bring your installation to a halt.

Oracle can be a little tough to install, but if you carefully follow the directions and meet the prerequisites, the installation usually runs well. Because the prerequisites change from release to release, always review the Oracle documentation first to prevent headaches.

Here are the supported versions of Linux for Oracle 12c:

- Oracle Enterprise Linux 5
- Oracle Enterprise Linux 6
- Red Hat Enterprise Linux 5
- Red Hat Enterprise Linux 6
- SUSE Enterprise Linux 11

To see what version of Linux you're on, follow these steps:

1. **Open a command prompt on your OS.**

2. **Type**

   ```
   <cat /proc/version>
   ```

   You should see something like this:

   ```
   Linux version 2.6.39-400.17.2.el6uek.x86_64
       (mockbuild@ca-build44.us.oracle.com)
       (gcc version 4.4.7 20120313 (Red Hat 4.4.7-3) (GCC) ) #1 SMP
   ```

3. **Type**

   ```
   <cat /etc/oracle-release>
   ```

   You should see something like this, which shows you whether you're running a version on which Oracle 12c is certified:

   ```
   Oracle Linux Server release 6.4
   ```

Checking your kernel version

The *kernel* is essentially the core operating version of Linux OS. It's kind of akin to a Service Pack in Windows. For Oracle to be certified, you also need to be on a certified kernel version.

Oracle Linux 6 with the Unbreakable Enterprise kernel's required kernel version is 2.6.39 or later. To see your kernel version, type

```
<uname -r>
```

You should see something like this:

```
2.6.39-400.17.2.el6uek.x86_64
```

 If you don't like command line interface for these checks, you can choose System⇨About This Computer (via the Gnome GUI desktop) to find your kernel release information and memory, processor, and disk specifics on one screen.

Checking your OS packages

Packages are modular pieces of the OS that you can install to activate certain features. For Oracle to run on Linux, it requires particular packages. These packages vary from release to release of Oracle, so reviewing the Oracle documentation specific to the version you are attempting to install is critical.

Both Oracle Linux 6 and Red Hat Enterprise Linux 6 require the following packages (or later versions) be installed:

- ✔ binutils-2.20.51.0.2-5.11.el6 (x86_64)
- ✔ compat-libcap1-1.10-1 (x86_64)
- ✔ compat-libstdc++-33-3.2.3-69.el6 (x86_64 and i686)
- ✔ gcc-4.4.4-13.el6 (x86_64)
- ✔ gcc-c++-4.4.4-13.el6 (x86_64)
- ✔ glibc-2.12-1.7.el6 (x86_64 and i686)
- ✔ glibc-devel-2.12-1.7.el6 (x86_64 and i686)
- ✔ ksh
- ✔ libgcc-4.4.4-13.el6 (x86_64 and i686)
- ✔ libstdc++-4.4.4-13.el6 (x86_6464 and i686)
- ✔ libstdc++-devel-4.4.4-13.el6 (x86_64 and i686)
- ✔ libaio-0.3.107-10.el6 (x86_64 and i686)

- libaio-devel-0.3.107-10.el6 (x86_64 and i686)
- libXext-1.1 (x86_64 and i686)
- libXtst-1.0.99.2 (x86_64 and i686)
- libX11-1.3 (x86_64 and i686)
- libXau-1.0.5 (x86_64 and i686)
- libxcb-1.5 (x86_64 and i686)
- libXi-1.3 (x86_64 and i686)
- sysstat-9.0.4-11.el6 (x86_64)

To see whether a required package is installed, use RedHat Package Manager (rpm). For example, to check the *make* package, type

```
rpm -q make
```

You should see something like this:

```
make-3.81-20.el6.x86_64
```

If you find some packages not installed or that don't meet the required version, get them from the Linux distribution installation media or the appropriate Linux vendor's download site.

Creating Linux OS groups and users

Linux best practices entail creating specific groups and users to install, own, and maintain the Oracle software.

Oracle requires two OS groups for the software:

- **dba** controls what users can do on the database server using OS authentication.
- **oinstall** controls which users are allowed to modify the Oracle software. Software modification includes installs, upgrades, and patching.

To perform the commands that follow, log in to the Linux computer as a Linux super user (root).

To create the groups, type

```
<groupadd dba><enter>
<groupadd oinstall><enter>
```

These commands have no output if the groups add successfully. If errors occur, review the details and fix as appropriate.

Do *not* add any users to Linux groups unless they're approved database administrators (DBAs). Members of these groups can see almost any data they want or damage the database and Oracle installation.

Creating the Oracle Software Owner

On a Linux installation of Oracle, best practice is to create a special user to own the Oracle software. Although you can name the user whatever you want, the best practice is to typically call that user *oracle* or some name with *ora* in it (such as *ora12c*):

```
useradd -c "Oracle Software Owner" -d /home/oracle -m -g oinstall
-s /usr/bin/ksh -G dba oracle
```

This command creates

- ✔ A user called *oracle*
- ✔ With the primary group *oinstall*
- ✔ In a secondary group *dba*
- ✔ With a home directory /home/oracle
- ✔ With korn shell as the default shell

After you create this user, change its password to something that you will remember, but not something too easy (such as "oracle").

To change the password for the user oracle, type

```
<password oracle>
```

It prompts you for the new password.

Configuring the Linux Kernel Parameters

The Linux OS has a set of kernel parameters that control how memory and processes function on the system. Installing Oracle typically involves adjusting these parameters. The parameters are found in the /etc directory in the sysctl.conf file.

Edit the sysctl.conf file (make a backup first!) and modify the following parameters to have the specified values:

```
fs.aio-max-nr = 1048576
fs.file-max = 6815744
kernel.shmall = 2097152
kernel.shmmax = 536870912
kernel.shmmni = 4096
kernel.sem = 250 32000 100 128
net.ipv4.ip_local_port_range = 9000 65500
net.core.rmem_default = 262144
net.core.rmem_max = 4194304
net.core.wmem_default = 262144
net.core.wmem_max = 1048586
```

If one of the parameters doesn't exist, add it just as it looks here. To make the changes take effect, type the following command:

```
/sbin/sysctl -p
```

Creating the ORACLE_BASE directory

The ORACLE_BASE directory serves as the starting point for all your Oracle installation files. Choosing this directory carefully is important. Ideally, it will be on its own drive or mount point.

A typical ORACLE_BASE might be /u01/app/oracle.

1. **Create the ORACLE_BASE directory:**

   ```
   mkdir /u01/app/oracle
   ```

2. **Change the ownership of the directory so that the owner is *oracle*, and the group is *oinstall*:**

   ```
   chown -R oracle:oinstall /u01/app/oracle
   ```

3. **Change the permissions on the directory:**

   ```
   chmod -R 775 /u01/app/oracle
   ```

   Now the owner can read, write, and execute; all other users can read and execute recursively.

Configuring the Oracle user environment

When you create the user oracle, the user has the korn shell. The korn shell is controlled by a .profile file in the user's home directory.

To set up the user's (oracle) environment, follow these steps:

1. **Log in to an OS terminal window as the user oracle.**

   You are in the home directory /home/oracle.

2. **Edit the .profile file and add the following lines.**

```
export PATH=/usr/kerberos/sbin:/usr/kerberos/bin:
           /usr/local/sbin:/usr/local/bin:/sbin:/bin:/usr/sbin:/usr/bin:.
export ORACLE_BASE=/u01/app/oracle
export ORACLE_HOME=/u01/app/oracle/product/12.1.0
export ORACLE_SID=dev12c
export LD_LIBRARY_PATH=$ORACLE_HOME/lib
export PATH=$ORACLE_HOME/bin:$PATH
```

If the file already exists, make sure to add the lines to the bottom of the file.

3. **Save and exit the .profile file.**

4. **Run the following command to make the changes take effect:**

```
<. .profile>
```

There is no output.

5. **See whether the changes worked:**

```
<env |grep ORA>
```

You should see something like this:

```
ORACLE_SID=dev12c
ORACLE_BASE=/u01/app/oracle
ORACLE_HOME=/u01/app/oracle/product/12.1.0
```

Congratulations! You're ready to install the software.

Installing the Oracle 12c database software

The following steps walk you through a quick start installation of the Oracle 12c database software. The steps at this point are almost identical across all operating systems, so your skills will translate very easily from OS to OS.

1. **Download the software from the Oracle website at**

```
www.oracle.com/technetwork/database/enterprise-
           edition/downloads/index.html
```

Be sure to read and understand the license agreement and then click Accept to continue the download.

You can order the software from the Oracle store, but we recommend downloading it because it's free for development use and the same thing you would get from the store. You can always burn it to DVD later.

2. **Copy the files to the database server's hard drive.**

3. **Create a directory to hold the software.**

Choose something like one of these:

- /u01/app/oracle/stage
- /u01/app/oracle/software/stage

Unzip your downloaded files into the directory you created. After unzipping, you should see a folder named database.

4. **Open a terminal window and go to the software directory.**

5. **Type cd to change directory to the database directory and execute the runInstaller program:**

```
<./runInstaller>
```

It might take a minute or two, depending on your machine speed. You're welcomed by the screen shown in Figure A-1.

6. **(Optional) Enter your e-mail and Oracle Support information to allow automated notifications from Oracle and set up the configuration manager. Then click Next to continue.**

This option establishes a link between your system and Oracle Support. Although there are many benefits to this, some companies or government agencies are barred from doing this.

7. **(Optional) Download software updates.**

You can provide your Oracle Support credentials to download the latest security patches and bug fixes.

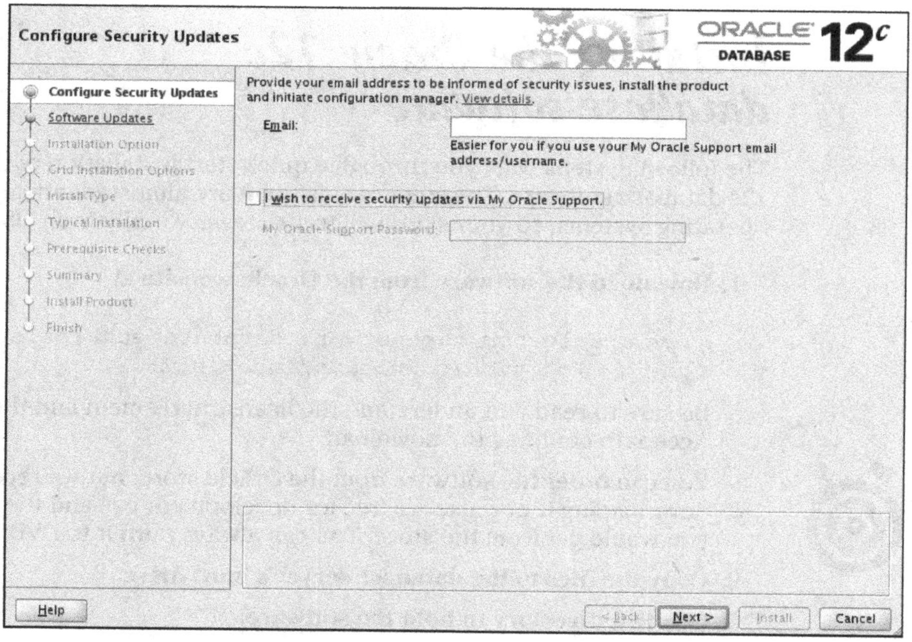

Figure A-1:
The Oracle Universal Installer screen welcomes you.

Downloading the updates ensures you have all the features in this book.

8. Select Install Database Software Only and then click Next.

You can create a starter database with your installation or just install the Oracle software binaries. We recommend *not* creating a starter database when you first install the software.

Getting the software installed is a big enough milestone. After you make sure the software installed correctly, go to Chapter 4 and create the database yourself. This gives you more control and the opportunity to understand the database creation process. If you let the installer do it, many of the steps are behind the scenes.

9. Determine the type of database installation you want to perform.

You may choose between a simple, single instance database installation or the more complex (and capable) Real Application Cluster (RAC) database installations. For simplicity with your first 12c install, select the single instance option.

10. Select the product language to install.

Verify English is selected (our assumption) and then click Next.

11. Identify the database edition you want to install.

Three versions of Oracle database software are available, each targeted (and priced) for different corporate audiences. For your company, you want to carefully determine which installation version meets your business needs and license restrictions. Because this is just a development database for you to learn on, select Enterprise Edition so you'll have the complete set of options available.

12. Enter the ORACLE_BASE and ORACLE_HOME directory information.

If your environment variables properly configured before running the installer, the values will populate for you. Otherwise, you may manually enter your ORACLE_BASE and ORACLE_HOME full Linux path names.

13. Identify the oraInventory directory and oraInventory group owner and then click Next.

The oraInventory directory stores metadata about the Oracle software you installed. This is valuable information when doing future installations or applying patches to ensure you don't encounter software conflicts.

14. Select privileged operating system groups and then click Next.

This screen determines the group file permissions for various administrative tasks. As you gain more experience and your environment grows, you may fine-tune these parameters. For your first Oracle install, the defaults of group dba are fine for all options except database operator, which is group oper. (See Figure A-2.) Oper is optional and many people do not use it.

The installer will quickly run pre-installation checks to ensure your install will be successful. Assuming no problems were identified, the installer automatically advances to the next screen after the prerequisite checks are completed.

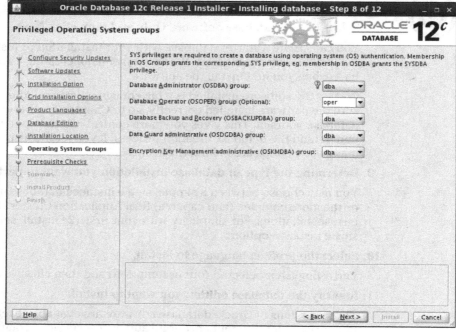

Figure A-2:
Select
group
dba for all
options
except
database
operator,
which is
group oper.

15. Review the summary screen to confirm the install options selected and then click Install.

This is your last chance to verify your installation locations and parameters before the installation.

The total time to install depends on the speed of the machine, network, options selected, and of course if problems are encountered. Be patient if a step seems to stall for a few minutes. For a small install on a fast machine with no network latency, the install can be as fast as 10 minutes.

16. If problems occur, diagnose and correct the issue, and then select Retry to continue.

Assuming the installation didn't encounter any errors, or you were able to fix the errors that did occur, you should now be at a screen stating the installation was successful.

17. Click Close.

You should have a fully functioning database software code tree.

Note you have not built any databases yet; see how to do that in Chapter 4.

Index

• B •

• C •

About the Author

Chris Ruel lives in Indianapolis, Indiana, and works as an Oracle DBA for a large financial investment company. He graduated from Wabash College in 1997 and has been working with Oracle ever since. His background has varied from 4 years of training to 10 years as an Oracle consultant. Occasionally, he can be seen speaking at local Oracle related events (Oracle Tech Days). He served as an Oracle University Instructor from 2000-2004, traveling the country teaching Oracle's DBA curriculum. Chris is certified in Oracle 8i-11g. He is also a RAC Certified Expert and has his Security+ certification.

When not working on Oracle, Chris enjoys working on old German cars (mostly BMW and Mercedes). He is also a big fan of Formula 1 auto racing, grilling out with his friends, and watching the Indianapolis Colts play football.

Michael Wessler received his bachelor's degree in computer technology from Purdue University in West Lafayette, Indiana. He is an Oracle Certified Database Administrator for Oracle 10g, 8i, and 8 and an Oracle Certified Web Administrator for 9iAS. Michael also holds a CISSP security certification. He has administered Oracle databases on Windows and various flavors of UNIX and Linux, including clustered Oracle Parallel Server (OPS) environments. He also performs database and SQL/PLSQL tuning for applications. Michael has worked in many IT shops ranging from small dot-com start-ups to large government agencies and corporations. Currently, Michael is an IT supervisor within the U.S. government.

In addition to Oracle DBA consulting, Michael works extensively as an Oracle web application server administrator and web application architect. He manages multiple web applications for the U.S. government and consults at various government agencies and in the private sector. Michael also frequently lectures on Oracle web technologies and teaches Oracle Performance Tuning classes. Michael is the author of *Oracle DBA on UNIX and Linux* and coauthor of *Oracle 11g For Dummies, Oracle Application Server 10g: J2EE Deployment and Administration, Oracle Unleashed*, Second Edition, *UNIX Primer Plus*, Third Edition, *COBOL Unleashed, UNIX Unleashed*, Fourth Edition, and *High Availability: Successful Implementation for the Data-Driven Enterprise*. Michael has also authored internal works on Oracle Exadata, Oracle Exalogic, cloud computing, and big data analytics.

Dedication

Chris Ruel: I dedicate this book to my parents who raised me well. If it wasn't for them, I don't know what I would be doing today. My dad always said that I would be digging ditches when he scolded me for not applying myself.

Michael Wessler: For my Dad, Jon Wessler. Thanks for always having a level head and keeping me (usually) pointed in the right direction. And now I can also thank you for being such a great Grandpa to my son, Garrick.

Author's Acknowledgments

Chris Ruel: A special thanks to the Wiley team, Constance and Brian; all my former co-workers at PTI in Indianapolis, IN; and Marshall Pyle for making sure the technical portion of this book did not get lost in 2:30 a.m. ramblings before deadlines. In addition, I'd like to thank my current co-workers who may find their names here and there in code examples . . . except for one who requested (as it were) to remain nameless. Lastly, I cannot forget the rest of the editors who, due to the amount of red ink on my review documents, must have thought I never graduated grammar school. Believe me, it's not that, I just have a bad babit of not froofreading what I typped.

Michael Wessler: I would like to thank my wonderful wife, Angela, for her endless support while I'm writing these projects. I know she must cringe when I say, "Good news, I have a new project", but she never lets on and works extra hard to watch our son as I sit in front of the computer for hours. I'd also like to recognize my brother, Dan Wilson, for getting me started in the Oracle world and helping me along the way: Thank you. Finally, I'd like to thank my co-author Chris Ruel and the Wiley team for another great experience!

Publisher's Acknowledgments

Acquisitions Editor: Constance Santisteban

Project Editor: Brian H. Walls

Copy Editor: Virginia Sanders

Technical Editor: Marshall Pyle

Editorial Assistant: Anne Sullivan

Sr. Editorial Assistant: Cherie Case

Project Coordinator: Kristie Rees

Cover Image: ©iStockphoto.com/Sirgunhik